3ds max 7 New Features and Production Workflow

12810-010000-1700-A
November 2004

3ds max 7 New Features and Production Workflow

discreet®

ELSEVIER

AMSTERDAM • BOSTON • HEIDELBERG • LONDON
NEW YORK • OXFORD • PARIS • SAN DIEGO
SAN FRANCISCO • SINGAPORE • SYDNEY • TOKYO

Focal Press is an imprint of Elsevier

Focal Press

Acquisitions Editor: *Elinor Actipis*
Project Manager: *Simon Crump*
Editorial Assistant: *Cara Anderson*
Marketing Manager: *Christine Degon*
Cover Design: *discreet*
Interior Design: *discreet*

Focal Press is an imprint of Elsevier
30 Corporate Drive, Suite 400, Burlington, MA 01803, USA
Linacre House, Jordan Hill, Oxford OX2 8DP, UK

Library of Congress Cataloging-in-Publication Data
Application submitted

British Library Cataloguing-in-Publication Data
A catalogue record for this book is available from the British Library.

ISBN: 0-240-80775-8

For information on all Focal Press publications
visit our website at www.books.elsevier.com

05 06 07 08 09 10 10 9 8 7 6 5 4 3 2 1

Printed in the United States of America

ISBN: 1-56444-985-8

Contents

1 Modeling a Cape and Pendant

Objectives

After completing this chapter, you should be able to:

- Model procedurally with Edit Poly.
- Subdivide using Turbo Smooth.
- Generate a Reactor Cloth solution.
- Use the Skin Wrap modifier.
- Use Preserve UV inside the Edit Poly modifier.

Introduction

This chapter concentrates on many of the new modeling features and techniques found in **3ds max 7**. You start modeling a cape and a pendant for a completed knight model. You model two capes: a low-poly version using Editable Poly and a high-poly version using Edit Poly and Turbo Smooth. The low-poly version acts as a template for the high-poly version. Edit Poly procedurally adds detail to the cape while Turbo Smooth generates a high-poly version of the cape.

You use Reactor to calculate the low-poly version of the cape to fit over the knight's shoulders. The Skin Wrap modifier is then added to the high-poly version of the cape and it uses the low-poly version to access the Reactor solution. This way you don't recalculate the Reactor solution for the high-poly version of the cape.

Finally, you use Preserve UVs to add geometry to the hips of the knight and maintain the knight's UVW coordinates.

Modeling the Low-Poly Cape

Starting with a Plane

1. Open *knightCape01.max*.
2. On the command panels, choose Create > Geometry > Plane.
3. In the Top viewport, create a Plane.
4. In the Parameters rollout, set Length to **424** and Width to **215**.
5. Change the Length Segs to **6** and Width Segs to 4.
6. On the main toolbar, right-click Move and set Absolute World: X: **0.0**, Y: **257.0**, Z: **741.0**.
7. Close the Move Transform Type-In dialog.
8. In the Name and Color rollout, type **Knight_GEO_LowResCape**.

   This object is used to create a low-resolution version of the cape.

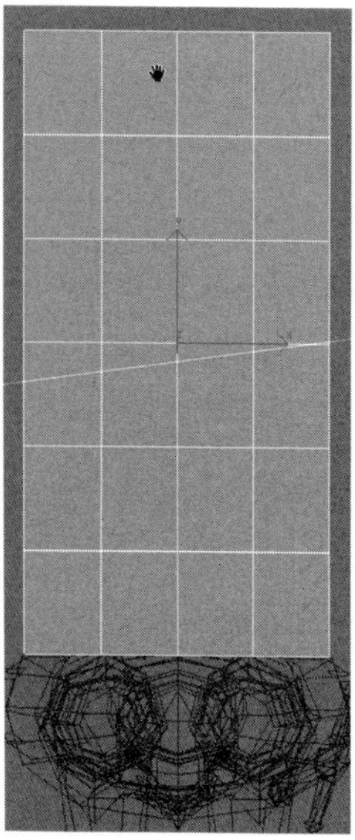

9. Press **F4** on the keyboard to activate Edged Faces in the Top viewport.
10. In the Top viewport, right-click and choose Convert to Editable Poly from the quad menu.
11. In the Selection rollout, choose Polygon.

12. In the Top viewport, choose the polygons on the left side of the cape and then choose Delete.

    Tip: F2 is the keyboard shortcut to display Shaded Faces.

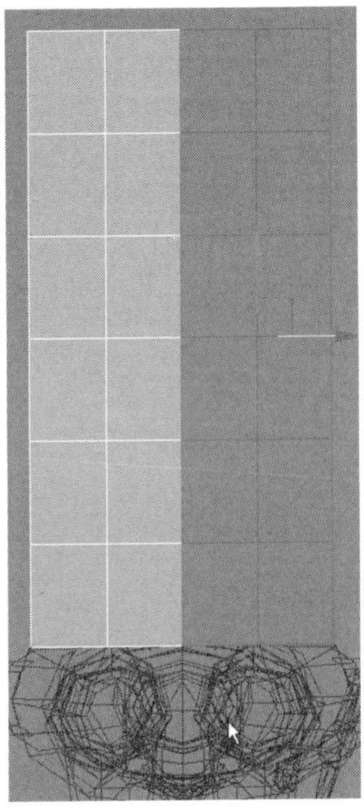

13. Save the file as **knightCape02.max.**

Adding Symmetry

Next, you add the Symmetry modifier to the plane object. This way, you work on half of the plane and the other half is affected automatically.

1. Continue from the previous exercise, or open *knightCape02.max.*
2. Exit Polygon Sub-object.
3. Make sure Knight_GEO_LowResCape is selected.
4. On the Modifier List drop-down, choose Symmetry.

5. In the Parameters rollout, turn off Slice Along Mirror.

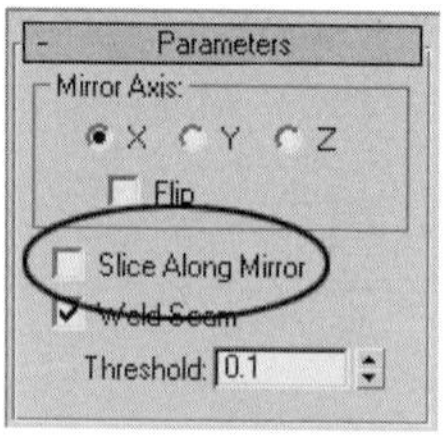

If you move a vertex across the center line, you'll know to fix it. If you let Symmetry do the slicing, then incorrect subdividing results can occur when MeshSmooth or Turbo Smooth are added.

6. In the Modify Stack display, choose Editable Poly.
7. In the Modify Stack display toolbar, turn on Show End Result.

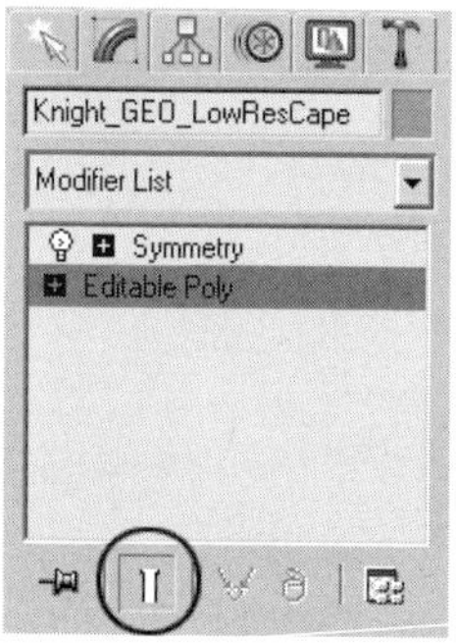

You want to see the effect of the Symmetry modifier while you model at the base level.

8. Press **2** to enter Sub-Object Edge.
9. Adjust one of your viewports to a User viewport.
10. In the User viewport, choose edge **4** behind the Knight's right shoulder.
11. You begin to copy edges by using SHIFT+Move to create the cape.
12. In the Top or User viewport, SHIFT+Move edge 4 on the Y-axis to create a new edge above the shoulder.

13. SHIFT+Move another edge down and forward to appear in front of the shoulder.

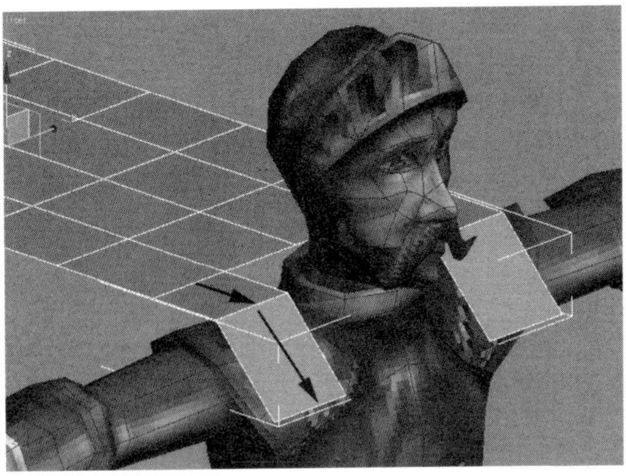

14. Press A to turn on Angle Snap.
15. Press E to choose Rotate.
16. SHIFT+Rotate the selected edge **–90** on the Y-axis.
17. Move the rotated edge toward the center of the character.

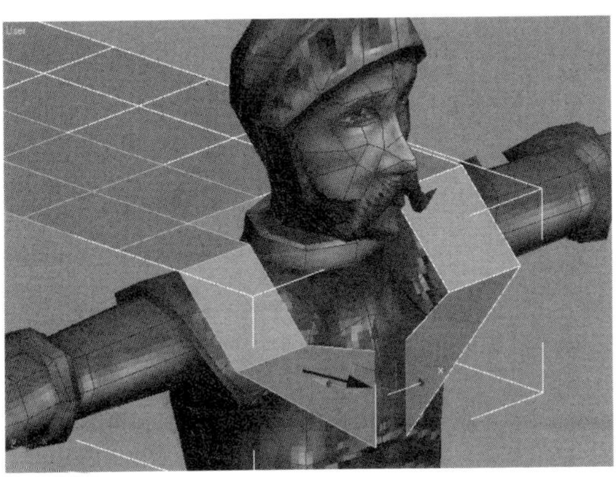

18. Select the edge behind the character's head and move it away from the character.

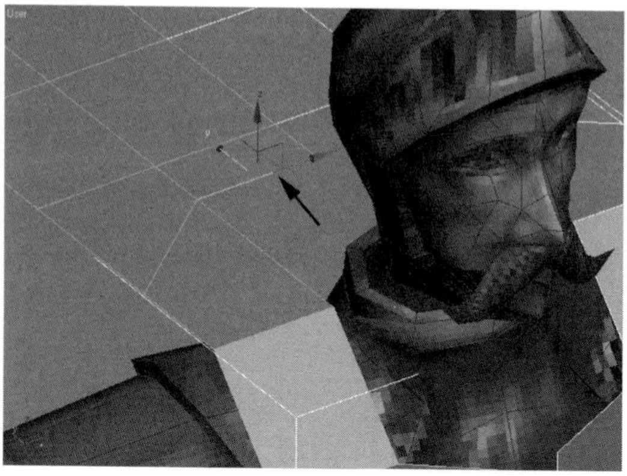

This helps form where the cape will hang down in the back.

19. Press **1** to choose Sub-Object Vertex.

20. Move the vertices to form over the Knight's shoulders. Make sure the cape vertices don't intersect with the character's geometry.

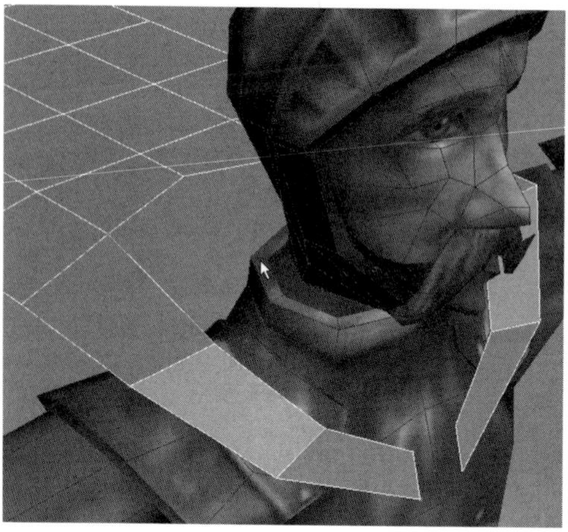

21. Press **2** to go to Sub-Object Edge.

22. In the User viewport, select the four edges on the inside of the neck area.

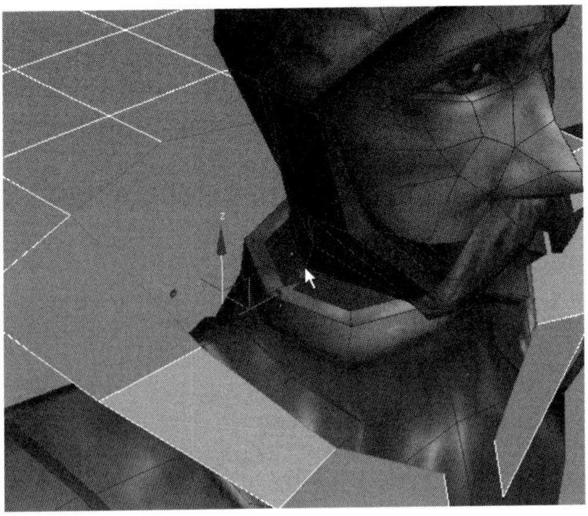

23. In the Edit Edges rollout, choose the Settings button next to Extrude.

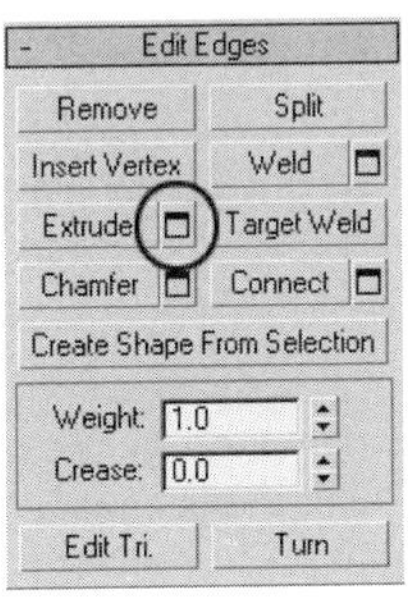

24. In the Extrude Edges dialog, set Extrusion Height to **0.0**, and Extrusion Base Width to **8.0** and then press OK.

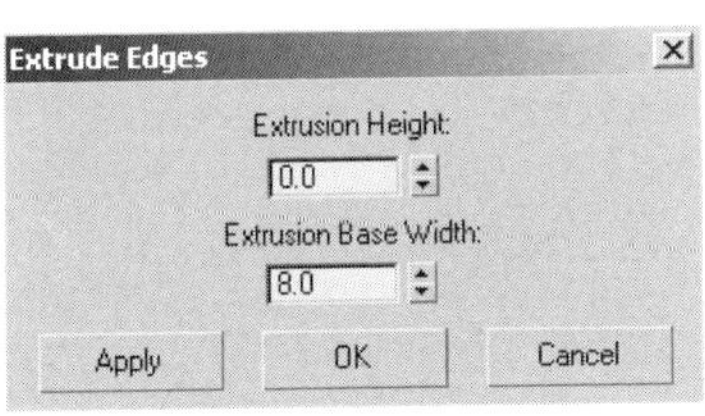

25. In the Top viewport, hold down CTRL to select the new edges.

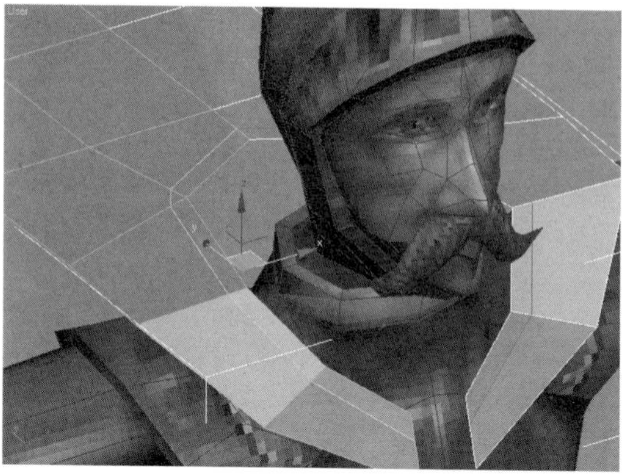

26. In the Top and User viewport, move the edges away from the neck of the character keeping the center line intact.

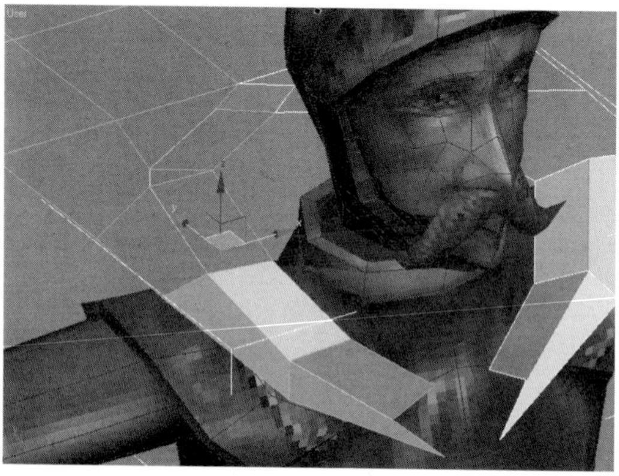

27. Press **1** to choose Sub-Object Vertex.

28. Move the back vertex into position by typing 0.0 on the X-axis in the Transform Type-In.

29. Move the front center vertex into position.

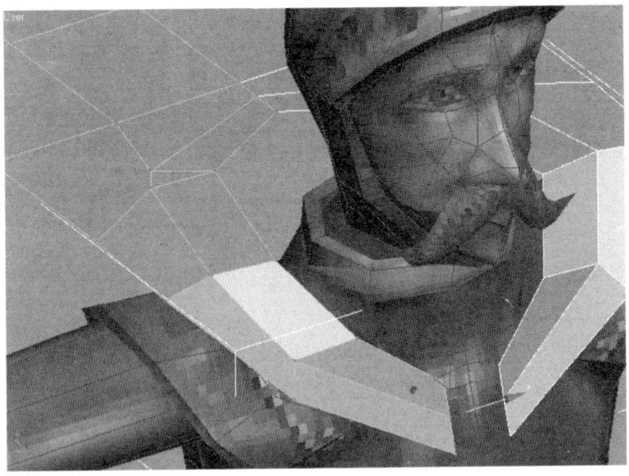

30. Spend some time moving the particular vertices to get an image similar to the following one.

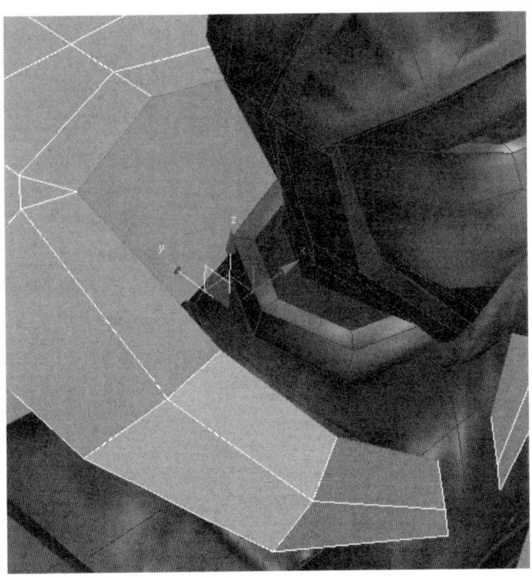

31. In the User viewport, choose the two vertices that have created a triangle.

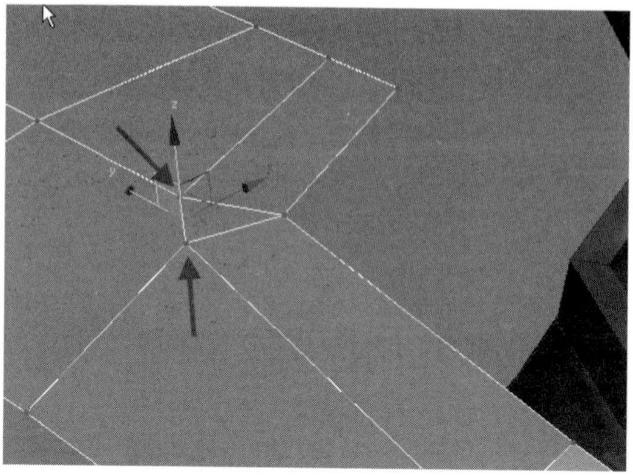

32. In the Edit Geometry rollout, choose Collapse.

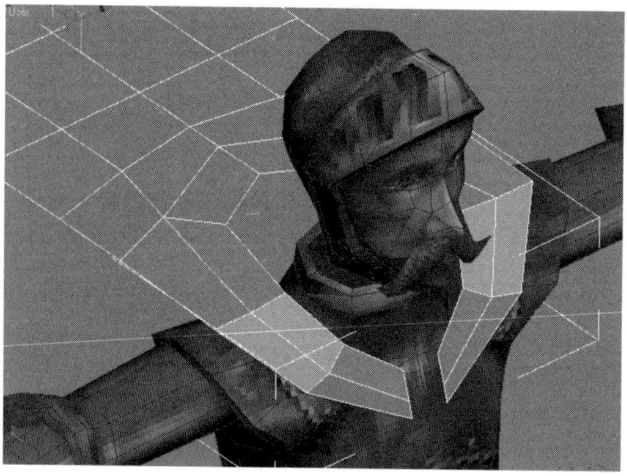

You modeled an edge ring around the neck opening for the cape. This helps to create the high-resolution model with folds and wrinkles.

33. Save the file as **knightCape03.max**.

Creating the Pendant

The next model you build is a pendant that holds the cape around the neck of the knight. You use several primitives and modifiers to create this object. Specifically, you use the Edit Poly modifier. Edit Poly retains most features of the Editable Poly object type with the added functionality of procedural modeling. This means you can add multiple Edit Poly modifiers onto your stack while modeling.

Edit Poly vs. Editable Poly

Feature	Edit Poly	Editable Poly
Procedural Modeling	Yes	No
Sub-Object Animation	Yes	Yes
Animation with Cage	Yes	No
Preserve UVs	Yes	Yes
SHIFT+Move to Copy	Yes	Yes
Paint Deformation	Yes	Yes
Vertex Properties	No	Yes
Subdivision Surface	No	Yes
Soft Selection	Yes	Yes

1. Continue from the previous exercise, or open *knightCape03.max*.
2. On the command panels, choose Create > Geometry > Extended Primitives > Oil Tank.
3. In the Front viewport, create an Oil Tank.
4. In the Parameters rollout, set the following values:
   Radius: **10.0**
   Height: **8.0**
   Cap Height: **3.5**
   Sides: **24**

5. In the Name and Color rollout, type **Knight_GEO_pendantCenter**.

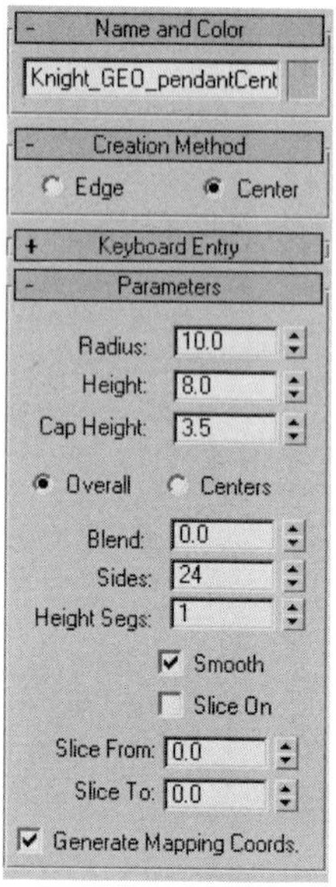

6. On the main toolbar, right-click Move and set Absolute World: to X: 0.0, Y: –46.0, and Z: 680.0. Close the Transform Type-In dialog.

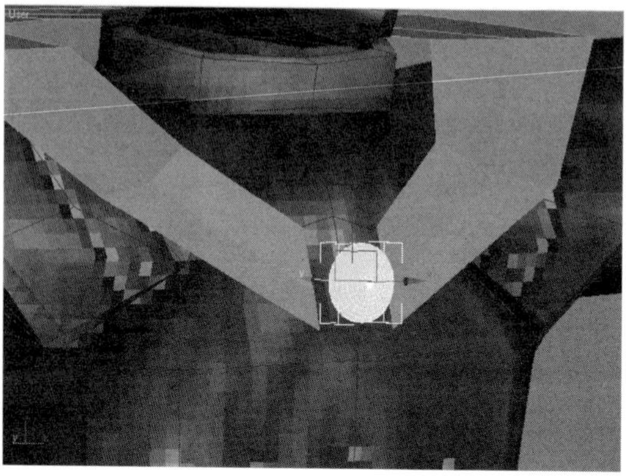

7. In the Top viewport, create a ChamferBox with the following values:
Length: **1.6**
Width: **10.0**
Height: **18.0**
Fillet: **0.2**
Length Segs: **1**
Width Segs: **3**

Height Segs: **4**
Fillet Segs: **1**

8. In the Name and Color rollout, type **Knight_GEO_pendantTop**.

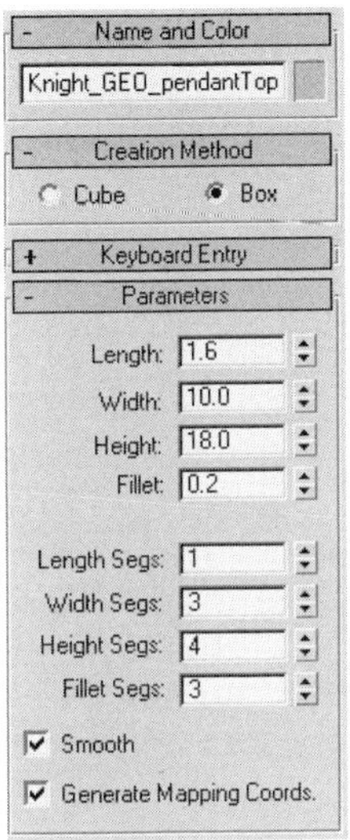

9. 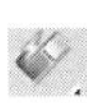 On the main toolbar, click Quick Align.

   Note: Quick Align aligns objects based on their pivot points.

10. In the Front viewport, choose Knight_GEO_pendantCenter.
11. In the User viewport, move the box approximately 2.8 units on the Z-axis.
12. On the command panels, choose Modify.
13. On the Modifier List drop-down, choose Taper.

14. In the Parameters rollout, set the Amount to 0.72.

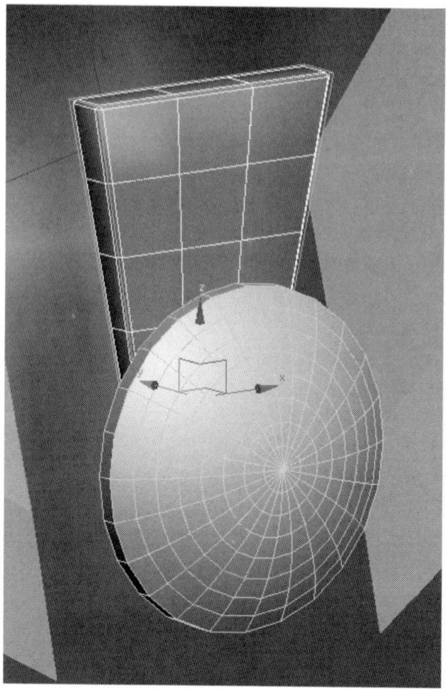

15. On the Modifier List drop-down, choose Edit Poly.
16. Press 1 to get to Sub-Object Vertex.
17. In the Edit Geometry rollout > Constraints drop-down list, choose Edge.

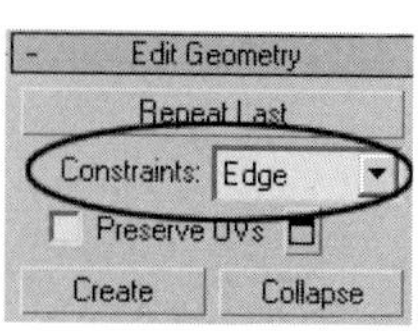

18.  On the main toolbar, turn on Percent Snap Toggle.

19. In the Front viewport, select all vertices in the two vertical center rows and scale them 240% on the X-axis.

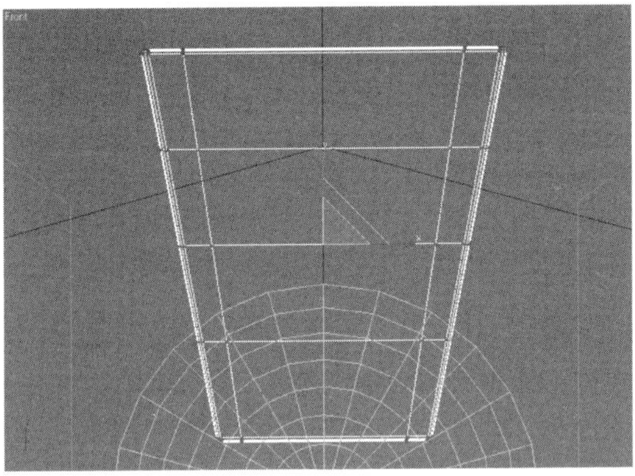

20. 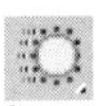 On the main toolbar, choose Paint Selection Region from the selection flyout.

Note: Paint Selection allows you to click and drag to select the specific sub-object option.

21. In the Front viewport, click and drag to select all vertices in the three horizontal middle rows.

22. In the User viewport, scale them 170% on the Z-axis.

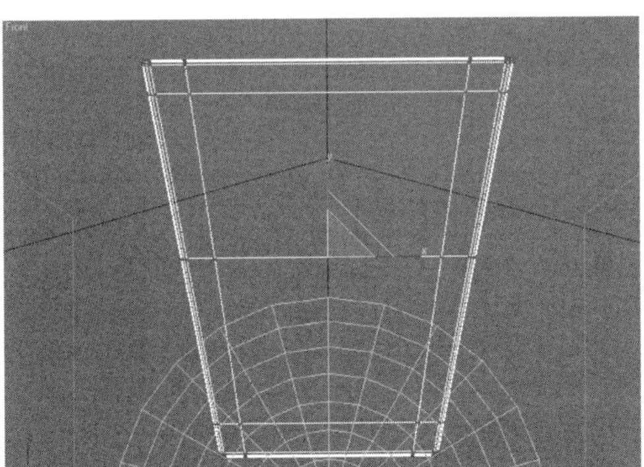

23. Press 4 to go to Sub-Object Poly.

24. In the Front viewport, choose the two polygons in the front center of the object.

25. In the Edit Polygons rollout, choose the Settings button next to Bevel.

26. In the Bevel Polygons rollout, set the Height to –0.3 and the Outline Amount to –0.3 and press OK.
27. Press the Settings button next to Extrude.
28. In the Extrude Polygons dialog, set the Extrusion Height to –0.5 and press OK.

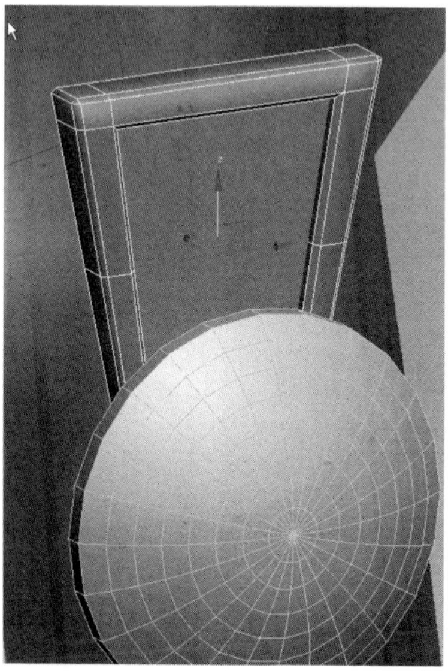

29. Save the file as **knightCape04.max**.

Finishing the Pendant

You create the rest of the pendant by creating clones using Array.

1. Continue from the previous exercise, or open *knightCape04.max*.
2. Make sure Knight_GEO_pendantTop is selected and you have exited every sub-object.
3. On the main toolbar, choose Pick from the Reference Coordinate System drop-down list.
4. In the Front viewport, choose Knight_GEO_pendantCenter.
5.  On the main toolbar, choose Use Transform Coordinate Center from the flyout.
6. This allows the Pendant Top to use the Pivot Point of the Pendant Center for transforms.
7. Make sure Knight_GEO_pendantTop is selected.

8. On the menu bar, choose Tools > Array.
9. In the Array dialog > Incremental area, set Z Rotation to 90.
10. In the Type of Object group, make sure Instance is chosen.
11. In the Array Dimensions group, set 1D Count to 4.
12. In the Preview group, turn on Preview.

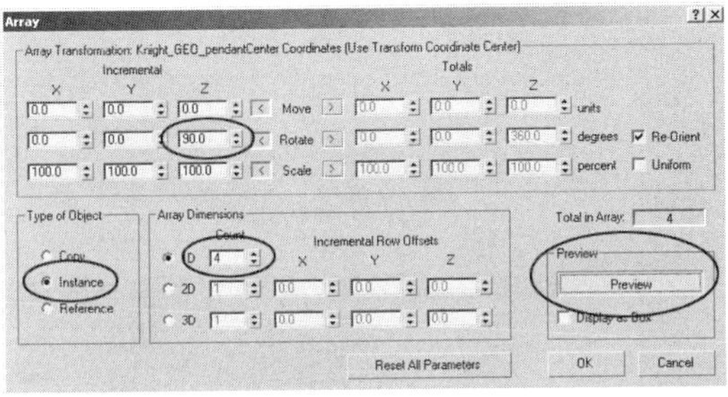

You are able preview the result of the array before accepting the settings.

13. Press OK to accept the settings and create additional pendant pieces.
14. In the User viewport, choose Knight_GEO_pendantTop02.
15.  On the Modify panel > Modify Stack display toolbar, choose Make Unique.
16. This option changes the object from an Instance to a Clone. Now you can add modifiers to this object and not affect other objects.
17. On the Modifier List drop-down, choose X-Form.
18. On the main toolbar, choose Scale.
19. On the main toolbar, set the Reference Coordinate System to Local.

20. In the Front viewport, Scale the gizmo 140% on the Z-axis.

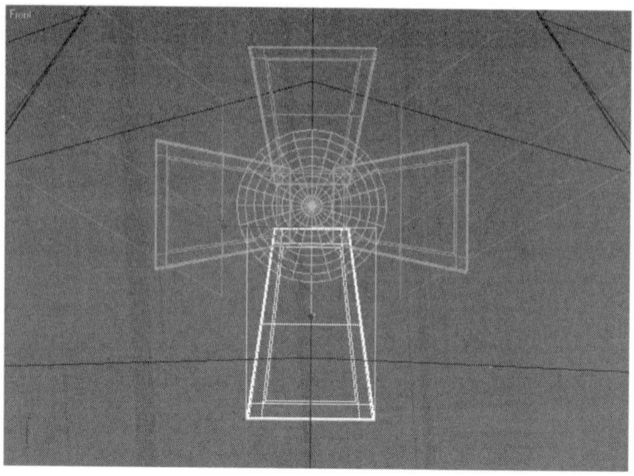

Creating the Back of the Crest

You start with a Chamfer Cylinder and then add Edit Poly to create the Crest.

1. Continue from the previous exercise.
2. In the Front viewport, create a Chamfer Cylinder with the following values:
   Radius: **19.0**
   Height: **1.5**
   Fillet: **0.3**
   Sides: **32**
   Cap Segs: **2**

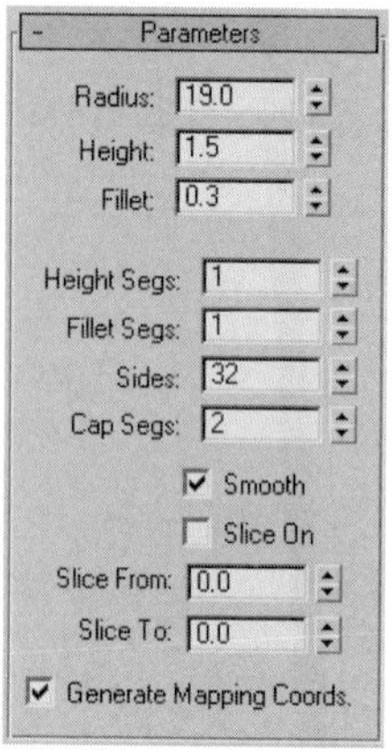

3. In the Name and Color rollout, type **Knight_GEO_pendantBack**.

4. On the main toolbar, right-click Select and Move and set the Absolute World to: X: 0.0, Y: –44.0, and Z: 680.0. Close the Transform Type-In.

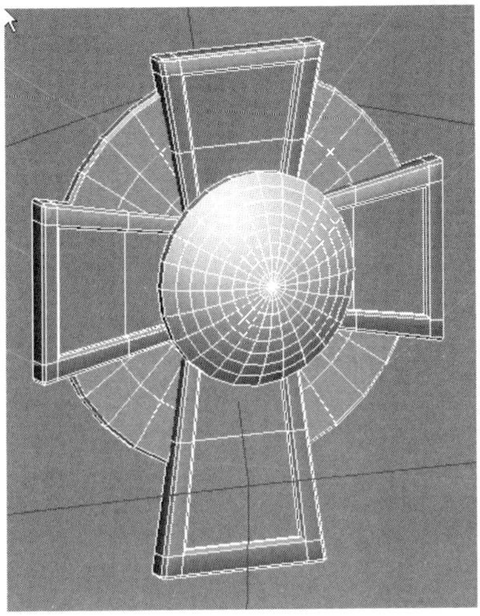

5. On the Modify panel > Modifier List drop-down, choose Edit Poly.
6. Press 2 to choose Sub-Object Edge.
7. In the Selection rollout, turn on Ignore Backfacing.
8. In the Front viewport, select one edge of the cap in the front of the object.
9. In the Selection rollout, choose Loop.

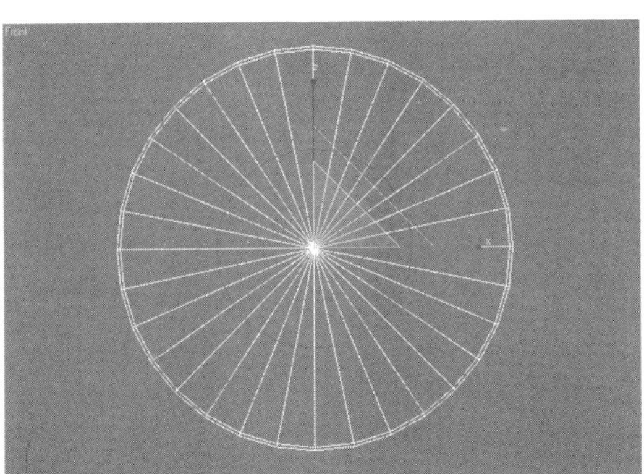

This selects all the edges in a loop around the top of the cylinder.

Tip: To display selected objects only, use Isolate mode, ALT+Q, while not in any sub-object mode.

10. On the main toolbar, set the Reference Coordinate System to View.
11. In the User viewport, scale the edges 140% on the X and Z-axes.

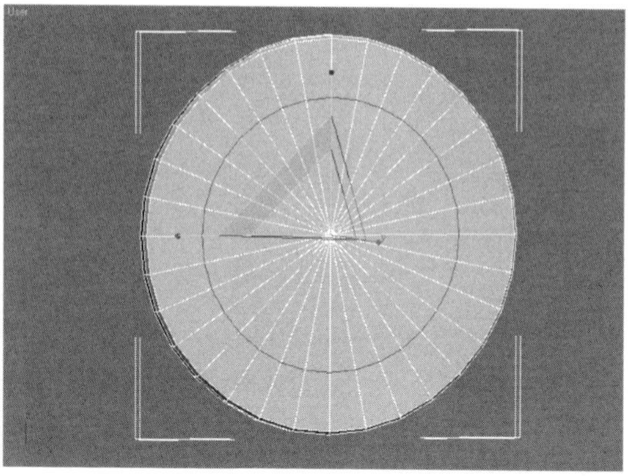

12. In the Edit Edges rollout, choose the Settings button next to Chamfer Edge.
13. In the Chamfer Edges dialog, set Chamfer Amount to 0.5 and press OK.

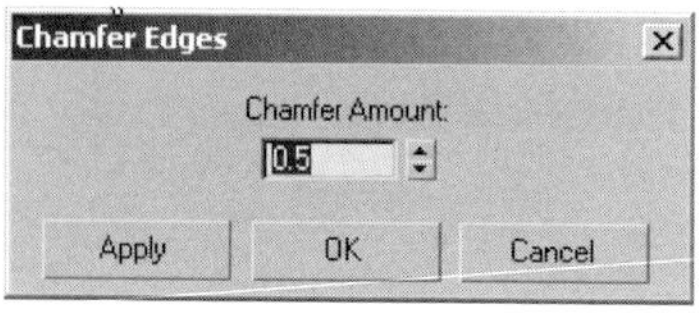

14. Press 4 to get to Sub-Object Polygon.
15. Make sure Ignore Backfacing is on.
16. On the main toolbar, choose Paint Selection Region from the flyout.
17. On the main toolbar, choose the Selection Object tool.

18. In the User viewport, select the Polygons as shown in the following diagram.

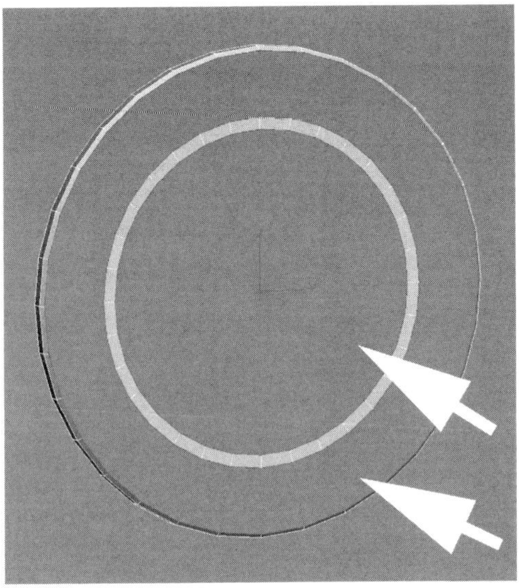

Tip: If you right-click the Paint Selection Region icon on the main toolbar, the Preferences Settings dialog is displayed, allowing you to change the size of the Paint Selection Brush.

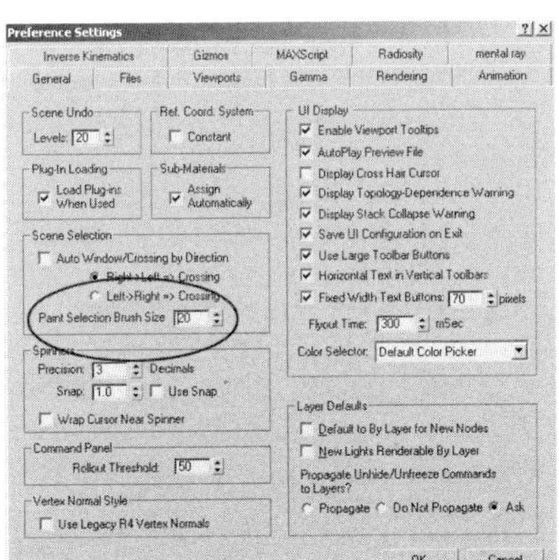

19. In the Edit Polygon rollout, choose the Settings button next to Bevel.

20. In the Bevel Polygons dialog > Bevel Type group, choose By Polygon.

21. Set the Height to –0.4 and the Outline Amount to –0.4 and press OK.

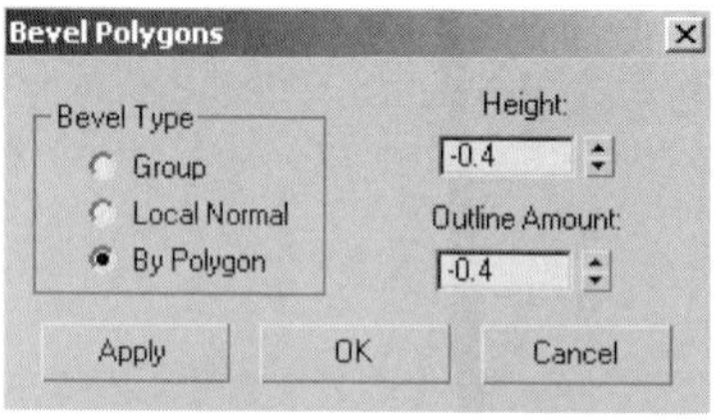

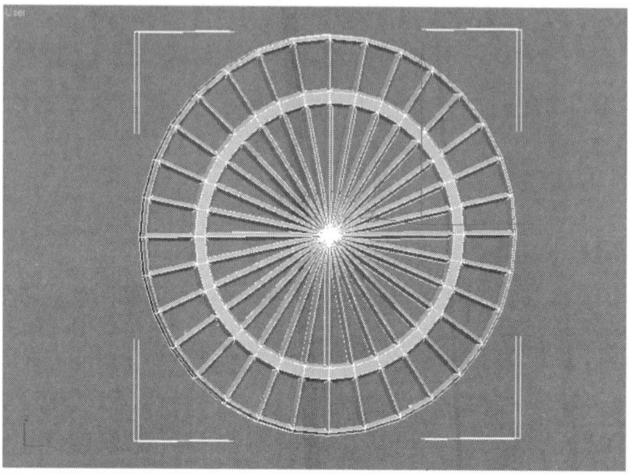

Creating the Ribbon

You use the Torus Knot to create the ribbon for the pendant. To add geometry to the Torus Knot, you use Turbo Smooth, which is an optimized version of Mesh Smooth. This modifier displays incredible speed while performing viewport operations.

Before you continue to embellish the pendant, familiarize yourself with the difference between Mesh Smooth and Turbo Smooth.

Turbo Smooth vs. Mesh Smooth

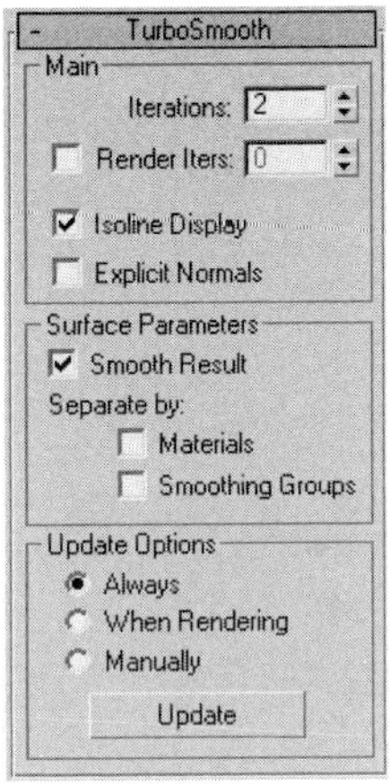

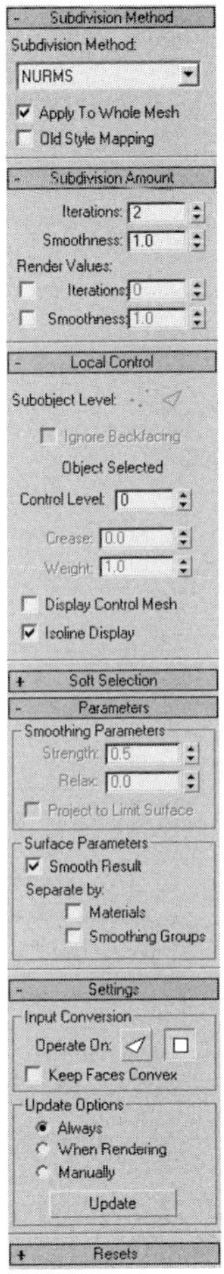

Feature	Turbo Smooth	Mesh Smooth
Subdivision Method	NURMS	Classic, Quad, NURMS
Sub-Object	No	Yes
Iterations	Yes	Yes
Smoothness	No	Yes
Render Values	Yes	Yes
Isoline Display	Yes (see note)	Yes
Explicit Normals	Yes (see note)	No
Surface Parameters	Yes	Yes
Soft Selection	No	Yes

Note: Isoline display hides all edges in the result that are indirectly descended from an original edge.

Turbo Smooth produces a TriMesh output, rather than a PolyMesh. Like Mesh Smooth, the only way to get this display to work is to actually hide all these edges, which means that the output suffers if converted into polygons. Turn on Isoline when Turbo Smooth is the last modifier in the stack.

Note: Explicit Normals indicates that Turbo Smooth should produce Explicit Normals in the result. These are normals set to particular values.

This option is unavailable in MeshSmooth. Its purpose is to improve display speed: the Turbo Smooth modifier can actually compute normals for its output faster than the standard method the mesh uses to compute normals from smoothing groups. Consequently, if the Turbo Smooth result is used directly for display or rendering, it will generally be faster using this option. (The quality of the normals will also be slightly higher.) However, if the user has topology-affecting modifiers on top of the Turbo Smooth, such as Edit Mesh or Edit Poly, these normals will be lost and new ones computed This means that overall, there would be a net performance hit if explicit normals were computed. There is no point in computing normals at the Turbo Smooth level if you add a modifier on top and essentially remove the normals. Ultimately, you want to use this option when Turbo Smooth is the last modifier in the stack.

Other Important Turbo Smooth Differences

- Quickly apply subdivision over any arbitrary mesh.
- Twice as fast as Mesh Smooth and can be faster in some cases.
- Produces a TriMesh Output.

Typical Turbo Smooth Workflow

- Create parametric object.
- Convert object to a surface type such as Poly or Mesh. Alternatively, add either an Edit Mesh or Edit Poly modifier.
- Edit the object to build the desired 3D model.
- Add Turbo Smooth to subdivide the surface.

1. Continue from the previous exercise.
2. On the Create panel, choose Create > Geometry > Extended Primitives > Torus Knot.
3. In the Front viewport, create a Torus Knot with the following values:
   Base Curve:
   Radius: **5.2**
   Segments: **52**
   Cross Section:
   Radius: **5.2**
   Sides: **6**
   Eccentricity: **0.65**
   Lump Height: **0.28**
   Lump Offset: **37.0**
4. In the Name and Color rollout, type **Knight_GEO_pendantKnots**.
5. Right-click Select and Move and set the Absolute World to X: –21.0, Y: –41.0, Z: 684.0.

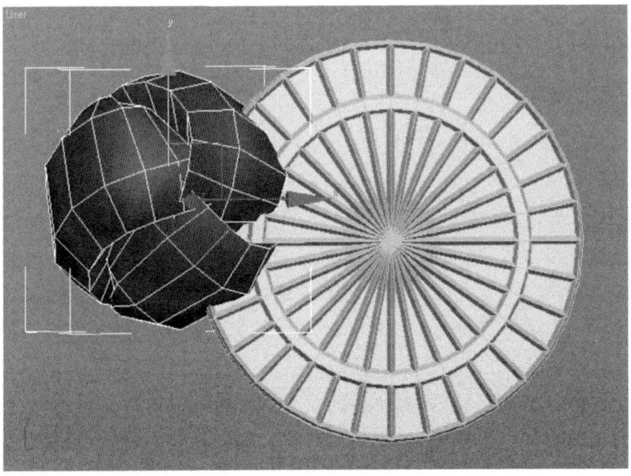

6. On the Modify panel > Modifier List drop-down, choose XForm.

7. In the User viewport, Scale the gizmo down 40% on Y-axis and up 150% on the Z-axis.
8. Press E to choose Select and Rotate and Rotate the gizmo 15° on the Y-axis.

   Tip: Type A on the keyboard to turn on Angle Snap and constrain the rotation in five-degree increments.

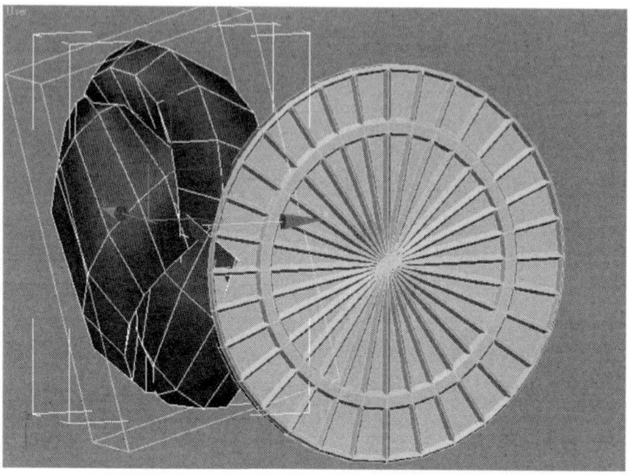

9. On the Modify panel > Modifier List drop-down, choose Mirror.
10. In the Modify Stack display, open Mirror and choose Sub-Object Mirror Center.
11. Right-click Select and Move, and set Absolute World: X: 0.0.
12. In the Parameters rollout > Options group, turn on Copy.

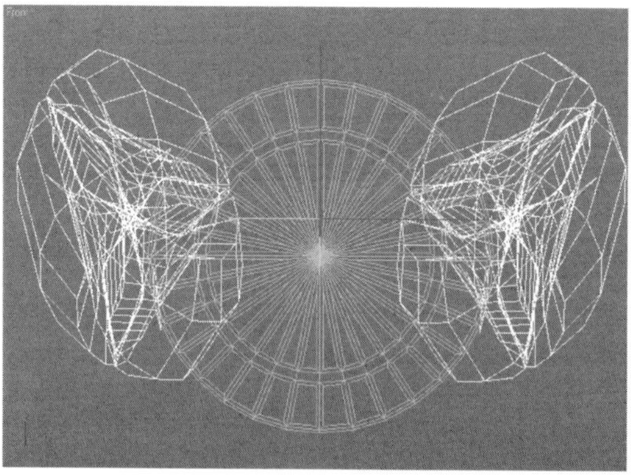

13. On the Modifier List drop-down, choose TurboSmooth.
14. In the TurboSmooth rollout > Main group, set Iterations to 2.

Tip: Do not drag the spinner for the Iterations value.

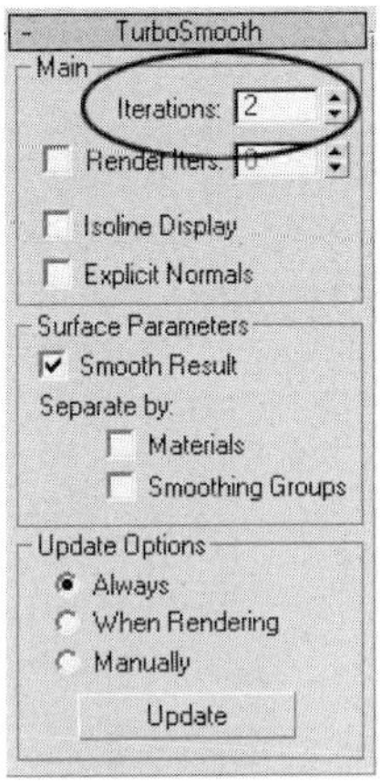

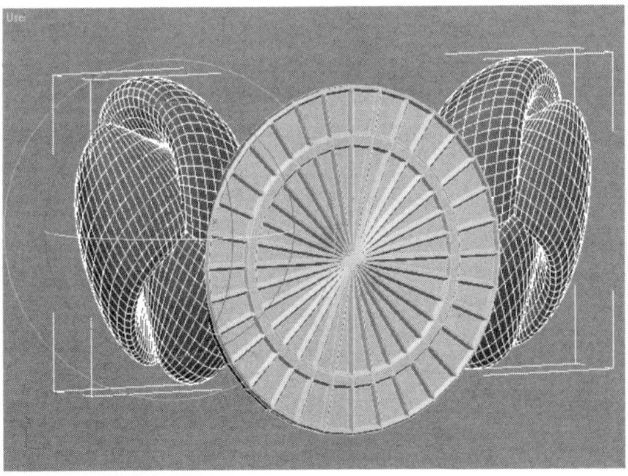

Creating a Point Helper and Linking

Next, you create a Point Helper object to act as the Parent to all parts of the pendant. You use Select and Link to create a hierarchy.

1. Continue from the previous exercise.
2. Exit the Isolation mode.
3. On the command panels, choose Create > Helpers > Point.
4. In the Parameters rollout, turn on Box, and leave Cross on and Size 20.
5. In the Top viewport, click anywhere to create the Point Helper.
6. On the main toolbar, choose Align and then choose Knight_GEO_pendantCenter.

7. In the Align Selection dialog, turn on X, Y, and Z Position.
8. Turn on Pivot Point for both Current and Target Object. Click OK.

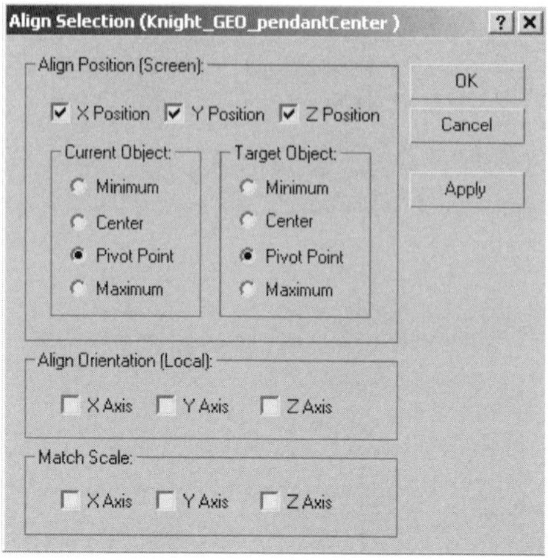

9. In the Name and Color rollout, type Knight_HLP_pendant.
10. Press H and choose all Pendant parts.
11. On the main toolbar, choose Select and Link.
12. In the Front viewport, click and drag from the child to the parent Helper Object (Knight_HLP_pendant).
13. Rotate and Move the Point Helper so the pendant appears to be resting on the character's chest.

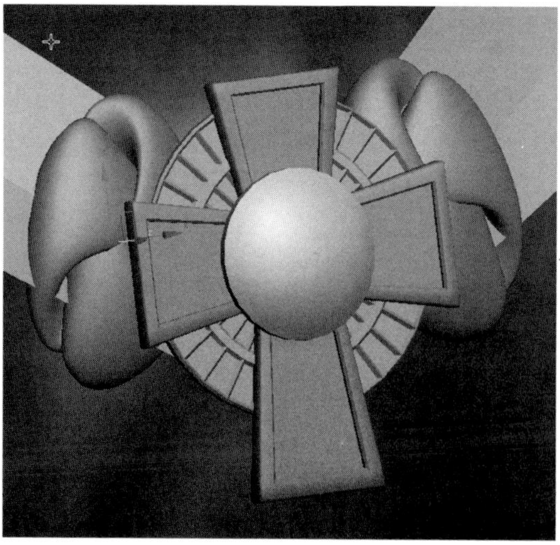

14. Save the file as **knightCape05.max**.

Modeling the High-Resolution Cape

Next, you model a high-resolution version of the cape. This will be used for the Skin Wrap modifier later in the chapter. You use Edit Poly to procedurally model changes to the cape, and Turbo Smooth to subdivide the geometry.

1. Continue from the previous exercise, or open *knightCape05.max*.
2. Select Knight_GEO_LowResCape.
3. On the menu bar, choose Tools > Snapshot.
4. In the Snapshot dialog > Clone Method group, choose Copy. Press OK.

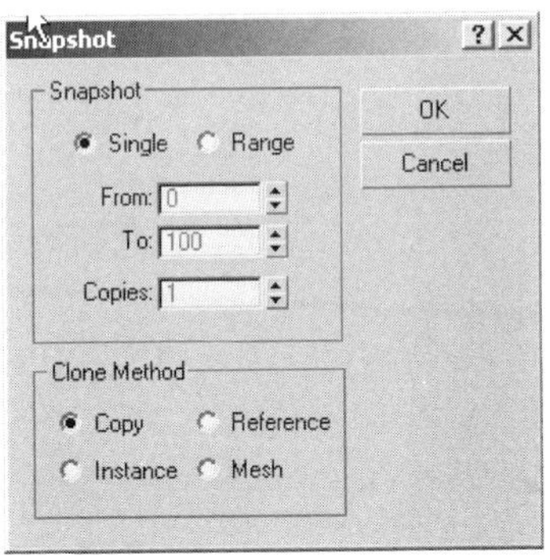

5. Right-click and choose Hide Selection from the quad menu to hide Knight_GEO_LowResCape.
6. Select Knight_GEO_LowResCape01 and rename it **Knight_GEO_HighResCape**.
7. On the Modifier drop-down list, choose TurboSmooth.
8. In the TurboSmooth rollout > Main group, set Iterations to 2 and turn on Isoline Display.

   Only the main edges are displayed.
9. In the Modify Stack display, choose Editable Poly.
10. On the Modifier List drop-down, choose Edit Poly.

11. In the Edit Poly Mode rollout, turn on Show Cage.

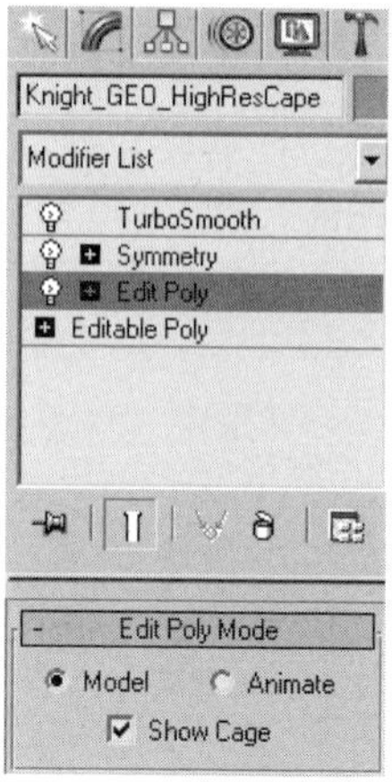

This option shows the object based on this level of the stack. Notice that when you add an Edit Poly modifier, Show End Result is on automatically.

To make a higher-poly cape, spread the edge loops around the neck of the cape so that you can cut the geometry and then add wrinkles.

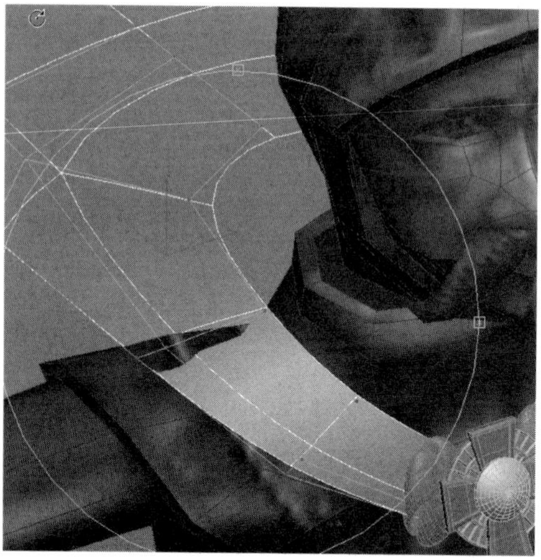

12. Press 2 to enter Sub-Object Edge.

13. In the User viewport, select an edge perpendicular to the ring of the neck.

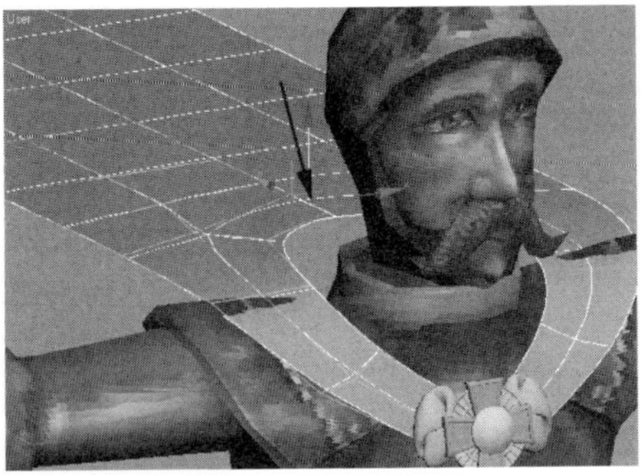

14. In the Selection rollout, choose Ring.
15. In the Edit Edges rollout, choose the Settings button next to Connect.
16. Change the Connect Edge Segments to 2 and press OK.

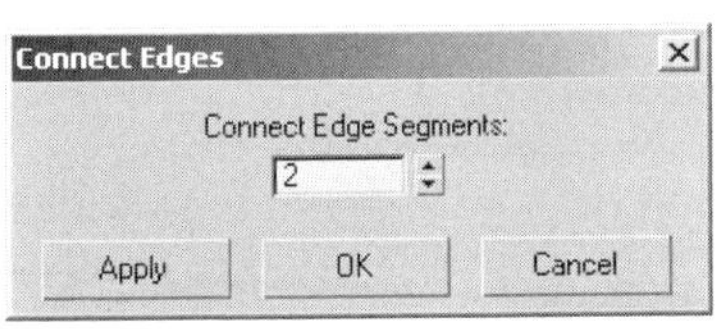

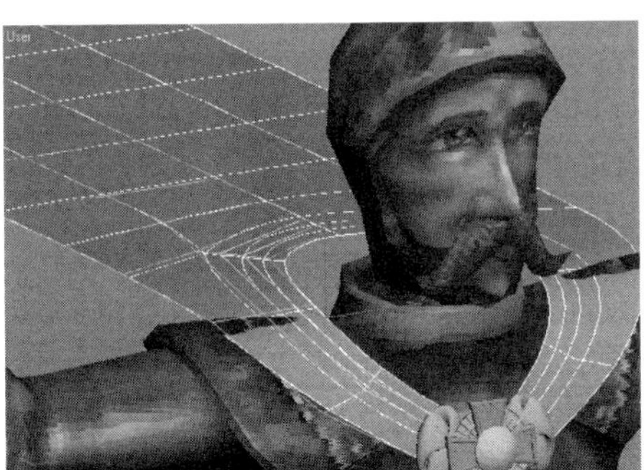

17. Press 1 to go to Sub-Object Vertex.

Tip: Holding down CTRL while choosing another sub-object selection creates the selection based on the previous sub-object selection.

18. Model the new vertices into a fold sticking up from the top of the cape.

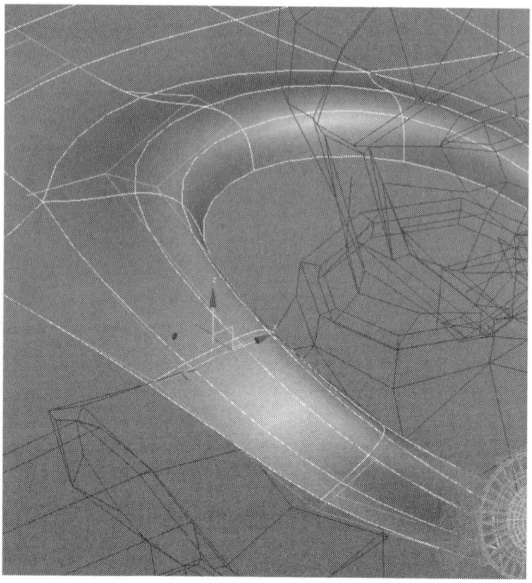

19. In the User viewport, choose Edge 54.
20. In the Selection rollout, choose Ring.

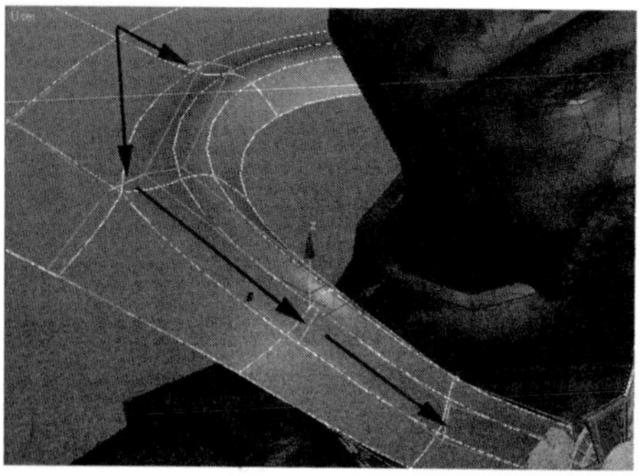

21. Choose the Settings button next to Connect and add two new Edge Loops.

Use the new vertices to model another fold.

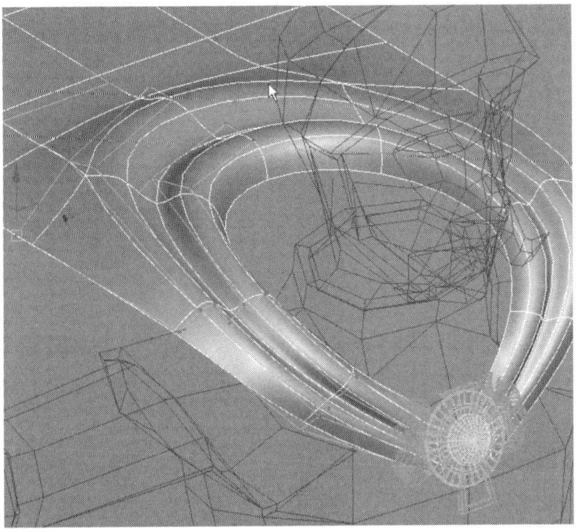

22. Save the file as **knightCape06.max**.

Adding More Detail

You continue modeling the high-resolution cape by adding details for the folds.

1. Continue from the previous exercise, or open *KnightCape06.max*.
2. Make sure Knight_GEO_highResCape is selected.
3. In the Modify Stack display, choose Edit Poly.
4. On the Modifier List drop-down, choose Edit Poly.
5. In the Edit Poly Mode rollout, turn on Show Cage.
6. Turn off Show End Result.

7. Select the edge rings that cross the shoulder portion of the cape.

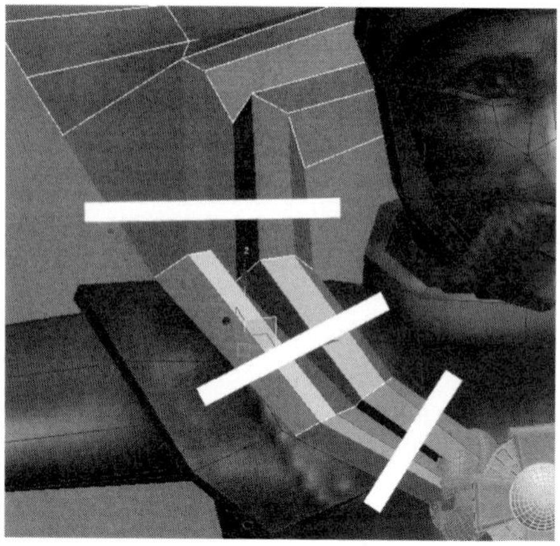

8. Choose the Settings button next to Connect and set the Connect Edge Segments to 1 and press OK.

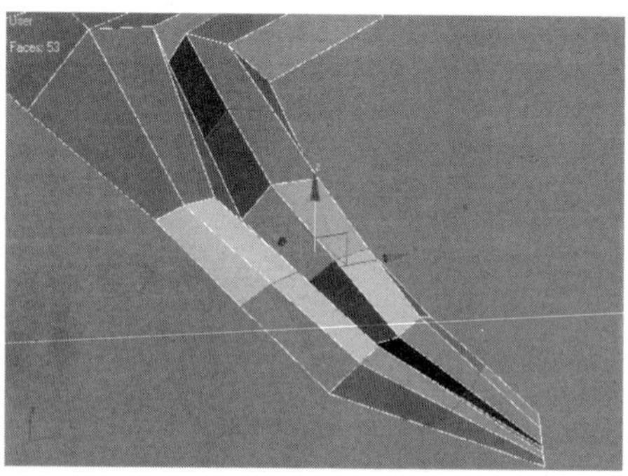

9. Edit the new vertices to make the cape look more natural as it curves over the shoulders of the character.

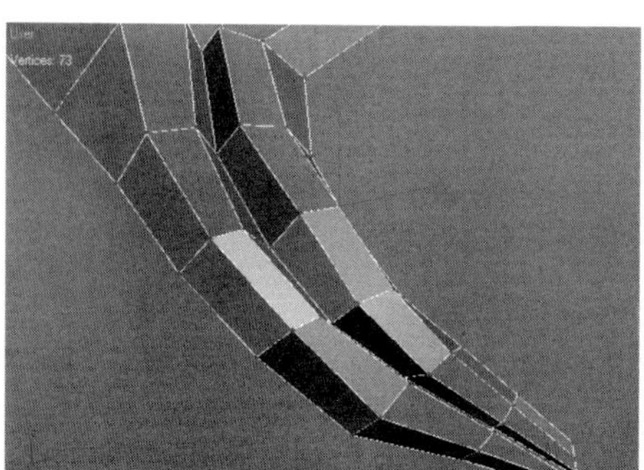

10. Exit Sub-Object.
11. On the Modifier List drop-down, choose Edit Poly.
12. Turn on Show Cage.
13. In the User viewport, select the two edges at the end of the Cape and press Ring in the Selection rollout.

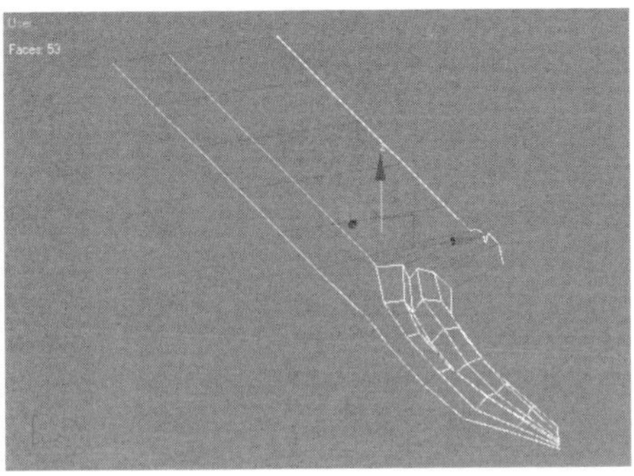

14. Choose the Settings button and set the Connection to 1.

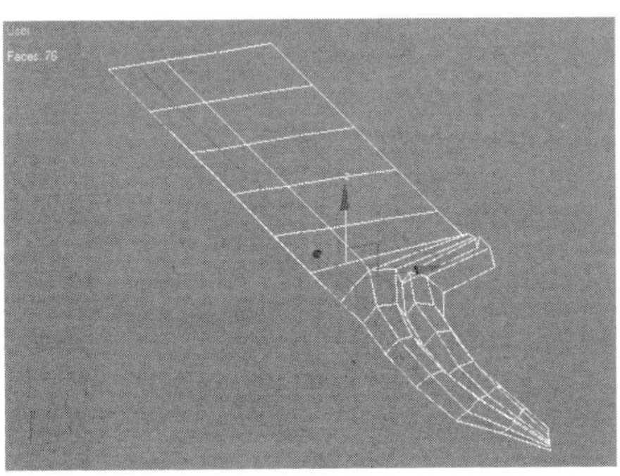

15. Edit the vertices to make the final cape model look similar to the following image.

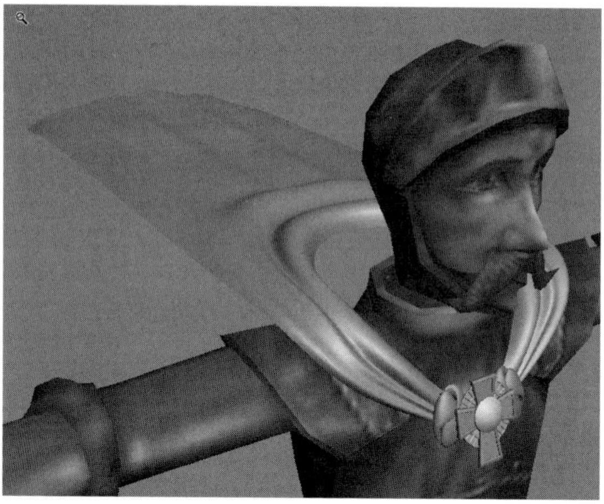

16. Save the file as ***knightCape07.max***.

Using Reactor

In this section, you drape the cape over the back of the character using Reactor. You use the low-resolution cape with the low-resolution character to solve the reactor cloth solution. You then use the Skin Wrap modifier on the high-resolution cape model and reference the low-resolution model. This approach assists the animation setup and makes the cape look natural as it hangs from the character.

You use the following three Reactor components:

- Cloth Collection and Modifier for the cape.
- Deforming Mesh Collection for the collision object on the low-resolution body.
- Rigid Body Collection as an anchor. This determines how the front of the cape drapes the chest.

1. Continue from the previous exercise, or open *KnightCap07.max*.
2. Unhide the low-resolution character and cape and hide the high-resolution character and cape.

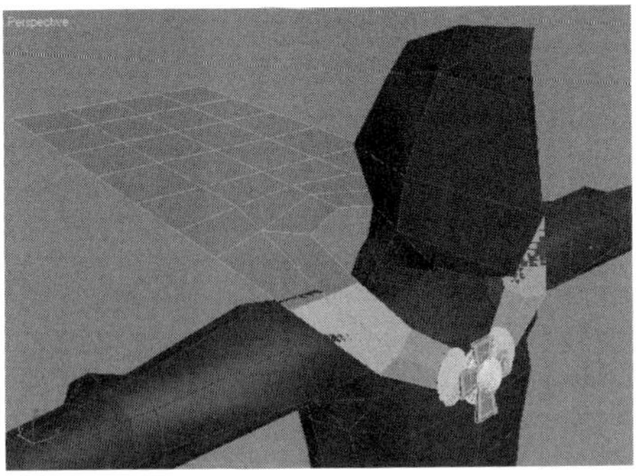

3. Select Knight_GEO_LowResCape.
4. Move the cape if it intersects the low-resolution model.

   Note: You might also want to add more edge loops across the shoulder area to make sure there are enough vertices to collide with the character. You can first make the solution and see the result before you start adding more geometry.
5. On the Reactor toolbar, choose Apply Cloth Modifier.
6. In the Modify Stack display, make sure the reactor Cloth modifier is on top of the stack.

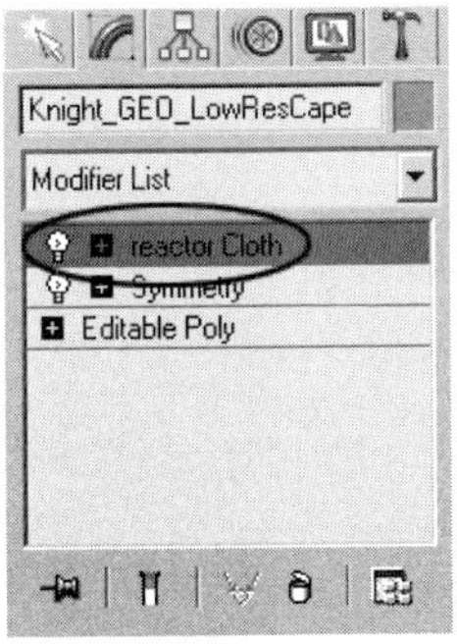

7. On the Reactor toolbar, choose Create Cloth Collection.

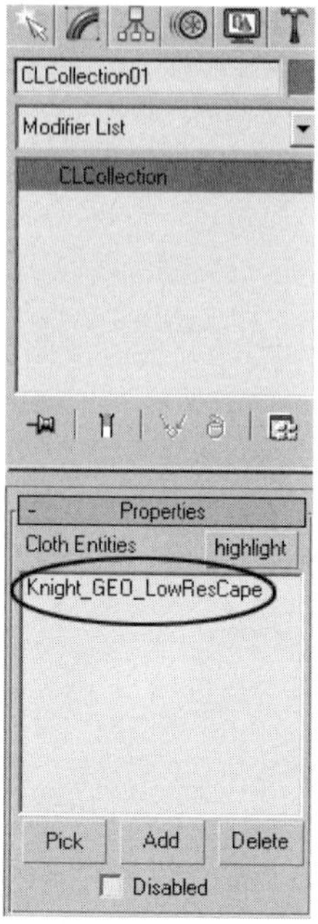

This adds a Cloth Collection object in the viewport and has added the Cape to its Properties.

8. In the User viewport, choose Knight_GEO_BodyLowRes.

9. From the Reactor toolbar, choose Create Deforming Mesh Collection.

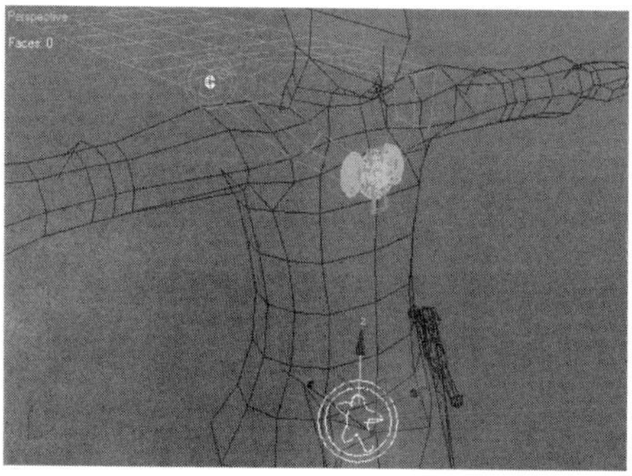

A Deforming Mesh Collection object is created in the viewport and the low-resolution mesh is added to its Properties.

10. In the User viewport, choose Knight_GEO_pendantCenter.

11. On the Reactor toolbar, choose Create Rigid Collection.

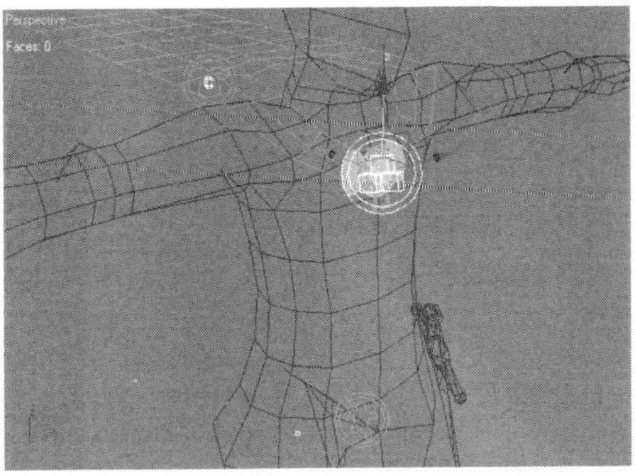

A Rigid Body Collection object is created and the Pendant is added to its Properties.

12. On the Reactor toolbar, choose Preview Animation.

Note: If you get an error stating there are interpenetrations, go to the cape and make sure no vertices have collided with the body of the character.

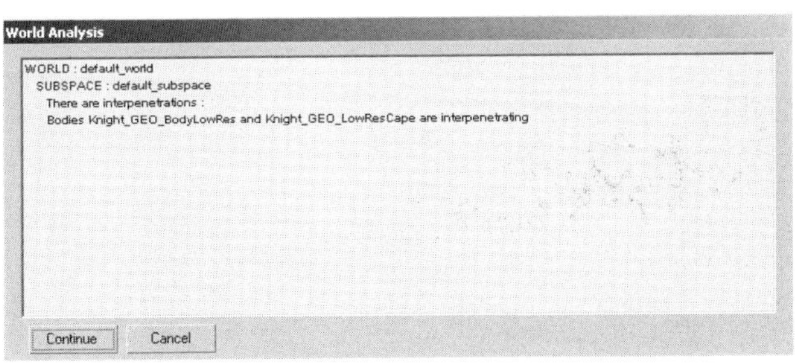

13. If there are no interpenetrations then a Reactor Real Time Preview dialog is displayed.

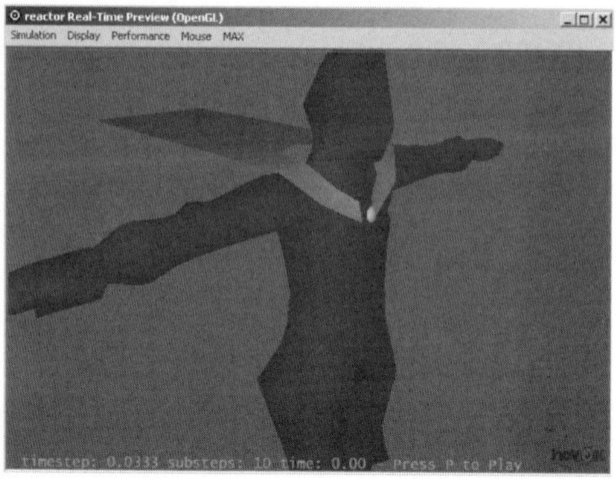

14. You may use your Left and Middle mouse buttons to navigate the preview window until you see the cape.
15. Press P to Play the simulation.

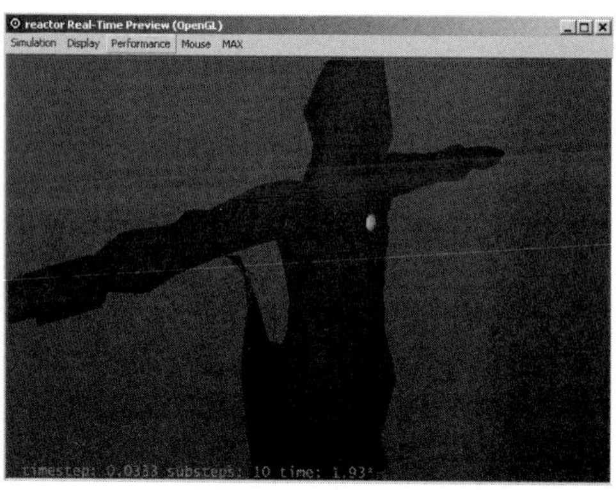

You see the cape collide with the character and drop down. You need to constrain the front of the cape to the pendant so the cape stays on the character.

16. In the User viewport, choose Knight_GEO_LowResCape.
17. In the Modify Stack display, open the Reactor Cloth modifier and choose Sub-Object vertex.

18. In the Perspective viewport, choose the vertices at the front of the cape behind the pendant.

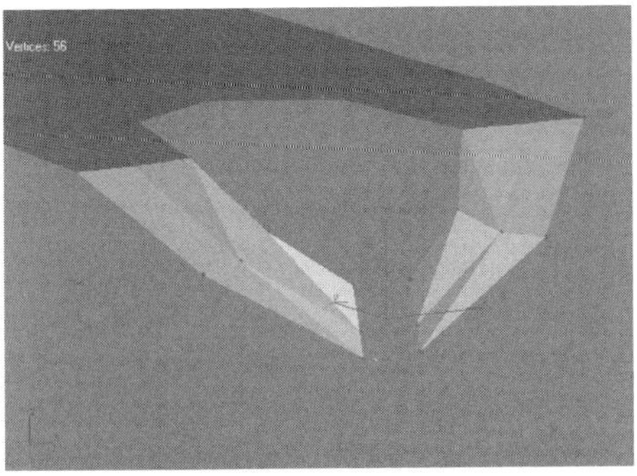

19. On the Modify panel > Constraints rollout, choose Attach To Rigid Body.

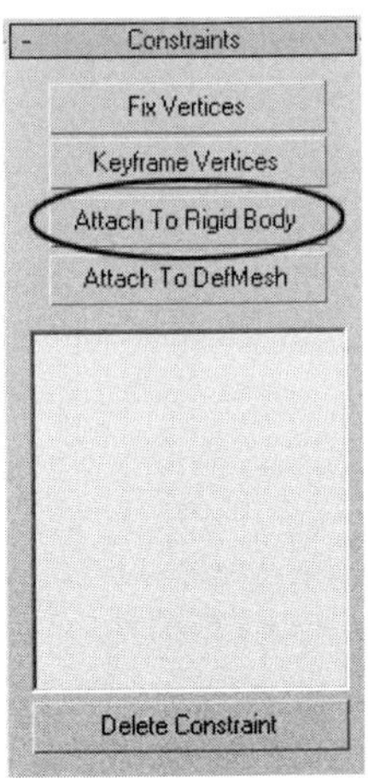

A new entry is displayed in the list.

20. In the Constraints rollout, choose Attach to Rigid Body from the list.

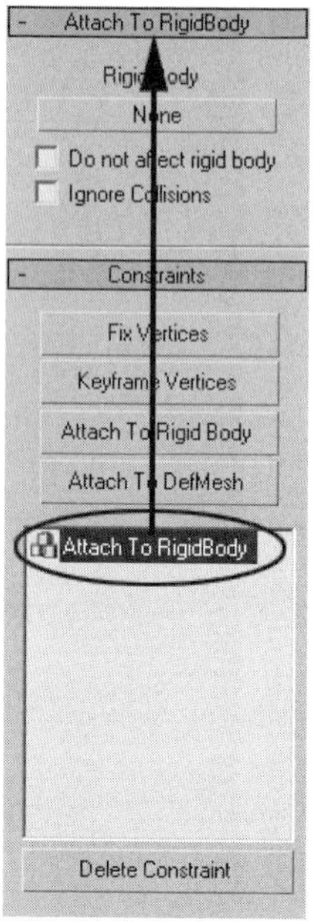

An Attach to RigidBody rolloutis displayed.

21. In the Attach to Rigid Body rollout, choose None.
22. In the User viewport, choose Knight_GEO_pendantCenter.

    The selected vertices are constrained to the pendant.

23. In the Reactor toolbar, choose Preview Animation.

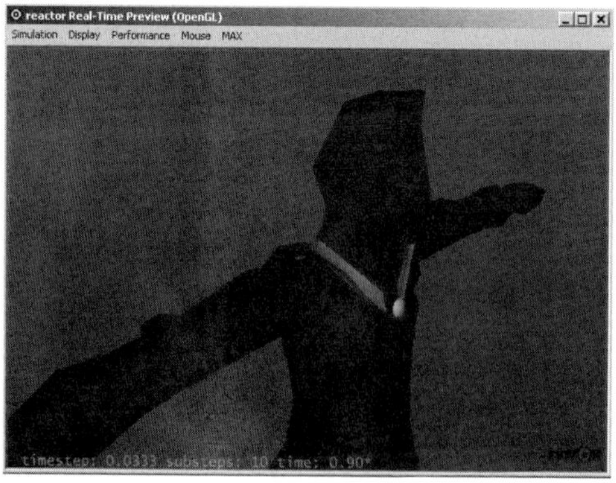

Note: If you didn't add geometry around the shoulder area you notice the cape does not form nicely. Spend time to add some geometry by adding an Edit Poly modifier above the Editable Poly object type and then make another Preview.

Tip: You might have to reselect the vertices in the Reactor Cloth modifier.

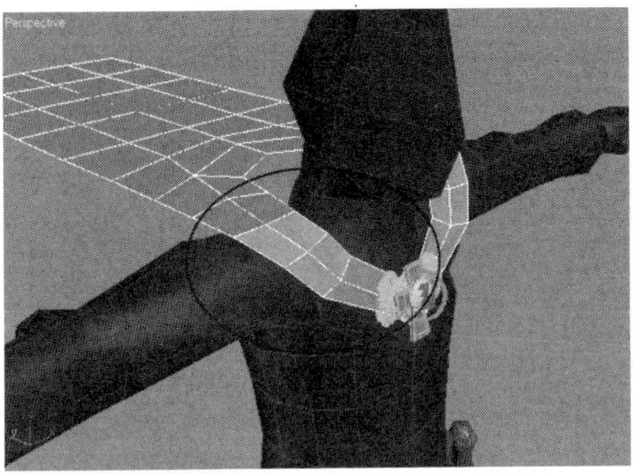

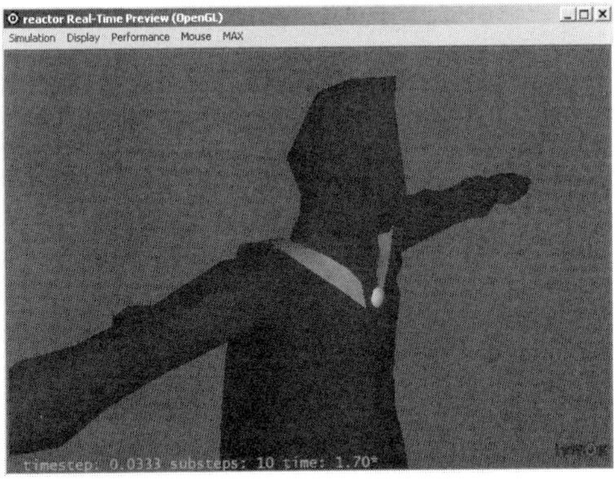

You need to give the cloth time to settle. The way to do this is to increase the total number of frames in your animation from 100 to 500. You then use the Utility panel to access Global controls for Reactor.

24. In the Time Controls, choose Time Configuration.
25. In the Time Configuration dialog > Animation group, set Length to 500.
26. On the command panels, choose Utility.
27. In the Utilities rollout, choose reactor.

28. In the Preview & Animation rollout, make sure the End Frame is set to 500.

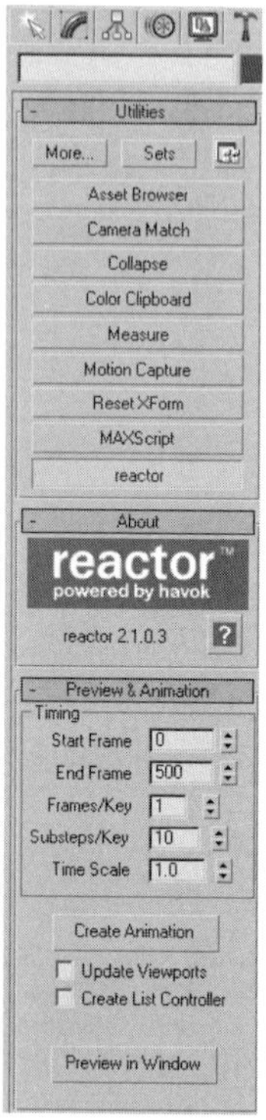

29. In the World rollout, set the Col. Tolerance to 6.

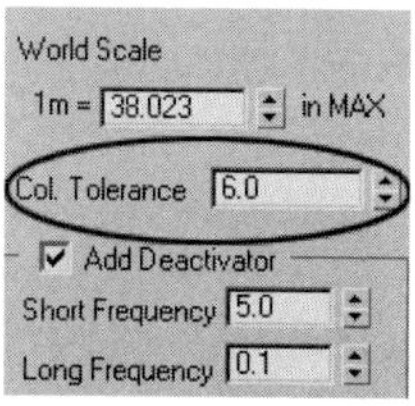

This keeps the cape from passing into the low-resolution character.

30. In the Preview & Animation rollout, choose Create Animation.

31. In the reactor dialog, choose OK.

32. It takes a few minutes to calculate the animation.

33. In the Time Controls, choose Play.

34. The cloth does not completely settle. You fix this by changing the Air Resistance to stop the cape sooner.
35. Select the low-resolution cape.
36. On the Modify panel > Properties rollout, set the Air Resistance to 0.2.
37. In the Force Model group, set the Stiffness to 1.0 and the Damping to 0.5.

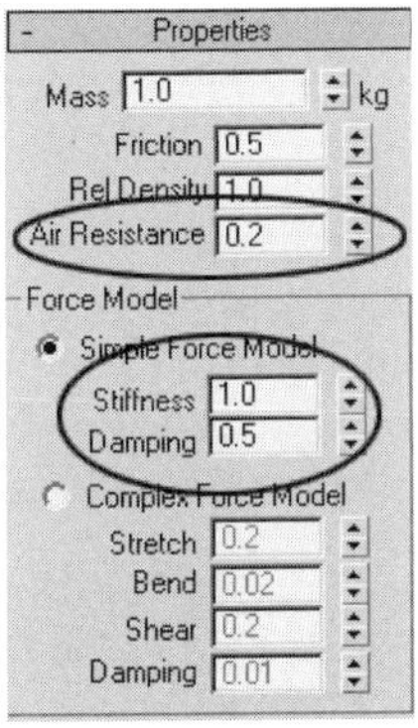

38. In the Reactor toolbar, choose Create Animation.
39. Play the animation.

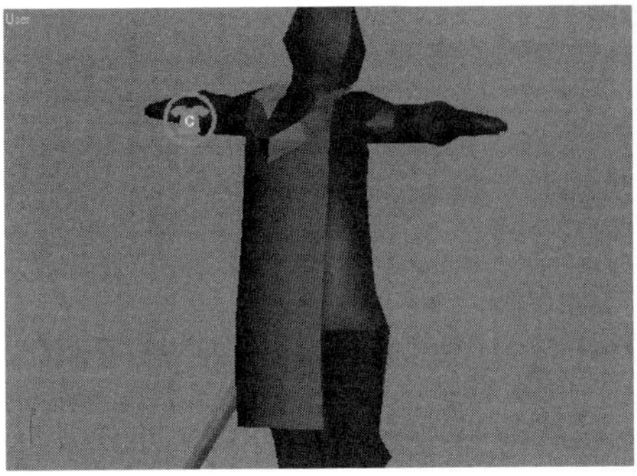

The cape now comes to a rest.

40. Save the file as **knightCape08.max**.

Skin Wrap

Next, you use Skin Wrap. Skin Wrap is a modifier that allows you to use another object to deform a mesh. The basic workflow is as follows:

- Create two models: one low-resolution and one high-resolution.
- Make sure these two objects are on top of each other.
- Animate the low-resolution model.
- Add the Skin Wrap modifier to the high-resolution object.
- In the Skin Wrap modifier, choose the low-resolution animated object.
- Scrub the time slider and watch how the high-resolution model is animated in the same way as the low-resolution mesh without adding any keyframes.

You add the Skin Wrap modifier to the high-resolution cape and then choose the low-resolution cape as the "wrapper" or "cage" object. Since you have calculated the cloth simulation using the low-resolution models, you can simply apply that same deformation to the high-resolution case by adding a Skin Wrap modifier. This saves you from recalculating the Reactor solution with the high-resolution models.

Skin Wrap Modifier

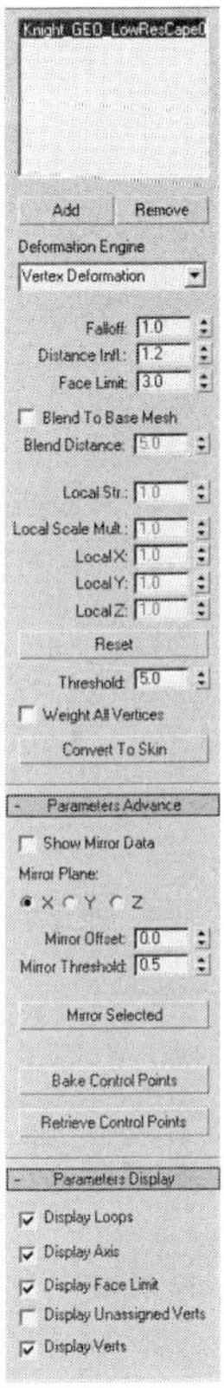

Skin Wrap supports two types of deformation engines: Vertex and Face. It defaults to Vertex, which is weighted and therefore generates a smooth result. Vertex also has more controls than Face. Face is rigid and lacks blending, which produces an uneven result. It has only one control named Falloff.

Note: No options in this modifier can be animated.

1. Continue from the previous exercise, or open **knightCape08.max**.
2. Unhide and then select Knight_GEO_highResCape.
3. On the Modify Stack display, choose Symmetry.
4. On the Modifier List drop-down, choose Skin Wrap.

5. In the Parameters rollout, choose Add and then select Knight_GEO_LowResCape from the viewport.

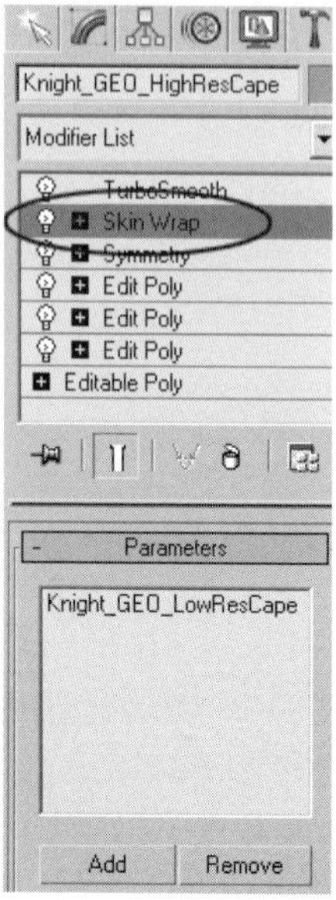

6. In the Parameters rollout, turn on Weight All Vertices.

   The rest of the default values work well.

7. In the Time controls, press play.

   Now the high-resolution cape follows the low-resolution cape.

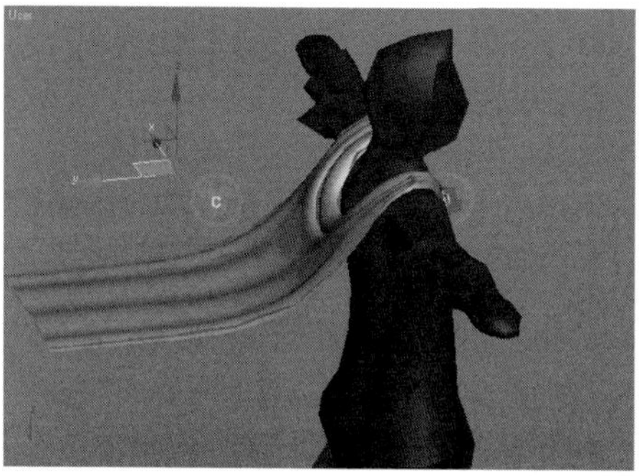

Making Snap Shots

Now that you have the capes draped over the character, use Snap Shot to copy both the high- and low-resolution meshes. Use Snap Shot also to remove the cloth simulation so that the cape, in its resting position, is the starting point.

1. Continue from the previous exercise.
2. In the User viewport, choose Knight_GEO_highResCape.
3. In the Modify Stack display, turn off TurboSmooth.

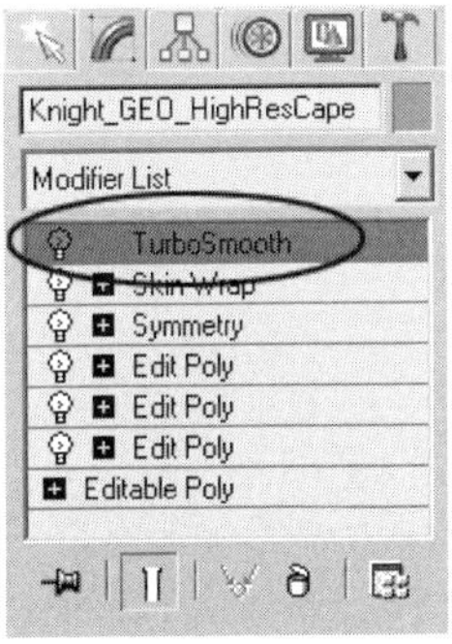

   You don't want to snapshot the mesh with TurboSmooth so that the poly count doesn't go up in the model until you decide.

4. Move the time slider to frame 500.
5. Select both the high- and low-resolution capes.
6. On the menu bar, choose Tools > Snapshot.
7. In the Snapshot dialog > Clone Method group, choose Mesh and then press OK.

8. Move the time slider to frame zero.

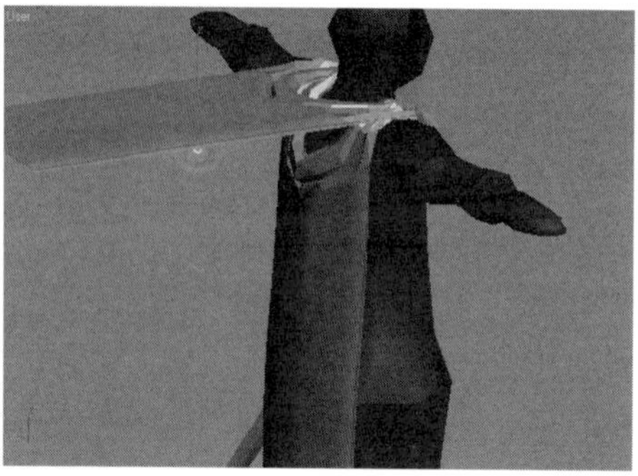

There are two new capes without the dynamics. These are the final models.

9. Select the two original capes and press Delete.

Note: You leave the dynamics icons to help you rig this character. You can reuse them for doing dynamics later.

10. Select the new high-resolution cape.

It is converted to an Editable Mesh object type.

11. On the Modifier List drop-down, choose TurboSmooth.
12. In the Main group, set Iterations to 2.
13. Press H and select the low-resolution object and reactor icons.
14. Right-click and choose Hide Selected.
15. Right-click and choose Unhide by Name.
16. Choose the high-resolution knight.

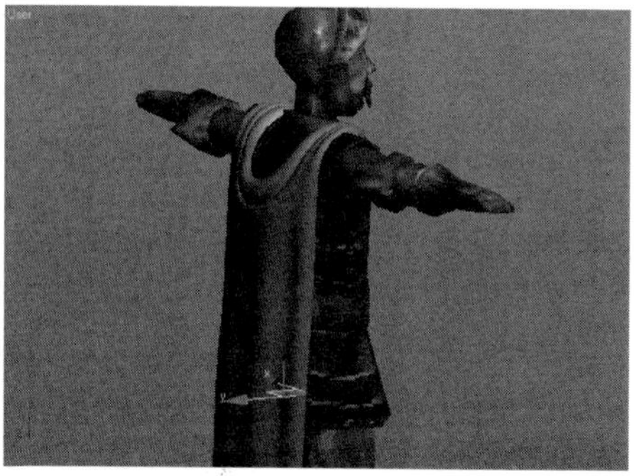

17. Save the file as **knightCape09.max**.

Using Preserve UVs

The next step is to add more edge loops to the character so that you can get better deformations in the hip area once you rig and skin this character.

Since the character is already mapped, adding geometry usually affects the UVW map coordinates. You use the Preserve UV feature built into the Edit Poly Modifier to rectify this problem.

1. Continue from the previous exercise, or open *knightCape09.max*.
2. Hide the Knight_GEO_BodyLowRes object.
3. In the User viewport, choose Knight_GEO_BodyHighRes.
4. In the Modify Stack display, choose Editable Mesh.
5. On the Modifier List drop-down, choose Edit Poly.
6. Press 2 to go to Sub-Object Edge.
7. In the Front viewport, select the vertical edges around the hip.

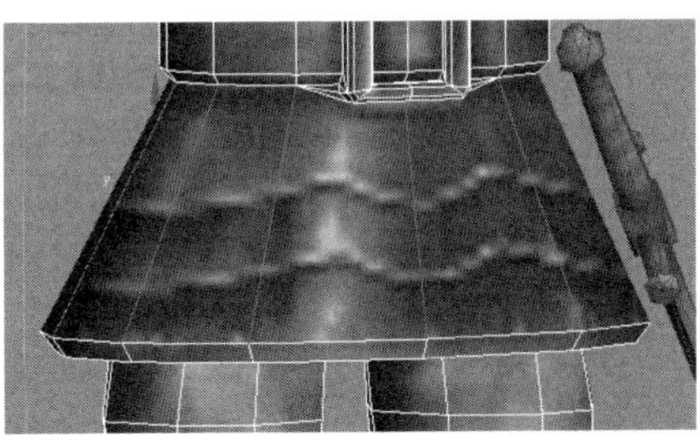

8. In the Edit Edges rollout, choose the Settings button next to Connect and leave the Connect Edge Segments set to 1.
9. In the Edit Geometry rollout > Constraints drop-down list, choose Edge.

10. In the Front viewport, move the new edges up and down.

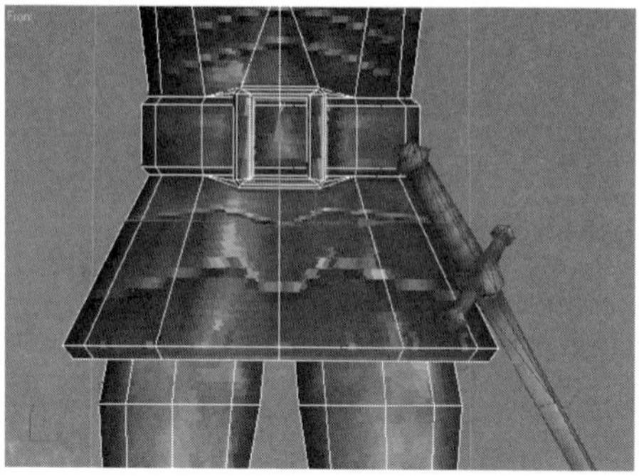

{bmc v_edges_stretch.bmp}

Notice the existing mapping coordinates are stretched.

11. Press CTRL+Z to undo the movement.

12. In the Edit Geometry rollout, turn on Preserve UVs.

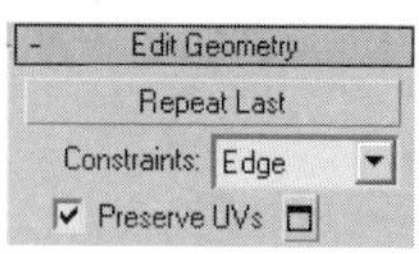

13. In the Front viewport, move the edges up and down again.

Notice how **3ds max** tries to preserve the UV coordinates. This way you can update models with little effect on the mapping.

Move the edge ring down to just above the next edge.

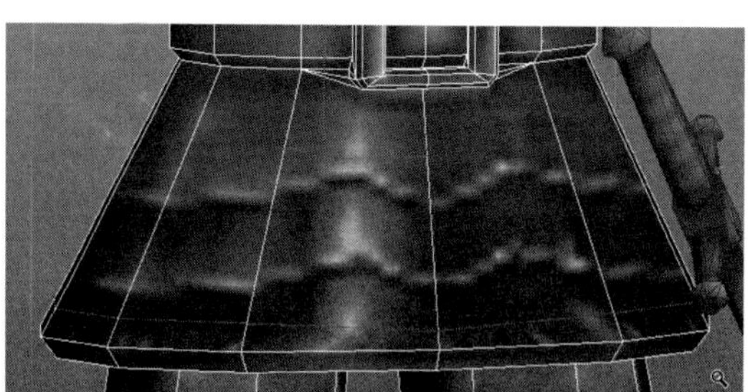

14. Select the edges around the hips again and press the Settings button next to Connect again.

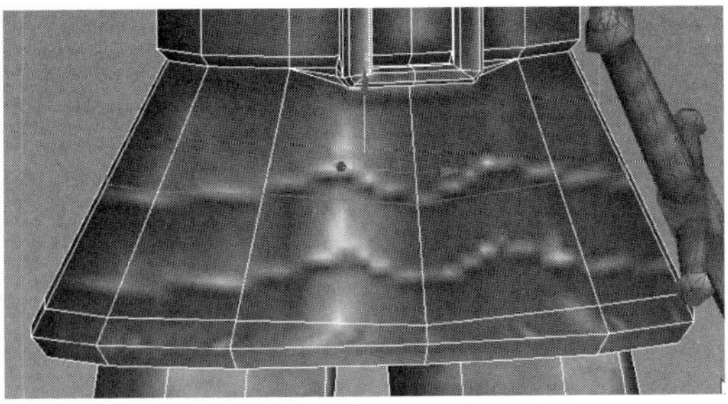

15. Move these edges up under the belt.
16. Add one more edge loop around the center of the hips.

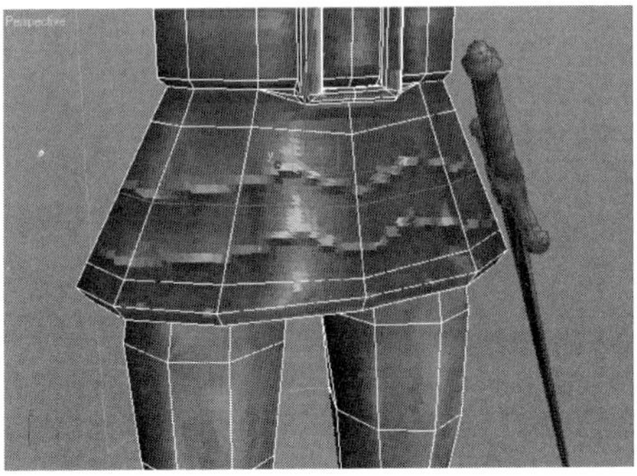

When the character is animated the hips will deform better.

Conclusion

This chapter concentrates on modeling in **3ds max 7**. Although there are always several ways to accomplish similar tasks, this chapter focuses on poly modeling using the procedural modifier, Edit Poly, and the poly object type, Editable Poly. You also become familiar with the Turbo Smooth modifier and when to use it rather than Mesh Smooth.

The versatility of Reactor was used in a modeling situation rather than in an animation. This allowed you to easily set up the necessary components in Skin Wrap. Finally, the chapter explores Preserve UVs, an option available in both Edit Poly and Editable Poly. It proved to be a versatile option to use after a character's UVs have been defined.

2 Materials and UVs

Objectives

After completing this chapter, you should be able to:

- Navigate and apply the new features in the UVW Unwrap dialog.
- Use Reactor Cloth to unwrap your models in real time.
- Create and apply Normal maps.
- Use the new Projection modifier to capture details from source objects for use on another.

Introduction

In this chapter, you start where the modeling phase ends and the texturing phase begins. You explore advances in **3ds max 7** for setting up and editing UVs, including an extremely creative use for Reactor Cloth.

You are also introduced to a new modifier called Projection. It is used to create normal maps as well as capture complex material data from multiple sources for use on a single object.

UVW Editing

You begin by editing some UVs that have already been set up and become familiar with some new features of the UVW Unwrap.

1. Open *Horse_EditUV.max* from the courseware CD.

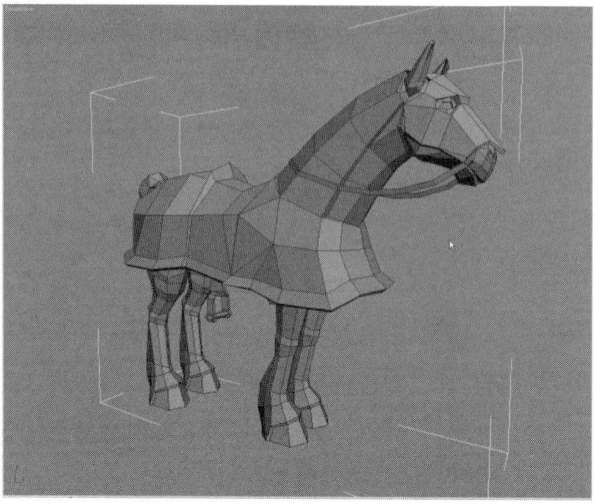

The horse from the previous chapter is displayed. The horse currently has a simple gray material applied. The first thing you do is create and apply a *Utility material* to see what is happening with the default mapping. A *Utility material* is an industry term that refers to a material used to easily see the material flow and scale on the geometry. Common *Utility materials* include checker patterns, grids, numbers, and other repeating geometric shapes and indexes.

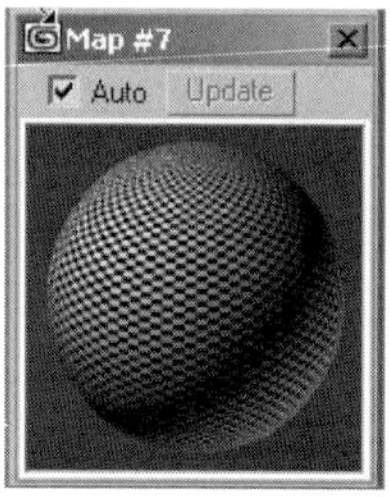

Tip: You typically turn on Edged Faces and change the shading from Smooth + Highlights to faceted when working with UVs, at least in the beginning stages. You then just toggle back and forth as needed. You might find it useful to set up these toggles as keyboard shortcuts.

Creating the Utility Material

1. Press **M** to open the Material Editor.

   In the Material Editor, the final horse material (called *Armored Horse*) is in the top left corner. Below it is the currently assigned modeling gray material.

2. Select the second material swatch called BasicStandard 8.
3. Rename it Checker TEST.
4. In the Blinn Basic Parameters rollout, choose the Map button next to Diffuse.
5. In the Material/Map Browser, double-click Checker.
6. In the Coordinates rollout, change the tiling values to **40** for both the U and V coordinates.

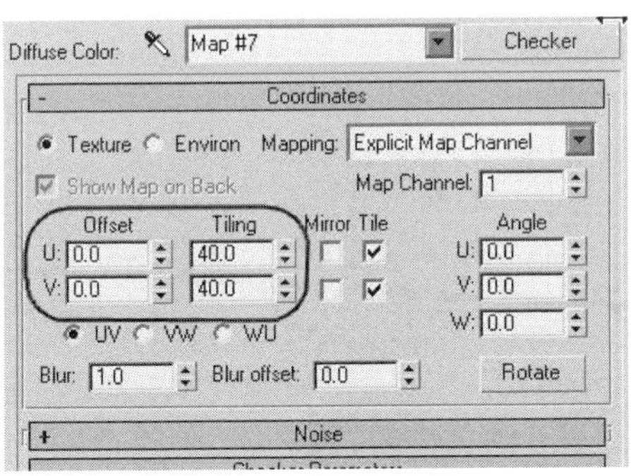

7. Click and drag the Material onto the horse.
8.  In the Material Editor's bottom toolbar, choose Show Map In Viewport.

Next, you need to look at the existing mapping and see if you spot any problems.

Spotting Problems in the UVs – Part 1

Once the checker Utility Material is applied to the horse, you begin to see problem areas clearly. The first problem is the scale of the checkered pattern on the right side of the neck.

1. Continue from the previous exercise, or open *Horse_EditUV_02.max* from the courseware CD.
2. Make sure the horse is selected.

3. On the Modifier List drop-down, choose Unwrap UVW.

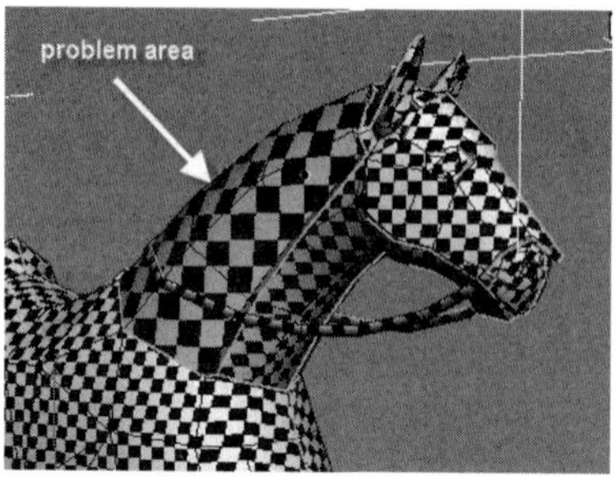

Note: Green lines are displayed on the model. You see the importance of these lines in the next few steps.

4. In the Parameters rollout, choose Edit.

   You use the Edit UVWs dialog to correct the texture coordinate scale on the right side of the horse's neck. First, move some elements so you clearly see what you are about to edit.

5. In the Edit UVW dialog toolbar, turn off Show Map.
6. In the Edit UVWs dialog, choose Options > Advanced Options from the menu bar.
7. In the Unwrap Options dialog, turn off Show Grid, and then click OK.

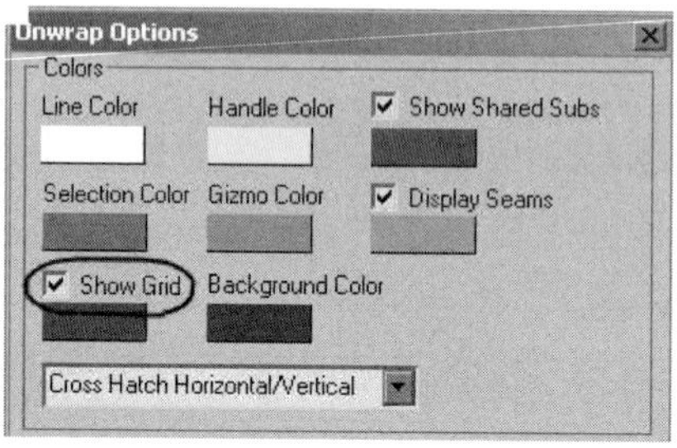

Note: All open edges are represented by green lines. These green lines correspond to the green lines in the viewport and clearly show the texture seams.

Tip: The green seam lines are sometimes easier to see when you have the model's Display Edge Faces turned off.

8. In the Edit UVWs dialog, choose Zoom Extents.

9. Pictured on the left is the side of the horse's body without the neck attached.

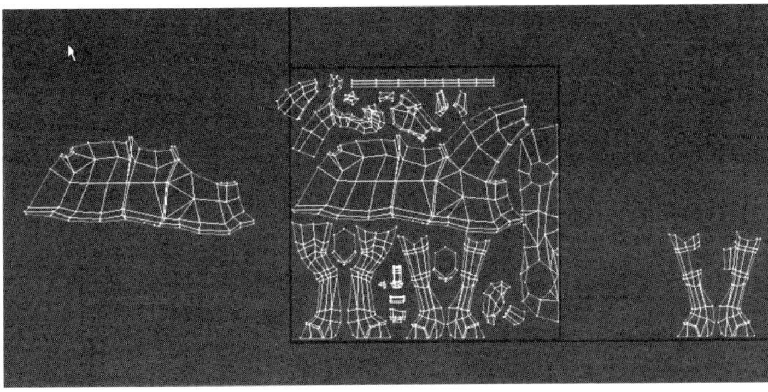

10. In the Edit UVW dialog, Zoom into this area and pay attention to the area where the neck should be.
11. Minimize the Edit UVW dialog and look at the horse in the viewport.
12. A corresponding green line (where the neck should be attached) appears on the right side of the horse, but no texture seam is visible on the left side.

    This indicates that to match the coordinates on the left side (which has correct texture scaling), you need to attach the right side of the neck and body.

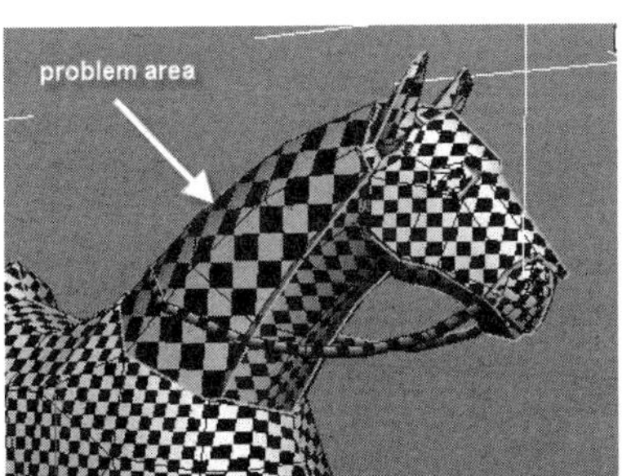

Right side has seam where the neck and body meet.

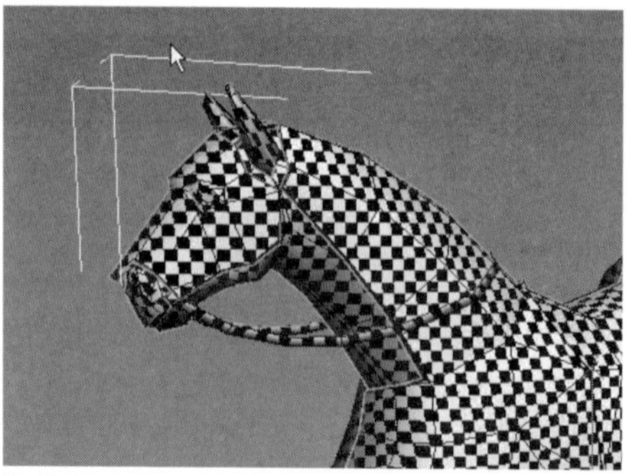

Left side does not have a seam where the neck and body meet.

13. Enlarge the Edit UVW dialog.
14. On the Edit UVW dialog menu bar, choose Display > Show Vertex Connections.
15. In the Edit UVW dialog, choose a Vertex on the body where the neck should attach.

    Tip: Make sure Vertex Sub-Object mode is chosen in the Selection Modes group at the bottom of the interface.

    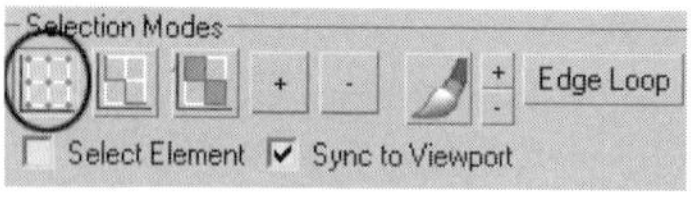

    The vertex's index number is displayed both on the selected vertex and on its corresponding vertex on the neck. This allows you to find the associated neck section quickly.

    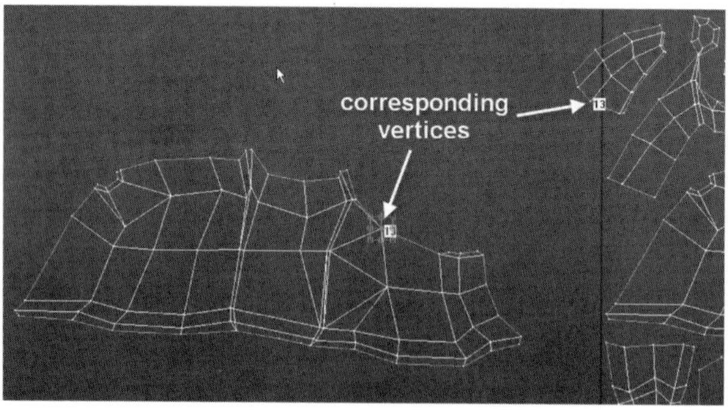

16. In the Edit UVW dialog's menu bar, choose Display > Show Vertex Connections to turn it off.
17. In the Selection Modes group, turn on Select Element.

Note: If the dialog is maximized, this area is not displayed.

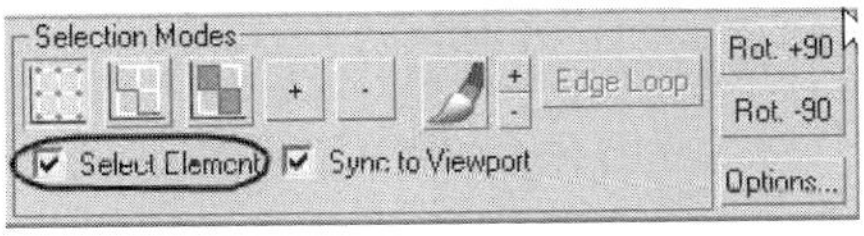

18. In the Edit UVW dialog, choose a vertex in the neck.
19. The whole neck is selected.
20. In the Edit UVW dialog, move the neck beside the body approximately where it should go.

    You can see that the neck is far too small compared to the body. You use an option called Stitch to attach these two pieces and adjust the size of the neck to the rest of the body.
21. In the Selection Modes group, choose Edge Sub-Object mode and turn off Select Element.
22. In the Edit UVW dialog, hold down CTRL to select the four edges on the body where the neck should be stitched.

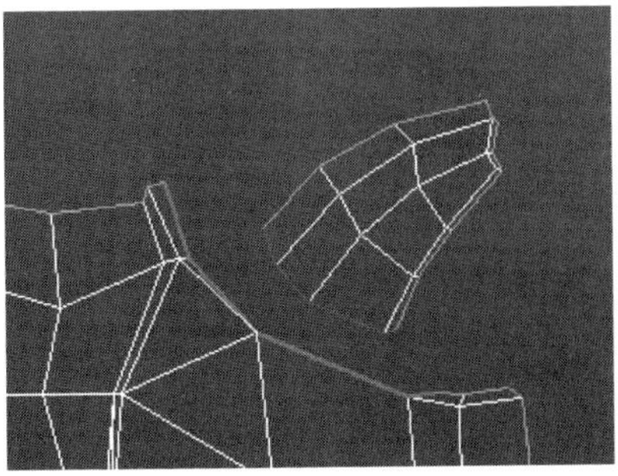

23. From the menu bar, choose Tools > Stitch Selected.

    The Stitch Tools dialog is displayed.

    The Edges are Stitched with the default setting in the Stitch Tool dialog.

24. In the Stitch Tool dialog, turn off Scale Clusters.

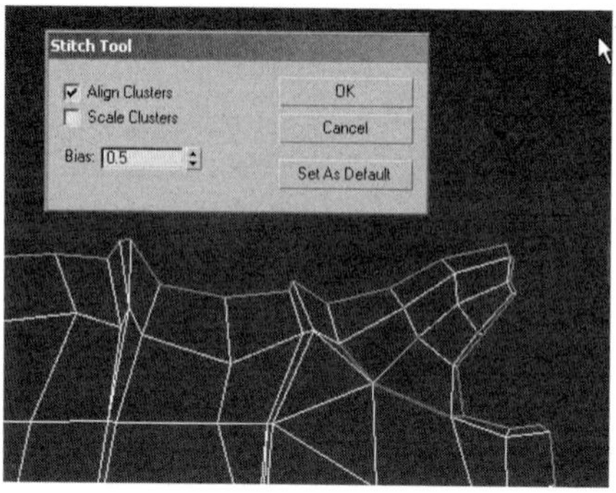

This is how the tool worked in previous versions of **3ds max**.

Note: With this option, instead of scaling the corresponding edges only, you can scale the entire element.

25. Turn Scale Cluster on.

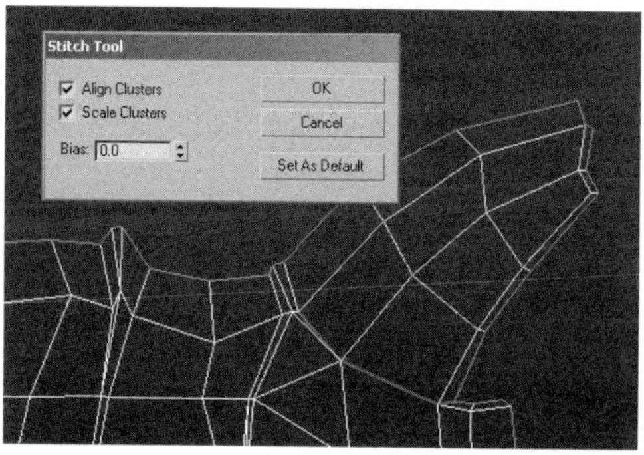

26. Change the Bias to **0**.

This option changes the neck's scale to match the scale of the body.

27. Click OK.

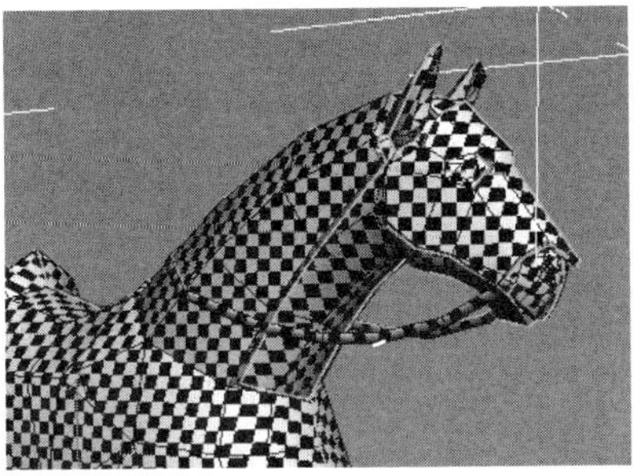

The scaling issue on the neck is correct. The green edge between the body and neck is gone in both the Edit UVWs dialog and the viewports, indicating the absence of a texture seam there. The *Utility Material* now flows correctly along the body and the neck on the right side, as it does on the left.

There is one finishing touch to the work on the body and the neck.

28. In the Selection Modes group, choose Vertex Sub-Object mode and turn on Select Element.

29. Select the body section you just stitched.

30. Move it to the right until it matches the other body section.

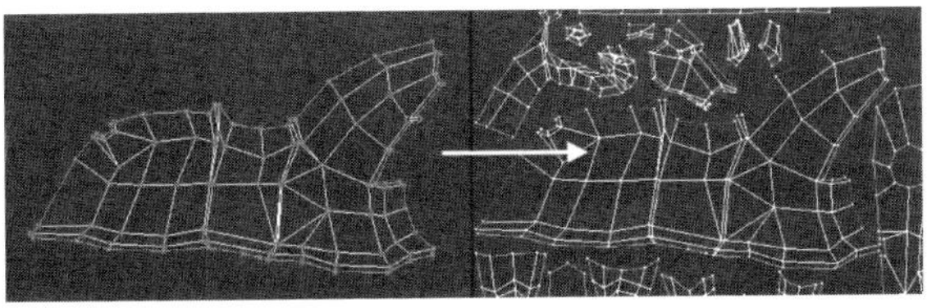

31. Close the Edit UVWs dialog.

Now that the texture scale issue with the neck is resolved, you need to check the model for any other problem areas. To do so, you make use of the new texture seam display (the green lines).

Texture Seams

Next, you turn off the material display in the viewport to see the green open edge displayed clearly. One option is to turn off Show Map in Viewport from the Material Editor. Another option is turn off Material Color from the Display panel. You do this next.

1. Continue from the previous exercise, or open *Horse_EditUV_03.max* from the courseware CD.
2. Select the horse.
3. On the command panels, choose Display.
4. In the Display Color rollout, turn on Object Color.

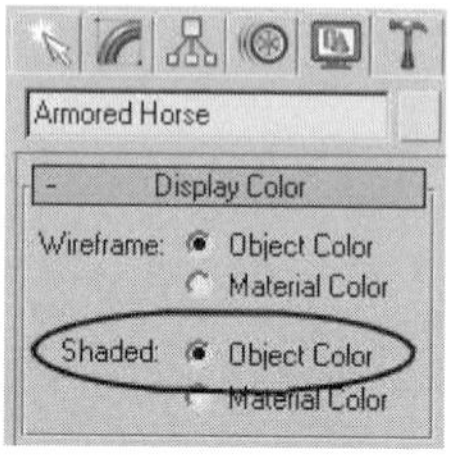

Tip: This is a fast way to turn on and off all maps in a viewport.

Next, you want to look for inconsistencies in the way the edge seams on the model are laid out.

5. On the command panels, choose Modify.
6. In the Perspective viewport, rotate the view so that you are looking at the underside/back of the horse's front legs.

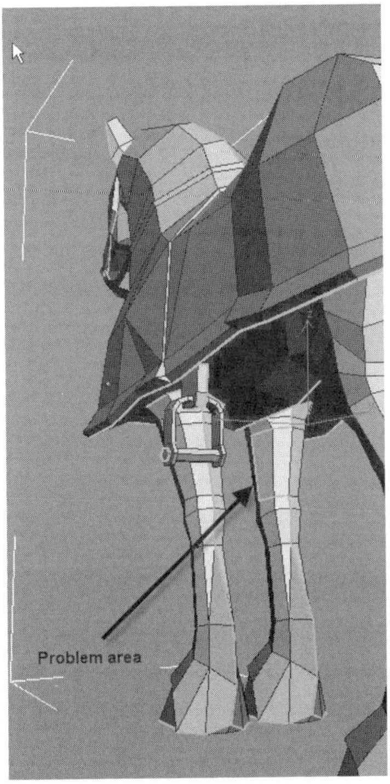

There is a problem with the way the right leg has been unwrapped.

7. On the Modify panel > Parameters rollout, choose Edit.
8. In the Edit UVW dialog, choose Zoom Extents.

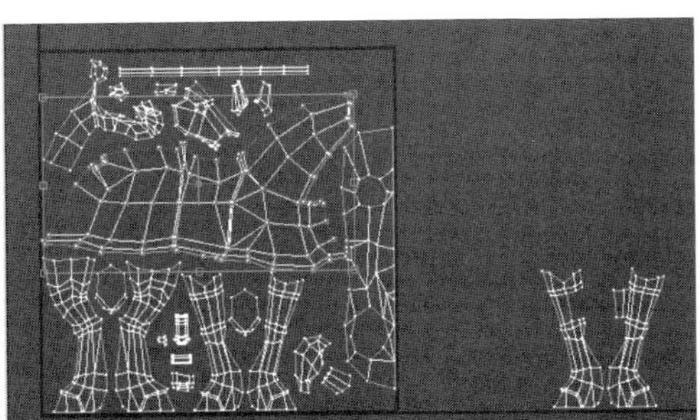

You see a leg split into two pieces with the disjointed unwrapping you saw in the viewport.

9. In the Selection Modes group, turn off Select Element, and then choose Sub-Object Vertex.

10.  In the Selection Modes group, turn on Paint Select.

    Note: This is a new option in **3ds max 7**.

    Tip: The Paint Select Mode option allows you to paint selections inside the Edit UVW dialog. There is also an option for changing the brush size. Use the Edge Loop button for selecting continuous edges at the Edge Sub-Object mode.

    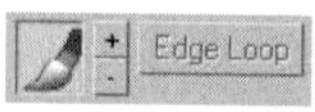

11. In the Edit UVW dialog, click and drag to select the two vertices where the extra faces are attached.
12. Right-click and then choose Break from the quad menu.

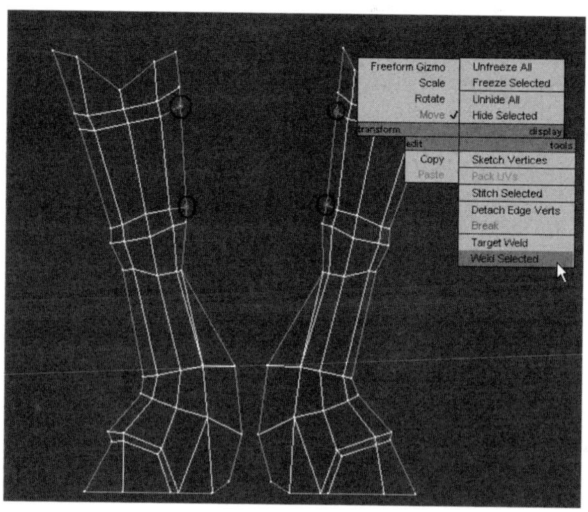

13. Turn off Paint Select.
14. In the Selection Modes group, turn on Edge.

15. On the left portion of the leg, hold down CTRL and select the edges that outline the hole where the pieces are missing.

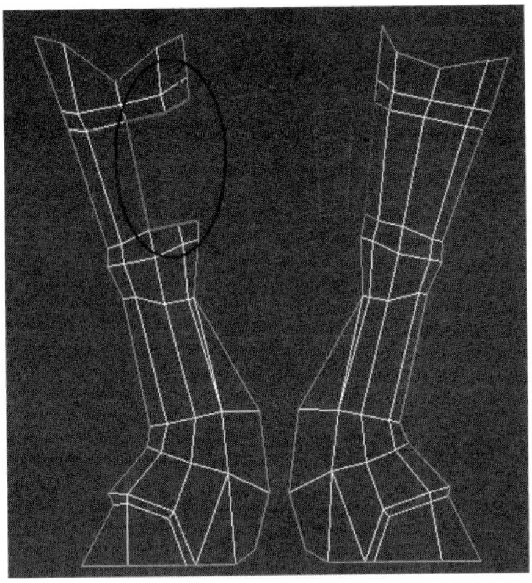

16. On the menu bar, choose Tools > Stitch Selected.
17. In the Stitch Tool dialog, change the Bias to **0**, and then click OK.

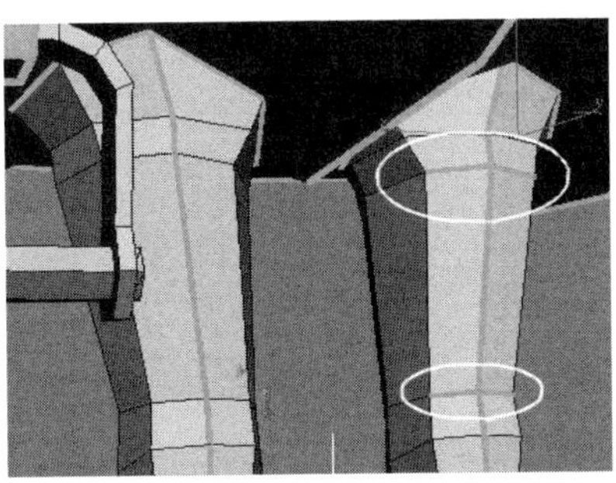

The UVs are now in the correct position but some clean-up is necessary. You need to weld the vertices where you broke off the extra piece. This is particularly apparent when looking at the underside of the front legs again in the viewport, where you see four texture seams breaking off the main vertical seam.

18. In Selection Modes, choose Vertex.
19. In the Edit UVWs dialog, region-select to choose the four vertices on the open edge of the offending texture seam (each leg piece has two).

20. Right-click and choose Weld Selected from the quad menu.

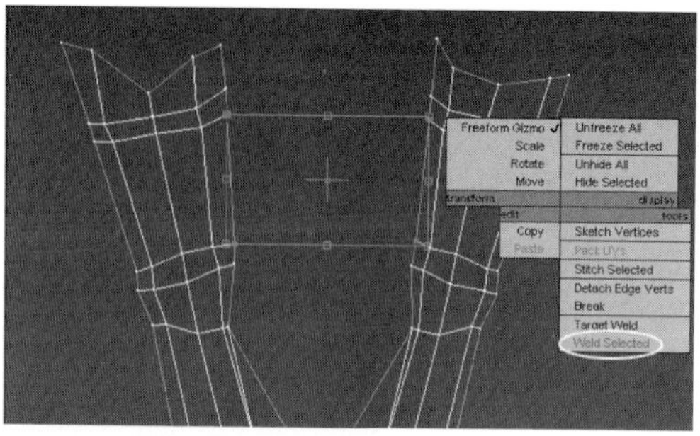

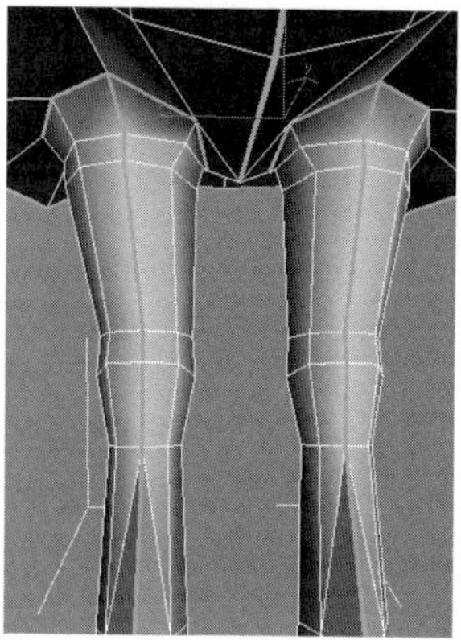

21. Select both pieces of the right leg. You can either select all vertices or use Select Element again. Move both leg pieces to the left until they line up exactly with the legs in the main group of objects.

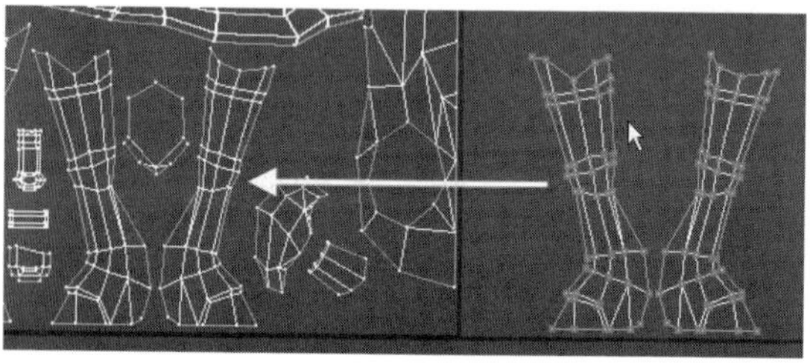

All UVs have been set. As a final step, you turn off the Show No Seams display in the viewport and apply the final material to the horse.

22. Close the Edit UVW dialog.

23. On the Modify panel > Parameters rollout > Display group, choose Show No Seams.

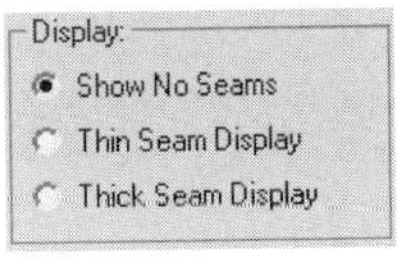

24. Press **M** to open the Material Editor.
25. Drag and drop the material named Armored Horse onto the Horse.
26. On the Display panel > Display Color rollout, turn on Material Color.

    You might want to turn off Edged faces as well.

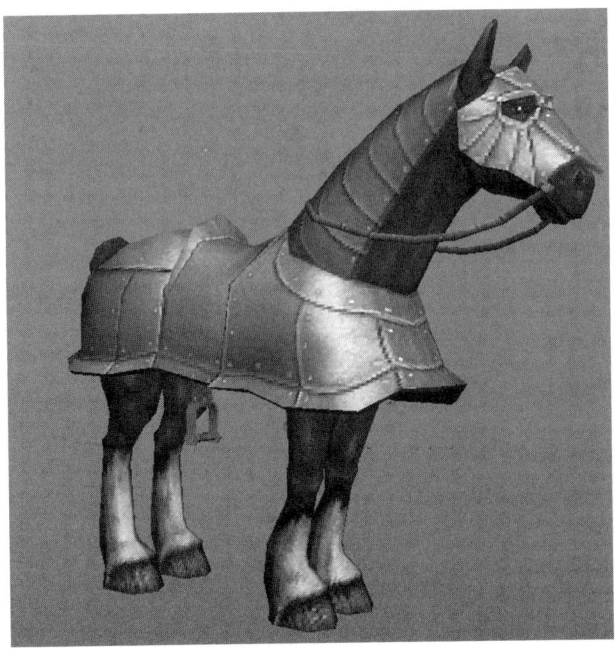

27. Save your file.

Real-Time UVW Unwrap with Reactor Cloth

Now that you are familiar with some of the new features for editing UVWs, you look at a creative way to create UVs. You use the built-in dynamics engine, Reactor Cloth and Vertex Channels, to create UVs in real time. This is an exciting and fast approach to creating UVs.

Your example model is a medieval tournament tent. The tent you work with is actually the low-res version of the final model. Later, you use the finished unwrapped low-res version that you complete in this section along with the high-res model to examine some new benefits in Render to Texture and the new Projection Modifier.

Prepping the Model

1. Open *Tent_ReactorUV.max*.
2. In the Perspective viewport, choose Tent_LowRes.
3. On the Modify panel > Modify Stack display, choose Sub-Object Edge.

   You need to plan the location of the texture seams on the model and then select them.
4. Select one vertical edge from each of the four corners.

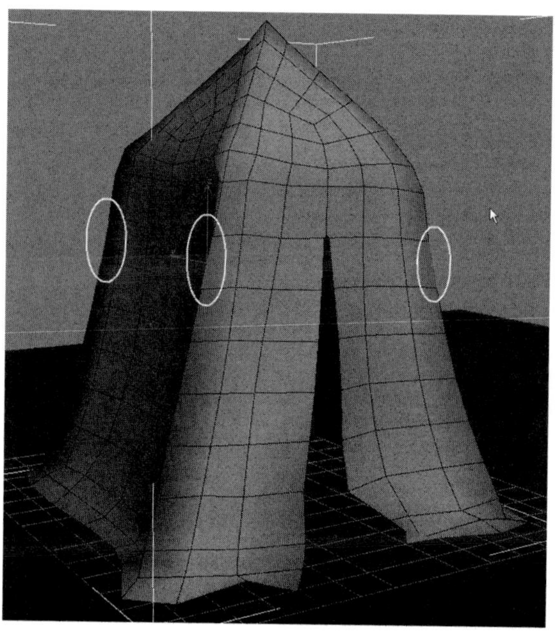

5. In the Selection rollout, choose Loop.

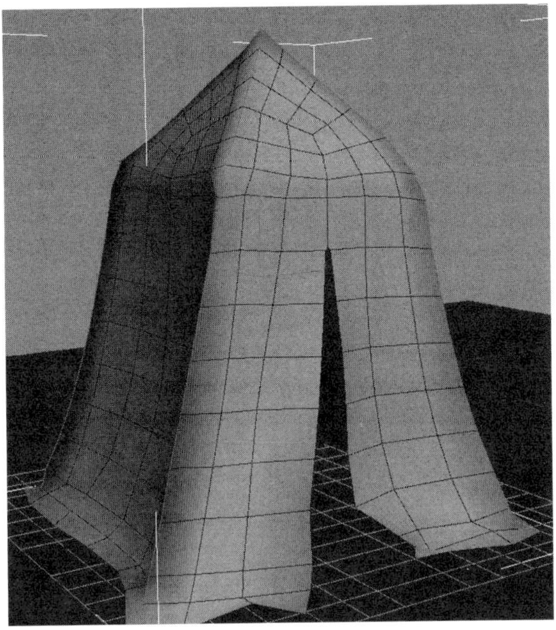

6. Hold ALT and then region select the edges for the top of the tent to deselect these edges. This leaves the vertical edges selected from each of the four corners on the side of the tent. These four edges determine the texture seams.

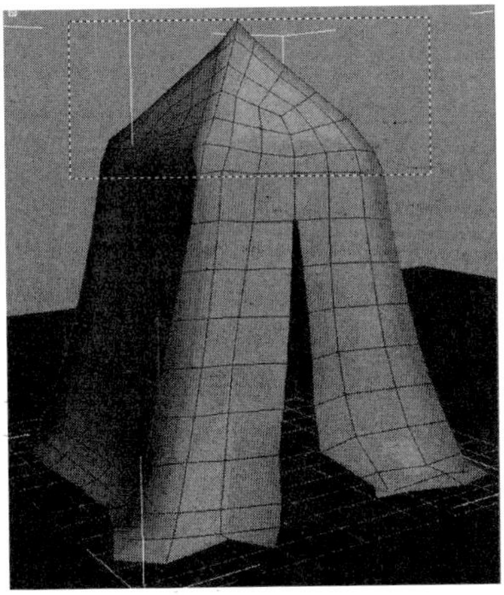

Now that the texture seams are determined, you need to prep them for the cloth simulation.

7. In the Edit Edges rollout, choose the Settings button next to Chamfer.
8. In the Chamfer Edges dialog, leave the Chamfer amount at **1** and click OK.

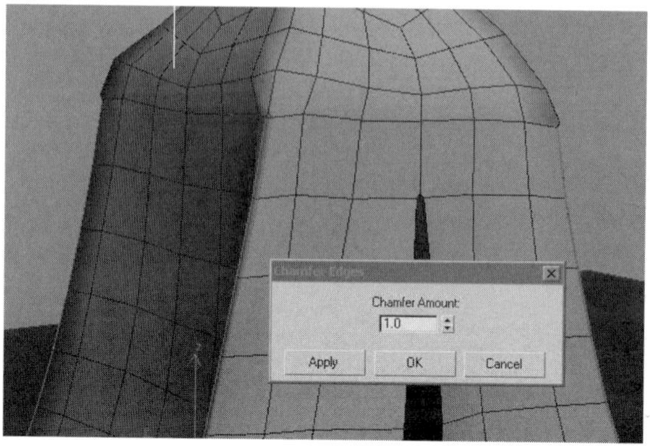

Next, you select the polygons just created from the Chamfer.

9. In the Selection rollout, hold down CTRL and then choose Sub-Object Polygon.

   This selects the polygons based on the previous edge selection.

10. In the Selection rollout, choose Shrink.

11. Hold CTRL and then add the missed polygons on each corner.

    Tip: You also want to select the three-sided polygon at the top of the quad selection at each corner.

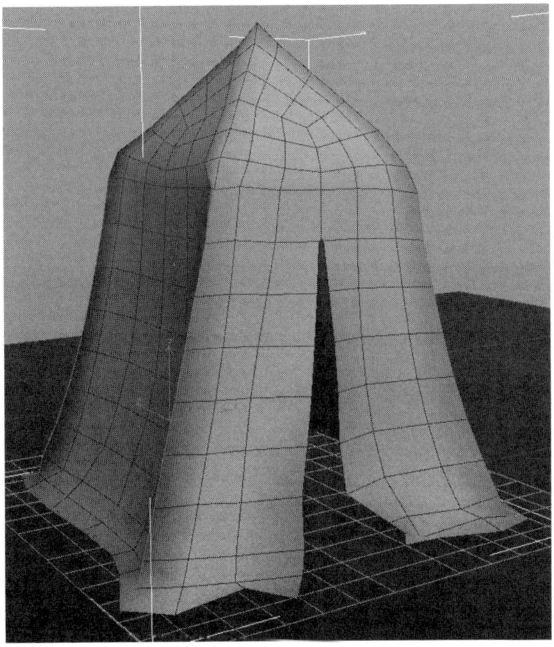

12. Press DELETE, and the texture seam preparations are done.

Using Channel Info

The next set of steps are important and integral to this technique. You store the model's vertex position information to use later in the exercise. To store this information, you use the Channel Info Tool, which provides access to all information saved to vertices such as UVs, Position, Vertex Color, etc.

1. Continue from the previous exercise, or open *Tent_ReactorUV_01.max*.
2. Make sure the tent_LowestRES object is selected and you are out of Sub-Object mode.
3. On the menu bar, choose Tools > Channel Info.
4. In the Map Channel Info dialog, look at the first entry.

   This first entry is where vertex position data is stored and you see this by looking at its ID, which reads poly.

5. Select the first entry.

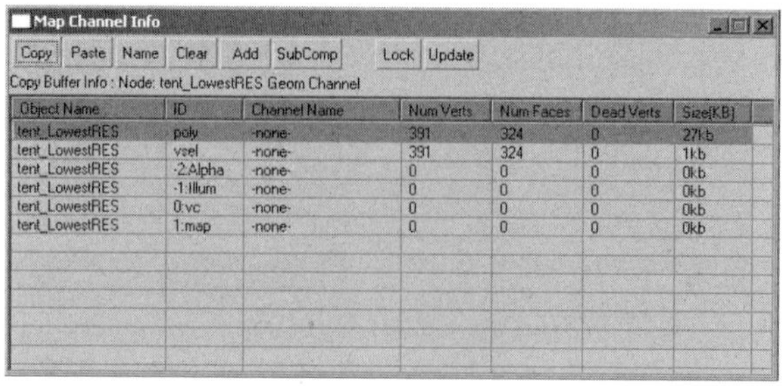

6. In the Map Channel Info dialog, choose Copy from the toolbar.
7. Right-click the first entry and then choose Add from the right-click menu.

   A new entry is added to the bottom of the list with an ID of 2:map
8. Choose the new entry.
9. On the toolbar, choose Paste.

   The Channel Name dialog is displayed.
10. In the Channel Name dialog, type Geo original and then click OK.

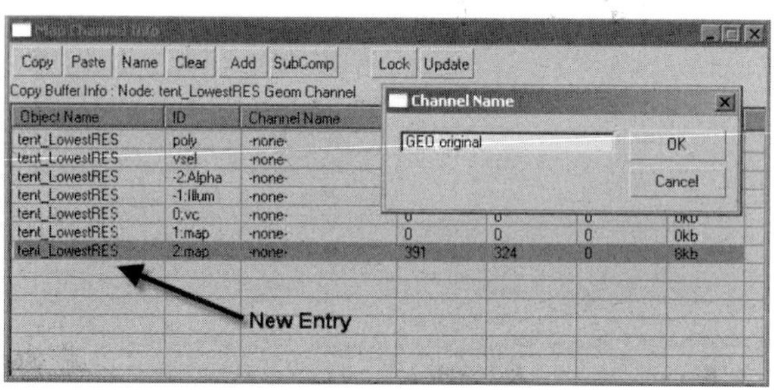

11. Close the Map Channel Info dialog.

    You just stored the current vertex position data in a new channel. This means you can modify the vertex position data as much as you like and are always able to retrieve the position data of the vertices as they look now.

12. Look at the Modify Stack display.

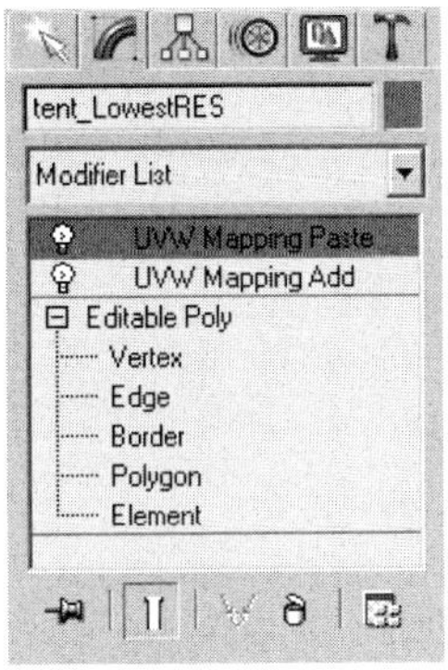

There are two new modifiers. This occurred by default based on the Add and Paste you did in the Channel Info dialog.

Next, you need to modify the geometry so that it simulates easily. This step is somewhat ambiguous since each model varies greatly. In some instances, this step is unnecessary. The point of modifying the geometry is to give it a starting position for the cloth simulation so the cloth falls flat on the floor without bunching. While performing this step, be careful not to change the relative position of the vertices too much.

13. Select the tent.
14. On the Modifier List drop-down, choose Edit Poly.
15. In the Selection rollout, choose Edge.
16. Select a horizontal edge on the second row from the bottom of the tent.

17. In the Selection rollout, choose Loop.

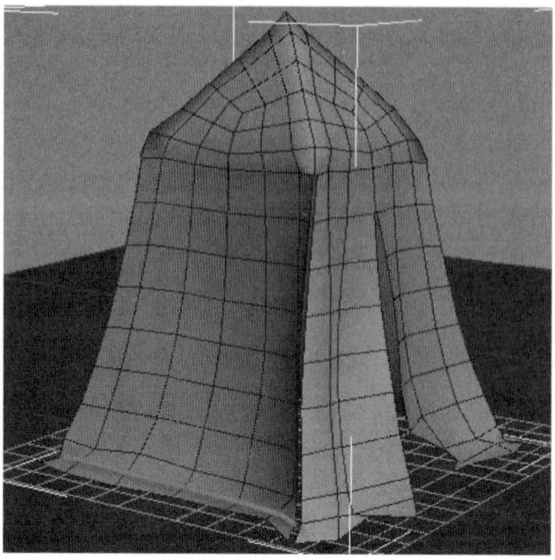

18. In the Selection rollout, choose Grow repeatedly until the selection reaches the top of the texture seam you created.

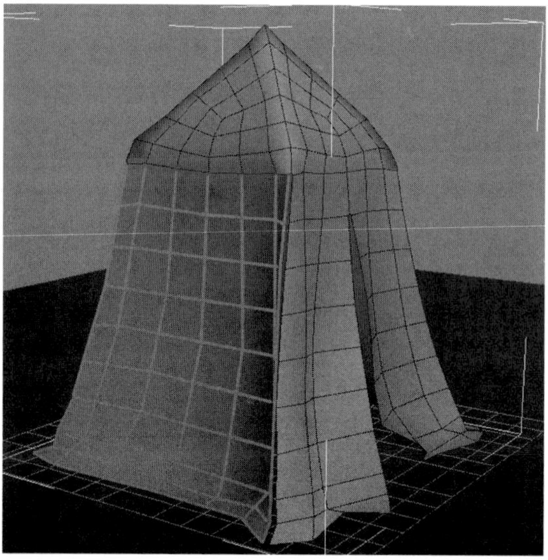

19. Rotate the selected edges approximately –90 or +90 degrees on the Y-axis so that the polygons lay flat on the ground.

20. Move the selected vertices up and out so that the relative distance between the selected and non-selected vertices is the same as previously.

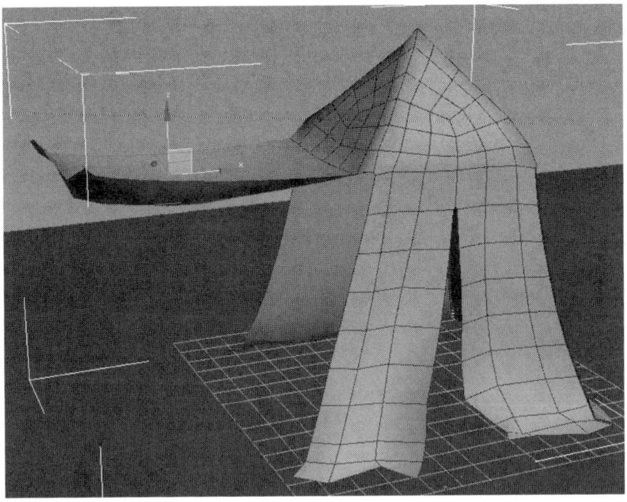

21. Repeat the previous step for each side of the tent.

Tip: It is easier to transform the two pieces in the front of the tent if you treat them as one selection.

22. In the Selection rollout, choose Element and then choose the entire tent.

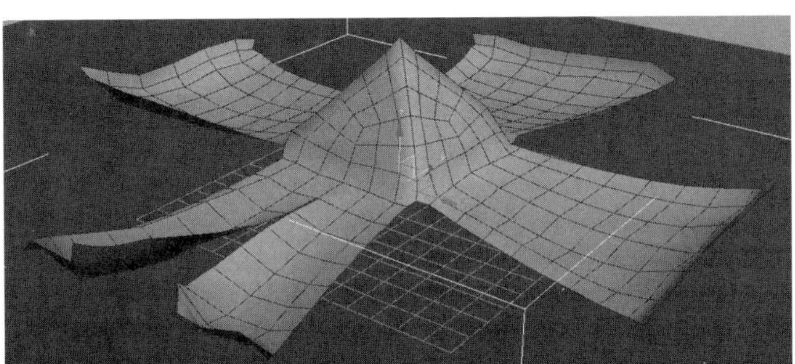

23. Move the tent down so that it is only a few units above the ground plane.

Running the Simulation

Now that you have set up the tent, you are ready for the simulation.

1. Continue from the previous exercise, or open *Tent_ReactorUV_02.max*.
2. Select the tent and make sure you are not in Sub-Object mode.
3. From the Modifier drop-down list, choose Reactor Cloth.
4. In the Properties rollout, set Friction to **0.1**.
5. In the Force Model group, set Stiffness and Damping to **0.0**.

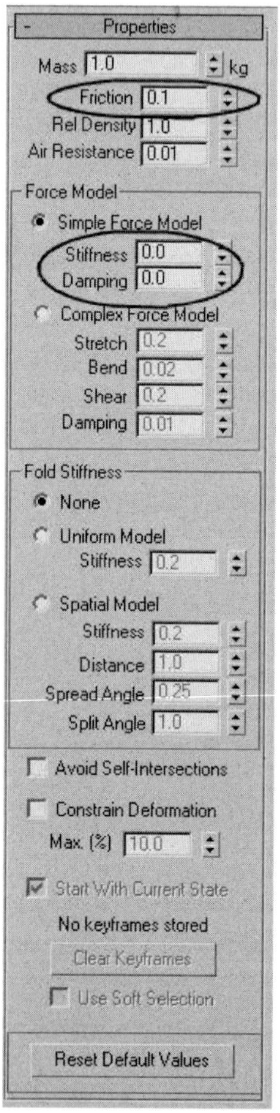

6. 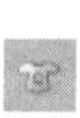 On the Reactor toolbar, choose Create Cloth Collection.

   A cloth collection is created and the tent is added.
7. In the Perspective viewport, choose GroundPlane.
8.  On the Reactor toolbar, choose Create Rigid Body Collection.

9. Select the GroundPlane.
10. On the menu bar, choose reactor > Open Property Editor.
11. In the Physical Properties rollout, leave Mass at **0.0**, Friction at **0.3**, and Elasticity at **0.3**.
12. Make sure Unyielding and Concave Mesh are turned on.

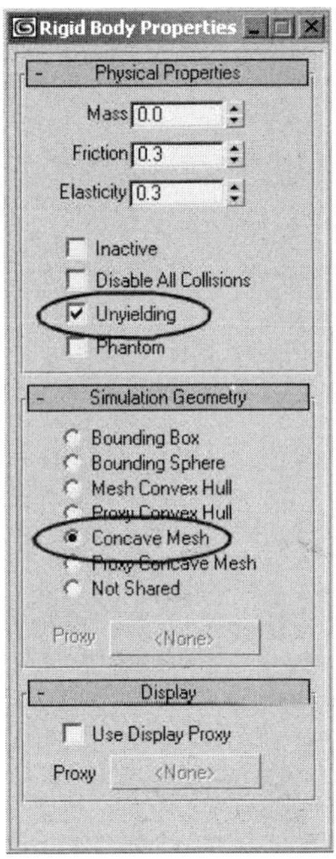

13. Close the Rigid Body Properties dialog.
14. 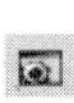 On the Reactor toolbar, choose Preview Animation.

The Reactor Real-Time Preview dialog is displayed.

15. Press **P** to start the simulation.

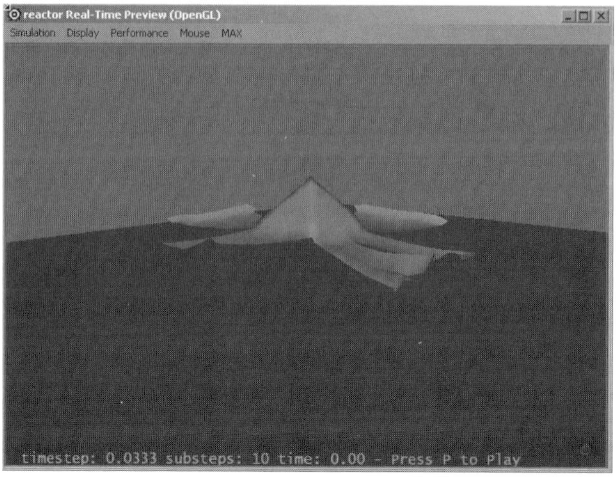

Tip: You can interactively drag the cloth around if you need to straighten things out by holding CTRL and the right mouse button down over part of the mesh.

16. Once you see the model get to a flat (Unwrapped) state you are happy with. On the menu bar, choose Max > Update Max.

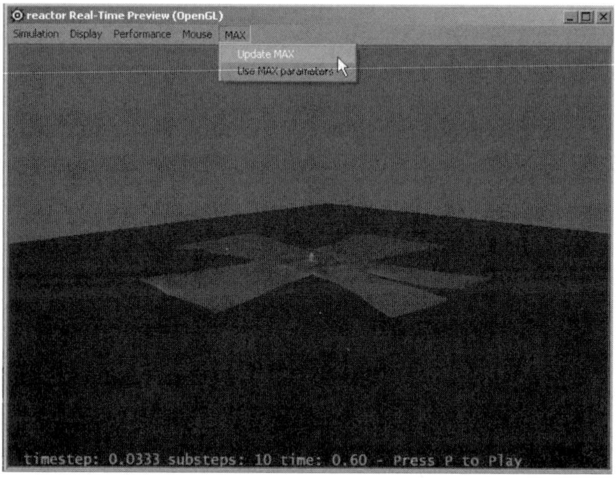

17. Close the Reactor Real-Time preview dialog.

18. In the viewports, you see your mesh is updated and is now in the fallen/unwrapped state.

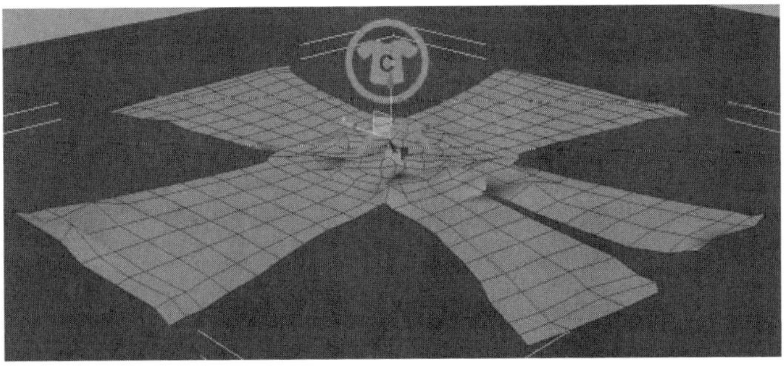

Restoring the Model

Now that reactor and the cloth simulation have done their job and flattened the model, you need to get this information into the UVs and return the model back to looking like a tent.

1. Continue from the previous exercise, or open *Tet_ReactorUV_03.max*.
2. Select the tent.
3. Right-click and choose Convert to > Editable Poly from the quad menu.
4. Delete both Reactor Collection helpers.
5. Select the tent.
6. On the menu bar, choose Tools > Channel Info.
7. Choose the first entry.

   This is the current vertex position information.
8. Copy this selection.
9. Select the 6th entry, which reads 1:map in its ID column.

10. Press Paste and enter the name **clothUV** when prompted for a name.

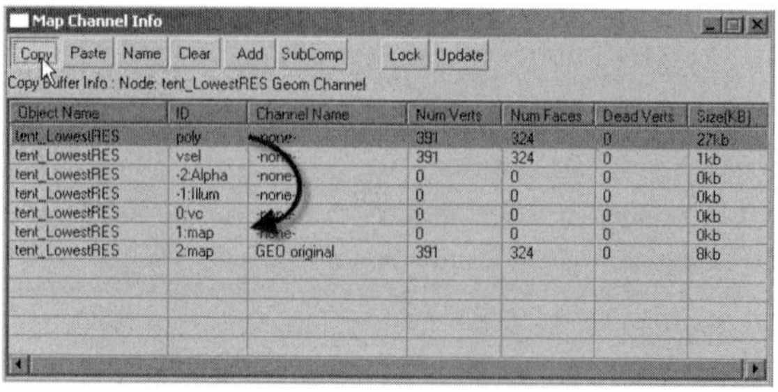

You copied the vertex position data (which is an unfolded mesh) into mapping channel 1. Now return to the original model and examine the results.

11. Select the last entry, that is, the entry you created previously that contains the original vertex position data, named GEO original.
12. On the Map Channel toolbar, choose Copy.
13. Select the current vertex position channel (the first entry).
14. On the Map Channel toolbar, choose Paste.

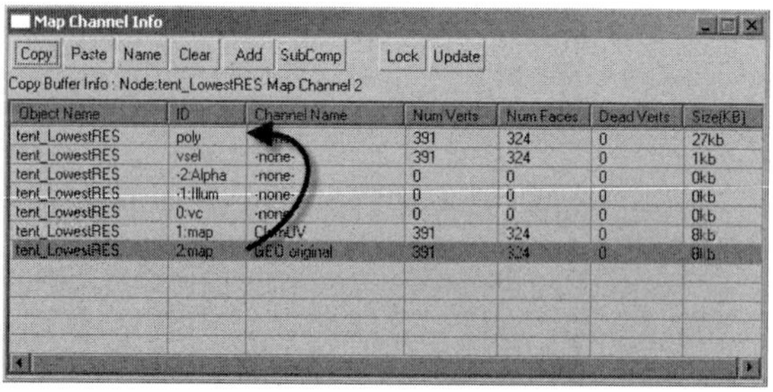

15. In the Channel Name dialog, type **OrigTent**.

    The tent returns to its original shape.

16. Close the Map Channel Info dialog.
17. Right-click and then choose Convert to > Editable Poly.
18. In the Selection rollout, choose Border.
19. Click and drag over the whole model to select all open edges.
20. In the Selection rollout, choose Edge.

21. Hold down ALT and then deselect all the bottom and door edges.

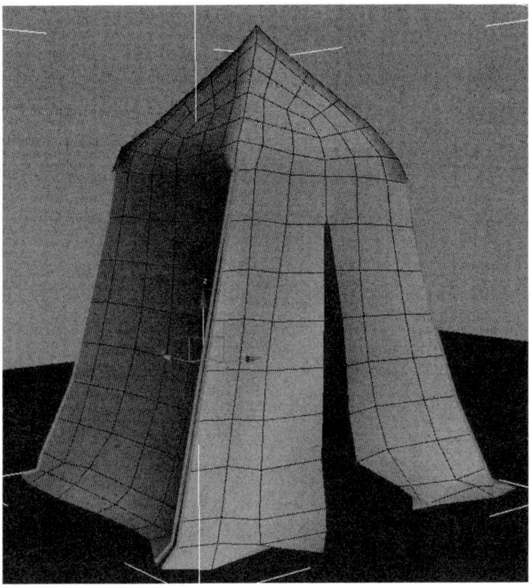

22. In the Edit Edges rollout, choose the Settings button next to Weld.

You want to weld the edges as in its original state.

23. In the Weld Edges dialog, change the Weld Threshold amount to approximately **2.0** - **2.3** or until everything is welded.

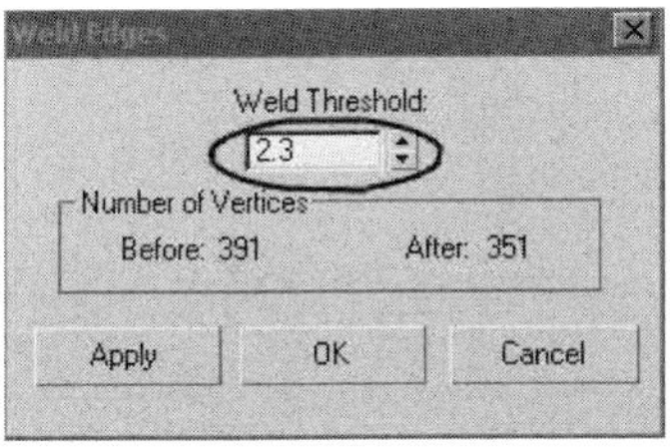

24. Click OK.

25. On the Modifier List drop-down, choose Unwrap UVW.

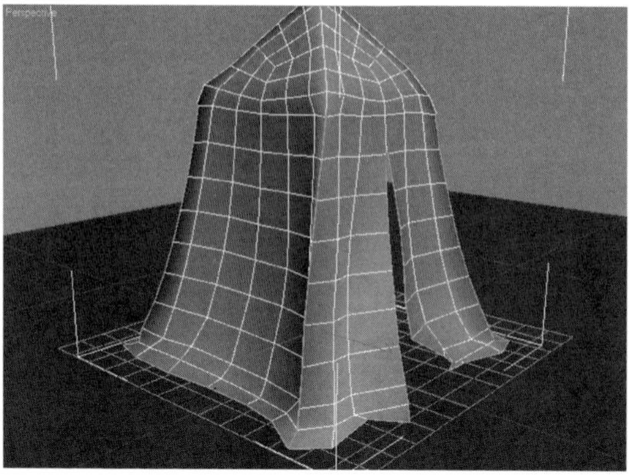

The green texture seams are in the exact location you selected at the beginning of this process.

26. In the Parameters rollout, choose Edit.

As you see, the unwrapped model is too big to fit in the texture square. You fix this next.

27. On the menu bar, choose Tools > Pack UVs.

28. In the Pack dialog, keep the default settings as is and click OK.

29. Press Zoom Extents Selected.

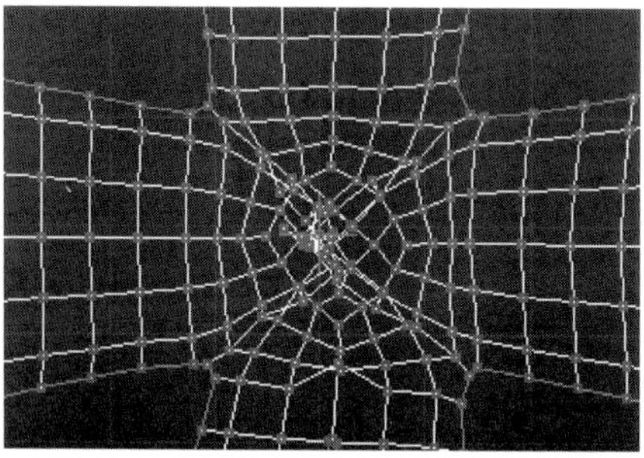

The model fits the texture square. However, the center vertices that correspond to the top of the tent look a bit tangled.

30. Select the vertex in the center of the unwrapped mesh.

31. In the Soft Selection group, turn on Soft Selection and then change the Falloff to **60**.

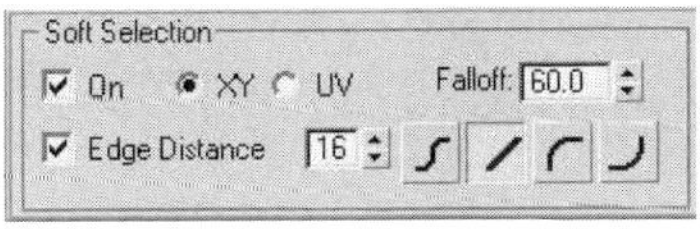

32. On the menu bar, choose Tools > Relax Dialog.

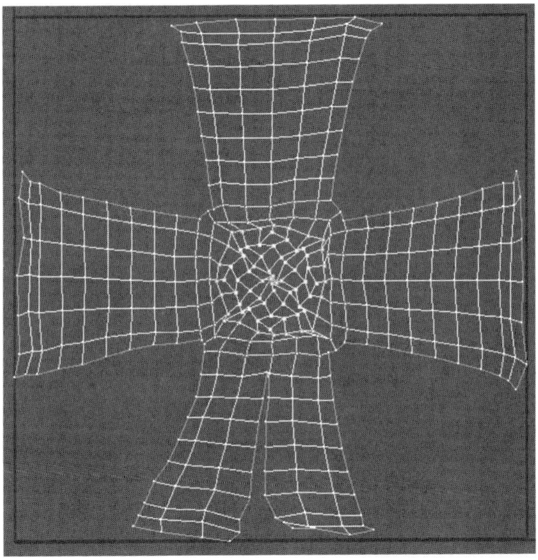

33. Change the iterations to **10** and click OK.

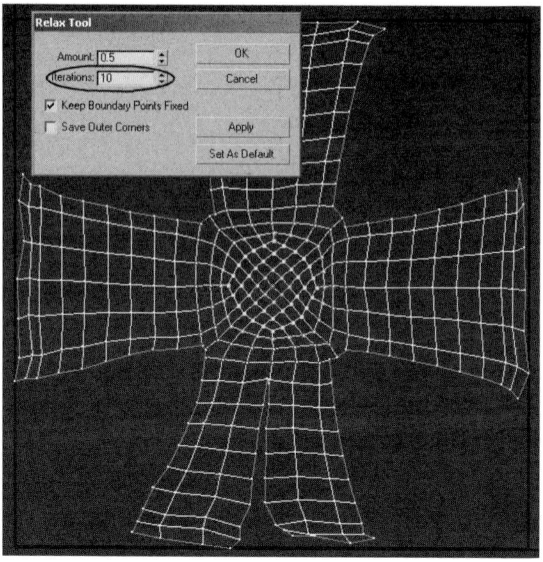

34. Close Edit UVs dialog.

You have created an unwrapped mesh using Reactor Cloth. On your own, apply a *Utility Material* with a Checker Map to see the results. You can continue to edit UVs based on what you have learned if you need to clean up other areas .

Render To Texture One-to-One

You continue to work with the tournament tent to add detail to the low-res model via the new Projection Modifier. You generate this detail using a Normal Map. This is common practice in games using DirectX shaders, which provide bump and displacement effects with normal maps.

However, while the process is certainly used for games, you see how this option is also useful for television and film visual effects.

For instance, imagine you want to create a crowd scene where you are looking over a medieval encampment. Tents are scattered everywhere, not to mention characters. You don't want to render all the tents and characters with a full- resolution hero mesh. But what if it looked like you did, without the rendering expense? You learn how with the next technique.

1. Open *Tent_RTT.max*.
2. Right-click and then choose Unhide by Name from the quad menu.
3. In the Unhide Objects dialog, choose *tent_HighRES_Compare*.

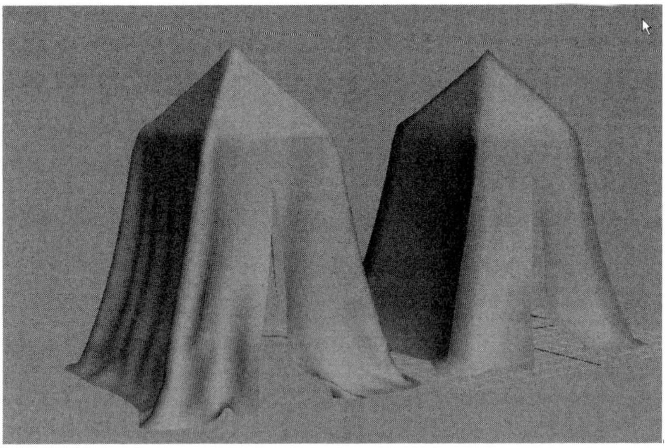

Here is the high-resolution mesh from which you get the normal information. As you see, it has a lot more detail, such as wrinkles and folds in certain areas.

4. Choose *tent_HighRES_Compare* and choose Hide Selection from the quad menu.
5. Press **M** to open the Material Editor.
6. In the Material Editor, choose the second material swatch (called plaster).
7. Drag it down to the slot below it to make a copy.

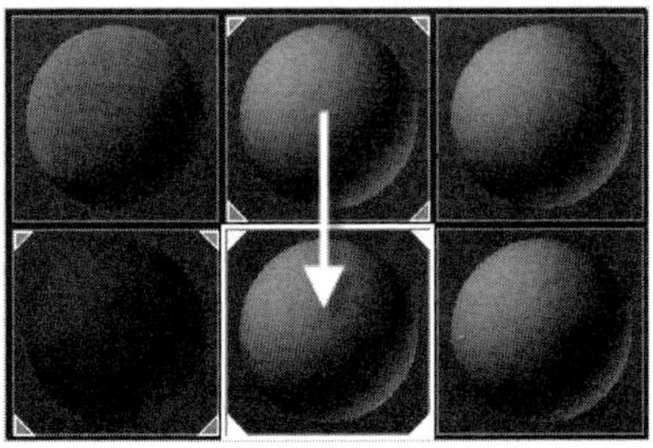

8. Rename this Material **LowRES Plaster**.

9. Click and drag to assign this material to the low-res tent.

   Tip: Simple gray materials (often referred to as plaster) are frequently used on objects to render lighting tests. The simple gray material allows you to focus on the lighting without being distracted with material-specific shaders. It can also be a great way to test Bump and Displacement maps since the details really stand out.

Setting up Render to Texture

1. Continue from the previous exercise.
2. Right-click and choose Unhide by Name from the quad menu.
3. In the Unhide Objects dialog, choose *tent_HighRES.*

   This object is the same one as previously; the only difference is its location in 3D space.
4. Select the low-resolution tent.
5. On the menu bar, choose Rendering > Render to Texture.

   Tip: You can also open this window with the default keyboard shortcut 0. Also, make sure the command panels are set to Modify.
6. In the Objects to Bake rollout > Projection Mapping group, turn on Enabled.
7. In the Projection Mapping group, choose Pick.
8. In the Add Targets dialog, choose tent_HighRES and then press Add.

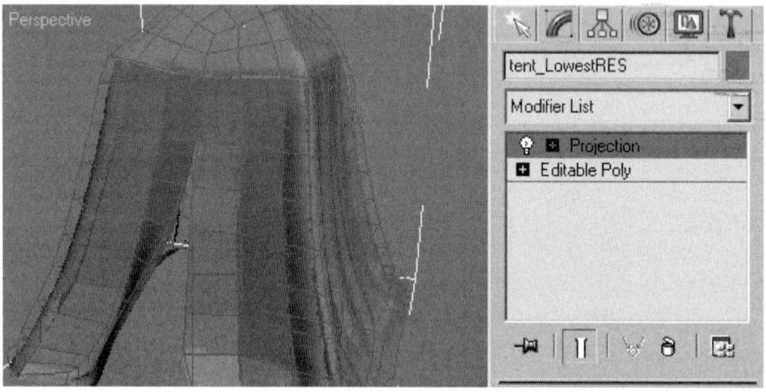

   A Projection modifier is added to the object and a blue wireframe cage surrounds the low-poly mesh. You learn the significance of the cage later.
9. In the Projection Mapping group, turn off Sub-Object Levels.

10. In the Mapping Coordinates group, make sure Use Existing Channel is on.

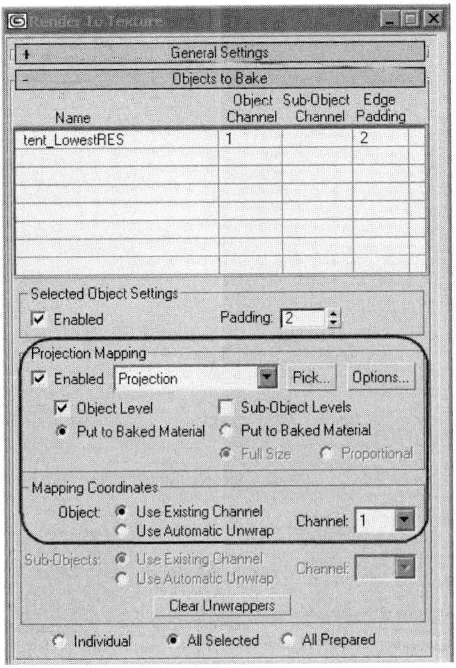

This tells the objects to use the current texture coordinates (the ones you created with Reactor cloth) for the projection. If you want, you could leave it set to automatic and **3ds max** would unwrap the mesh automatically. However, if you think you might do some touch-up painting on the generated maps, it is better to have organized the UV layout yourself.

11. In the Output rollout, choose Add.

12. In the Add Texture Elements dialog, choose Normals Map and then press Add Elements.

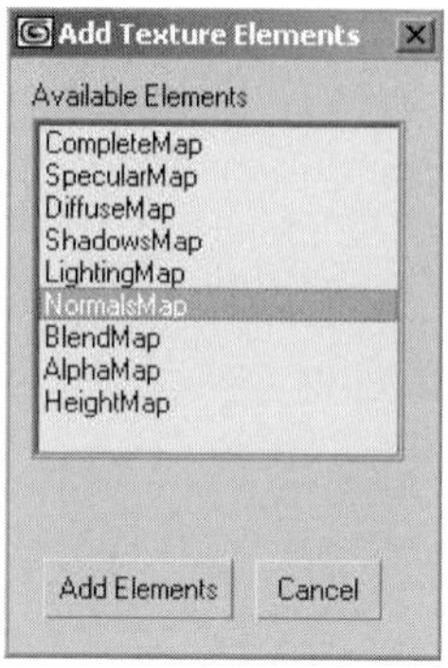

An entry is added to the output chart.

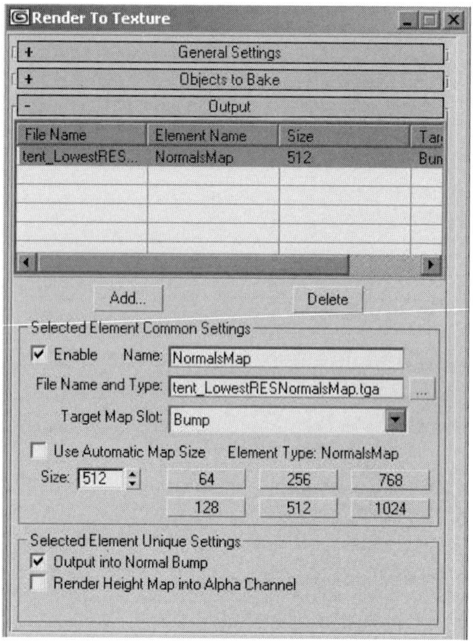

13. In the Selected Element Common Settings group > Target Map Slot drop-down list, choose Bump.
14. Change the output size to **1024**.

15. In the Selected Element Unique Settings group, turn on Output into Normal Bump.

    Tip: The Normal Bump is a new map type in **3ds max 7** that enables you to render a Normal map directly inside a **3ds max** render, be it scanline or mental ray. In the past, you were only able to use Normal maps with DirectX shaders for real-time rendering unless you purchased a plug-in.

16. In the Objects to Bake rollout > Projection Mapping group, choose Options.

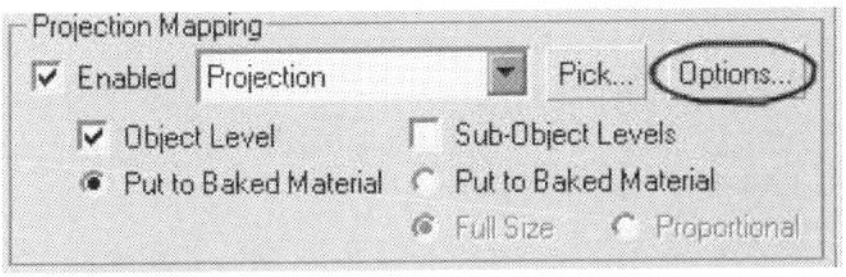

17. In the Projections Options dialog > Normal Map Space group, choose World.

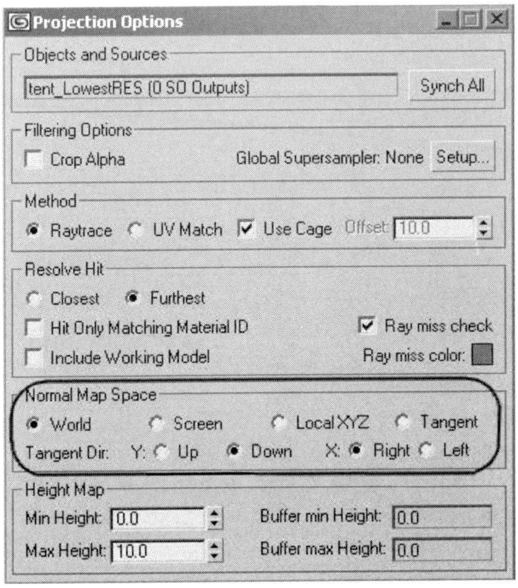

18. Close the Projection Options dialog.

19. In the Baked Material rollout > Baked Material Settings group, choose Output Into Source.

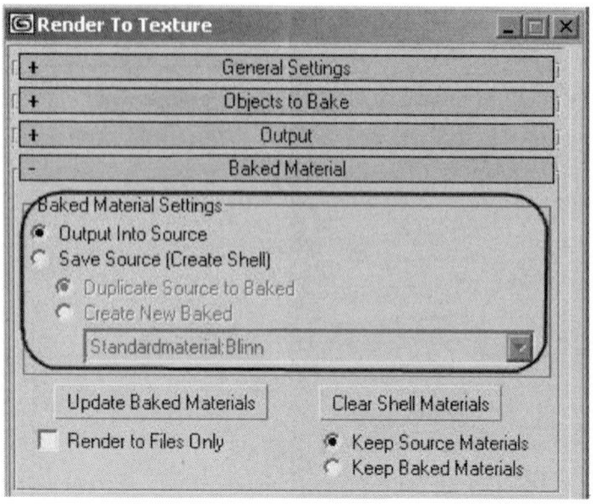

Tip: **3ds max** can create a Shell Material. This enables the addition of the newly rendered maps without changing any settings on your original material. However, it's unnecessary for this example.

20. Close the Render to Texture dialog.

Adjusting the Cage

The blue cage that surrounds the low-poly mesh defines the limits within which the projection takes place. The objective is for the cage to completely surround the high-res mesh. The cage can be adjusted by either changing its Push amount and/or moving the points in the cage the same way you edit vertices.

By default, as you pick a high-res mesh in the modifier to use with a low-res mesh, as you've done in the tent example, the cage separates outward from the original geometry to envelope the new geometry. This is referred to as best fit.

1. Continue from the previous exercise, or open tent_RTT_01.max.
2. Make sure the low-resolution tent is selected.
3. On the Modify panel > Cage rollout, turn on Shaded.

   By default, **3ds max** does a *best fit* of the cage to the object it's projecting to, but in most cases it's better to reset.
4. In the Cage rollout, choose Reset.

5. In the Push group, set the Amount to **4**.

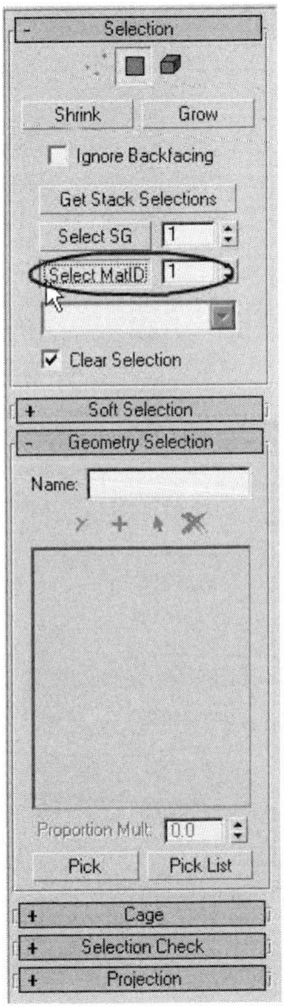

The high-resolution mesh still pokes through in a couple of spots.

6. In the Selection rollout, choose Vertex.

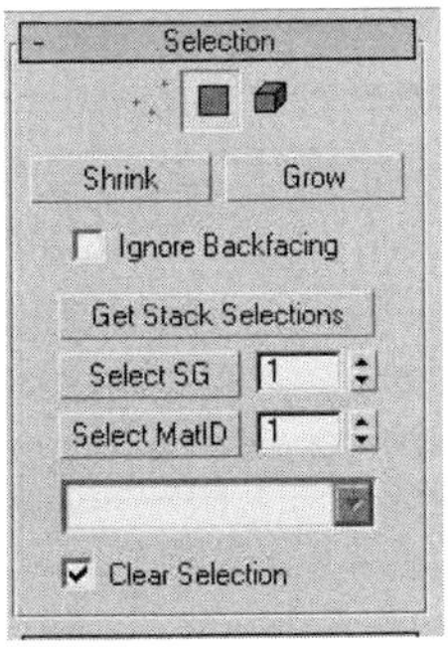

7. Go around the object and select vertices in areas that are poking through and move them out until they cover the underlying high-resolution mesh.

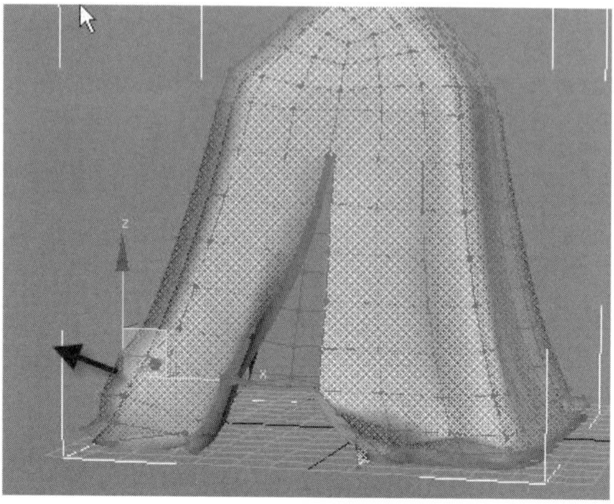

8. Exit sub-object mode.
9. Make sure the low-resolution tent still selected.
10. Press 0 to open Render to Texture.
11. Click Render.

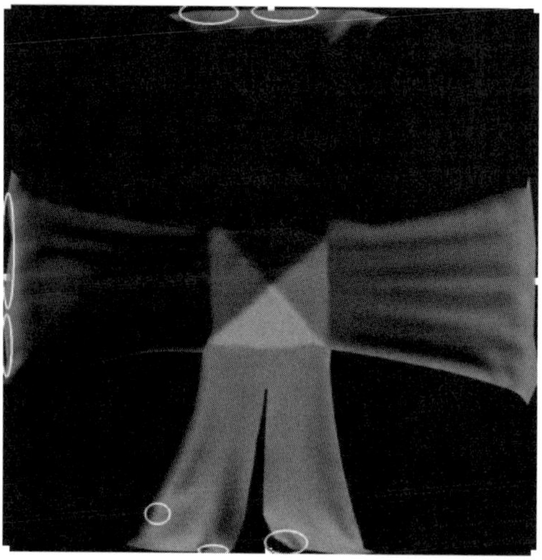

You notice the rendered image has some red areas. These red areas are spots that the rays from the Projection modifier didn't hit the high-resolution mesh. You fix this next.

12. In the Objects to Bake rollout, press Options.
13. In the Resolve Hit group, turn on Include Working Model.

    This renders the underlying low-resolution mesh where rays missed the high-res mesh.

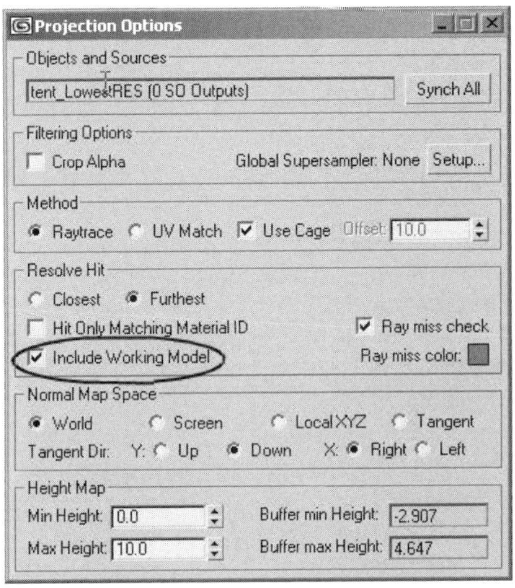

14. Close the Projection Options dialog and then press Render again.

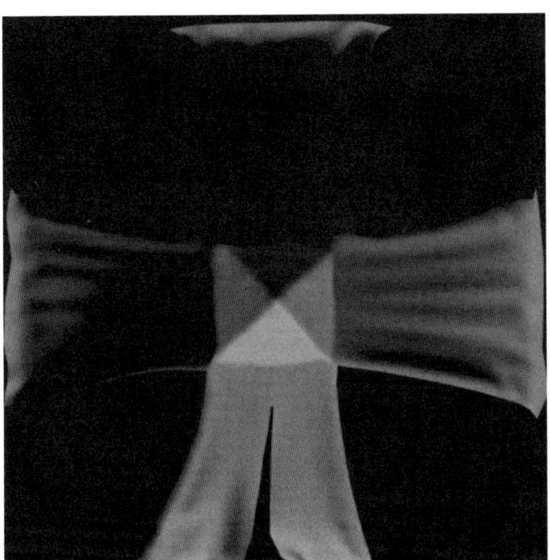

15. Answer Yes (Overwrite Files) in the Warning dialog.

16. Close the Render to Texture window.

Viewing and Working with the Results

1. Continue from the previous exercise.
2. Press **M** to open the Material Editor.
3. Select the LowRES_Plaster material.
4. Open the Maps rollout.

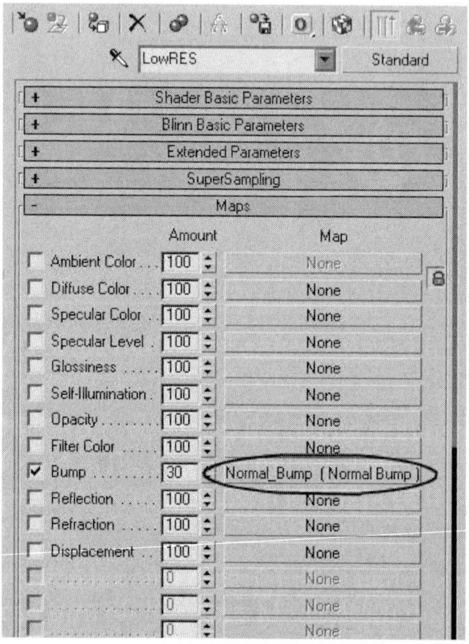

A Normal Bump map type has been added to the Bump Map channel. This is a new map type. This map type enables the rendering of normal maps inside the **3ds max** renderer. Notice that the method is set to World because that is what you set in the Render To Texture > Options dialog.

5. In the Maps rollout, choose the Bump map.

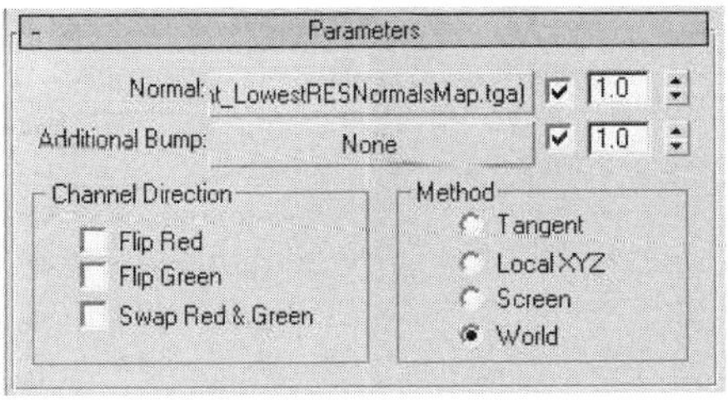

Tip: You can also layer other bump maps with the normal map for added bump effects by loading them into the additional bump slot.

6. Choose the button beside the Normal: label (it contains the computed normals map).
7. In the Bitmap parameters rollout, choose View Image.

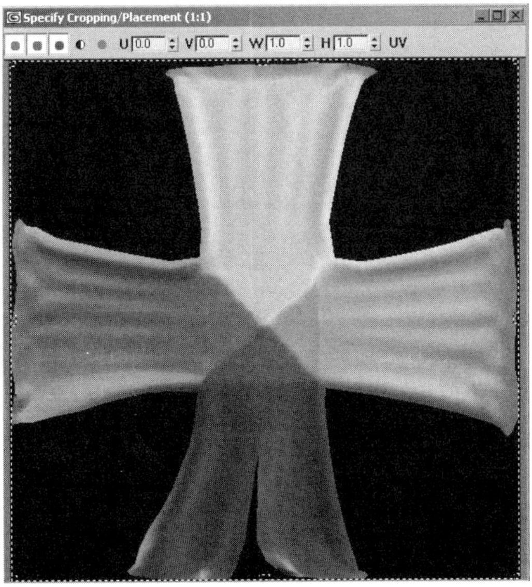

This is the normal map that was rendered.

Note: It follows the texture UV layout so adjusting the map in a 2D application such as Photoshop is straightforward.

8. Close the Material Editor.
9. Choose the high-resolution tent.
10. Right-click and choose Hide Selection from the quad menu.

11. Right-click and then choose Unhide by Name. Choose tent_HighRES_Compare.
12. Right-click to activate the Perspective viewport.
13. In the viewport navigation controls, choose Zoom Extents.
14. On the main toolbar, choose Quick Render.

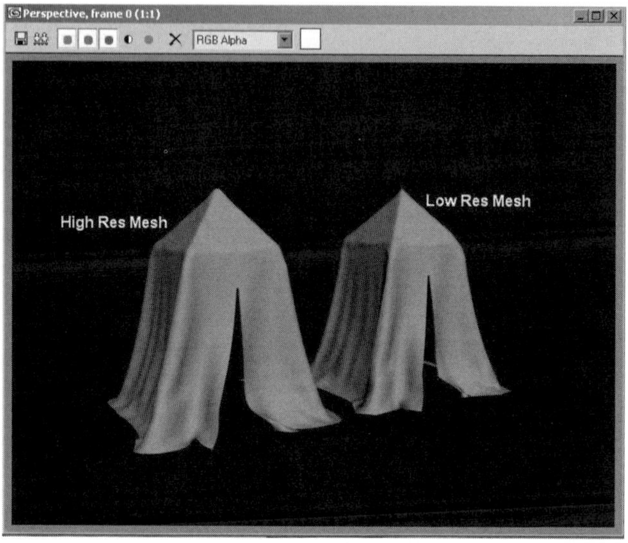

Clearly you see the difference a Normal map makes when rendering. Used as a Bump map, it has very little impact on render times.

Projection Modifier

Next, you open a new file and delve into the Projection modifier. In the previous example, the Projection modifier was used at its most rudimentary level. It works well for that scenario, but what happens when you need to capture a lot of complex data from many objects and bake that information into a single object?

When working with tutorials, you often open a scene already set up with only a few final steps left to do. Usually the preparations before the steps are most important in understanding the overall workflow and functionality of the specific tool. In this case, the pendant has been prepared with simple, routine steps, but the steps play an important role in understanding what is happening. First, open the file and become familiar with the setup.

1. Open *Pendant_RTT.max*.

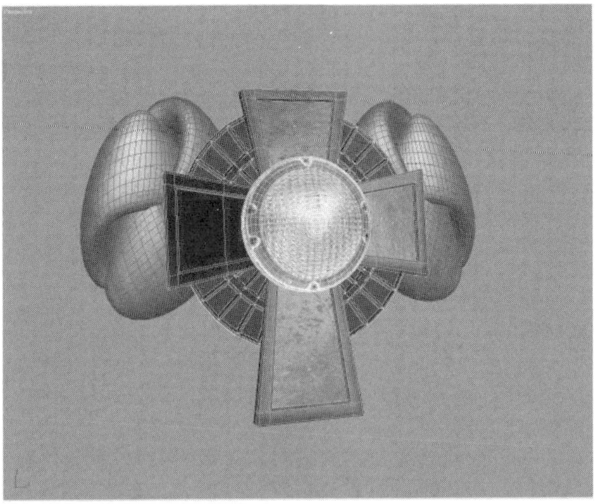

The high-resolution pendant you modeled in the previous chapter is loaded, however this one has mapping and materials applied.

2. Press **M** to open the Material Editor.

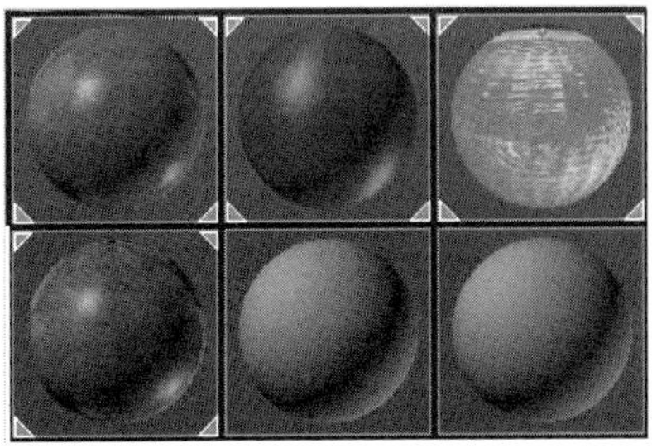

Tip: **M** also closes the dialog.

3. Examine the materials applied to the high-resolution pendant objects.

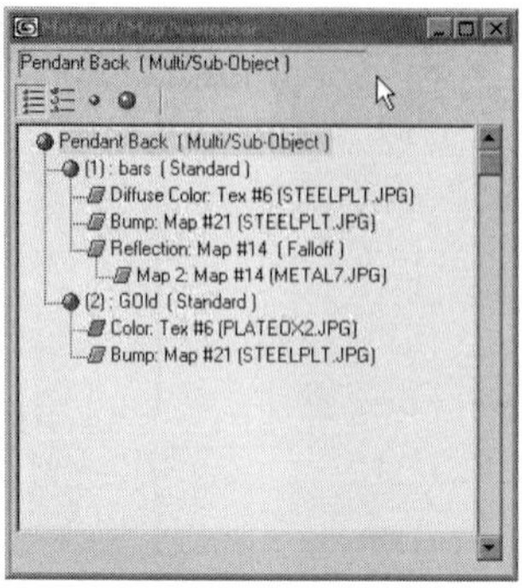

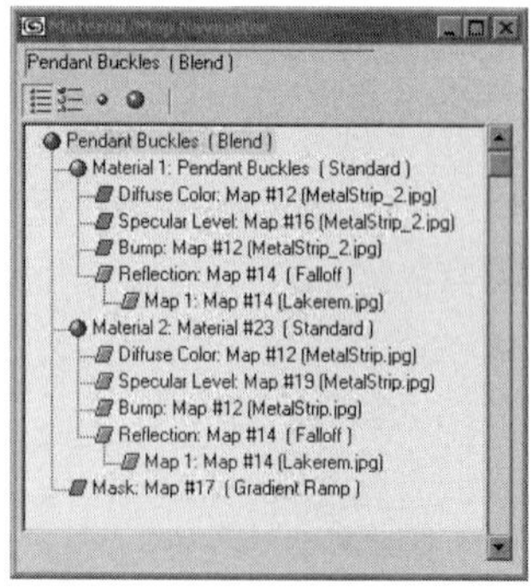

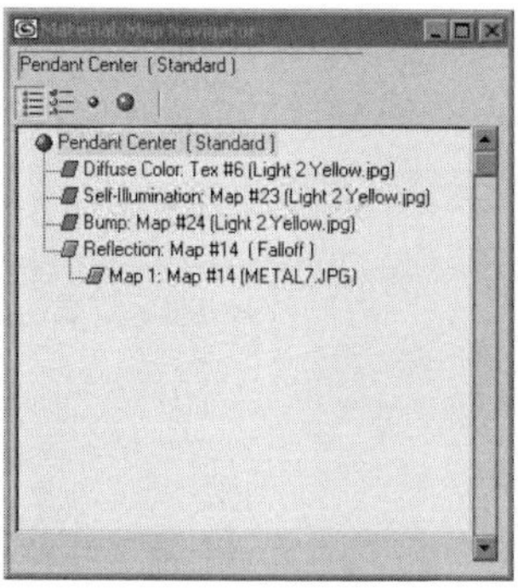

Note: The majority of the pendant pieces have complex materials. This means they include Material types such as Multi/Sub-Object and Blend. The Material Types use Map channels such as Self-Illumination, Specular Level, and Reflection. The Map Channels are defined by Map Types such as Mask, Falloff, and Gradient Ramps.

4. When you're done examining the materials, close the dialog by pressing **M**.

5.  On the main toolbar, choose Layer Manager.

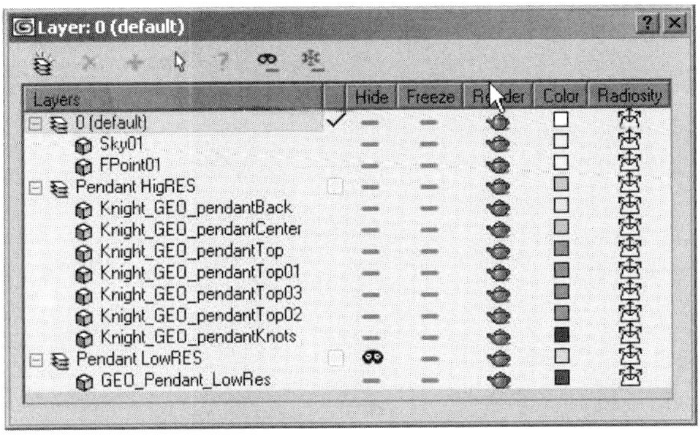

The Layer Manager has three layers: the default layer, and a separate layer for both the high-resolution and low-resolution pendants.

6. In the Layer dialog > Hide column, choose the dashed line next to Pendant HighRES.

7. Choose the dashed line next to Pendant LowRES to unhide it.

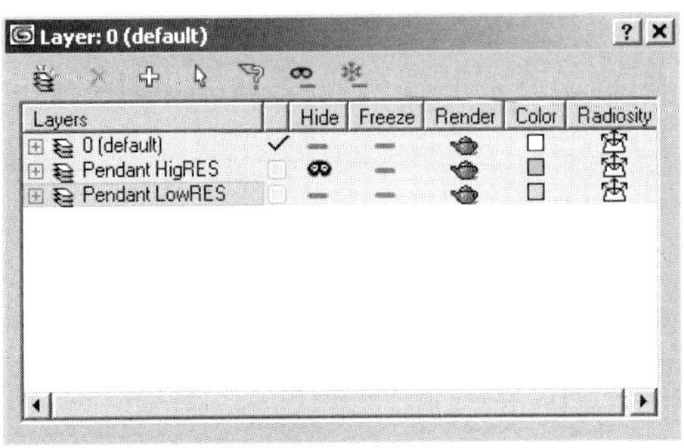

8. Close the Layers dialog.

9. In the Front viewport, choose the low-resolution pendant.

10. On the Modify panel > Parameters rollout, choose Edit.

11. You see that the texture unwrapping has been completed and the UVs are laid out in a sensible manner.

12. At the bottom of the dialog, choose the All ID's drop-down list.

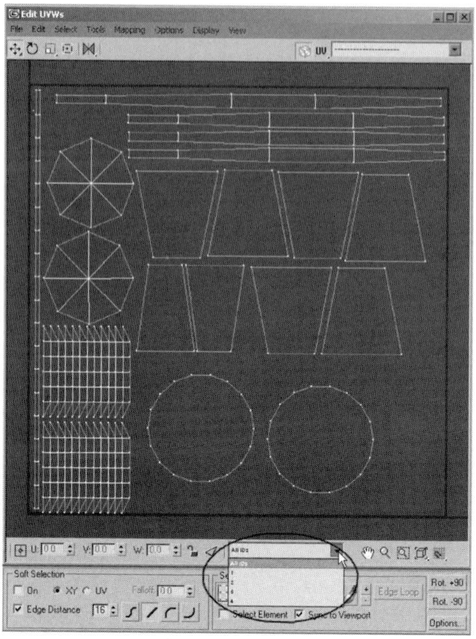

13. Choose the different Material IDs.

    By checking the ID's drop-down list, you see that the model has been given a few different Material IDs. The importance of these Material IDs is that there is one for each of the high-resolution objects. You use these IDs to control which high-resolution source objects get baked for use in the low-res object.

14. Close the Edit UVWs dialog.

Setting Up the Projection Modifier

1. Continue from the previous exercise.
2. Make sure the low-resolution pendant is selected.
3. Collapse the modifier stack.
4. Right-click in the Modify Stack display, and choose Collapse All from the right-click menu.
5. From the Modifier List drop-down, choose Projection.

   When you worked with baking the Normal maps into the tent, the projection modifier was handled internally for the most part. This time you want more control, specifically control at the sub-object level.

6. In the Selection rollout, choose Face.
7. Choose the Select MatID button.

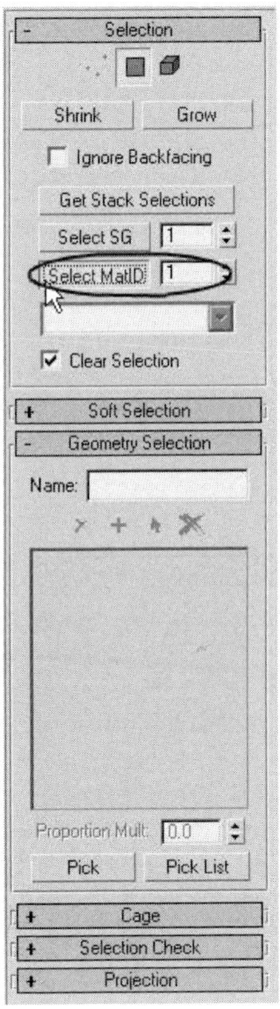

The faces associated with Material ID 1 are selected.

8. In the Geometry Selection rollout, type **BackPlate** to name the current face selection.

9.  Choose the Add button to add the name to the geometry selection list.

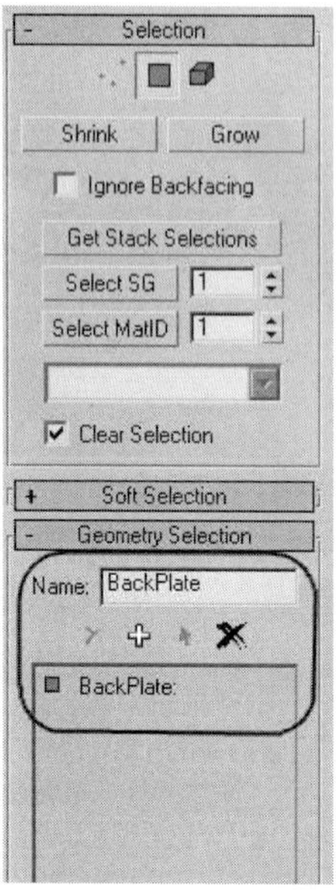

10. Repeat the previous steps for the remaining Material IDs.

Material ID	Name
2	Cross
3	Center
4	Buckles

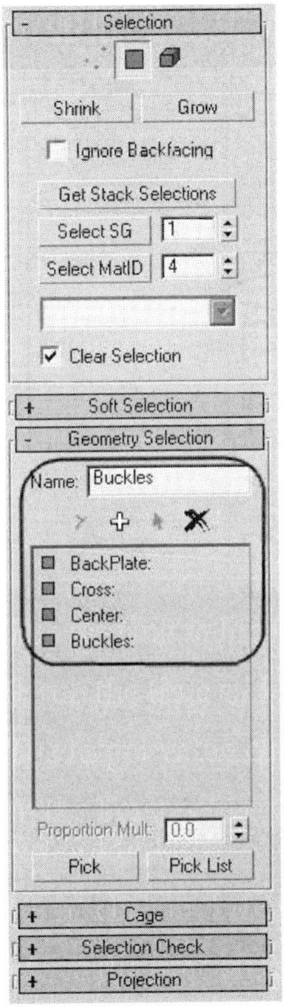

11. In the Selection rollout, turn off Face Sub-Object.

    The entries in the Geometry Selection list enable you to map different objects to various geometry selections without affecting other parts of the same object. You have the target selections set up, now you assign source objects to them.

12. On the main toolbar, choose Layer Manager.
13. Unhide the Pendant HighRES layer.
14. Make sure the low-resolution mesh is selected.

15. In the Geometry Selection rollout, choose BackPlate.

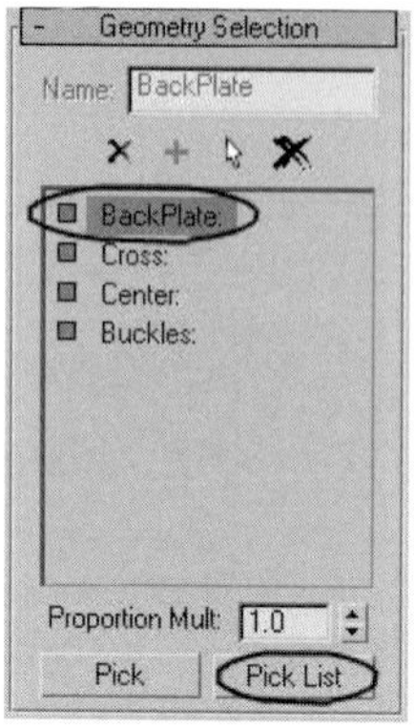

16. In the same rollout, choose Pick List.
17. Select Knight_GEO_pendantBack and then click Add.

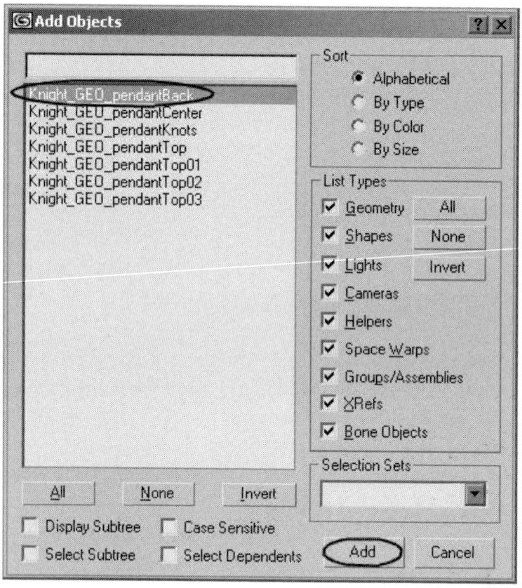

A new entry in the Geometry Selections list is displayed. This new entry is directly under the BakePlate entry and indicates that Knight_GEO_pendantBack is associated with it.

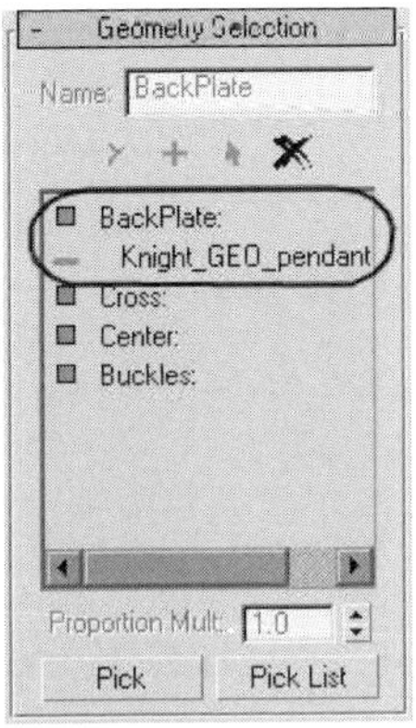

18. In the Geometry Selection rollout, choose Cross.
19. Click Pick List.
20. In the Add Objects dialog, select all four Knight_GEO_pendantTop objects and press Add.
21. Repeat these steps for both Center and Buckles, choosing Knight_GEO_pendantCenter and Knight_GEO_pendantKnots respectively.

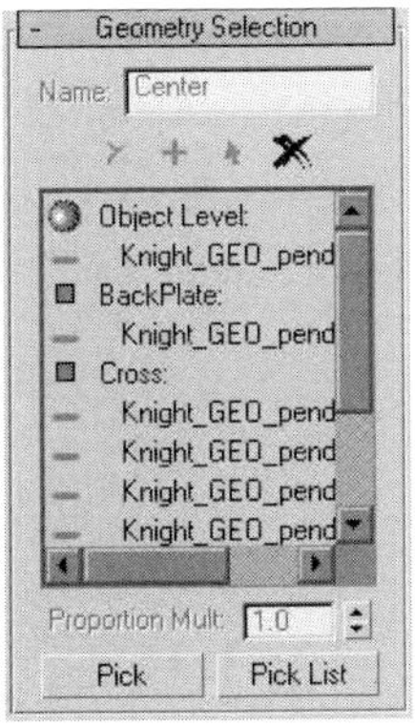

22. Now the geometry selections and their associated source objects are set up, but the cage looks a mess. You fix this next.

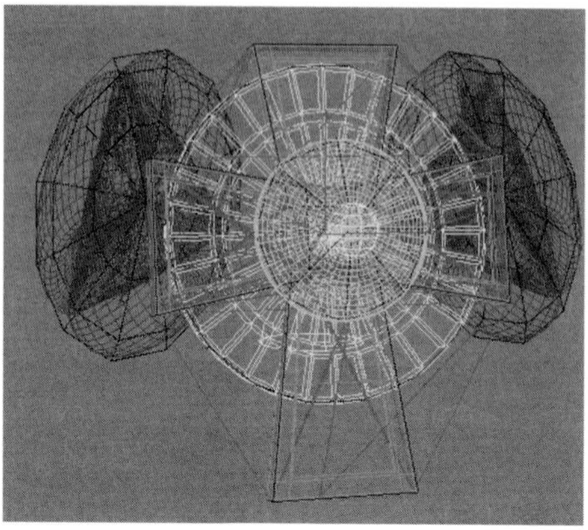

23. On the Modify panel > Cage rollout, choose Reset.
24. In the Display group, turn on Shaded.
25. In the Push group, change the Amount to **1.8**.

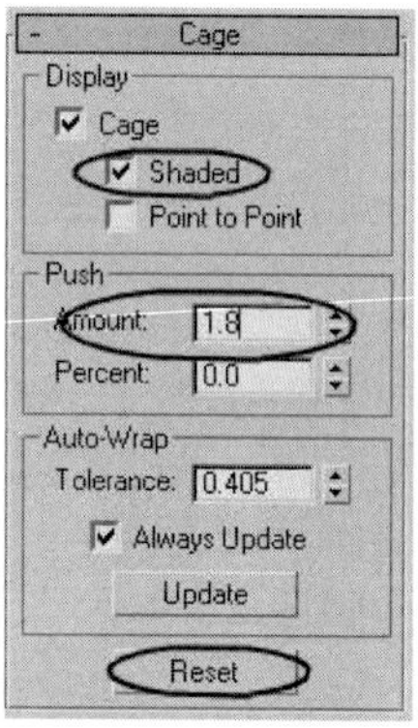

26. In the Perspective viewport, look closely at the centerpiece and the cage surrounding it.

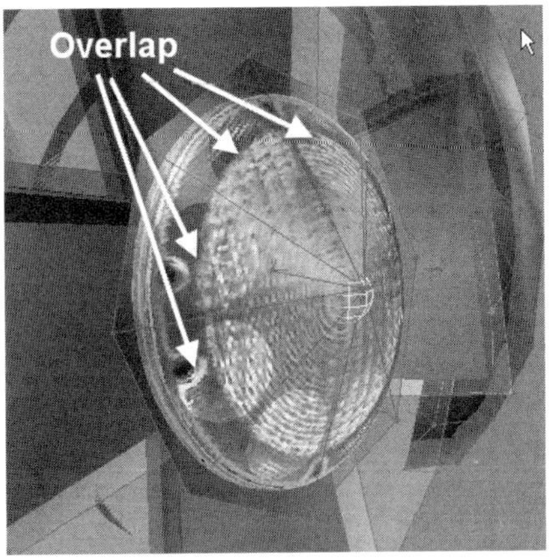

The high-resolution object is still cutting through the cage.

27. In the Selection rollout, choose Vertex.

28. Select one vertex on the centerpiece. In the Selection rollout, click the Grow button twice to select all of the vertices.

29. In the Push group, change the Amount until you can no longer see the high-resolution mesh intersecting the cage.

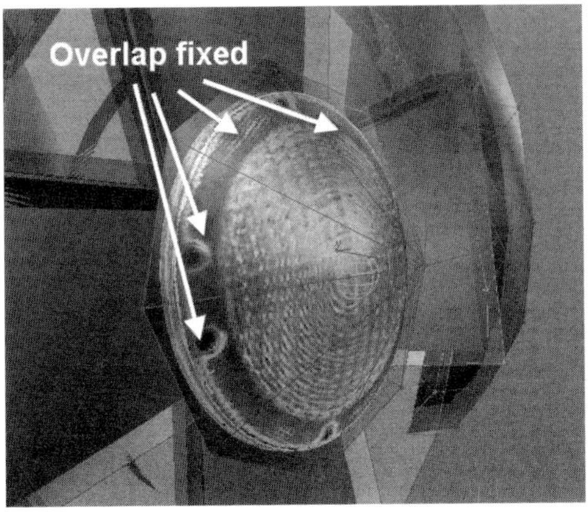

30. Repeat the previous step with the center vertex on the back of the object.

The Projection modifier is set up; next you use Render to Texture.

Baking with Render to Texture

1. Continue from the previous exercise, or open *pendant_RTT_02.max*.
2. Make sure that GEO_Pendant_LowRes is still selected.
3. Press 0 to open Render To Texture.
4. In the Objects to bake rollout > Projection Mapping group, turn on Enabled.

   Note: There is a difference between what you are doing now compared to what you did with the tent. When you worked with the tent, after you enabled the Projection mapping, you also used the Pick button to select which objects were the source objects. This time, you don't use that option because you have manually set up the source objects giving you control of the mapping on the target object at a sub-object level.

5. In the Projection Mapping group, turn off Sub-Object Levels and then choose Options.

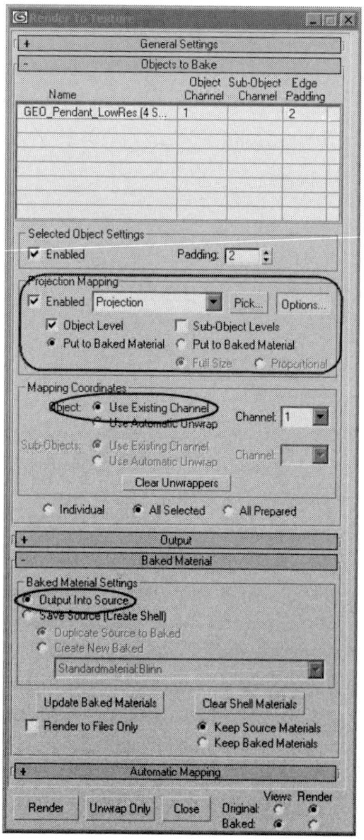

6. In the Projection Options dialog > Normal Map Space group, choose World and then close the options window.

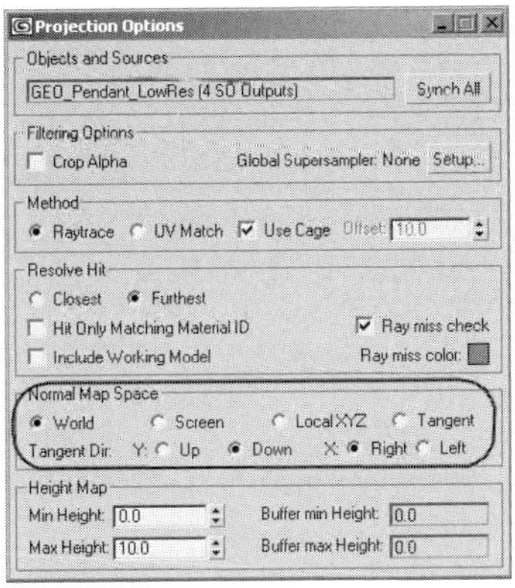

7. In the Baked Material rollout, choose Output Into Source.

   Next, you set up the Output maps. You render in two stages because of the complexity of the source objects.

8. In the Output rollout, choose Add.

9. In the Add Texture Elements dialog, choose BlendMap and then press Add Elements.

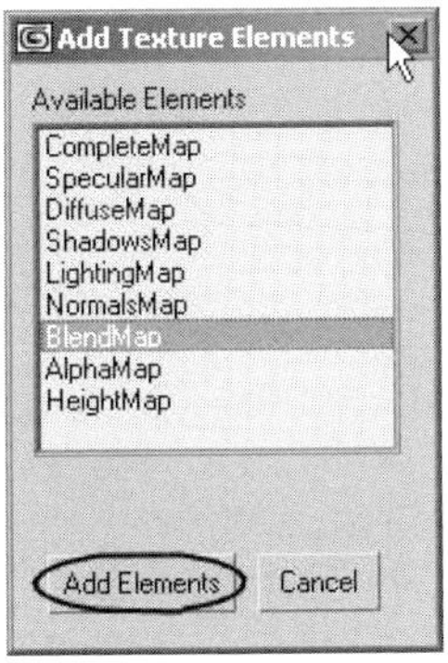

   The BlendMap type is a compilation of all other texture elements in the list plus a few more that aren't available individually. What makes it so powerful is that it also enables you to toggle on and off all these elements. The reason this is important is because there is no single element for Self-Illumination maps, so instead you use the BlendMap and just turn off all other elements.

You need the Self-Illumination map because one of the object's materials in the high-resolution pendants is Self-Illuminated whereas none of the others are. You need to change the Self-Illuminated control on the low-resolution mesh from being part of the Material type to being a Map type.

10. In the Select Element Unique Settings group, turn off all options except for Self-Illum.
11. Change the Output Size to **1024**.
12. Change the Target Map Slot to Self-Illumination.
13. Change the file name to **GEO_Pendant_lowResSelfIlluminationMap.tga**.

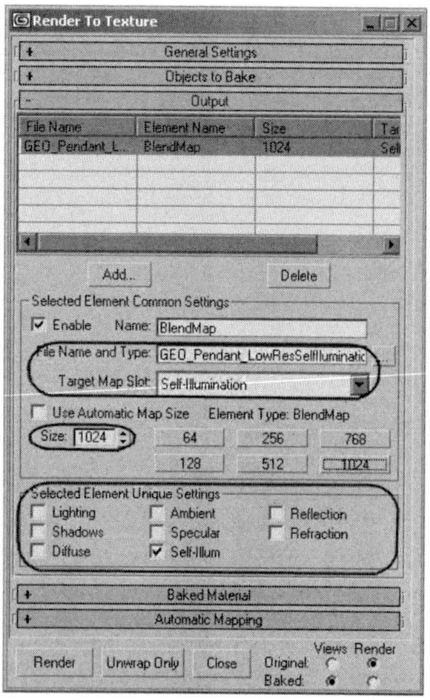

14. At the bottom of the dialog, choose Render.
15. Press **M** to open the Material Editor.
16. Choose the Material swatch named Pendant_LowRes.
17. On the side toolbar, choose the Material/Map Navigator.

There is an entry in the Self-Illumination slot.

18. In the Material/Map Navigator, choose the Self-Illumination Map channel.
19. In the Bitmap Parameters rollout, choose View Image.

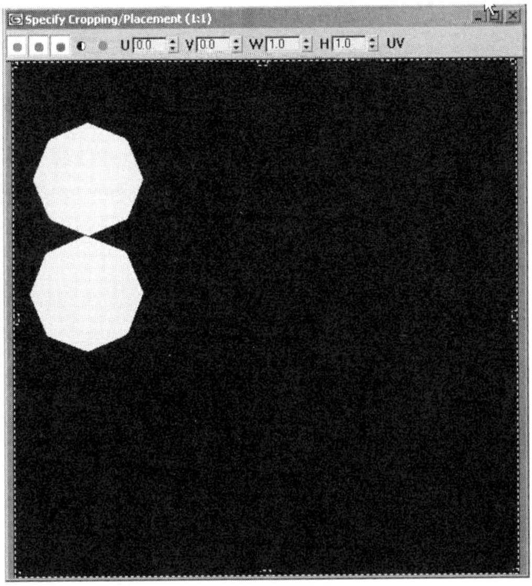

You can see that only the area on the map where values are something other than black is in the texture space containing the unwrapped centerpiece.

Creating a Diffuse Map and a Bump Map

1. Continue from the previous example.
2. Make sure Render to Texture is open.
3. In the Output rollout, select the entry you made for Self-Illumination and press DELETE.
4. In the Output rollout, choose Add, and then choose another BlendMap.
5. This time you use the Blend Map to produce a bitmap for the Diffuse Color Map Channel.
6. In the Target Map slot drop-down list, choose Diffuse Color.
7. In the Selected Element Unique Settings group, turn off Lighting and Shadows.
8. You continue to use the lights in the scene for lighting.

9. Set the Output size to **1024**.

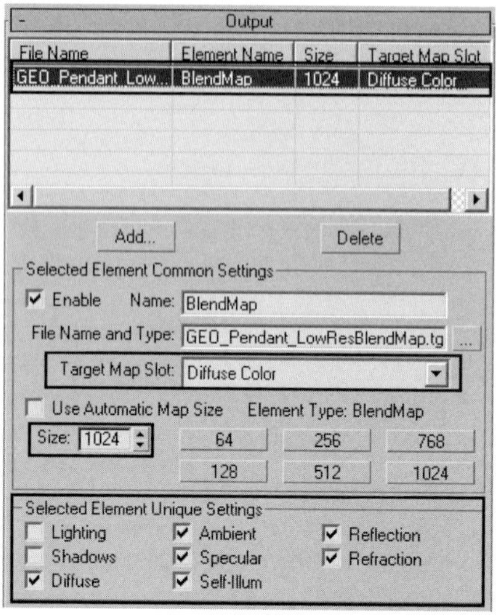

10. In the Output rollout, choose Add and then choose NormalsMap.
11. Make sure the Target Map Slot is set to Bump.
12. Set the Output size to **1024**.
13. In the Selected Element Unique Settings, turn on Output into Normal Bump.

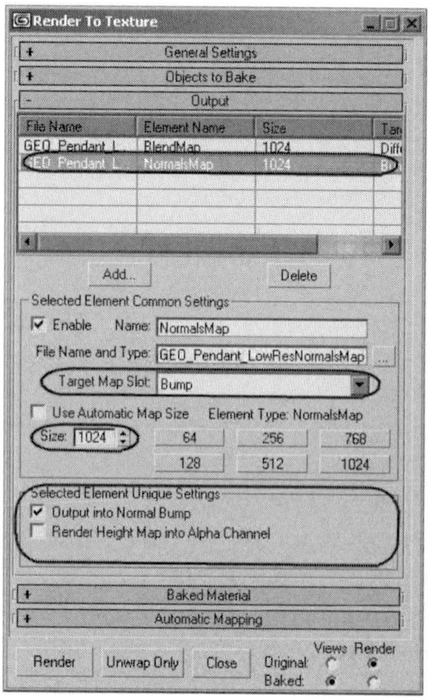

14. At the bottom of the dialog, choose Render.

How is the Scene Progressing?

1. Continue from the previous exercise.
2. Press 0 to close the Render To Texture dialog.
3. Press M to open the Material Editor.
4. Make sure the Pendant_LowRes Material is selected.

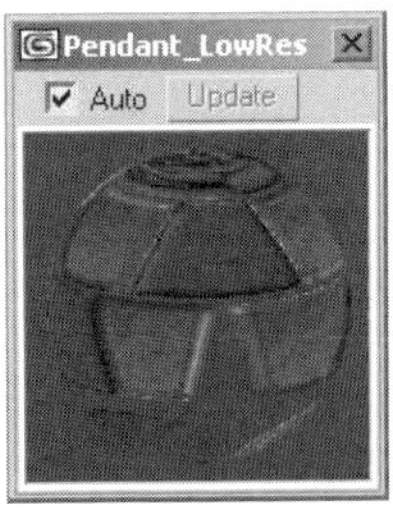

You see that two new map slots, Diffuse and Bump, also have entries.

5. Make sure the Material/Map Navigator is displayed.

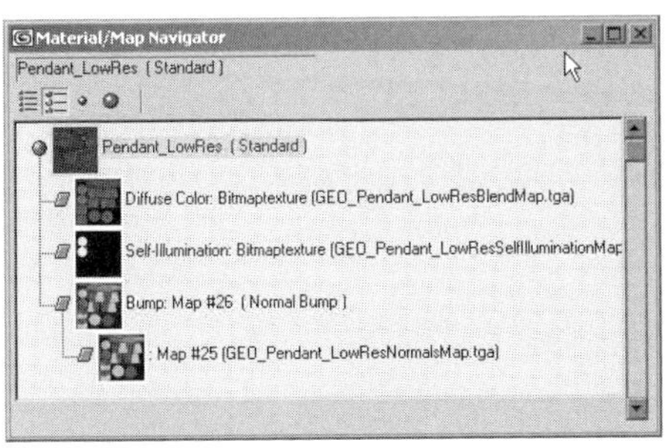

6. Use the Navigator to choose each Map Channel (Diffuse and Bump) and view the rendered bitmap by choosing View Image in the Bitmap Parameters rollout.

   Next, you render to compare the maps created with Render to Texture and used on the low-res object with the high-res object.

7. On the main toolbar, choose Layer Manager.
8. Hide the LowRES layer and unhide the HighRES layer in case it's hidden.
9. Make sure the Perspective viewport is active.
10. On the main toolbar, choose Quick Render.

11. On the Rendered Frame Window toolbar, choose Clone Rendered Frame Window.
12. In the Layer Manager, hide the HighRES layer and unhide the LowRES layer.
13. In the Front viewport, choose Fpoint01.
14. In the General Parameters rollout, turn off Shadows.

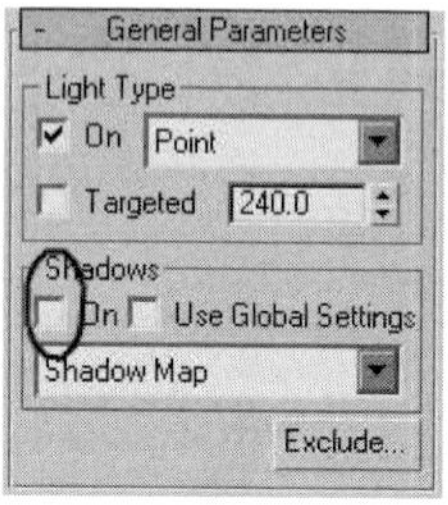

The reason you disable shadows is because in the high-resolution pendant, the centerpiece is excluded from casting shadows (because it's supposed to look like a light source itself.) The low-res pendant is all one object and unfortunately, there is no way to exclude shadows cast from certain faces only in an object. However, as you will see, the results are still quite good. If you really wanted the shadows, you could detach faces from the low-resolution pendant (the centerpiece) and make it a separate object, excluded from casting shadows.

15. Render the scene and compare the two renders.

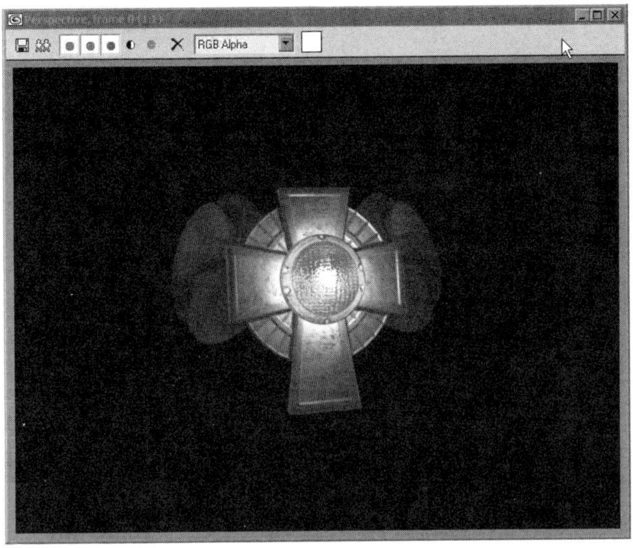

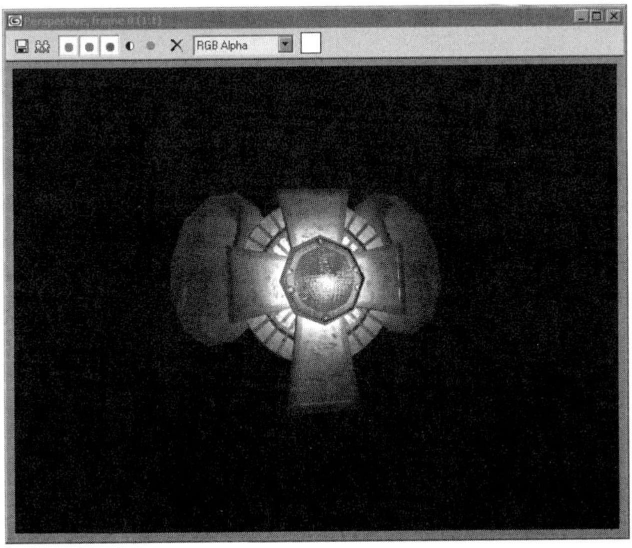

16. As you see, the low-resolution model holds up quite well compared to the high-resolution version. The low-resolution model is appropriate for a real-time game model or background/crowd model.

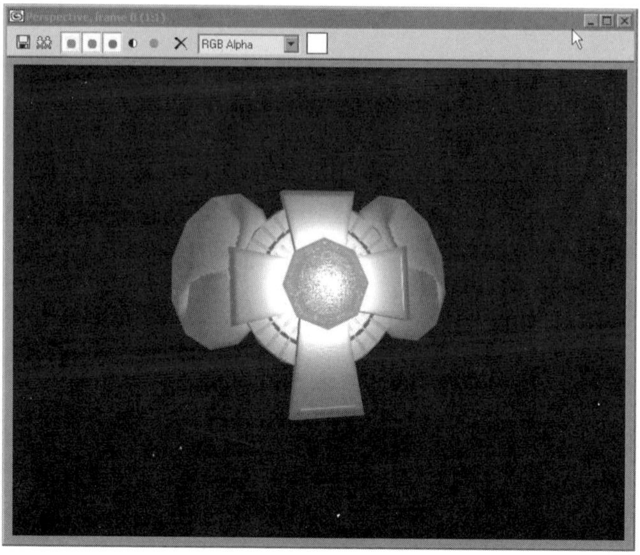

Tip: Another method you can try is to turn off the Diffuse Color Map channel of the Pendant_LowRes Material and render so you can see how much the Normal Map type contributes to the resulting image.

Conclusion

In this chapter, you have found new and more efficient ways of editing and trouble- shooting your texture coordinates. You have also explored the new projection modifier and have begun to see the power and potential it has to make your workflow easier. Moreover, you saw the benefits of using normal maps in non-game related work via the new Normal Bump map type. You also had fun doing UVs in real time with Reactor Cloth and Channel Info.

When you review what you have learned in this chapter, try to look beyond the simple steps and see the theory behind it. In doing so, you can apply what you have learned to new areas and combine it with other tools in **3ds max**. For instance, take the Projection modifier. You could use it to copy vertex colors, or use the power in Channel Info with the ability to create, copy, and store data in new channels.

3 IK/Scripting

Objectives

After completing this chapter, you should be able to:

- Mirror Bones.
- Assign Custom attributes.
- Use Script controllers.
- Mirror envelopes with the Skin modifier.
- Work with the Reaction Manager.
- Use the Extract Transform helper.

Introduction

Character rigging is a specialized area in 3D programs. As you load files with complete character rigs, you might notice that no two-character riggers create the same character rigs. However, most character rigs have similar components, which include:

- **Bones** – Non-renderable objects that fit inside your geometry.
- **Control Splines** – Non-renderable objects that act as animation handles.
- **IK Solvers** – Non-renderable objects that define how parented objects are transformed. IK Solvers define an IK Solution and can be assigned to any object type.

- **Custom Attributes** – Usually assigned to Control Splines to define custom interfaces.

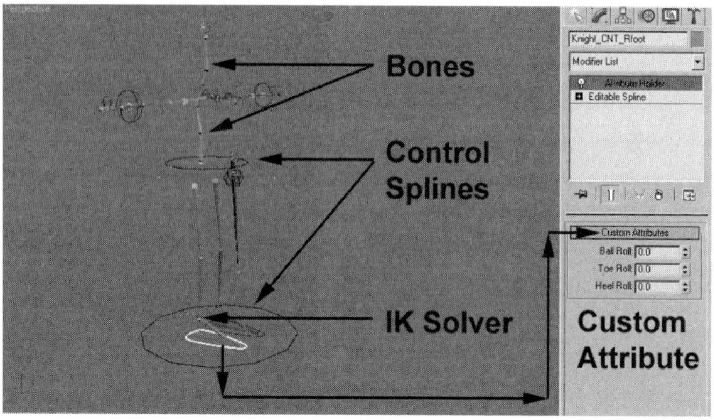

The setup in the foot of the knight has what is referred to as an inverse foot rig. It is called an inverse foot rig because the bones in the foot travel down the hierarchy in the opposite direction of the leg bones.

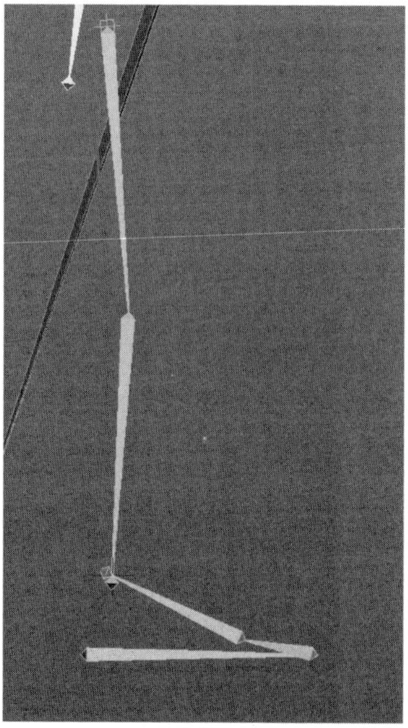

The inverse bones in the feet enable the rotation of the heel, toe, and ball of the foot, without setting up a lot of IK Solvers and complex hierarchies.

Another component included in this character rig is stretchy bones. Not every character rig requires this feature, but it is commonly used for animating cartoon-type characters. Even though the knight is not a cartoon character, stretching a leg in one direction only during animation is a useful approach.

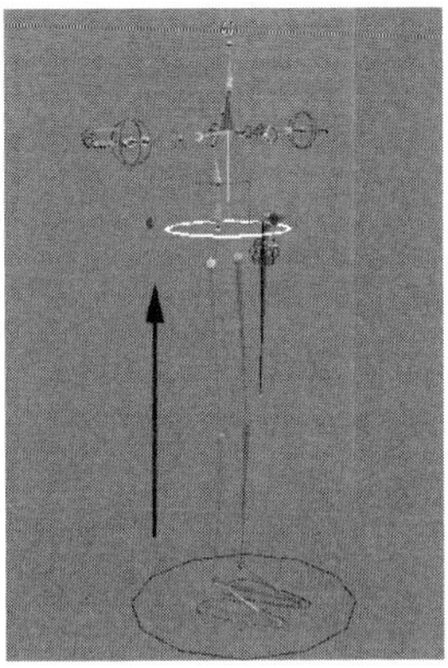

In this chapter, you open a file with most of the character rigging complete. You mirror the leg bones from the right side to the left side, create a History Independent (HI) Solver from the thigh bone to the ankle (or nub) and then add custom attributes for the right foot control spline.

You then use a Script Controller to create a stretchy leg effect. This chapter highlights that Script Controllers are name dependent. This means if an object's name changes in the scene that references the script, the script returns errors and does not run. You learn an approach to work around this issue.

At the end of the chapter, you use the Reaction Manager to assign three bones to one slider control. You also use the Expose Transform Helper to assist in an arm twist example.

Completing the Rig

1. Open *KnightRig01.max*.

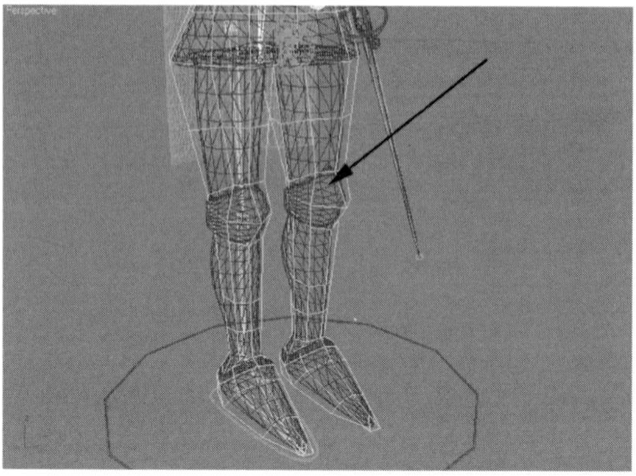

The rig for the whole character is complete except for the left leg.

2.  On the main toolbar, choose Layer Manager.

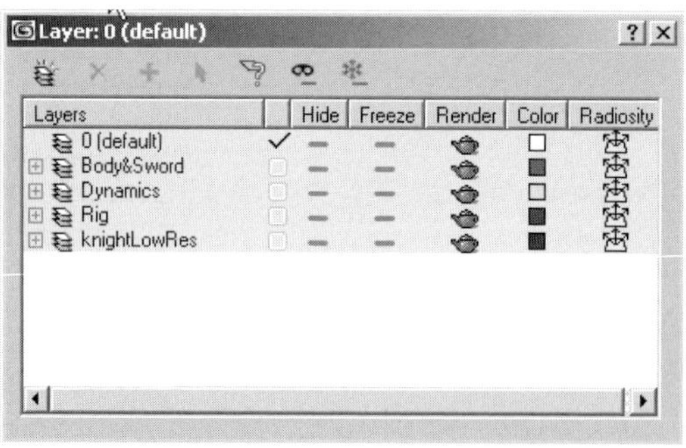

The Layer Manager dialog is displayed. Several layers are already assigned.

3. In the Layer dialog, choose the Hide icon next to the Body&Sword and kightLowRes layer names.

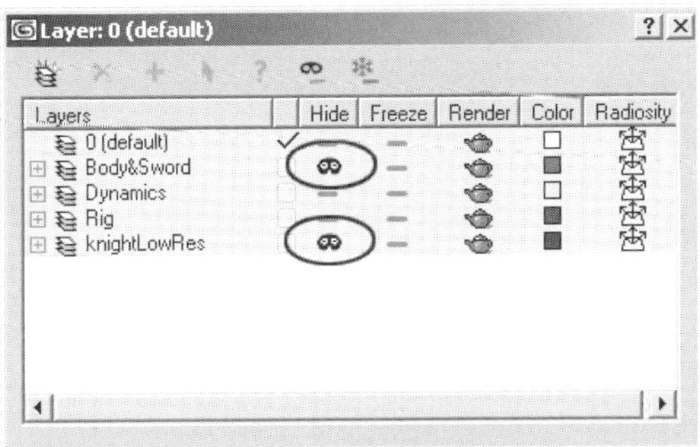

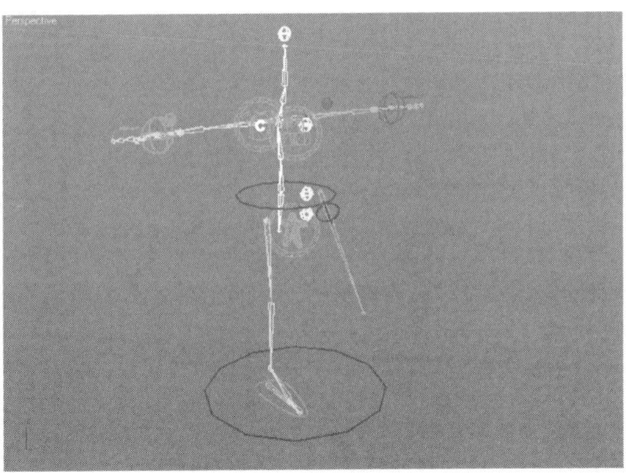

This hides all the objects associated with those layers.

Mirroring Bones

The leg you set up is an inverse foot rig. You use this type of rig because it is fast and easy to set up. It has one IK Solver only and offers a good range of motion. The first thing you do is mirror the bones from the right side.

Tip: The mirror bones option does not non-uniformly scale bones. This is appropriate since most game engines don't support scaled objects usually.

1. Continue from the previous exercise.
2. On the command panels, choose Create > Helpers > Point.
3. In the Top viewport, click anywhere to create a Point helper.
4. On the main toolbar, right-click Select and Move.

5. In the Transform Type-In dialog, set Absolute World X, Y, and Z to **0**.

   You use the helper object as a reference for the mirror bones dialog to ensure the bones are placed on the left side.

6. Make sure the Point helper is selected.

7. On the main toolbar, Selection Filter drop-down list, choose Bone.

8. In the User viewport, hold down CTRL and choose the bones in the right leg and foot.

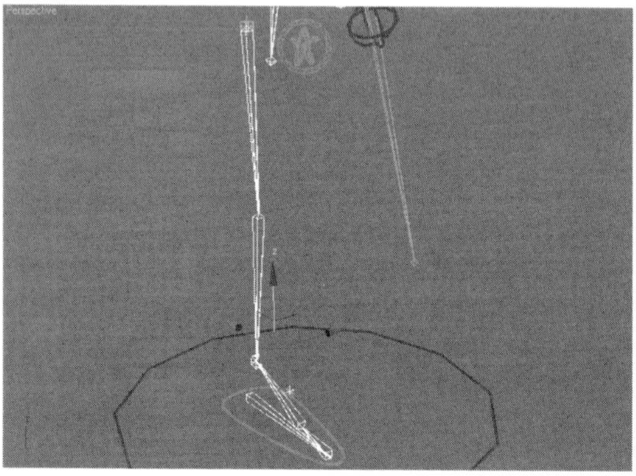

9. On the menu bar, choose Character > Bone Tools.

   You use the dialog to create and edit bones.

10. In the Bone Tools group, choose Mirror.

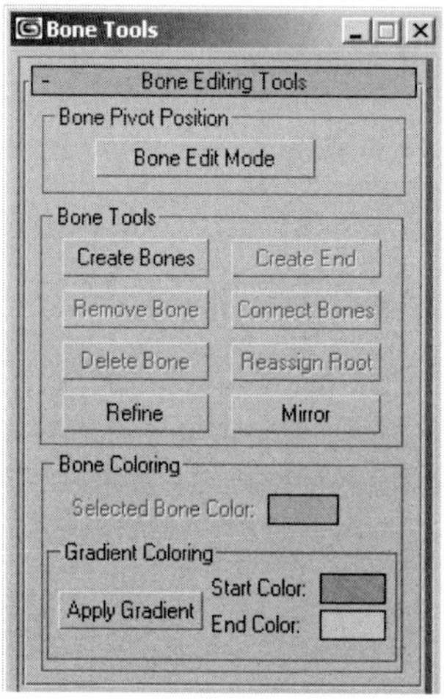

11. Two dialogs are displayed; answer Yes to proceed.

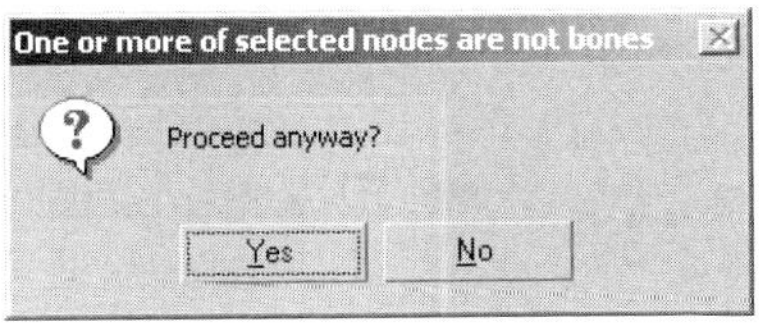

This dialog recognizes that a helper object is part of the selection.

12. In the Bone Mirror dialog, accept the defaults and then choose OK.

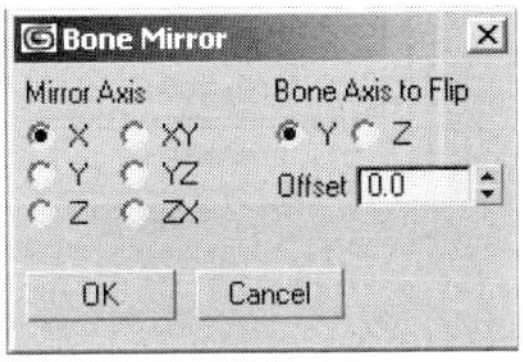

Note: You can choose a different axis to see how the bones are mirrored. You can see that the defaults work well.

Note: The mirrored bones are named with *(mirrored)* following their names.

13. On the command panels > Name and Color rollout, choose the Color Swatch.

14. In the Object Color dialog, choose the same color assigned to the left arm.

15. On the main toolbar > Selection Filter drop-down list, choose All.

16. In the User viewport, choose the Point Helper and press Delete.

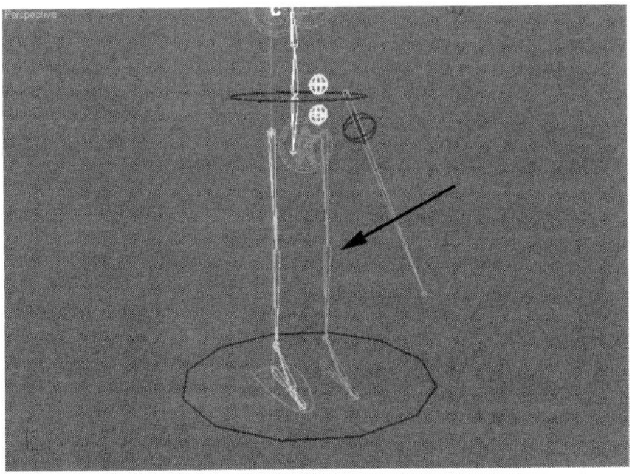

Cloning and Linking Controls

1. Continue from the previous exercise.
2. In the Top viewport, choose Knight_CNT_Rfoot.

   This is the control object for the right foot.
3. SHIFT+Move on the X-axis to copy the foot to the body's left side.
4. In the Clone Options dialog, rename the object **Knight_CNT_Lfoot**.
5. Change the color to the same shade of red as the left arm control.

   Tip: Use different colors for the right and left sides of the character. In this case, green and red are used but you can use any color scheme.
6.  On the main toolbar, choose Quick Align and choose the nub bone for either the leg or the foot, for example, Knight_Bone_Rleg02 (mirrored). This aligns the Knight_CNT_Lfoot to the bone nubs.
7. In the Perspective viewport, choose Knight_Bone_Rfoot00 (mirrored).
8. On the main toolbar, choose Select and Link.
9. Link the child Knight_Bone_Rfoot00 (mirrored) to the parent Knight_CNT_Lfoot.
10. Rename all mirrored bones by removing (mirrored) from the name and changing the R to an L.

Creating Point Helpers

1. Continue from the previous exercise.
2. In Top viewport, create a Point Helper object.
3. In the Parameters rollout, choose Box and Cross.
4. On the main toolbar, choose Align and then choose the Left Thigh bone.

5. In the Align Selection dialog, turn on Position X, Y, and Z for both objects' Pivot Points. Turn on every axis in the Align Orientation [Local] group. Click OK.

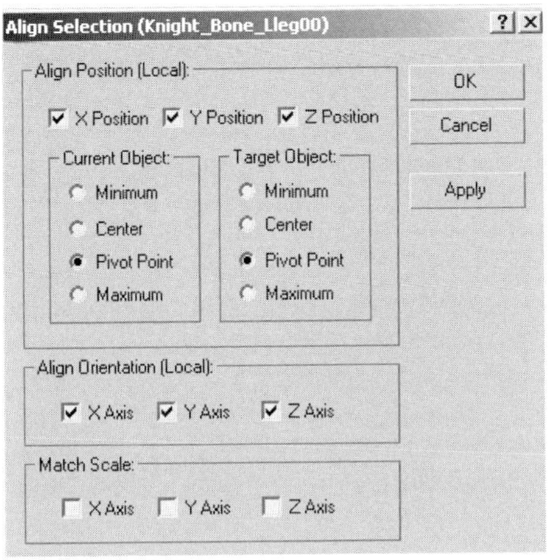

6. Change the name of the helper to Knight_HLP_Lleg00.
7. On the main toolbar, change the Reference Coordinate System to Local.

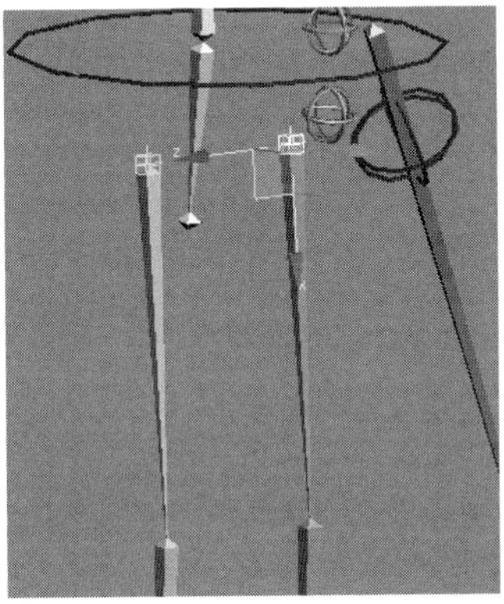

8. On the main toolbar, choose Select and Link and then make the following Child > Parent hierarchies:
9. Link the left thigh bone to Knight_HLP_Lleg00.

10. Link Knight_HLP_Lleg00 to Knight_Bone_Spine03.

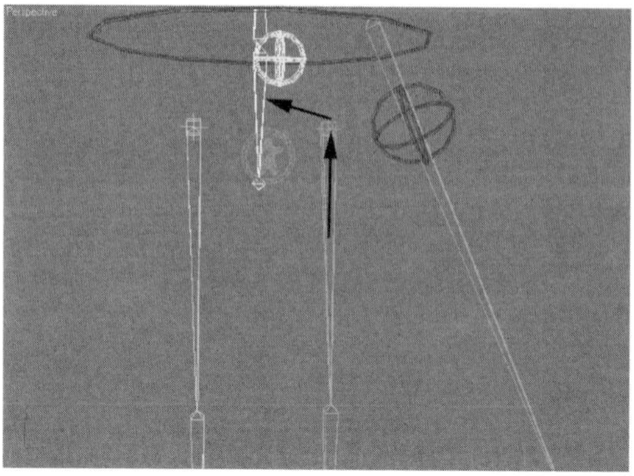

Point helpers are used for different bone chains because they make it easier to reposition the bones without moving its parent's bones.

11. Save this file as **knightRig02.max**.

Adding a Solver

Next, you add an IK Solver. The IK Solver you add is called History Independent or HI Solver. This is the preferred character animation solver. It is stable to use and fast, regardless of the length of animation.

1. Continue from the previous exercise, or open *KnightRig02.max*.
2. In the User viewport, choose Knight_Bone_Rleg00.
3. On the menu bar, choose Animation > IK Solvers > HI Solver and then choose Knight_Bone_Rleg02. It's the nub bone at the end of the leg.

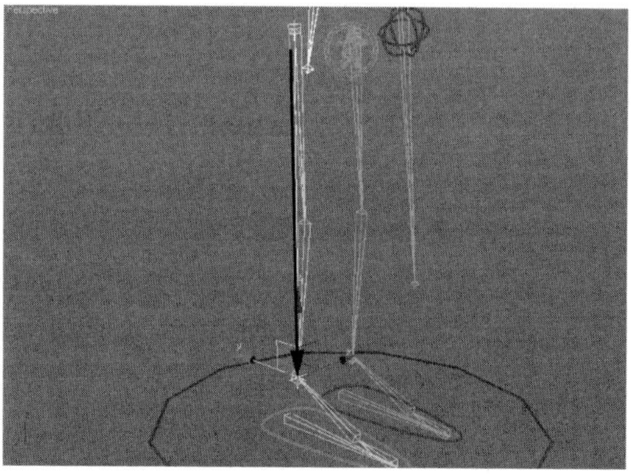

This adds a History Independent IK solver to the leg. The IK Solver now controls the rotation of the hip and knee.

Note: When you create IK Solvers, the command panels go directly to the Motion panel to display the controls for the specific solver.

4. In the User viewport, choose the IK Solver.
5. Move it along the Y and Z-axes to view the result of the IK solver.
6. Press CTRL+Z to undo the movement.
7. Rename the IK Chain **Knight_IK_Rleg**.
8. Zoom into the bones of the right foot.
9. Select a foot bone and rotate it on the Z-axis.

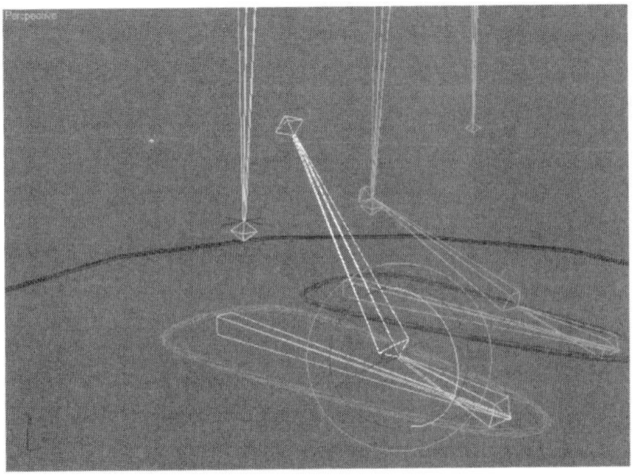

You see that the rotation does not affect the rest of the leg. You change that next by linking the Solver as a child to the foot nub.

10. Undo any rotation that you tried.
11. Use Select and Link to Child > Parent the following:
12. Knight_IK_Rleg to Knight_Bone_Rfoot03, which is the nub bone at the end of the foot.

13. Repeat the rotation on a foot bone.

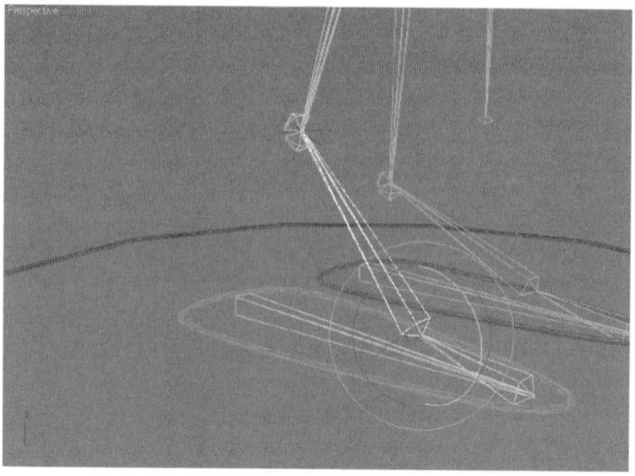

14. In the User viewport, choose Knight_IK_Rleg.
15. On the Motion panel > IK Solver Properties rollout > Parent Space group, turn on IK Goal.

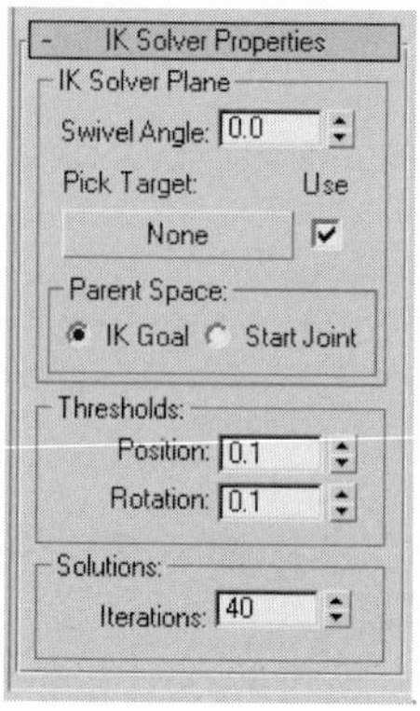

This ensures the knee rotates and stays aligned with the foot, as it is during animation.

Adding Custom Attributes

Next, you use custom attributes to create an interface for the object named Knight_CNT_Rfoot. When creating animation rigs, especially character rigs, you usually set keyframes for control objects rather than bones and/or IK Solvers.

Control objects are objects that you create using 2D shapes such as Lines or Circles. You can think of control objects as handles. They are non-renderable and easy to identify in the viewport.

1. Continue from the previous exercise.
2. In the User viewport, choose Knight_CNT_Rfoot.
3. On the Modify panel > Modifier List drop-down, choose Attribute Holder.

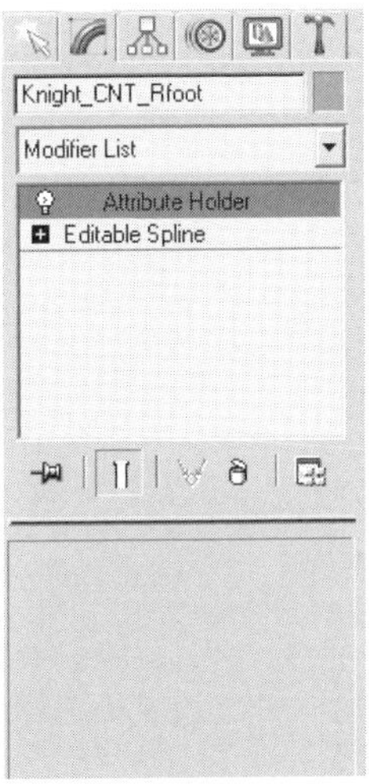

This is a blank modifier used to hold custom attributes.

4. On the menu bar, choose Animation > Parameter Editor.

   Tip: A Testing Attribute rollout at the bottom of the dialog displays the interface choices you make.

5. In the Attribute rollout, Add to Type group, make sure the drop-down list is set to Selected Object's Current Modifier.

   The interface you create in this dialog is placed in the Attribute Holder modifier.

6. In the UI Type group, change the name to Ball Roll.
7. In the Float UI Options rollout, Size group, type **110**.

8. In the Alignment group, choose Right.

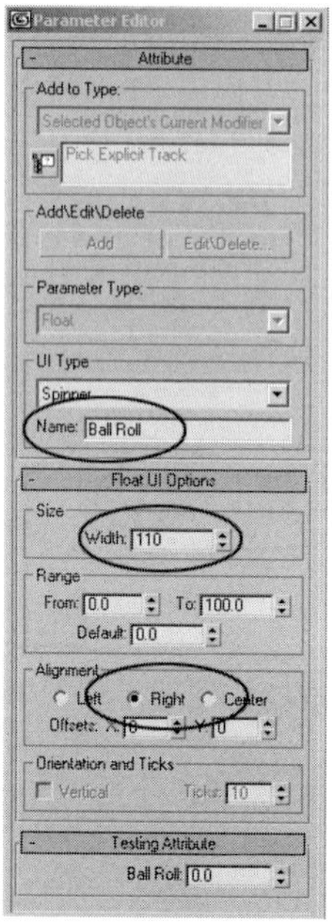

9. In the Add\Edit\Delete group, choose Add.

   This adds the spinner to the Attribute Holder modifier.

10. Add two more custom attribute spinners named Toe Roll and Heel Roll.

Note: You might have to adjust the width of the spinners for each roll if you want to keep the toe and heel aligned. The size is based on the width of the text and the spinner field.

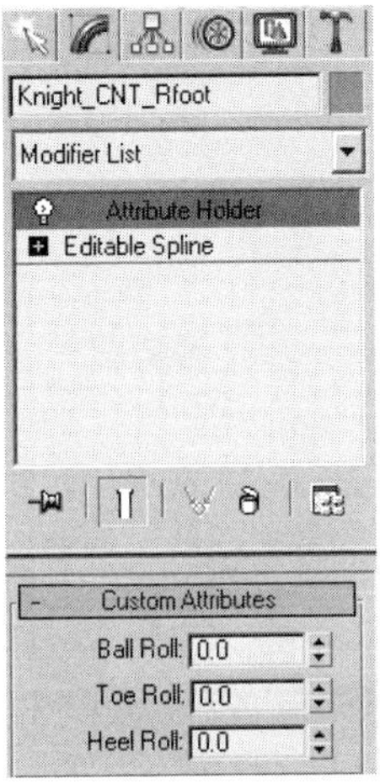

11. If you need to edit the Custom Attribute after you create it, you can choose Edit/Delete from the Add\Edit\Delete group.

12. In the Edit Attributes/Parameter dialog, choose the attribute you want to edit and then make changes in the Parameter Editor.

13. Once the changes are made, choose Apply Changes in the Edit Attributes dialog.

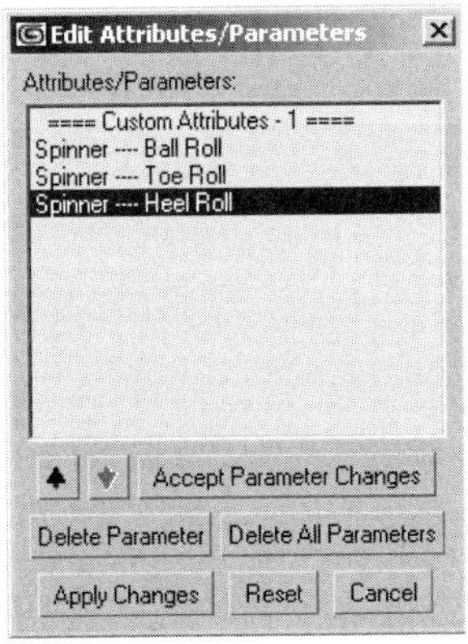

14. Save the file as **knightRig03.max**.

Parameter Wiring Setup

If you attempt to adjust the spinners you just created for the Right Control Foot, nothing happens. To fix this, you use Wire Parameters to connect the spinners with specific transform axes for the foot control object.

First, you apply List controllers to all bone objects in the foot and the control object so that they receive a zero value. This way when you wire the control object to the spinners, the bones' initial rotation angle does not change.

1. Continue from the previous exercise or open *KnightRig03.max*.
2. In the User viewport, choose a bone in the right foot.
3. On the command panels, choose Motion.
4. Open the Assign Controller rollout, and verify the default animation controller is set to Position XYZ.

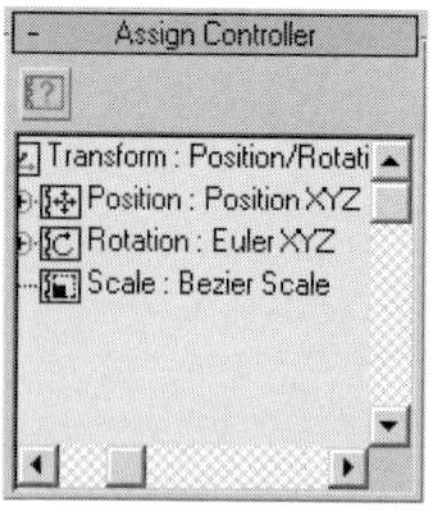

5. You change the animation controller next. You add a List Constraint to ensure an initial zero value.
6. In the User viewport, choose the three bones in the right foot and the right foot control object.
7. Press ALT+right-click to display the Animation quad menu.

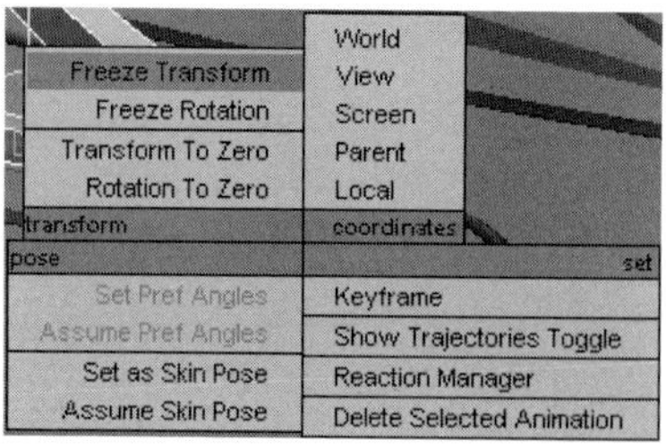

8. In the Transform quad, choose Freeze Transform.

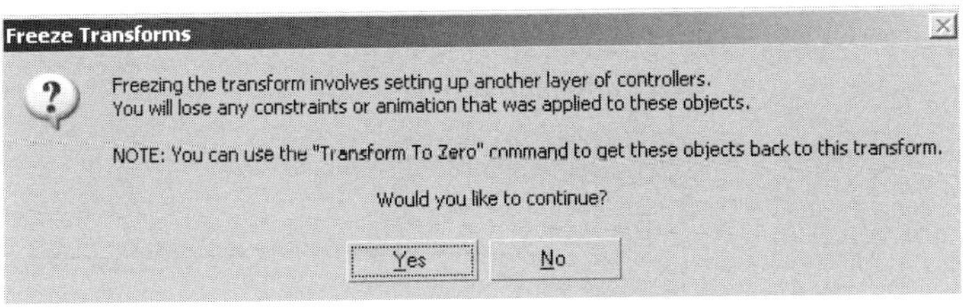

A dialog is displayed warning you about losing other controllers that were added.

9. Press Yes.

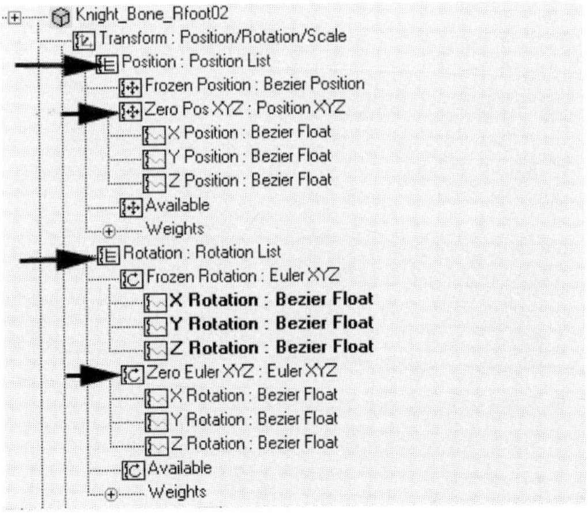

You can choose a bone and open the Curve Editor to view the change. A List Constraint is added to the Position and Rotation of the selected objects. A second controller is also added, which starts at a value of zero for each axis. Right-click the Filters icon on the toolbar in the Curve Editor and then choose Controller Types.

Now you are ready to use Wire Parameters. You first wire the Z Rotation of Knight_Bone_Rfoot02 to the Ball Roll spinner of the Control Object.

Parameter Wiring

1. Continue from the previous exercise.
2. In the User viewport, choose Knight_Bone_Rfoot02.
3. Right-click and choose Wire Parameters.

4. Choose Transform > Rotation > ZeroEuler XYZ > Z Rotation.

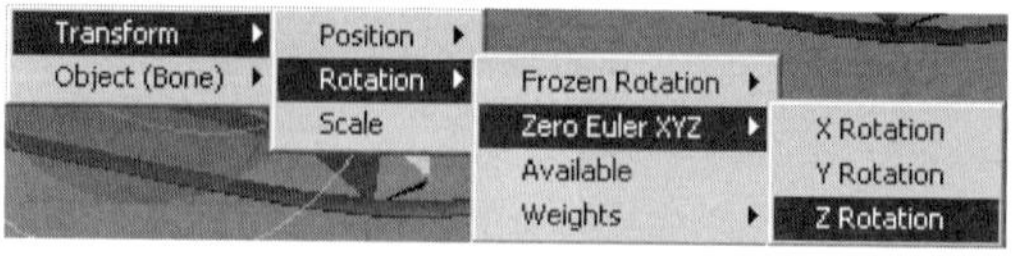

A dotted line follows your mouse.

5. In the User viewport, choose Knight_CNT_Rfoot.
6. Choose Modified Object > Attribute Holder > Custom_Attributes > Ball Roll.

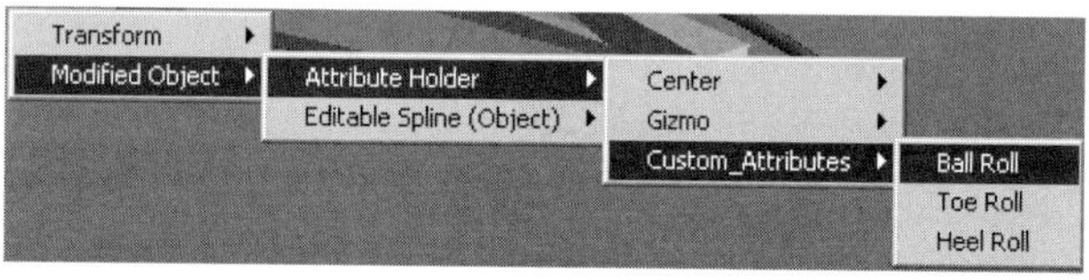

The Parameter Wiring dialog is displayed and the correct tracks are selected.

7. In the Parameter Wiring dialog, choose the arrow that points left.
8. In the Expression window, change the expression to read degToRad –Ball_Roll and then press Connect.

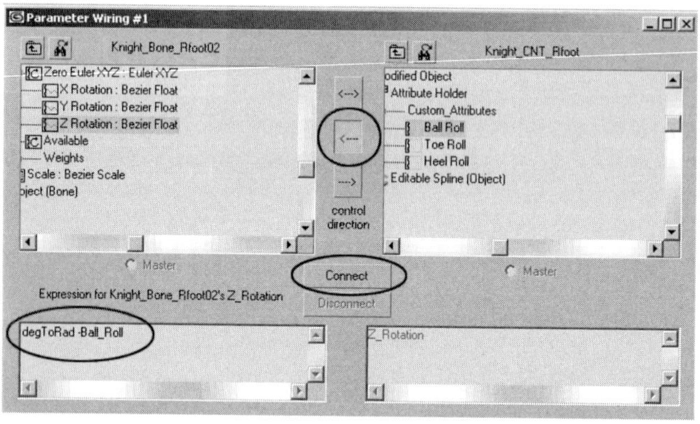

DegToRad converts degrees to radians and the – sign inverts the value so that it rotates in the correct direction.

9. In the User viewport, choose Knight_CNT_Rfoot.

10. On the Modify panel > Custom Attributes rollout, adjust the Ball Roll amount.

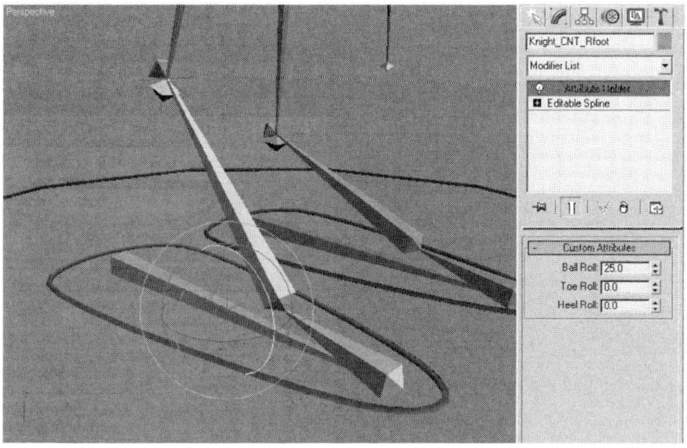

11. Repeat the previous steps to wire Knight_Bone_Rfoot01 to the Toe Roll custom attribute (degToRad –Toe_Roll).

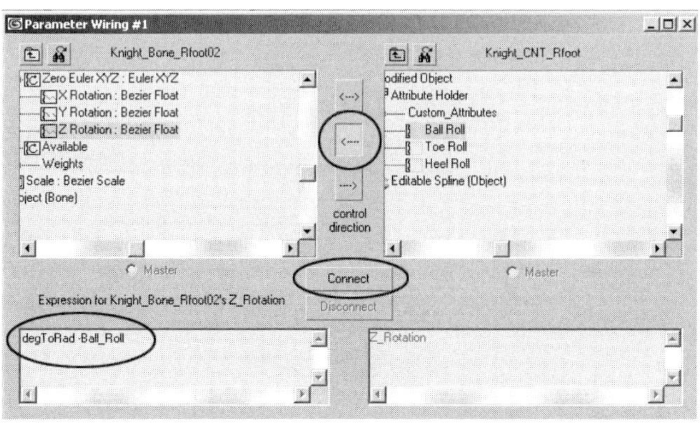

12. Make sure to test the attribute before wiring the next bone.

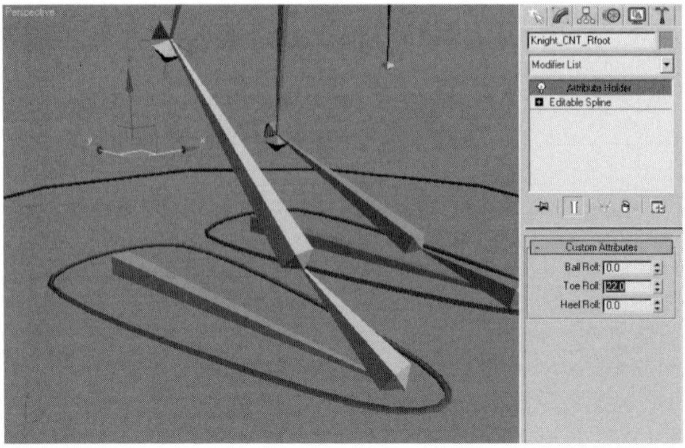

13. Wire Knight_Bone_Rfoot00 to the Heel Roll custom attribute (degToRad Heel_Roll).

14. In the Parameter Wiring > Expression window, don't use the – sign. This way, the heel rolls backward instead of forward.

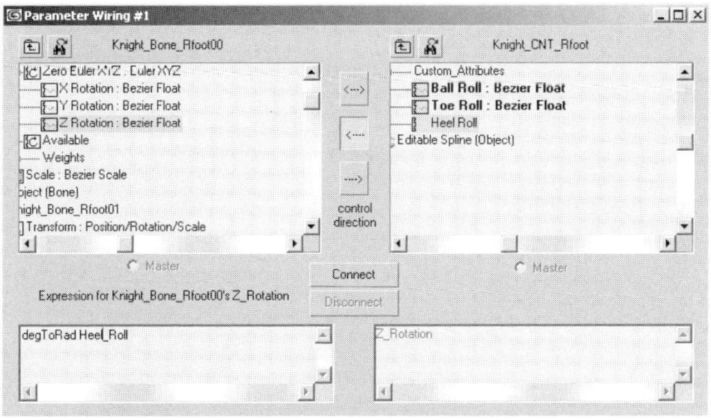

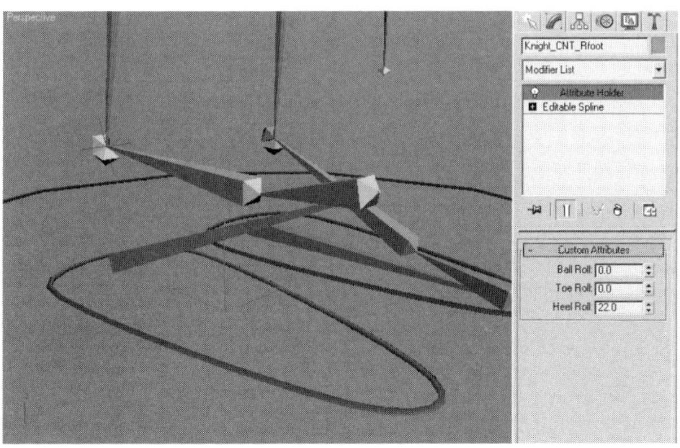

Stretchy Legs

Next, you set up a stretchy leg so the ankle doesn't separate from the foot when it is pulled too far.

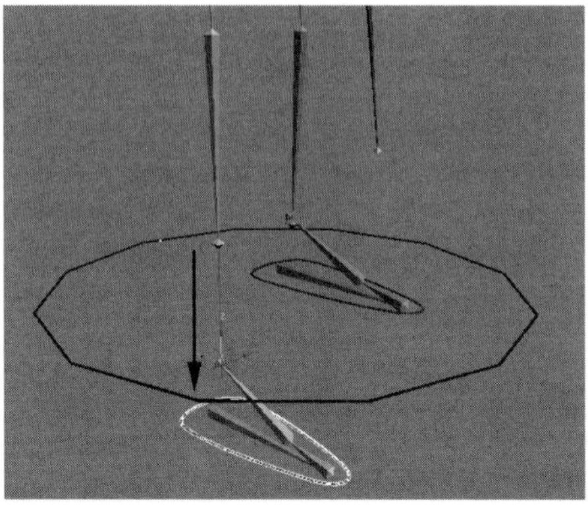

To set up the stretchy leg, the first step is to extract the distance from the hip to the foot and use that value to decide the length of the leg. You don't want to shorten the leg when the foot and hips get closer because you want the leg to bend. You only want the leg to lengthen once the foot starts to pull away from the ankle.

You use a Script controller to control the stretchy legs. Script controllers are quite powerful but have a name-dependent drawback. This means after setting up the script controllers, if changes occur to the names of referenced objects in the scene, the script controller displays errors and does not function.

To solve this problem, you use a set of custom attribute parameters added to the Script controller. This adds tracks to the Script controller for storing a reference to the objects that the script needs.

In the Script controller, you reference the custom attributes instead of the actual objects. This way, if the name of the object changes, the custom attribute updates automatically and the script continues to work.

The first step is to find the starting distance between the ankle and the hip so that you know when to start stretching the leg.

Before you continue, you can reference the following images to visually understand what you are about to do.

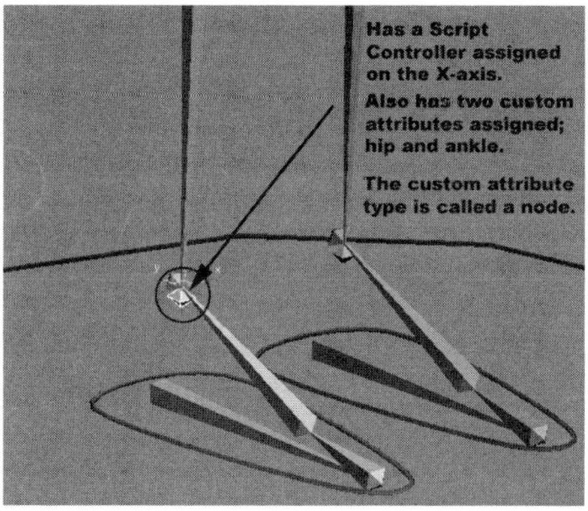

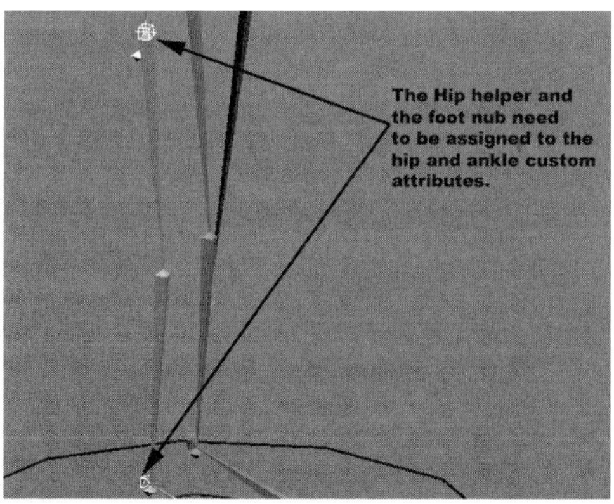

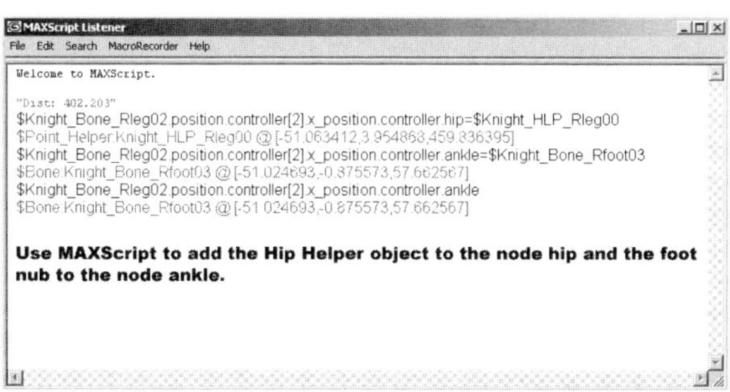

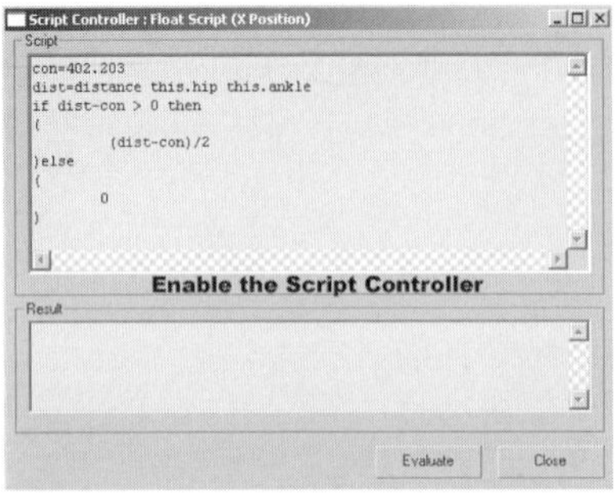

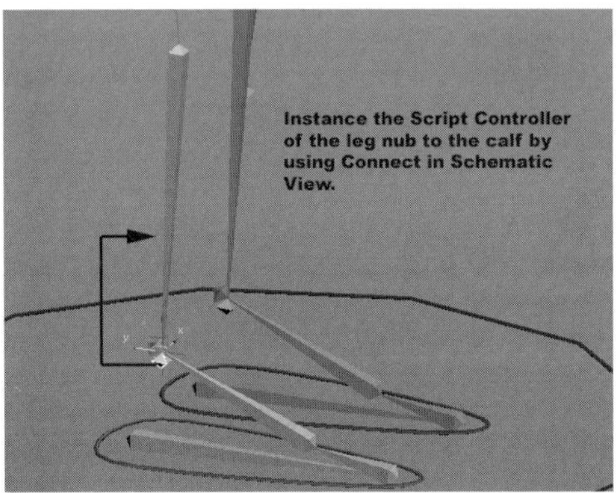

Measuring the Leg

1. Continue from the previous exercise or open *knightRig_control_wire.max*.
2. Press S to turn on Snap.
3.  On the main toolbar, right-click Snaps Toggle.
4. In the Grid and Snap Settings dialog, turn off all snap options except for Pivot.

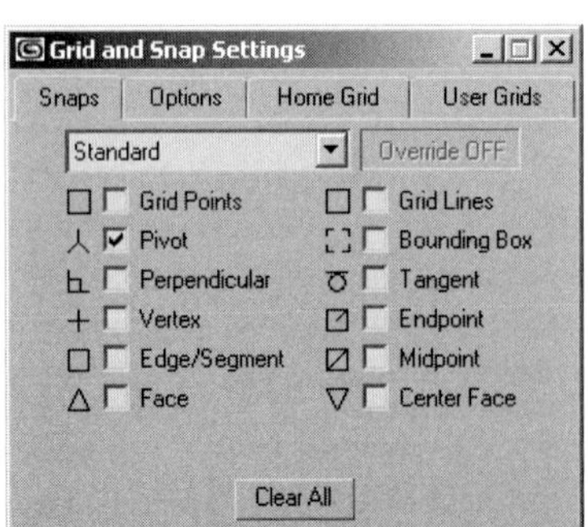

5. On the menu bar, choose Tools > Measure Distance.

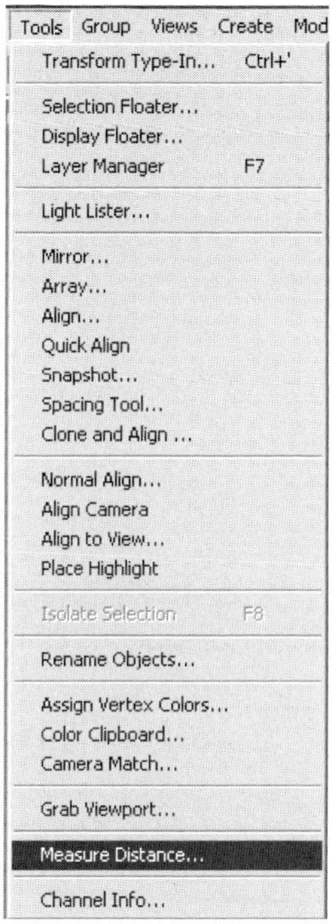

6. The Measure Distance option is active.
7. In the User viewport, choose Knight_HLP_Rleg00 at the hip and then choose Knight_Bone_Rfoot03 at the ankle.
8. The MAXScript Listener displays the distance between the two objects and reads Dist: 402.203.

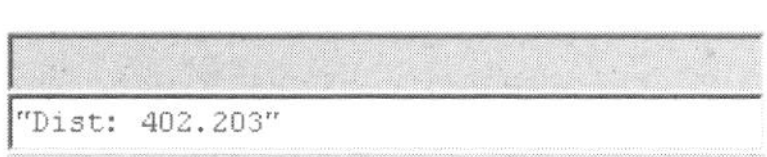

9. Right-click the MAXScript Listener, and choose Open Listener Window.
10. In the MAXScript Listener dialog, highlight the number and press CTRL+C to copy it to the clipboard.
11. Close the MAXScript Listener dialog.

Assigning the Float Script Controller

1. Continue from the previous exercise.
2. In the User viewport, choose Knight_Bone_Rleg01 and Knight_Bone_Rleg02.

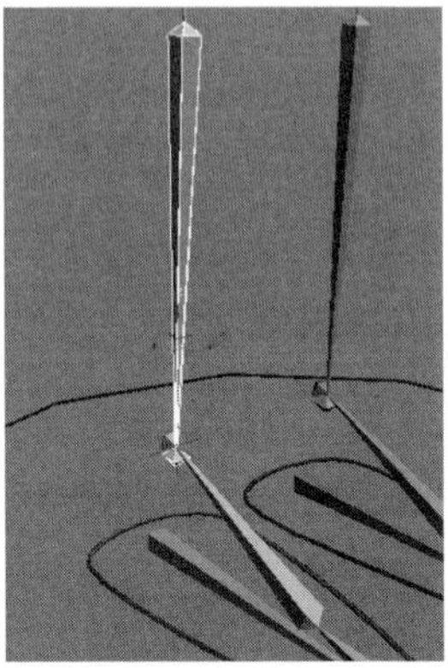

3. Press ALT+right-click and then choose Freeze Transform from the Animation quad menu.
4. Answer Yes in the dialog.
5. In the User viewport, choose Knight_Bone_Rleg02.

   This is the nub bone. You add the Script Controller to this bone.
6. On the main toolbar, choose Schematic View.
7. In the Display dialog, turn on Expand, Position (P), and Controllers.

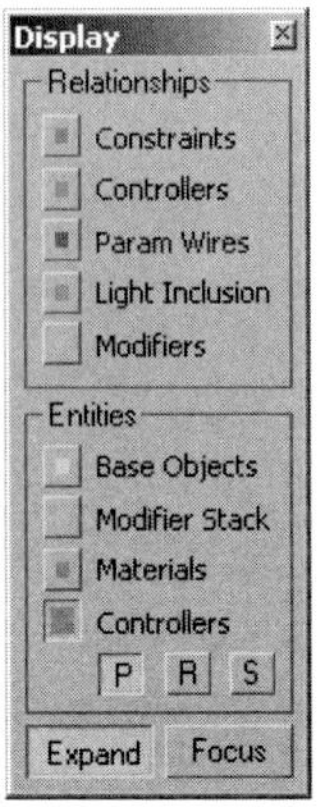

All the Controller information is displayed.

8. In Schematic View, viewport navigation controls, choose Zoom Extents Selected.

   This way you see the controllers for the selected object.

9.  On the Schematic View's main toolbar, choose Hierarchy Mode.

10. Choose the Bezier Float (X Position) controller for the Position XYZ (Zero Pos XYZ) controller.

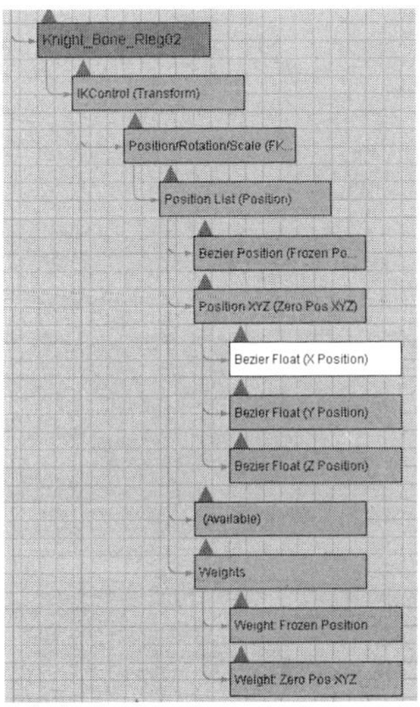

11. Right-click and then choose Assign Controller from the quad menu.

12. In the Assign Float Controller dialog, choose Float Script.

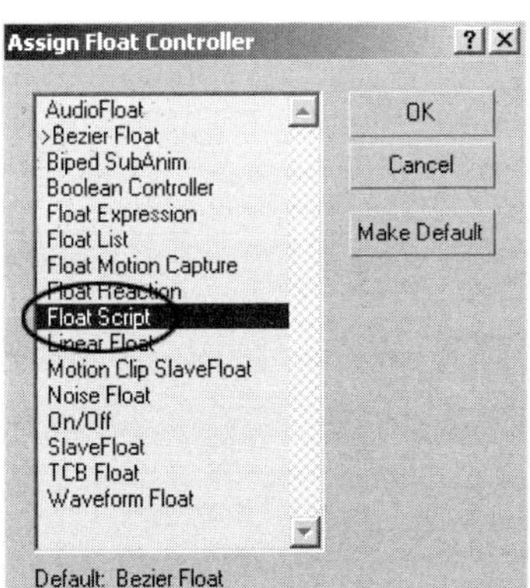

This changes the X Bezier Float controller to a Script Controller.

13. In Schematic View, double-click Float Script (X Position).

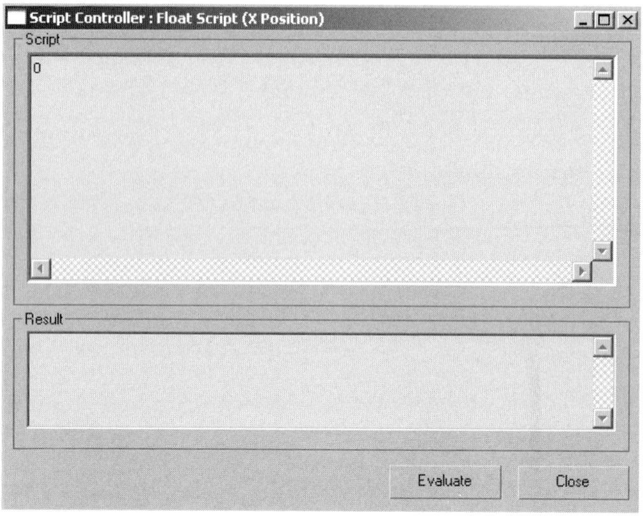

This opens the Script Controller dialog with the expression set to 0, which is the current value of the controller.

Note: Script controllers are name dependent, which means that if the name of the object changes, then errors occur when the script controller is called. To get around this, use custom attributes to store the nodes you need to reference.

Assigning Node Script Controllers

1. Continue from the previous exercise.
2. Close the Script Controller dialog.
3. In Schematic View, right-click Float Script (X position) and then choose Add/Edit Parameters from the quad menu.

   This opens the Parameter Editor dialog and has the Script Controller selected as the target for the parameters.

4. In the Parameter Type group drop-down list, choose Node.

   You use Node instead of a float value for the Parameter Type because you want to store a reference to an object in the **3ds max** scene. A Node refers to an object in **3ds max**. Using this option means you can store an object in the parameter (custom attribute) and reference that object from the Script Controller.

5. In the Name field, type *hip* and then press Add.

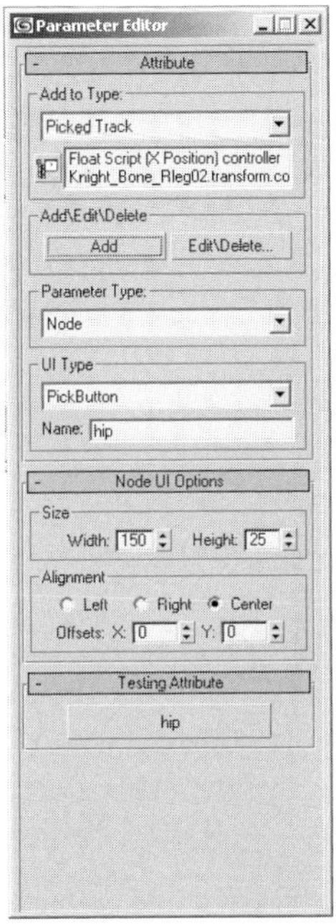

You can see the Custom Attribute added below the Float Script in Schematic View.

6. Repeat the previous steps, but change the name to *ankle* this time. Close the dialog when you are done.

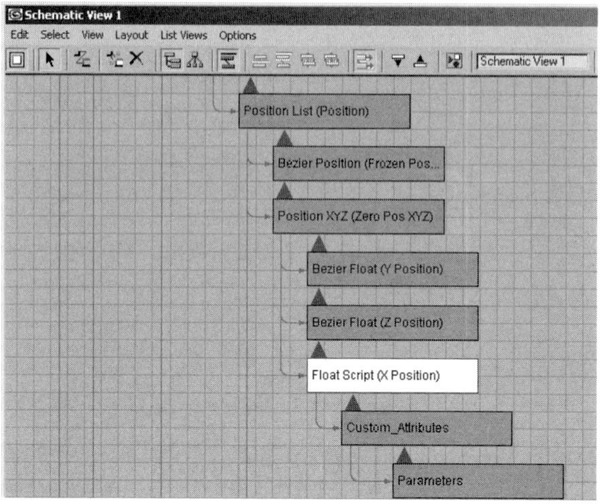

You have two nodes defined as custom attributes within the Script Controller of the leg nub. You need to reference the Helper object at the top of the leg to the node named *hip*. You also need to reference the nub of the foot to the node named *ankle*. You do this next by writing scripts in the MAXScript Listener and then adding text to the Script Controller.

Writing Scripts

Next, you add Knight_HLP_Rleg00 to the Hip custom attribute and Knight_Bone_Rfoot03 to the Ankle custom attribute by writing specific lines of MAXScript in the MAXScript Listener window.

1. Continue from the previous exercise or open *knightRig_prescript.max*.
2. Open the MAXScript Listener Window.

3. In the MAXScript Listener dialog, type:

```
$Knight_Bone_Rleg02.position.controller[2].x_position.
controller.
hip=$Knight_HLP_Rleg00
```

and press ENTER.

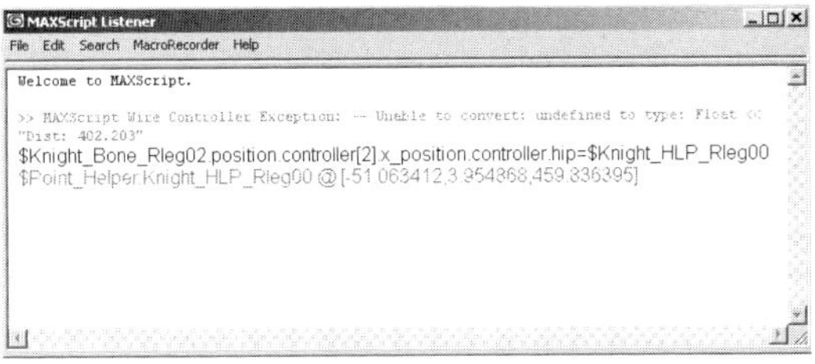

This adds Knight_HLP_Rleg00 to the Hip custom attribute in the Script Controller for the X-axis.

4. Now type:

```
$Knight_Bone_Rleg02.position.controller[2].x_position.
controller.ankle=$Knight_Bone_Rfoot03.
```

This adds Knight_Bone_Rfoot03 to the ankle custom attribute.

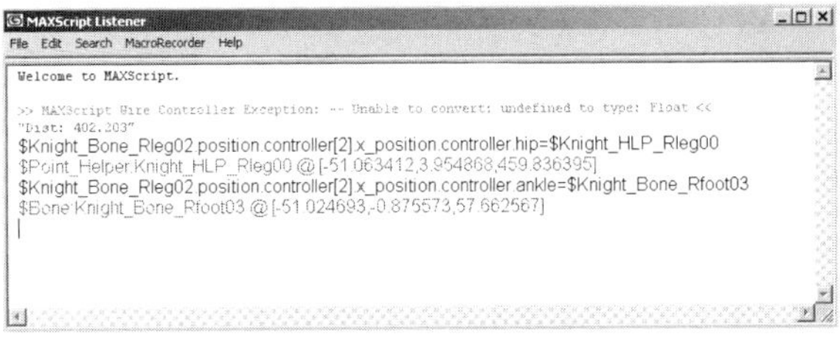

Next, you want to make sure the custom attributes are set correctly. You use a script to test your setup.

5. In the MAXScript Listener Window, type:

```
$Knight_Bone_Rleg02.position.controller[2].x_position.
controller.ankle
```

   and then press ENTER.

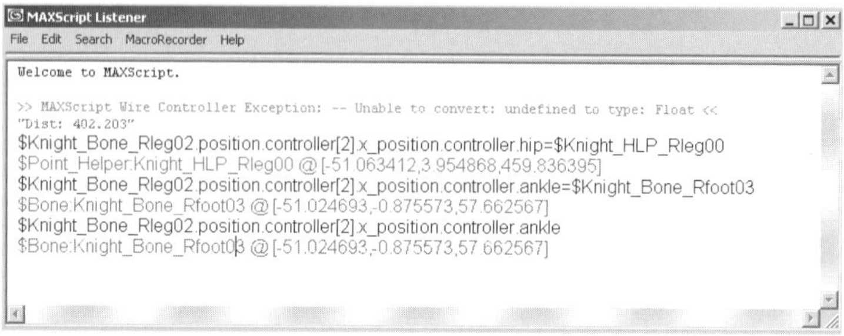

   Next, you break down the script to see what it does.

Testing Scripts

1. Continue from the previous exercise.
2. In the User viewport, choose Knight_Bone_Rleg02.
3. Open Schematic View, and then double-click Float Script (X Position).
4. In the Script Controller, type the following two lines to define two variables.

```
con=402.203
dist=distance this.hip this.ankle
```

   The first line defines the variable *con*. The variable is assigned the constant value of 402.203, which is the distance from the hip to the ankle.

   The second line defines the variable *dist*. This variable defines the distance from the hip to the ankle. The word *this* refers the script controller, so *this hip* refers to the custom attribute called hip in the Script controller. Remember that the object Knight_HLP_Rleg00 is now stored in that custom attribute.

   Note: A *variable* is a user-defined container to which you can assign a value, and later retrieve the value. A variable is identified by its name. Wherever the variable name is referenced, the value stored in that variable is used.

   Next, you use an *if* statement. This statement does most of the work for the script.

5. In the Script Controller dialog, type these lines under the variables:

```
if dist-con > 0 then
(
   (dist-con)/2
)else
(
   0
)
```

The *if* checks to see if the distance between the hip and ankle, minus the value of con, is greater then zero. If it is, it evaluates the first expression, which calculates the distance minus the starting value divided by two. It's divided by two because two bones share the distance.

If dist – con is less than or equal to zero, then the second expression is evaluated, that is 0.

6. In the Script Controller dialog, press Evaluate to execute the script.

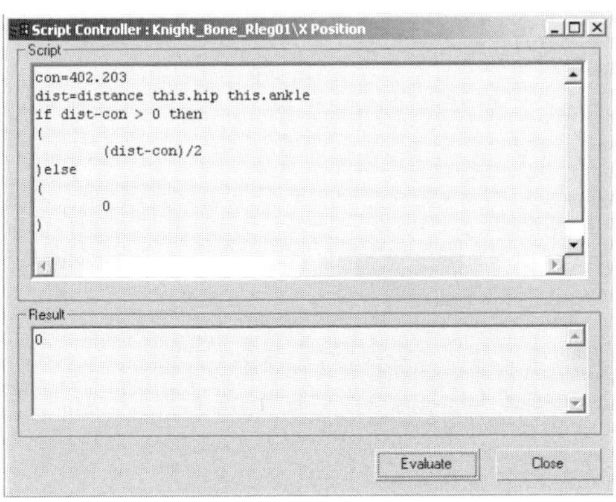

Note: If any errors occur in the syntax, they display in the MAXScript Listener Window. You must make the appropriate changes and then press evaluate again to update the script.

Instancing the Script Controller

To finish the stretchy right leg, you instance the Script Controller of Knight_Bone_Rleg02 to Knight_Bone_Rleg01.

1. Continue from the previous exercise or open *knightRig_postscript.max*.
2. Close all Script and MAXScript windows.

3. In Schematic View, locate Float Script (X Position) for Knight_Bone_Rleg02 and Bezier Float (X Position) for Knight_Bone_Rleg01.

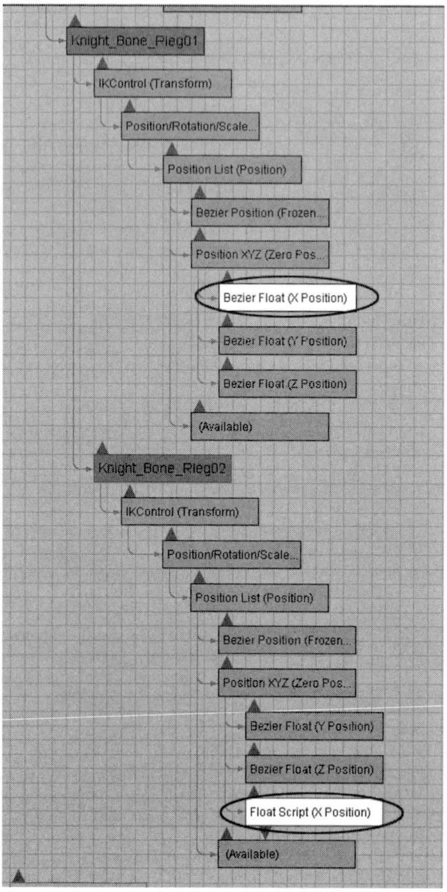

4.  On the Schematic View tool bar, choose Connect.

5. Click and drag from the Float Script controller to the X_Position of Knight_Bone_Rleg01.

6. In the Attach Controller dialog, choose Instance, and then press OK.

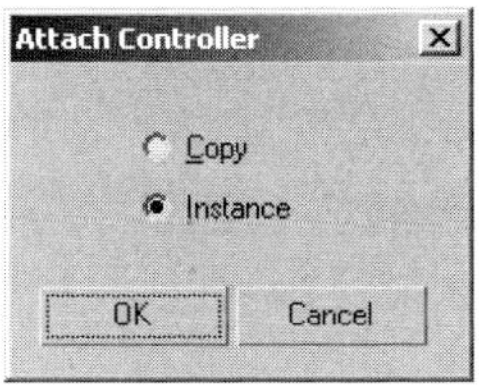

Testing the Stretch

1. Continue from the previous exercise.
2. Type **S** on the keyboard to turn off Snap.
3. In the User viewport, choose Knight_CNT_Rfoot.

4. Move the foot down and notice the bones stretching. Move it up and the bones bend at the knee.

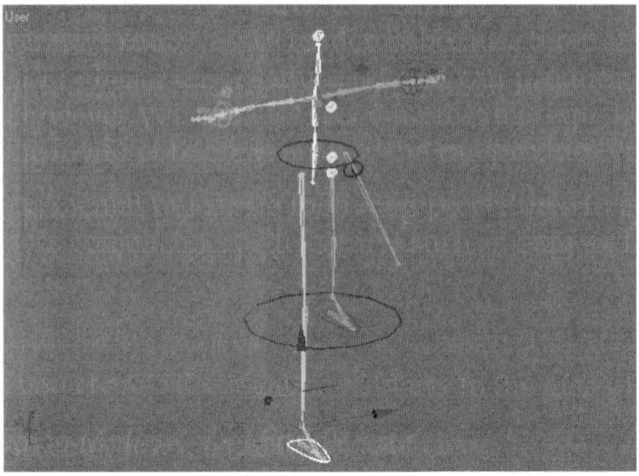

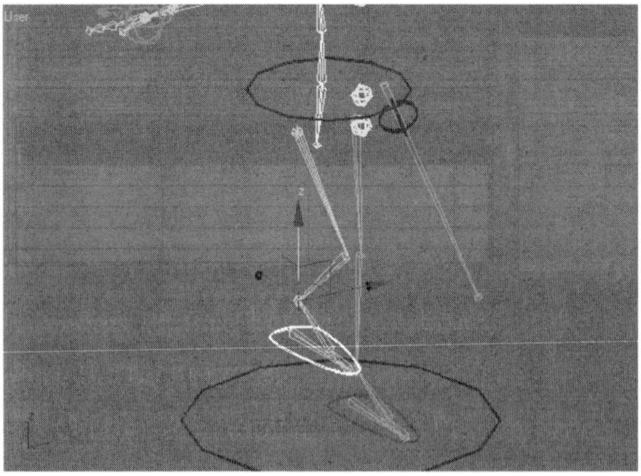

5. Save the file as *knightRig04.max*.

6. Repeat the steps for the left leg.

   Tip: To save time, you can copy the Attribute Holder modifier from the right foot control to the left foot control. You can also copy the Script controller that controls the stretch from the right leg to the left leg. Remember to reset the correct hip and ankle reference objects in the custom attribute definition.

7. Save the file as **knightRig05.max**.

Using Skin

Next, you add the bones you created to the Skin modifier and then Mirror the envelopes and weights from the right side.

1. Continue from the previous exercise or open *knightRig05.max*.
2. On the main toolbar, choose Layer Manager.
3. In the Layer dialog, choose the icon next to the Layer named knight-LowRes to unhide the layer.

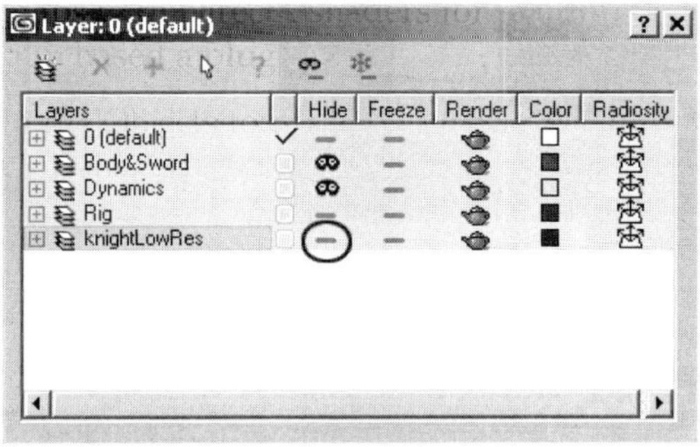

4. The low-resolution body and cape are displayed.
5. Close the Layer dialog.
6. In the User viewport, choose Knight_GEO_BodyLowRes.
7. On the Modify panel > Skin modifier > Parameters rollout, choose Edit Envelopes.

8. In the Parameters rollout, choose Add.

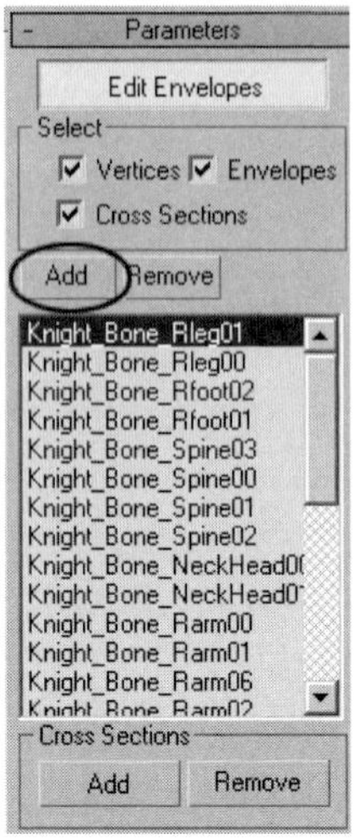

The Select Bones dialog is displayed.

Tip: Choose Display Subtree in the dialog to see the linking hierarchy.

9. In the Select Bones dialog, choose Knight_Bone_Lleg00 and Knight_Bone_Lleg01 and Knight_Bone_Lfoot01,Knight_Bone_Lfoot02, and then press Select.

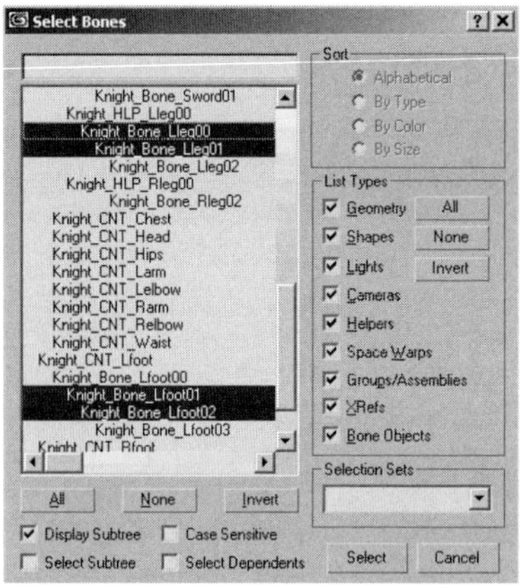

The bones are added to the Skin modifier and default envelopes are created.

10. In the Front viewport, choose the Envelope for the right thigh bone.

11. In the Parameters rollout > Envelope Properties group, turn on Envelope visibility.

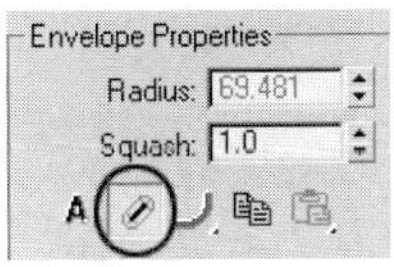

12. In the Front viewport, choose the Envelope for the left thigh bone.

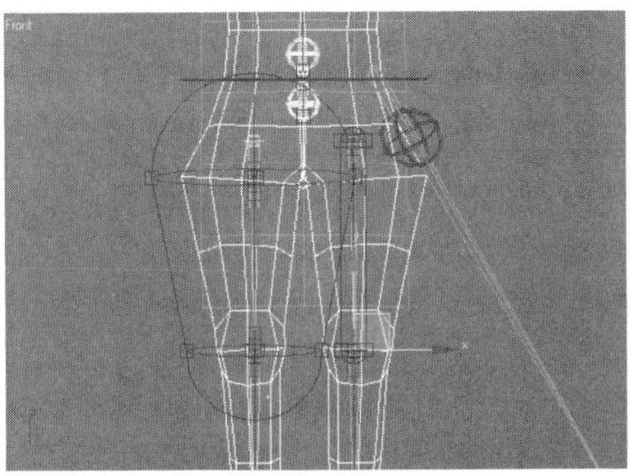

You see that the envelopes are edited on the right side and not on the left. You use the Mirror option to mirror the envelope information from the right to the left side.

13. In the Mirror Parameters rollout, turn on Mirror Mode.

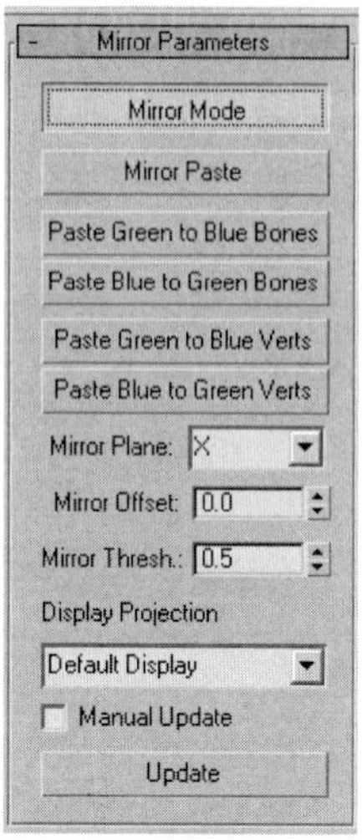

The right side of the character's bone length is displayed in green and the left side in blue.

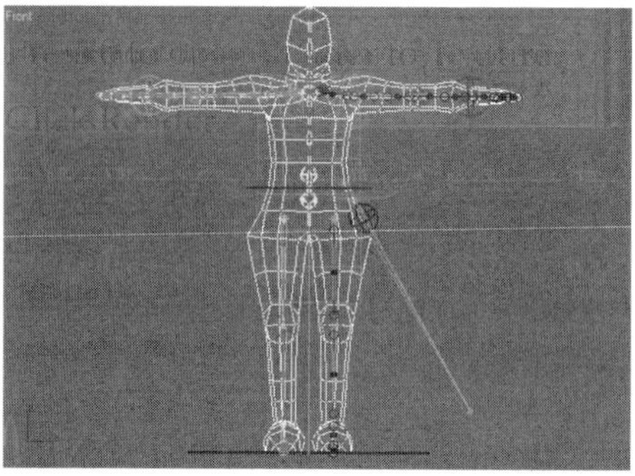

14. Since the right side is complete, you can simply use Paste Green to Blue Bones to transfer the envelope information from the right to the left side.

15. Turn off Mirror Mode.

Note: Everything is lined up because the geometry's pivot point is at 0 on the X-axis. You can adjust the mirror axis by using the Offset spinner but this usually means more work than setting up the model correctly from the beginning.

16. In the Front viewport, choose envelopes from the right and left side.

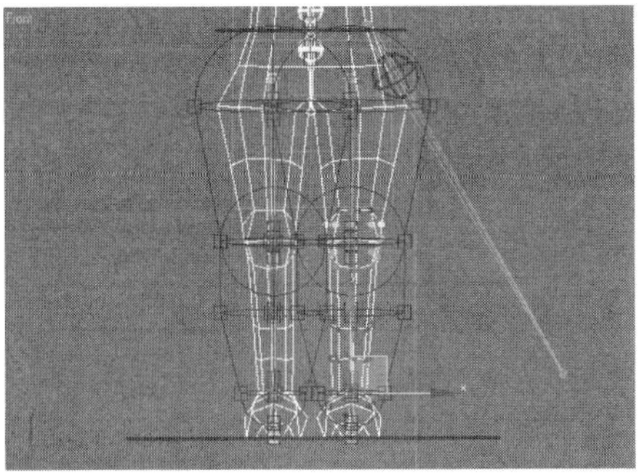

The envelopes on the left side are the same as the right side.

17. Save the file as **knightRig06.max**.

What Is the Reaction Manager?

The Reaction Manager is a tool that allows you to edit an animatable track of one object and affect an animatable track of another object. It does this using the following terminology: Master, Slave, and State.

- Master – Any animatable object in **3ds max**.
- Slave – Any animatable object in **3ds max**.
- State – The result of editing the master object and having it affect the slave object.

For example, you have two objects, a box and a sphere. You want the box's position to affect the sphere's rotation. As the box moves up and down, you want the sphere to rotate in a positive and negative direction. The box is the Master and the Sphere is the Slave. As the box moves up, the sphere rotates in a positive direction on the Z-axis. You interactively edit the box's position in the viewport along with the sphere's rotation, and then you define a State in the Reaction Manager.

Why Use the Reaction Manager?

You use Reactions in a scene to make it easier to animate objects. You can set up complex interactions and then drive those interactions with one slider. A master object can control many slave objects using one control. This control can be a custom attribute that you have set up previously or it can be done interactively by transforming the object in the viewport. All this control is contained in a simple and unified interface.

Reaction Manager Workflow

The following sample workflow is for a character rig, but the Reaction Manager can be used for any object in any type of scene.

- Create a character rig.
- Choose a Control Spline, such as the foot control.
- Assign a Custom Attribute to the control spline for one of its Transforms, such as Rotation. This custom attribute can be a slider or a spinner.
- Open the Reaction Manager by choosing Animation > Reaction Manager from the menu bar.
- In the Reaction Manager dialog, choose your Master Object. In this case, the Master Object is the foot control spline.
- In the viewport, select the bones the Master Object is going to control and assign them in the Reaction Manager dialog as Slaves. These are the foot bones in the character rig.
- Use the Custom Attribute and the bones in the viewport to identify states and record them as states in the Reaction Manager dialog. An example of this is a toe roll.
- Repeat this process for however many states you want to define.
- Use the Custom Attribute Slider to animate the states you defined.

Reaction Manager UI

The Reaction Manager displays information about your scene in a dialog that contains three separate areas or windows.

- The first window, called Reactions, shows all Master and Slaves connections.

- The second window, called States, shows all States for the master and slaves and allows you to edit them as needed.
- The third window shows the function curves for each of the states. This allows you to control the speed at which any given state reacts to the master.

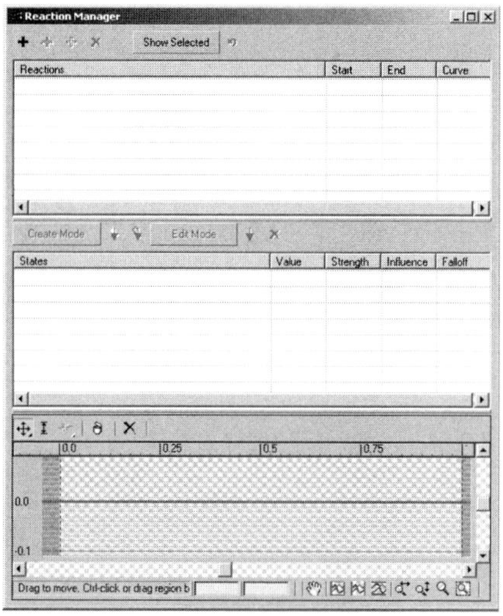

Using the Reaction Manager

Use the Reaction Manger to define the foot control as the Master and the foot bones as the Slaves. You then adjust the custom attribute of the Master object and the bones of the slave objects to define states. At the end, as you adjust your custom attribute, it displays the states you define.

1. Open *knightRig_ReactionFoot_Start.max*.
2. Choose Knight_CNT_Rfoot.
3. Go to the Modify panel.

   There is an Attribute Holder modifier assigned to the foot control spline. The Attribute Holder is assigned two custom attributes assigned: a spinner and a slider.
4. Adjust the spinner and then adjust the slider.
5. Notice the spinner and slider are both affected. They have two-way wiring. Many animators like to use the slider for animation, but the slider does not display numbers. Therefore, as the slider adjusts, you can keep track of the amount with the spinner.

6. Set the spinner to 0.
7. Choose a bone in the foot.
8. Go to the Motion panel.
9. Both the Position tracks and Rotation tracks are Frozen.

   This is a good habit to get into when animating Rotations.
10. On the menu bar, choose Animation > Reaction Manager.

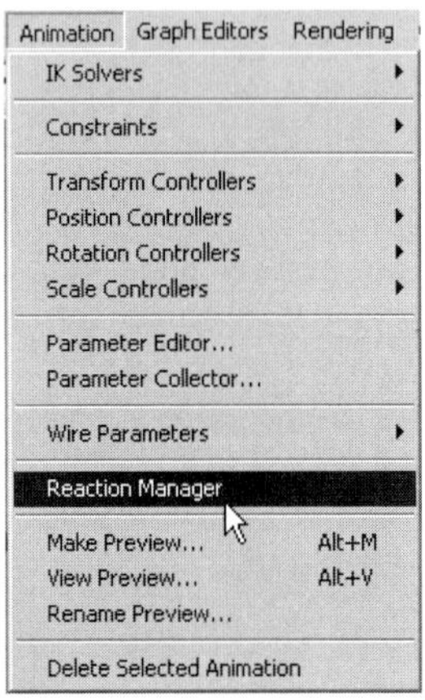

11. 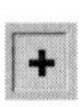 In the Reaction Manager dialog > top toolbar, choose Add Master.
12. In the User viewport, choose Knight_CNT_Rfoot.
13. From the menu, choose Modified Object > Attribute Holder > Custom_Attributes > Foot Roll > Foot_Roll Animation.

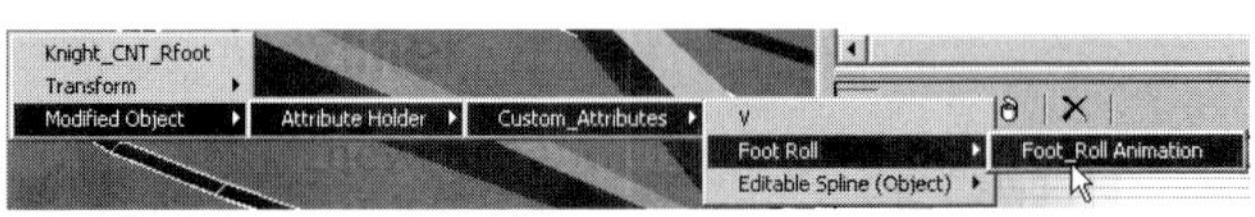

   The Foot Roll Custom Attribute of Knight_CNT_Rfoot is the Master object.

   Now that the Master is defined, you need to define the Slave objects. You can define an individual object or a selection of objects. Since you want the three foot bones as slaves, you decide to define the slaves by selection.
14. In the User viewport, choose Knight_Bone_Rfoot00, Knight_Bone_Rfoot01, and Knight_Bone_Rfoot02.

15. [In the Reaction Manager dialog > top toolbar, choose Add Selected.

16. From the menu, choose Transform > Rotation > Zero Euler XYZ > Z Rotation.

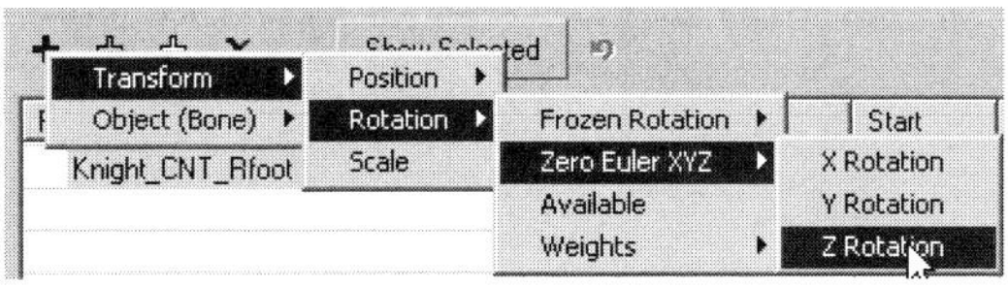

The Z Rotation of the three foot bones are added as slaves to the Master control, which is the foot spline. Their current rotation angle, which is zero, is added as a first state in the States window below the Master window.

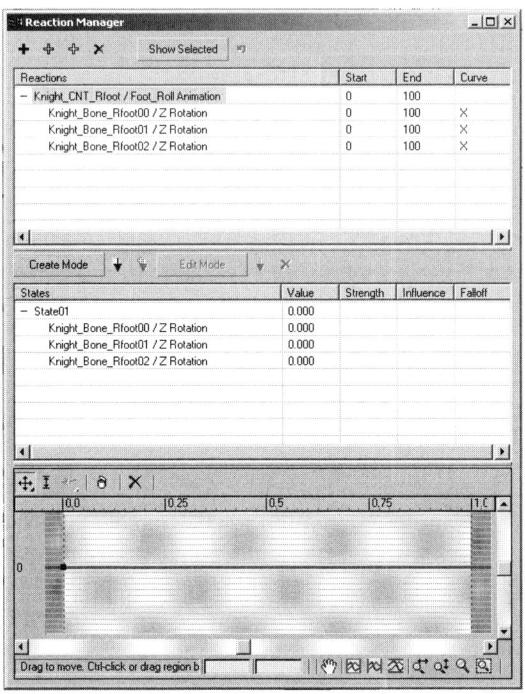

Defining the Heel Roll State

1. Continue from the previous exercise.

2. In the User viewport, choose Knight_CNT_Rfoot.

3.  In the Modify Stack > bottom toolbar, choose Pin Stack.

   This ensures the control spline is always displayed even when other objects are selected.

4. In the Custom Attributes rollout, change the slider to **–100**.

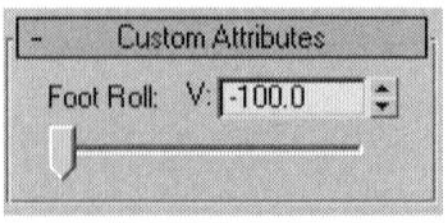

5. In the Reaction Manager dialog > Reactions window, choose the Master object and then choose the Create Mode button.

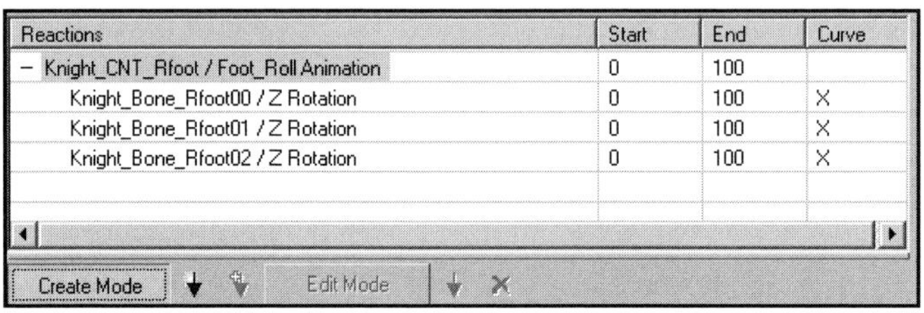

6. In the User viewport, choose Knight_Bone_Rfoot00.
7. On the main toolbar, choose Rotate.
8. On the main toolbar, choose the Local Reference Coordinate System.
9. Press **A** to turn on Angle Snap.
10. In the User viewport, rotate Knight_Bone_Rfoot00 **90** degrees on the Local Z-axis.

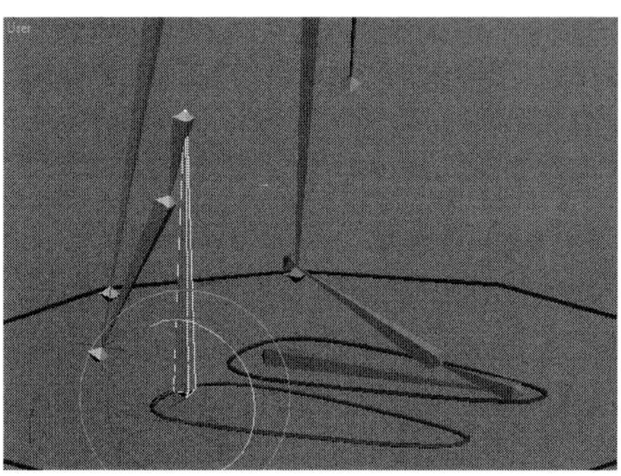

11. In the Reaction Manager dialog, choose Create State.

    This is the heel roll state.

States	Value	Strength	Influence	Falloff
− State01	0.000			
Knight_Bone_Rfoot00 / Z Rotation	0.000			
Knight_Bone_Rfoot01 / Z Rotation	0.000			
Knight_Bone_Rfoot02 / Z Rotation	0.000			
− State02	-100.000			
Knight_Bone_Rfoot00 / Z Rotation	90.000			
Knight_Bone_Rfoot01 / Z Rotation	0.000			
Knight_Bone_Rfoot02 / Z Rotation	0.000			

    The three slave tracks are included in State02.

    Tip: You can add one track to a state by selecting that slave track in the Reactions list.

12. In the Reaction Manager, turn off Create Mode.
13. In the States window, click and then click again State02. Rename the state Heel Roll.

    This is not quite a double-click since you have to activate the name and then click again to rename.

14. In the Attribute Holder rollout, adjust the slider and notice the bone is affected.

Adding the Ball Roll State

Next, you add another state for the ball roll.

1. Continue from the previous exercise.
2. In the Custom Attribute rollout, set the Foot Roll slider to 50.
3. In the Reaction Manager dialog, turn on Create Mode.
4. In the User viewport, choose Knight_Bone_Rfoot02.

5. Rotate the bone **–60** degrees on the Local Z-axis.

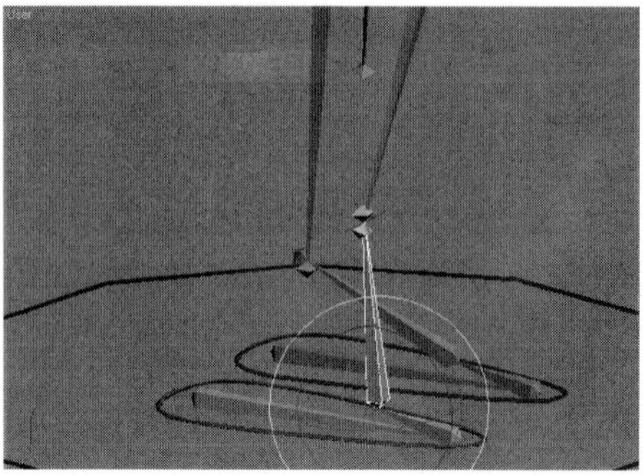

6.  In the Reaction Manager dialog, choose Create State.
7. In the States window, rename the state **Ball Roll**.

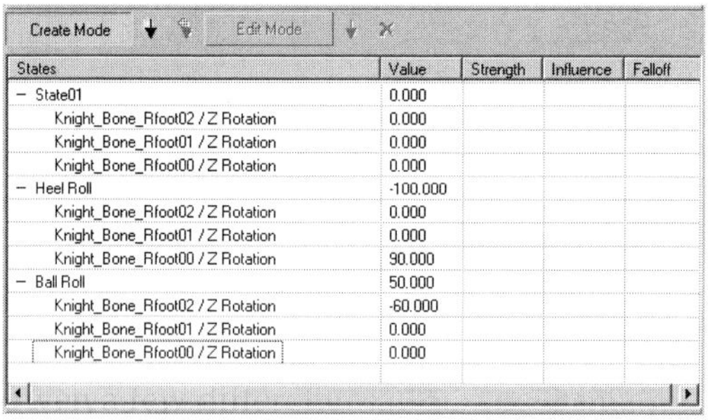

States	Value	Strength	Influence	Falloff
– State01	0.000			
Knight_Bone_Rfoot02 / Z Rotation	0.000			
Knight_Bone_Rfoot01 / Z Rotation	0.000			
Knight_Bone_Rfoot00 / Z Rotation	0.000			
– Heel Roll	-100.000			
Knight_Bone_Rfoot02 / Z Rotation	0.000			
Knight_Bone_Rfoot01 / Z Rotation	0.000			
Knight_Bone_Rfoot00 / Z Rotation	90.000			
– Ball Roll	50.000			
Knight_Bone_Rfoot02 / Z Rotation	-60.000			
Knight_Bone_Rfoot01 / Z Rotation	0.000			
Knight_Bone_Rfoot00 / Z Rotation	0.000			

8. In the Reaction Manager, turn off Create Mode.
9. Adjust the slider to view the bones.

Adding the Toe Roll State

Next, you add the toe roll state.

1. Continue from the previous exercise.
2. In the Custom Attribute rollout, set the Foot Roll slider to **100**.
3. In the Reaction Manager dialog, turn on Create Mode.
4. In the User viewport, choose Knight_Bone_Rfoot02.
5. Rotate it **60** degrees on the Local Z-axis so it returns to its starting value.
6. In the User viewport, choose Knight_Bone_Rfoot01.

7. Rotate it **–90** degrees on the Local Z-axis.

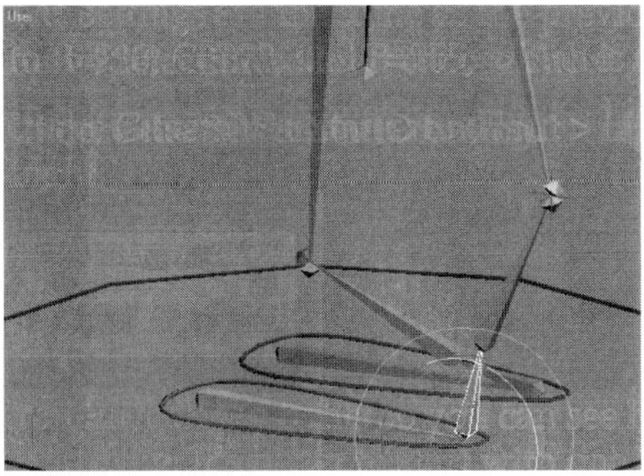

8. In the Reaction Manager dialog, choose Create State.
9. Change the name of the state to Toe Roll.
10. Turn off Create Mode.

States	Value	Strength	Influence	Falloff
– State01	0.000			
Knight_Bone_Rfoot00 / Z Rotation	0.000			
Knight_Bone_Rfoot01 / Z Rotation	0.000			
Knight_Bone_Rfoot02 / Z Rotation	0.000			
– State02	-100.000			
Knight_Bone_Rfoot00 / Z Rotation	90.000			
Knight_Bone_Rfoot01 / Z Rotation	0.000			
Knight_Bone_Rfoot02 / Z Rotation	0.000			
– State04	50.000			
Knight_Bone_Rfoot00 / Z Rotation	0.000			
Knight_Bone_Rfoot01 / Z Rotation	0.000			
Knight_Bone_Rfoot02 / Z Rotation	-60.000			
– State05	100.000			
Knight_Bone_Rfoot00 / Z Rotation	0.000			
Knight_Bone_Rfoot01 / Z Rotation	-90.000			
Knight_Bone_Rfoot02 / Z Rotation	0.000			

Tip: You can double-click any value in the States window to change its value. You can also click and scrub to change the value.

11. Scrub the Foot Roll slider from –100 to 100.

    The foot rolls through the full range of motion.

Editing the Function Curves

Every time you create a state, a curve in the third window of the Reaction Manager dialog is displayed. You notice the linear points of transition from one state to another, making the motion appear stiff. In the next steps, you adjust the curves to smooth the motion so the animation flows more smoothly.

1. Continue from the previous exercise.
2. In the Reaction Manager dialog > Function Curve area, the curves for the three states are displayed.

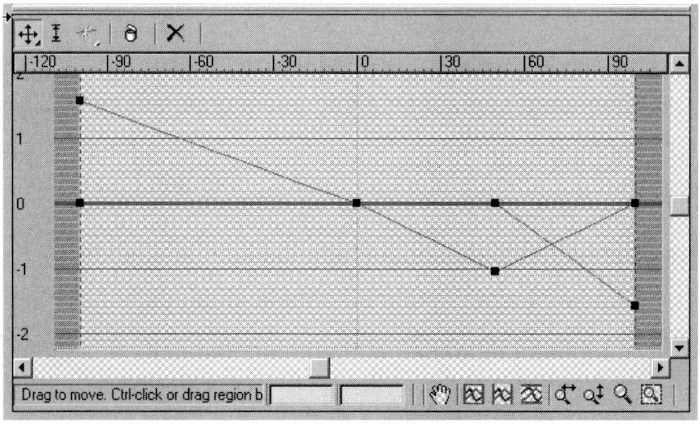

You work on the transition points from heel to the ball of the foot and then the ball to the toe roll.

3. In the Reaction Manager dialog > Reactions window, choose Knight_Bone_Rfoot00 / Z Rotation.

   Its curve is displayed in the Curve window.

4. In the Curves area, right-click the keyframe at frame 0 and choose Bezier Corner from the right-click menu.

5. Adjust the left handle of the curve so it is flat.

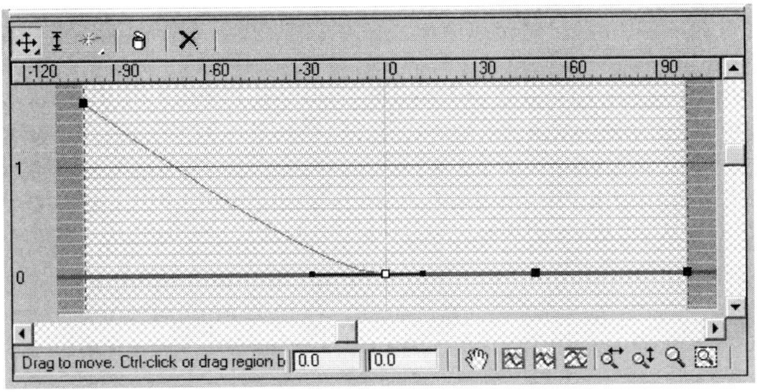

6. In the Reaction Manager dialog, choose Knight_Bone_Rfoot02 / Z Rotation.
7. In the Reaction Manager dialog, region-select the keys at **0** and **100**.
8. Right-click and then choose Bezier Corner from the right-click menu.
9. Move the handles so they are flat.
10. Right-click the key at 50, and then choose Bezier Smooth.

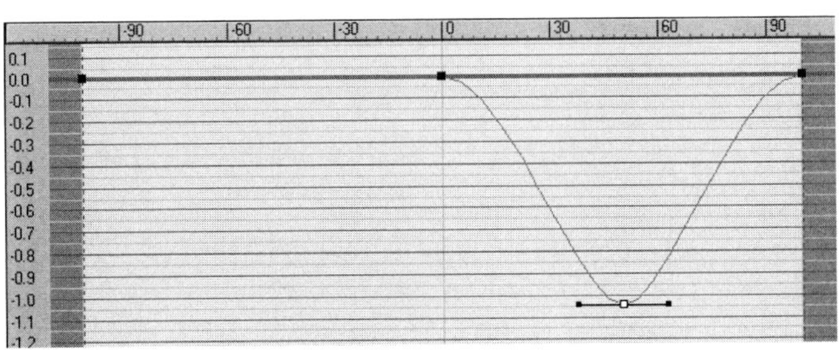

11. In the Reaction Manager dialog > Reactions window, choose Knight_Bone_Rfoot01 / Z Rotation.
12. In the Curve area, right-click the key at **50** and choose Bezier Corner.
13. Choose the right handle and move it up so it's flat.

    This creates a slight ease out. Make sure you don't drag the handle too far to the right because this makes the ease greater and starts to affect the timing on the foot roll during animation.
14. Scrub the Foot Roll slider and notice the action is smoother.
15. Save your file.

Note: Repeat all steps for the left leg and foot so that it works the same way. It is also possible to layer list controllers on the foot bones and have more than one custom attribute affect each joint. This way, you can set up individual sliders for each joint in case you can't get the desired effect with one main slider.

Expose Transform

Expose Transform is a helper object used to extract transform information from an object. In previous versions of **3ds max**, it was impossible to use wire parameters or expressions on a rotation value in a joint driven by IK, Orientation Constraints, or LookAt Constraints. The options to retrieve the data involved a lot of work. Expose Transform resolves that issue by allowing you to choose an object to expose the transform. You can also have a reference object in case the parent of the exposed object is not the one you wanted to use as a reference.

Why Use Expose Transform?

One use for Expose Transform is to set up a forearm twist. Twisting solutions are needed in the forearm to correct collapsing geometry. The way a human forearm works is quite complex. The ulna and radius bones run from the elbow to the wrist and allow the forearm to twist along the length of the arm. This creates a soft deformation of the skin in the forearm. Rotating the wrist up and down or side to side creates a sharp deformation in the skin. If you try and create a forearm rig without bones to simulate what the ulna and radius do, you will lack the necessary full range of motion for the forearm.

Expose Transform UI

The Expose Transform helper object has the following three rollouts.

- Parameters rollout – Allows you to choose the object to expose the transform.
- Display rollout – Changes the display of the object.

- Expose Values rollout – Displays the data so you see the values.

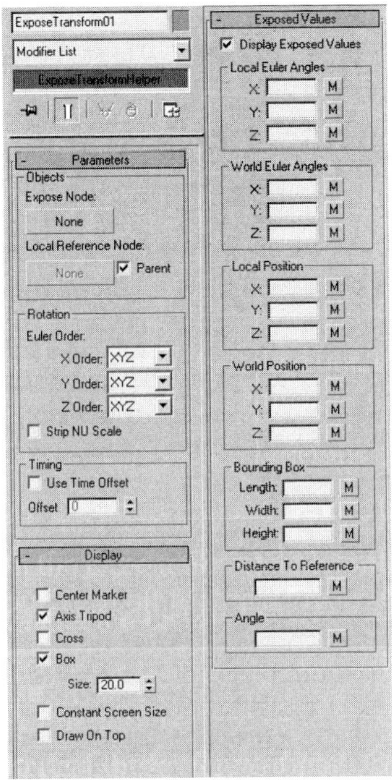

Using Expose Transform

You use the Extract Transform helper object to extract the rotation values from the wrist so you can drive a twist bone in the forearm.

1. Open *knightRig_armTwist01.max*.
2. On the command panels, choose Create > Helpers > ExposeTm.

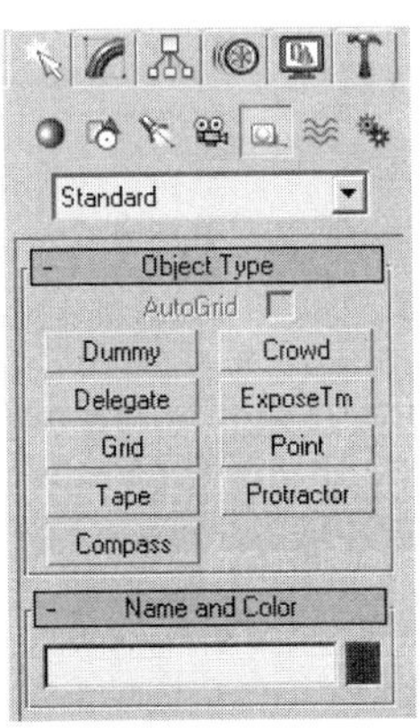

3. In the User viewport, click near the wrist to create the ExposeTm helper object.

   No values display because you have not selected an Expose Node.

4. On the command panels, choose Modify.

   The ExposeTm helper looks a lot like a Point Helper. You edit its properties so it's easy to distinguish between helper objects.

5. In the Display rollout, turn on Axis Tripod, and then turn off Cross. Turn on Box and then set the size to **40**.

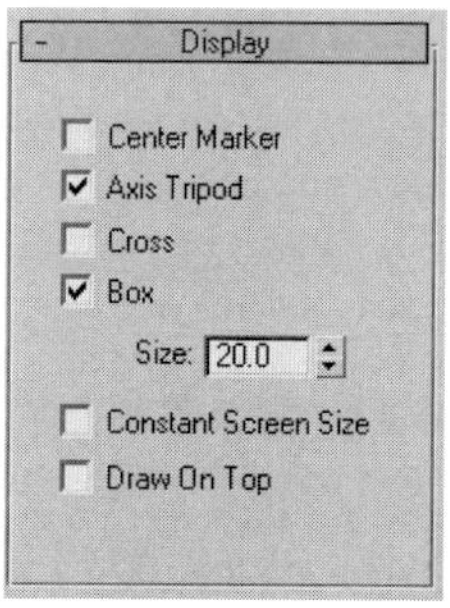

6. On the main toolbar, choose Align.
7. Press **H** and choose Knight_Bone_Rhand00.
8. In the Align Selection dialog > Align Position group, turn on X, Y, and Z.
9. Choose Pivot Point for Current and Target.
10. In the Align Orientation group, choose X, Y, and Z.

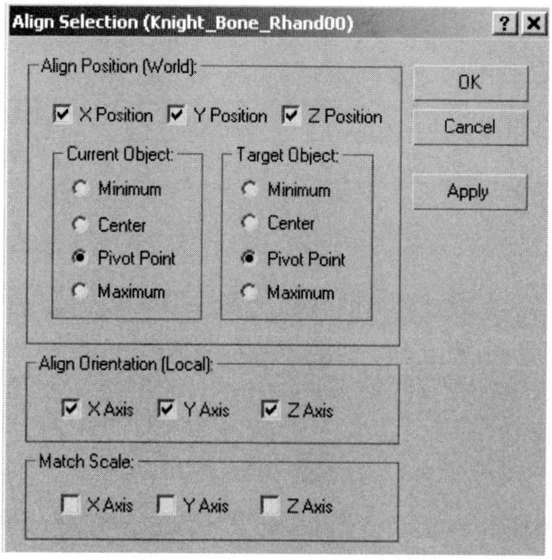

11. On the main toolbar, choose Select and Link.
12. In the User viewport, link ExposeTransform01 to Knight_Bone_Rhand00.
13. On the main toolbar, choose Select Object.
14. On the Modify panel > Parameters rollout > Objects group, choose Expose Node: None.
15. In the User viewport, choose Knight_HLP_Rarm02.

    This node is the root object of the hand and aligned to the forearm so you know you start with a Rotation value of 0 on all three axes.

    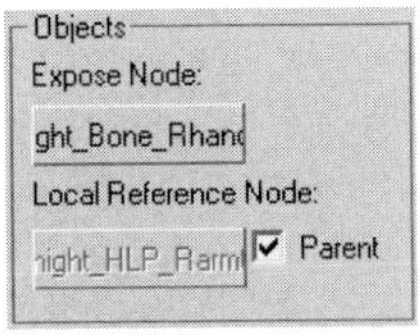

    Now that you have added the Expose Node, you see the values exposed in the Exposed Values rollout. It is the Local Euler Angles you are interested in for the twist bone. You see they are X:0.0, Y:0.0, and Z:0.0.

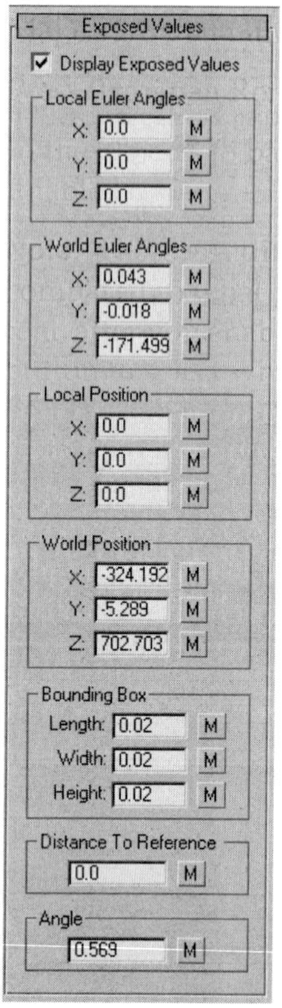

16. Save your file.

Using Wire Parameters with Expose Transform

The next step is to use wire parameters to connect the twist bone to the needed values in the Expose Transform helper object.

1. Continue from the previous exercise, or open *knightRig_armTwist02.max*.
2. In the User viewport, choose Knight_CNT_Rarm.
3. On the main toolbar, choose Select and Rotate and set the Reference Coordinate System to Local.
4. In the User viewport, rotate the control object on each axis and then undo each rotation.

5. As you rotate, notice Knight_Bone_Rarm04 does not rotate.
6. In the User viewport, choose Knight_Bone_Rarm04.

   This is the small twist bone in the lower part of the arm.

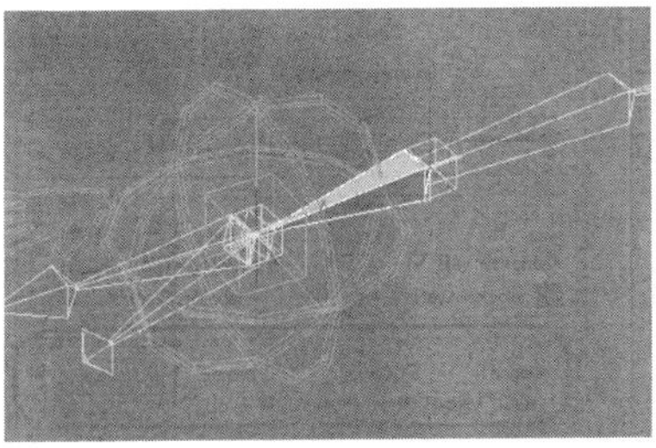

7. Right-click in the viewport and then choose Wire Parameters from the quad menu.
8. Choose Transform > Rotation > Zero Euler XYZ > X Rotation.

   The local X-axis of a bone runs along its length.

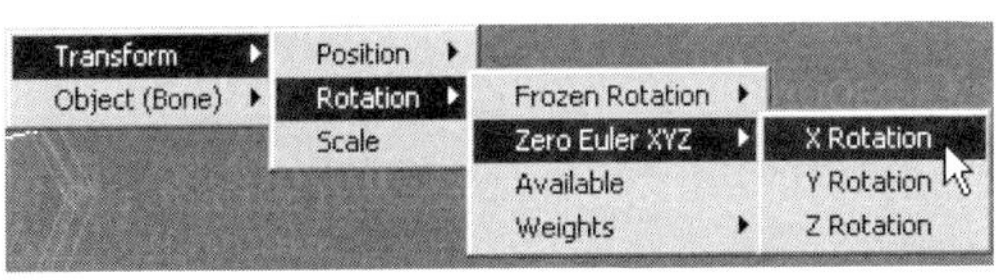

9. In the User viewport, choose ExposeTransform01 helper and then choose Object (ExposeTransformHelper) > Local Euler X.

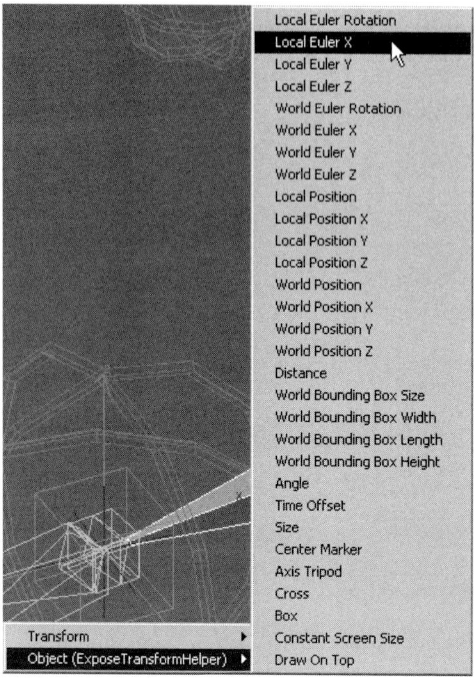

The Parameter Wiring dialog is displayed.

10. In the Parameter Wiring dialog, choose the one-way connection left button and then press Connect.

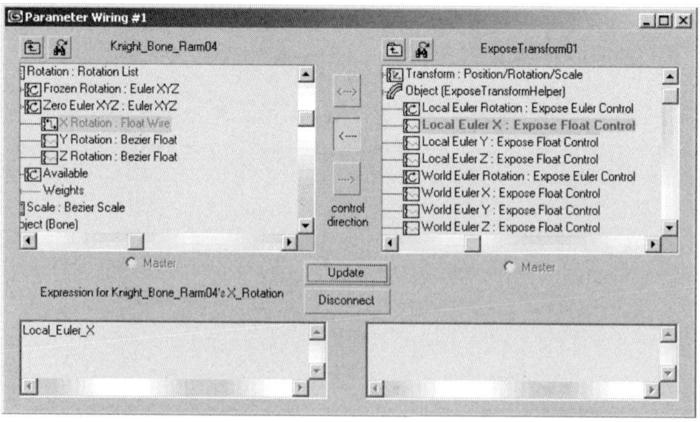

11. In the User viewport, choose Knight_CNT_Rarm.

12. In the User viewport, rotate Knight_CNT_Rarm on each axis, one at a time.

    With the hand, the twist bone in the wrist rotates on the X-axis only. The twist bone stays aligned to the forearm in the Y and Z-axes.

13. Save your file.

14. Open *knightRig_armTwist03.max* to view the finished file.

Conclusion

In this chapter, you learned the principles of character rigging. You assigned IK Solvers, created Custom Attributes, and used Script Controllers. At first glance, character rigging appears technical, but you have seen several approaches to setting up a character for animation, and that process is quite creative.

4 Animation

Objectives

After completing this chapter, you should be able to:

- Use Skin Morph.
- Use Skin Wrap.
- Use Parameter Collector.

Introduction

In this chapter, you finish setting up the deformation on the low- and high-resolution mesh objects of the knight. The low-resolution mesh was set up with the Skin modifier in Chapter 3.

To complete the low-resolution mesh, you use a new tool in **3ds max 7** called Skin Morph. To complete the high-resolution mesh, you use another new tool called Skin Wrap. This chapter shows you how to use these modifiers efficiently and effectively for any production.

You then use Parameter Collector to add your custom attributes set to the hands and feet in an organized dialog.

What Is Skin Morph?

Skin Morph is a modifier that is usually applied above the Skin modifier. It expands the Angle Deformer tools currently found in the Skin modifier. Skin Morph and Skin allow you to use a bone's rotation to drive a morph target. The difference is that Skin's Joint and Bulge Angle Deformers apply a cage around the area you want to edit, whereas Skin Morph allows direct manipulation on the mesh using its Points sub-object level.

Why Use Skin Morph?

Skin Morph enables you to add morph targets to problem areas of a character, such as elbows, knees, hips, and shoulders. These joints are usually the toughest parts of a character to deform correctly.

A good character rig commonly consists of twist bones, well placed joints, excellent envelope adjustments, and vertex weighting. However, these elements don't prevent joints from collapsing or deforming incorrectly. To fix this, you add more bones, or use the Angle Deformers found in the Skin modifier. You can also use the Morpher modifier.

Using the Morpher modifier to create morph targets is a slow, disjointed process. Separate targets need to be modeled, added to the modifier, and then tested. This editing is done at the base pose so it is hard to know the results once the joint is rotated. Workarounds are available, however it's never easy. Also, left and right joints need separate targets because you cannot mirror a morph target.

Skin Morph relieves you of this process and makes the task of fixing and working with problem joints easy.

Typical Skin Morph Workflow

- Model an object that is a mesh, poly, or patch surface type.
- Rig the character with bones, such as biped or **3ds max** bones.
- Apply the Skin modifier to the surface and add the bones to the Skin modifier.
- Adjust envelopes and weight vertices where applicable.
- Add keyframes to control objects to test your character rig.
- Fine-tune areas such as the shoulders and hips, which generally need more attention.
- Instead of adding extra bones or helpers to the rig and to the Skin modifier, add Skin Morph above the Skin modifier.
- Pick the troubled bone in the Skin Morph modifier.
- Go to the frame that best displays the problem areas and choose Create Morph.
- Go to the Points Sub-Object level and edit the geometry directly.
- Adjust the Influence Angle so the Morph Target does not affect the base pose.

- Continue to add Morph targets to fix the troubled bones.
- When complete, mirror the Morph targets on the opposite side.

Skin Morph UI

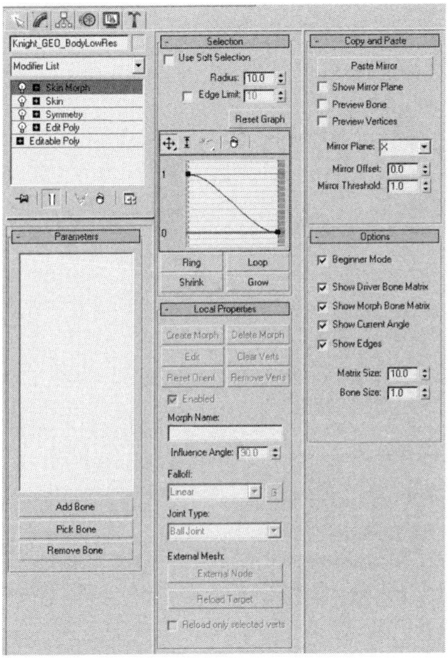

The interface for Skin Morph has the following five rollouts.

- **Parameters** – Lists the joints to be calculated that drive the morph targets.
- **Selection** – Enables selection of vertices for shaping targets. Soft selections, creating edge loops and rings, and growing and shrinking the selections speed up the process.

  Note: You can create targets from separate geometry so you can use all the modeling tools available to create your targets.

- **Local Properties** – Allows you to edit the morph shapes, add external shapes, and set up the types of joints used.
- **Copy and Paste** – Allows you mirror targets from one side to the other. This saves a lot of time because only half of the character needs to be set up and then mirrored.
- **Options** – Shows different interface items that help you see what you are working on.

Adding Skin Morph

You work with the right elbow of the low-resolution version of the knight object. This file is rigged and animated.

1. Open *knightSkin01.max*.
2. Scrub the time slider to see the animation.

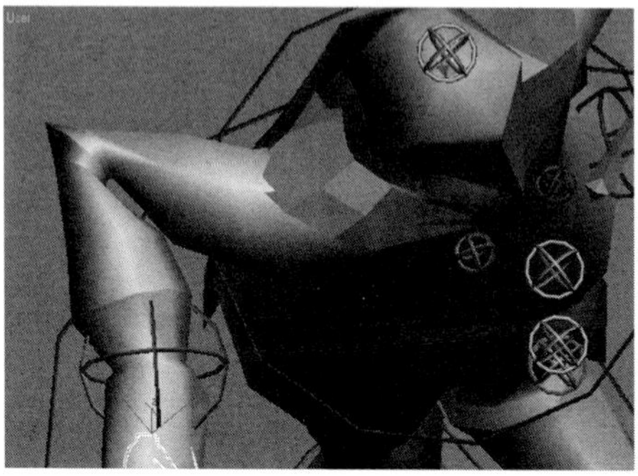

   View the problems in the Joint areas.

3. In the User viewport, choose Knight_GEO_BodyLowRes.
4. Go to frame 0.
5. On the command panels, choose Modify.
6. On the Modifier List drop-down, choose Skin Morph.

   Skin Morph needs to be above Skin so that it can act on the mesh after it has been deformed.

7. In the Parameters rollout, choose Add Bone.

8. In the Select Bones dialog, choose Knight_Bone_Rarm02.

   It's the right forearm bone.

9. Scrub the time slider to frame **70**.

   The elbow is bent to the maximum.

10. In the Parameters rollout, choose the bone from the list.

11. In the Local Properties rollout, choose Create Morph.

This adds a target value for the current angle of the elbow.

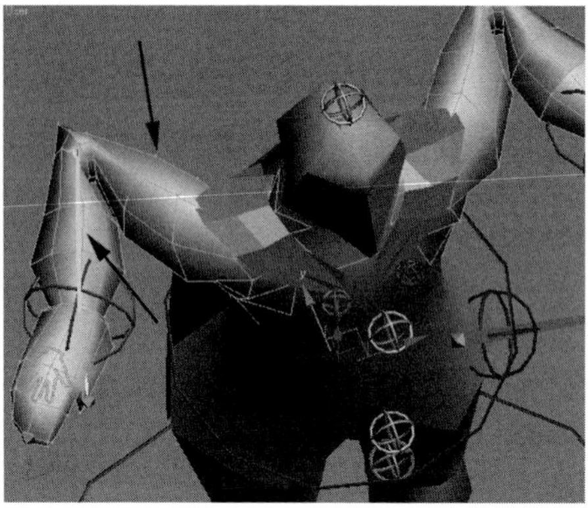

An orange gizmo surrounding the geometry and a yellow line highlighting the selected bone are displayed in the viewport.

12. Change the Morph Name to **RelbowBend** and the Joint Type to Planar Joint.

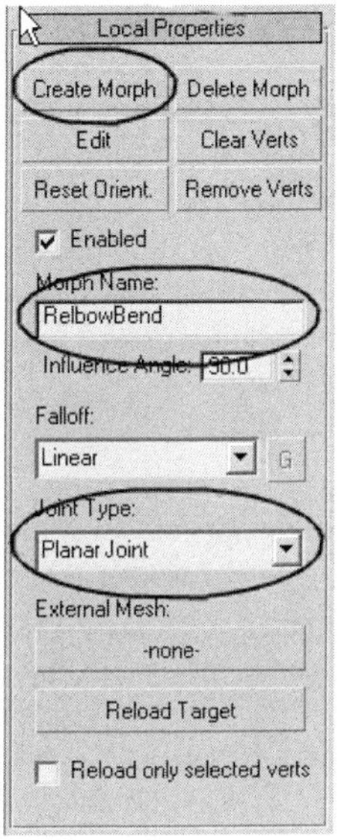

There are two Joint Types: Ball and Planar. Ball Joint is the default and designed to work with bones such as the hip and shoulder. However, getting the right setup is usually challenging, considering the way rotations work in 3D space. Planar Joints work with bones that have one axis of rotation, like the elbow. Try to use Planar Joints more often than Ball Joints.

Next, you edit the morph target. The most common problem with elbow and knee joints is that the geometry around the joints appears to collapse when only the Skin modifier is used.

13. In the Local Properties rollout, choose Edit.

You are at the Points sub-object level.

14. Model the vertices around the elbow so that the shape and volume of the elbow remain consistent with its original shape.

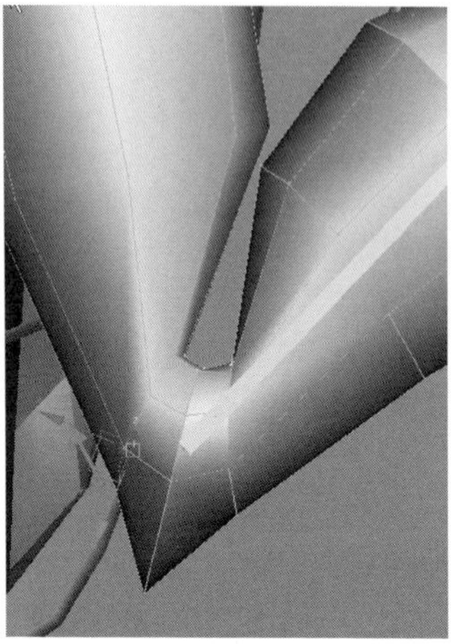

Elbow before editing

15. Move the points out around the elbow to keep its shape.
16. Edit the point at the end of the elbow to protrude when the elbow bends.

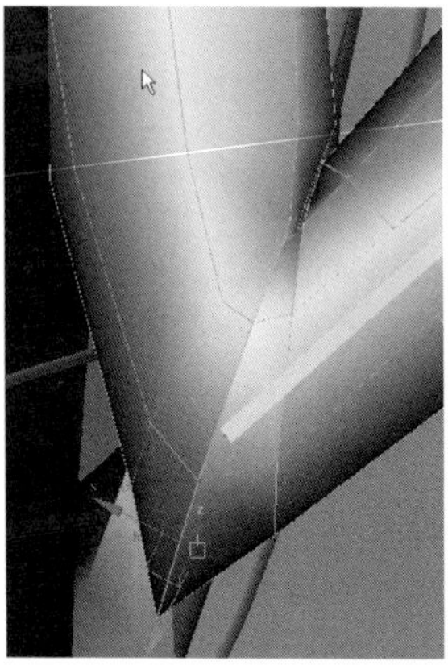

Elbow after editing

17. In the Local Properties rollout, turn off Edit.

18. Scrub the time slider between frames **60** and **70**.

    You see the elbow morphs into its target shape as the angle in the elbow changes.

19. Save the file as **knightSkin02.max**.

Mirror the Morph Target

Next, you add the left elbow to the Skin Morph bone list and mirror the right elbow's morph target.

1. Continue from the previous exercise, or open *knightSkin02.max*.
2. Make sure you are at frame 0.
3. Select Knight_GEO_BodyLowRes and make sure Skin Morph is chosen in the Modify Stack display.
4. In the Parameters rollout, choose Add Bone.
5. In the Select Bones dialog, choose Knight_Bone_Larm02.

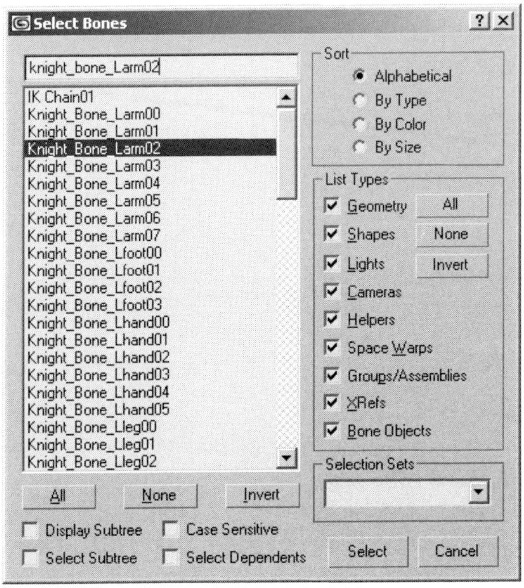

6. In the Parameters rollout, expand the Knight_Bone_Rarm02 entry. Choose RelbowBend, which you created previously.

7. In the Copy and Paste rollout, turn on the Show Mirror Plane and Preview Bone check boxes.

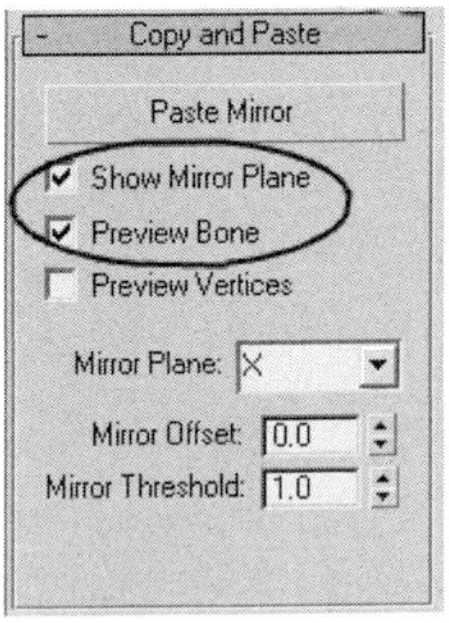

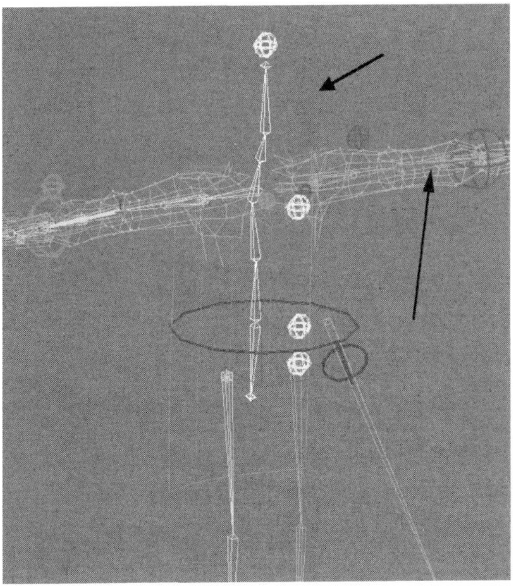

This displays a large red rectangle down the center of the character and a red line over the bone you want to mirror.

The red rectangular gizmo is the Show Mirror Plane. It is in the correct location because the character was modeled with the pivot set to the center of the mesh. You can use the Mirror Offset spinner in the Copy and Paste rollout to change the mirror axis if your character was not modeled with the pivot point set at the center of the mesh. Keep in mind that proper workflow indicates starting with your pivot point set in the correct location rather than having to use the offset options found here and in other locations such as Skin.

The Preview Bone option creates the red line over the bone that becomes mirrored. If the bone isn't highlighted, it might mean the bone is not exactly on the mirror side of the object. To fix it, you can increase the Mirror Threshold to allow for a variance in the position of the bone. Make sure you mirror bones correctly otherwise options such as mirroring skin weights, skin targets, and other tools do not work well. The same principle applies to Offset. The higher the Threshold, the greater the chance for error.

8. In the Copy and Paste rollout, choose Paste Mirror.

   In the Parameters rollout, a new morph target is displayed.

9. In the Local Properties rollout > Morph Name, type **LelbowBend** and then set the Joint Type to Planar.

10. Scrub the time slider from frame **60** to **70**.

    Both elbows morph and keep their volume.

11. Save the file as *knightSkin03.max*.

Shoulder Joint

Shoulders are a difficult area on a character to skin correctly because you must consider the amount of motion on three axes. A big mistake is trying to deform the shoulder joint correctly for rotations that are impossible for a human to make, as in making the upper arm rotate above the clavicle bone. The human body only rotates the upper arm in line with the clavicle. To raise your arm above your head, you need to raise your clavicle, not your arm.

Rotations that are active on all three axes can cause problems due to gimble lock and axis order. Getting the correct values for a shoulder joint requires you limit the axes you deal with to limit the problem. One approach is to create a twist bone in the upper arm and have it rotate only on the Y and Z-axes. The upper arm stays aligned to the clavicle on the X-axis. You do this by adding a LookAt Constraint to the twist bone looking at the forearm and using the clavicle as the up node.

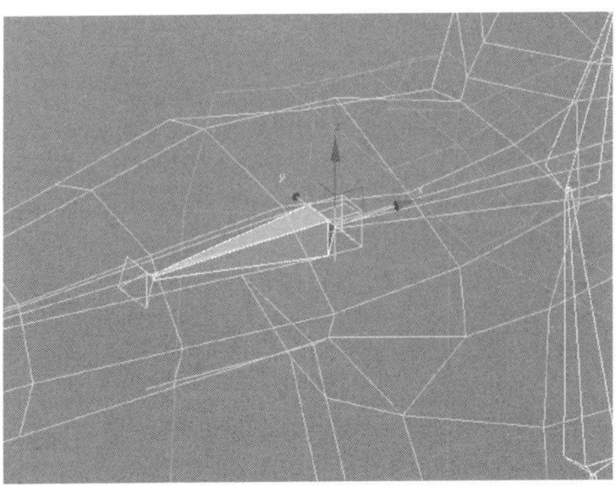

1. Open *knightSkin04.max*.
2. In the Perspective viewport, choose the Cape.
3. Right-click and then choose Hide Selection.
4. Scrub the animation and watch Knight_Bone_Rarm06.

   This bone stays aligned to the clavicle effectively, rotating on two axes only.

   You correct the deformation for the forward position first.
5. Scrub the time slider to frame **80**.
6. Select Knight_GEO_BodyLowRes.
7. On the Modify panel > Modify Sack display, choose Skin Morph.

8. In the Parameters rollout, choose Add Bone.
9. In the Select Bones dialog, choose Knight_Bone_Rarm06.

   It is the twist bone in the upper arm.
10. In the Parameters rollout > Bone list, choose Knight_Bone_Rarm06.

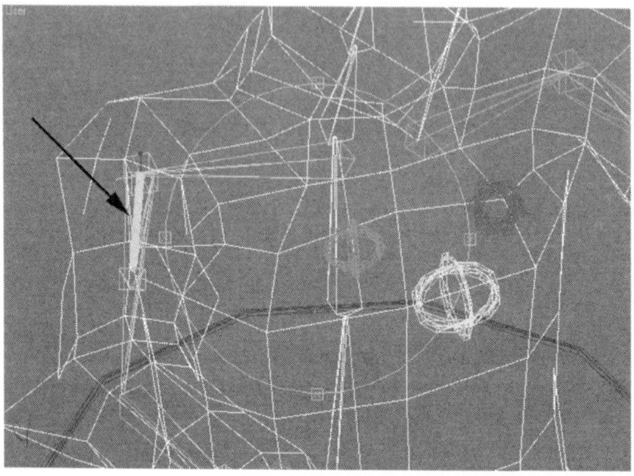

A yellow indicator bar is displayed in the viewport to confirm the bone is selected.

In the procedure for the elbow, you used Beginner Mode, which is found in the Options rollout. This is a "safe mode" that forces you to press the Create Morph and Edit buttons in the Local Properties rollout.

As you become more familiar with the workflow in Skin Morph, you can turn off Beginner Mode. With this option off, targets are created automatically as you edit the Points in the Skin Morph modifier.

If you want to edit an existing target, make sure the angle of the joint is where it was when you first created it, otherwise a new target is added. With Beginner Mode turned off, you can inadvertently add targets. This file has Beginner Mode turned off.

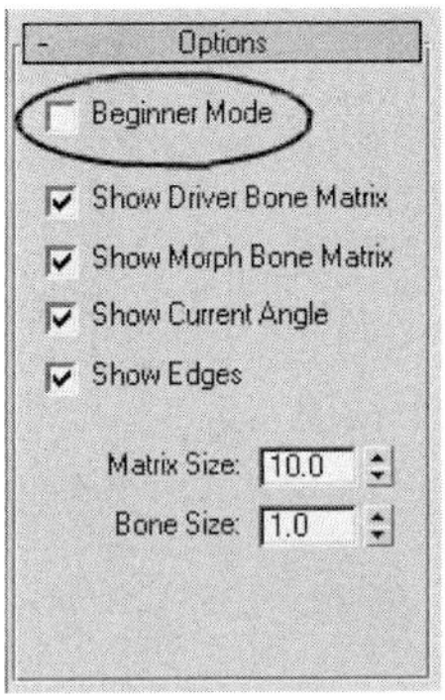

11. In the Modify Stack display, choose Points.

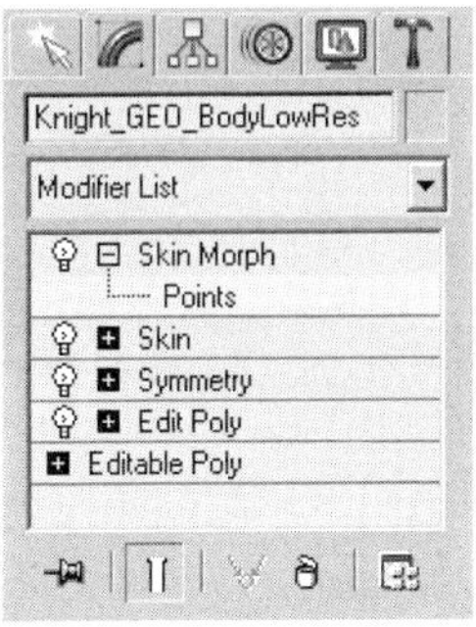

12. In the Perspective or User viewport, select the vertices around the shoulder area.
13. Move the vertices to correct the collapsing.

    Tip: It's easier if you edit the geometry with the viewport set to Smooth + Highlights.

14. You might also want to bulge the chest muscles and slide the skin over the back of the shoulder.

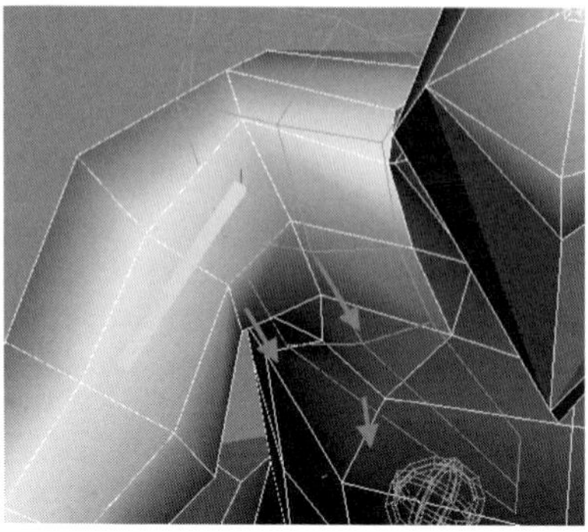

15. In the Parameters rollout, a new target is added to the joint in the bone list.

16. In the Local Parameters rollout, rename the new target RshoulderFront.

17. Model the shoulder area based on the following image.

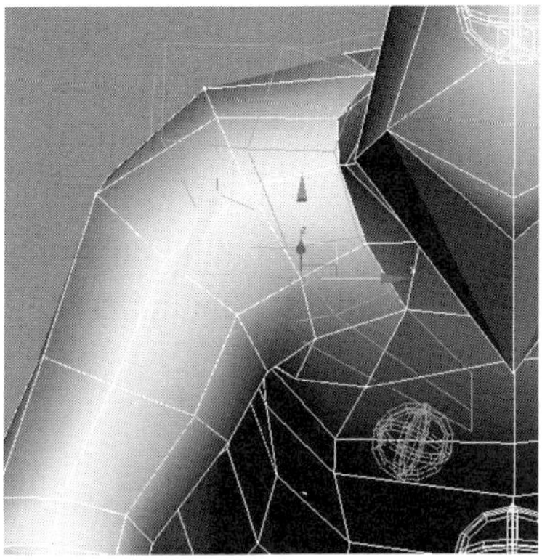

18. Move the time slider to frame **60**.

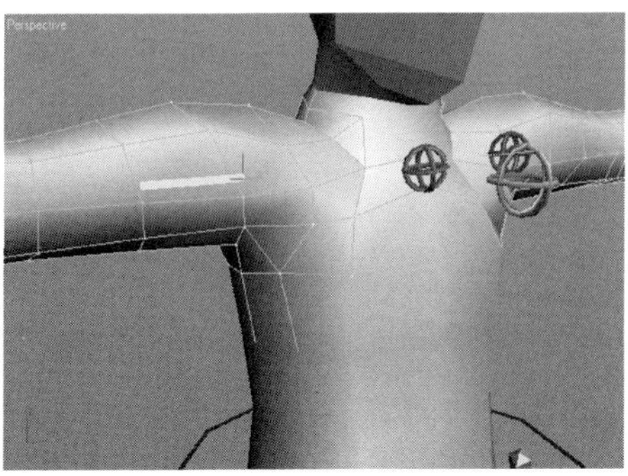

The knight is in its default pose. You notice the new target is affecting the shape of the shoulder area. To fix it, you need to set an option called Influece Angle.

19. In the Parameters rollout, the value for this target is **23.3** at frame **60**.

20. In the Local Parameters rollout, the Influence Angle is set to **90**.

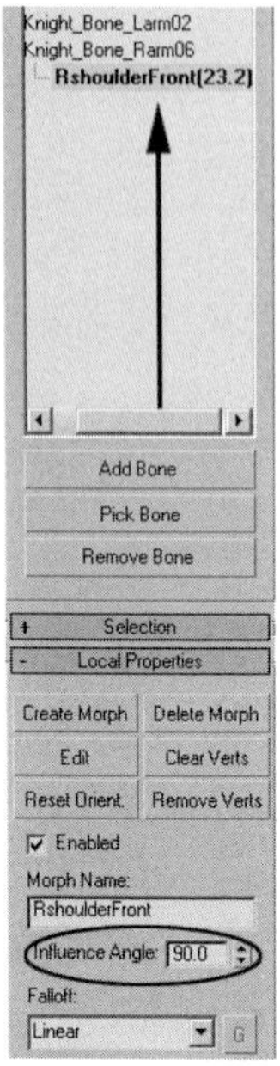

21. In the Local Parameters rollout > Influence Angle, drag the spinner down and watch both the mesh and the morph target value.

As you lower the Influence Angle, you see the mesh return to its shape.

22. Set the Influence Angle to **69**. The Target Value is set to **0.0**.

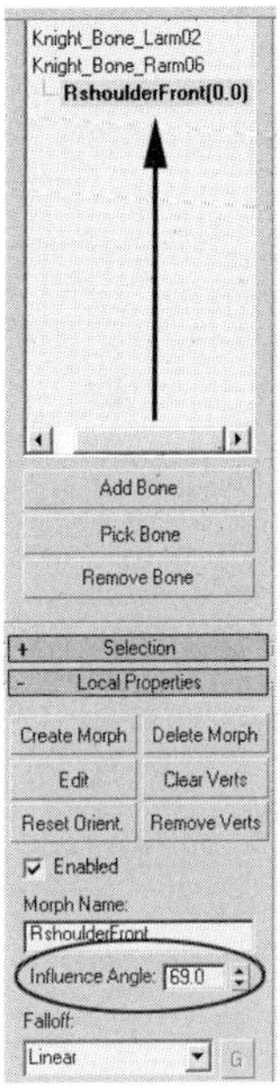

Tip: You mirror the morph targets after all the targets have been made because you mirror the Bone properties, not individual targets.

Using Snapshot with Skin Morph

Next, you manipulate the back side of the shoulder to complete the shoulder joint. Instead of applying the same technique you used in the previous procedure, you use Snapshot to create the morph targets.

One use of snapshot is to extract a single mesh object at any frame of its animation. In this case, you want to snapshot the current pose without the effect of Skin Morph. Skin Morph affects the elbows and you want to start with an unedited version of the mesh.

1. Continue from the previous exercise.
2. On the Modify panel > Parameters rollout, choose Knight_Bone_Rarm02.

3. In the Modify Stack display, choose the light bulb next to Skin Morph to turn it off.

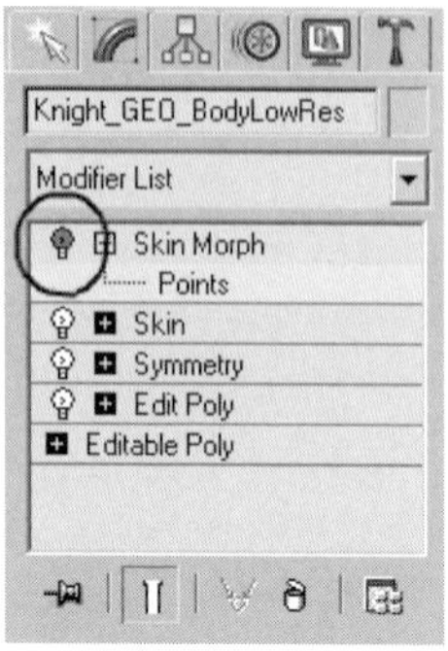

4. Move the time slider to frame **90**.
5. On the menu bar, choose Tools > Snapshot.
6. In the Snapshot dialog, make sure Single and Mesh are chosen, and then press OK.

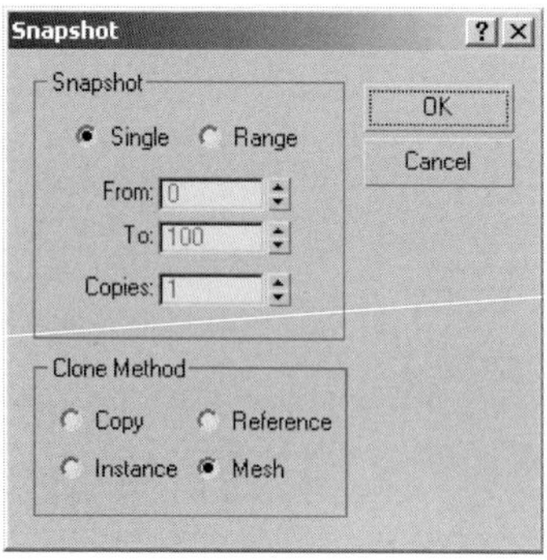

7. In the Modify Stack display, turn on Skin Morph.
8. Press **H** and choose Knight_GEO_BodyLowRes01.

9. In the Perspective viewport, move the new mesh in front of the original.

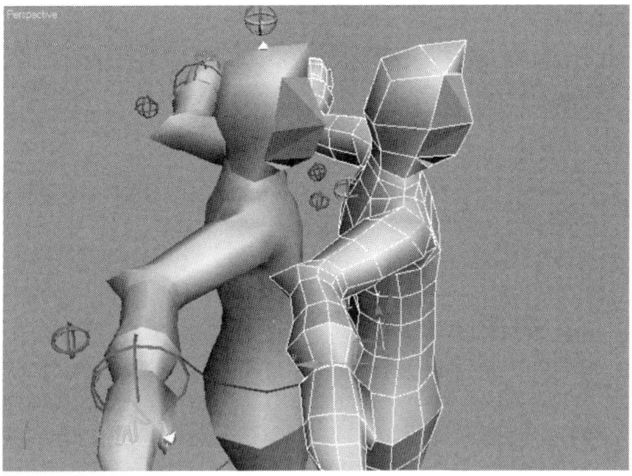

10. On the Modify panel > Name area, type **RshoulderBack**.
11. On the Modifier List drop-down, choose Edit Poly.
12. Use the options in Edit Poly to reshape the back of the shoulder area.

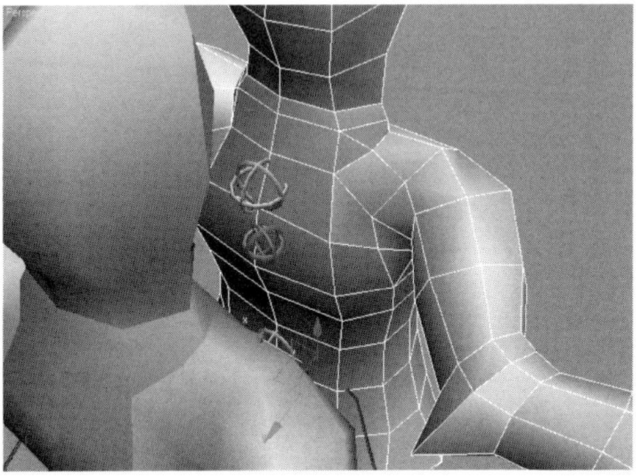

Before Edit Poly

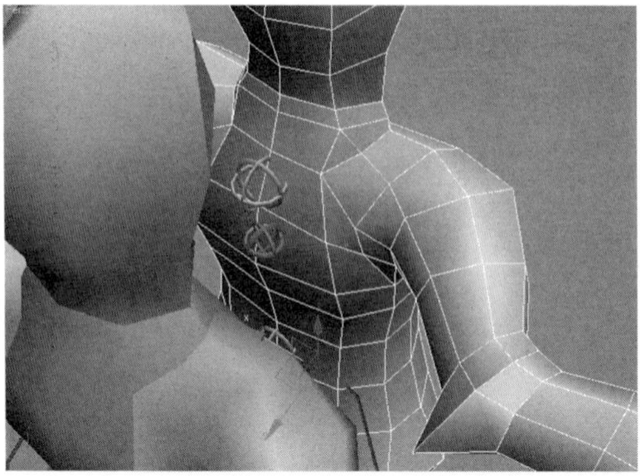

After Edit Poly

13. In the User viewport, choose Knight_GEO_BodyLowRes.
14. On the Modify panel > Modify Stack display, choose Skin Morph.
15. In the Parameters rollout, choose rshoulderFront under Knight_Bone06_Rarm06.
16. Make sure you are at frame **90**.
17. In the Local Properties rollout, choose Create Morph.

    This adds a new target.
18. Rename this target RshoulderBack.
19. In the External Mesh area, choose None, and then choose the target geometry from one of the viewports.
20. Scrub the time slider from frames **0 – 90** and notice the morph target amount.

    The value changes when the arms are still. The value should only change when the arm is animating.

    Next, you reset the values for the Influence Angle so that the object isn't deformed at the base pose.
21. Make sure you are at frame 90.
22. Set the Influence Angle to **45**.

    Note: Make sure to go to frame 0 before you add a bone in the Parameters rollout of Skin Morph.

23. Scrub the time slider from 0 to 60.

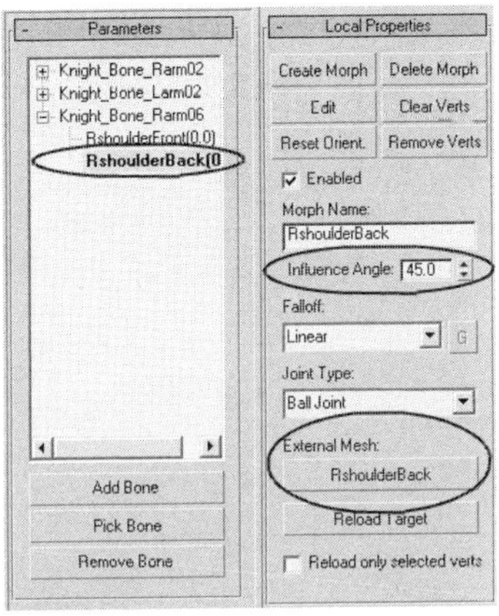

The starting value for the target is set to **0.0** from frames 0 to 60.

24. Scrub the time slider to frames 60 to 100.

    The target value changes accordingly.

25. In the Perspective viewport, choose the snapshot mesh, RshoulderBack.
26. Right-click and then choose Hide Selection.
27. Move the time slider to frame 100.
28. In the Local Properties rollout, choose Create Morph to add a third target for the down position.
29. Edit the location with one of the methods you learned.
30. Set the Influence Angle to **66**.

Mirroring the Left Shoulder

1. Continue from the previous exercise.
2. In the Parameters rollout, choose Add Bone.
3. In the Select Bones dialog, choose Knight_Bone_Larm06.
4. In the Parameters rollout, choose Knight_Bone_Rarm06.
5. In the Copy and Paste rollout, turn on Show Mirror Plane and Preview Bone. Choose Paste Mirror.

6. Change the names of the morph targets for the left arm.

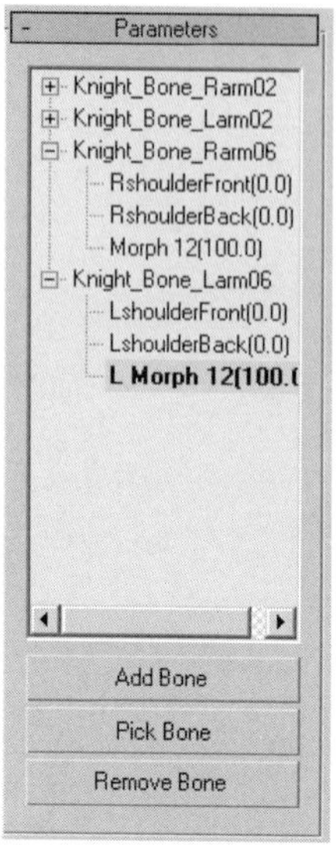

On your own, continue to set targets for the knees and hips. Experiment with the Falloff types to set different curves to affect how fast the targets are reached. Choosing Slow sets the target to slow into the target shape, while choosing Custom enables you to create a custom curve.

7. Save the file as **knightSkin05.max**.

What Is Skin Wrap?

Skin Wrap is a modifier usually applied below modifiers such as TurboSmooth and MeshSmooth. It has its own sub-object level called Control Vertices. The modifier allows one or more objects to deform another.

The object you apply to the Skin Wrap modifier is called the Base Object. The object you pick to deform the Base Object is called the Control Object. The Base object can be any deformable surface type.

Why Use Skin Wrap?

The advantage of using a Skin Wrap modifier instead of just Skinning the high-resolution mesh to the bones involves the issue of weighting. You typically use a low-resolution mesh as your control object. This object has the Skin modifier applied and since it is low-poly, you don't have to weight so many vertices. You apply the Skin Wrap modifier to the high-resolution mesh, and it becomes your base object. You add the control mesh to the Skin Wrap modifier and make minor adjustments to see the effects on the high-resolution mesh.

At any time, you can change the topology of the high-resolution mesh without affecting the weighting in the Skin modifier. The reason for this is because no Skin modifier is applied to the base object.

The high-resolution mesh can change the amount of vertices or shape, and it continues to follow and deform correctly with the low-resolution control mesh. This sort of flexibility is outstanding, especially if you have many characters that are all about the same proportions. You can set up cycles on one and then replace the high-resolution mesh with the one required for the animation.

Typical Skin Wrap Workflow

- Create a low-resolution model with any surface type.
- Make a copy and apply TurboSmooth or MeshSmooth to create a high-poly version.
- Rig the low-resolution version with bones, helpers, and so forth.
- Apply a Skin modifier to the low-poly object and assign all bones.
- Animate the helpers in the rig.
- Select the high-resolution object.
- Apply a Skin Wrap modifier. It is now your base object.
- Determine the Threshold amount.
- Decide a Deformation Engine: Vertex or Face.
- Choose Add and then select the low-resolution object. It is now your control object.
- Scrub the time slider to see how the control object affects your base object.
- Make Global and Local adjustments.

- Choose Convert to Skin.
- A Skin modifier is applied above the TurboSmooth or MeshSmooth modifiers. Skin Wrap is turned off automatically.
- Continue to fine-tune vertex weighting.

Skin Wrap UI

Skin Wrap has three rollouts for controlling all options.

- **Parameters** – Contains global and local parameters for controlling the deformation of the geometry.
- **Advanced Parameters** – Contains options for Mirroring using mirroring tools.
- **Display Parameters** – Controls the viewport display for visual reference.

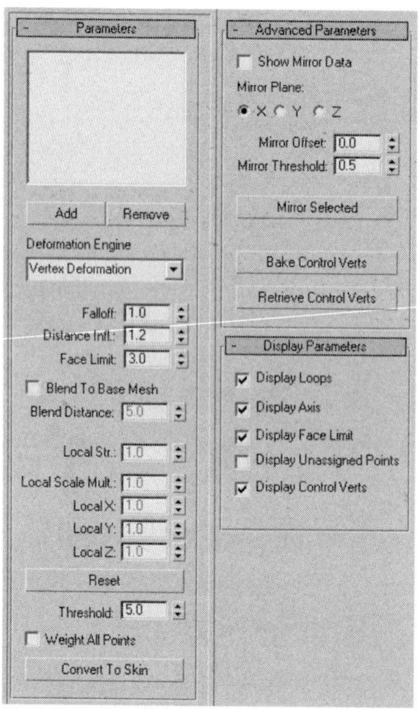

Assigning Skin Wrap

1. Open *knightSkin05.max*.
2.  On the main toolbar, choose Layer Manager.
3. In the Layer Manager dialog, unhide the Body & Sword layer.
4. Close the Layer dialog.

5. Scrub the time slider.

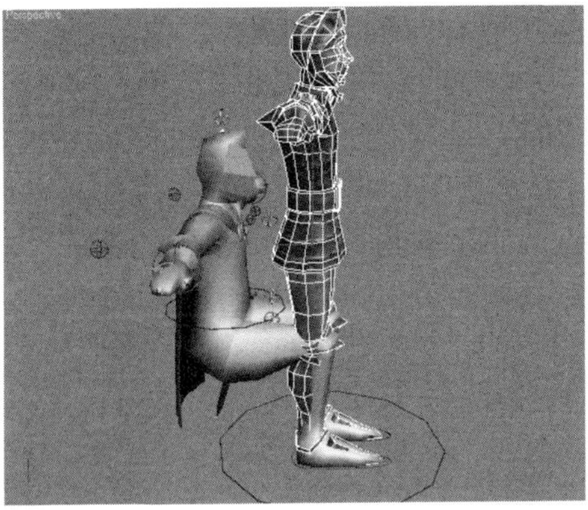

Notice the high-resolution mesh is not animated.

6. Go to frame **0**.
7. Press **H** and choose Knight_GEO_BodyHighRes.
8. On the Modify panel > Modify Stack display, choose the Edit Poly below TurboSmooth.

   You want TurboSmooth at the top of the stack so that Skin Wrap doesn't have to work on four times the amount of vertices.

9. On the Modifier List drop-down, choose Skin Wrap.

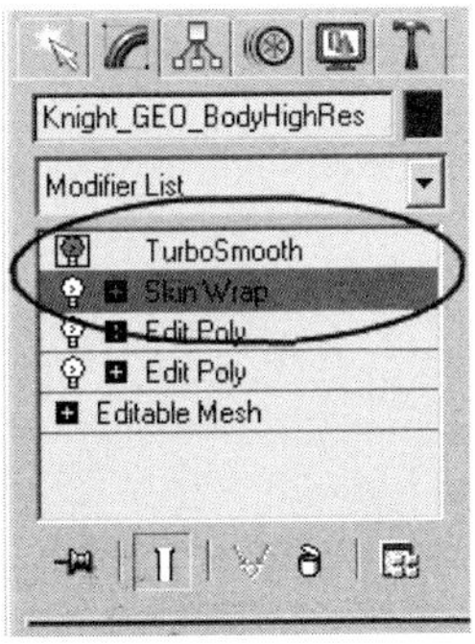

At this time, the most important option is the Threshold setting.

This option determines the distance in system units that the software uses to find the closest face to a control vertex. The greater the distance by which the control object's and base object's surfaces deviate, the higher the Threshold value needs to be and the slower it calculates. Default=**5.0**. The lowest amount is **0.001**.

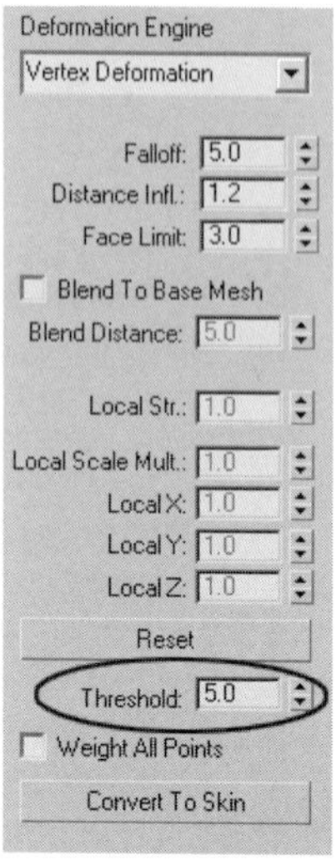

It's important to have the objects aligned or close to one another in 3D space. In this case, both knights are on top of one another.

First, you add a new controlling mesh.

Adding a Controlling Mesh

1. In the Parameters rollout, change the Threshold to **1.0**.
2. In the Parameters rollout, choose Add.
3. In the Perspective viewport, choose Knight_GEO_BodyLowRes.

   You can add as many controlling objects as you like. This is a good feature in case you have a low-resolution mesh in separate pieces.
4. Turn off Add.

5. Scrub the time slider.

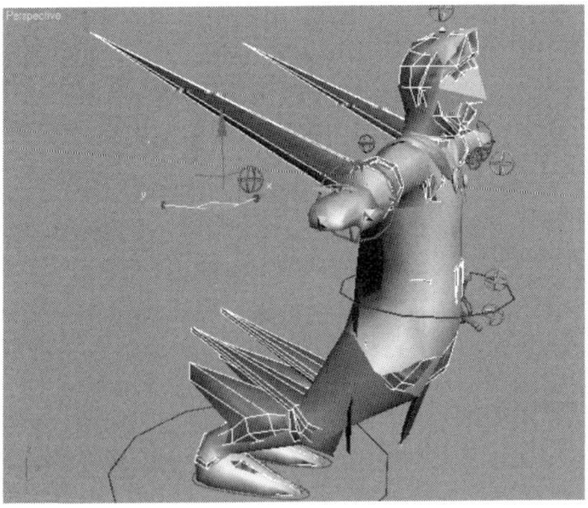

The high-resolution mesh follows the low-resolution mesh but there are many unassigned vertices.

6. Go to frame **0** to return the character to its base pose.
7. In the Display Parameters rollout, turn on Display Unassigned Points.

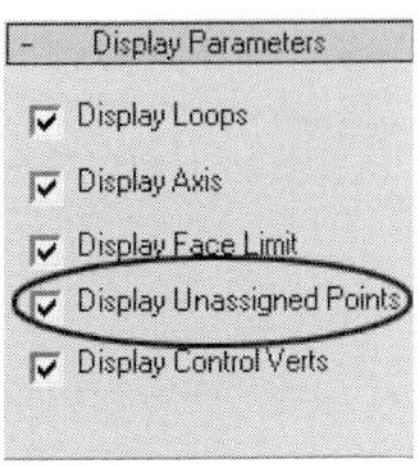

8. In the Modify Stack display, choose sub-object Control Vertices.
9. Change the Threshold to **5** and then press Reset.

10. Scrub the time slider.

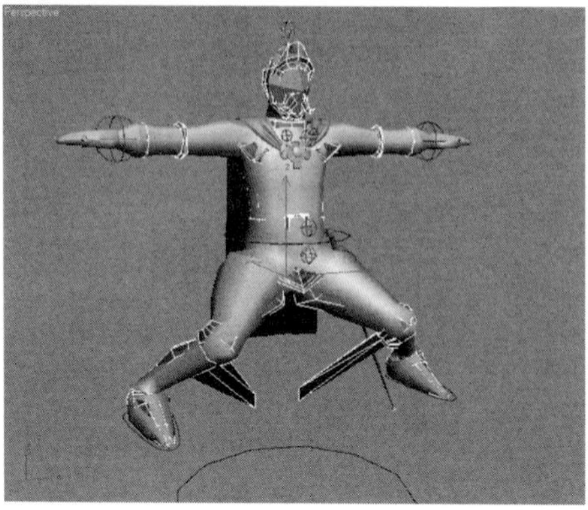

Now there are only a few unassigned vertices at the back of the calf.

11. Scrub the time slider.

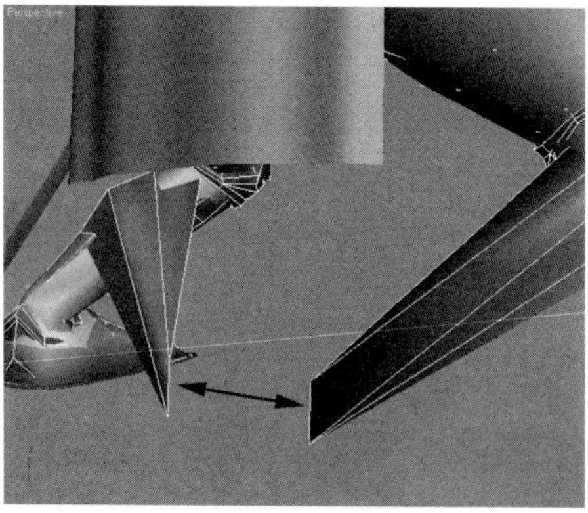

12. Two red boxes surround vertices on the mesh.

The red boxes indicate the vertices are not assigned.

13. Move the time slider to frame **0**.

14. In the Parameters rollout, turn on Weight All Points.

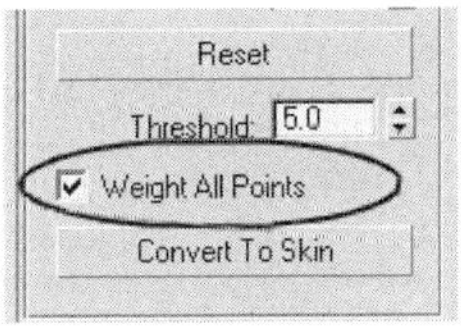

This forces all base-object points to have weights. Since you only have a couple of points that are not weighted, this method is acceptable. If several points are not weighted, then adjusting the Threshold is a better solution. If a large number of base-object points are unassigned, it can take a long time to calculate.

Note: This option needs to happen at the base pose so that Skin Wrap knows the starting point for the deformations.

15. Scrub the time slider.

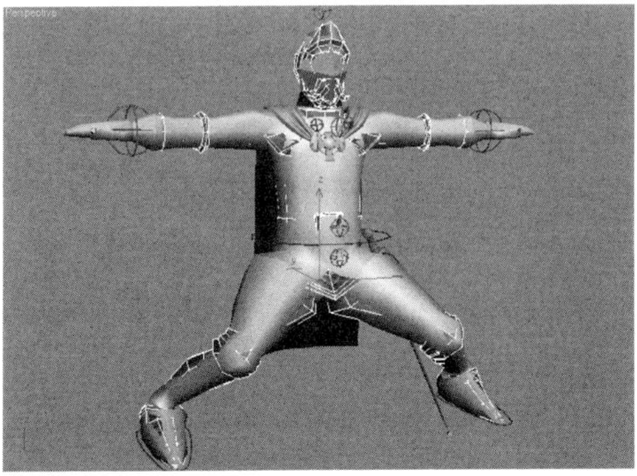

16. Save the file as **knightSkin06.max**.

Local Adjustment

Local adjustments are needed on the control vertices to get problem areas to work better. Hips, shoulders, and other joints might need some attention so that the high-resolution mesh deforms closer to the low-resolution mesh.

Skin Wrap has two Deformation Engines: Vertex and Face. The Vertex Deformation engine is a weighted engine. It uses vertex proximity to drive the deformation, meaning each vertex in the control object affects nearby points in the high-resolution (base) mesh. When Vertex is chosen, you have three controls: Falloff, Distance Influence, and Face Limit.

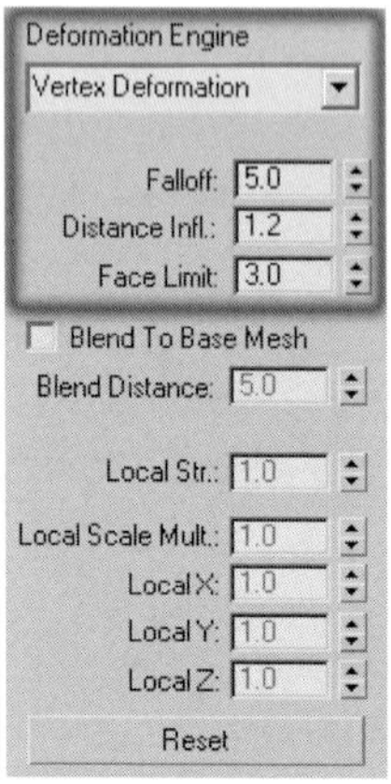

{The Vertex Engine surrounds each vertex with an envelope. You can access the sub-object level, select the control points, and manipulate the size of the envelope using the local controls.

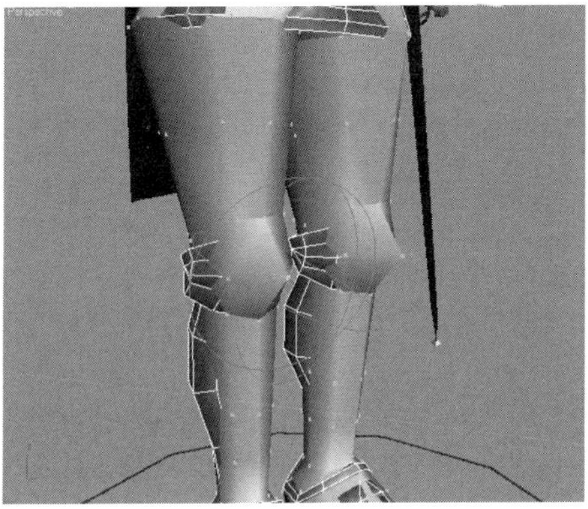

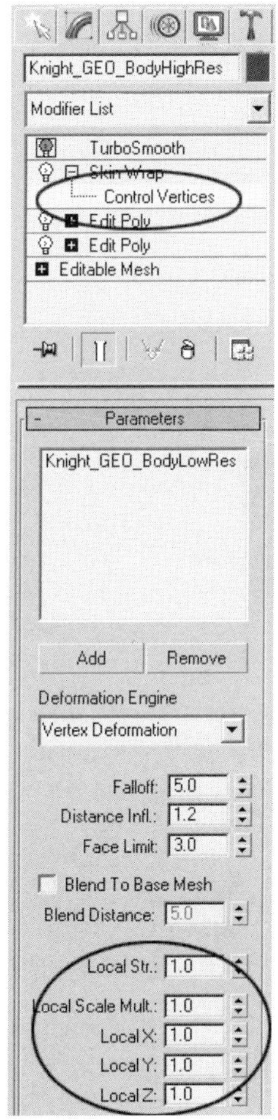

With the Face Deformation engine, each control vertex is tied to the closest face in the base object. Face deformation can use Falloff, or be a rigid deformation by setting Falloff to **0.001**, the lowest possible value. With Face chosen, you have the Falloff control only.

Note: No envelopes surround control points when you use the Face Deformation engine.

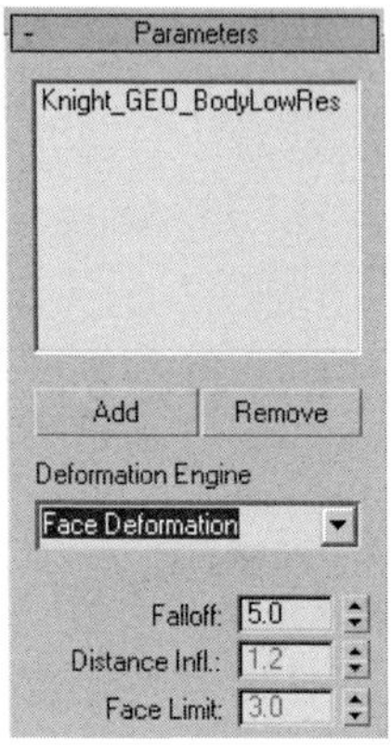

Using the Vertex Deformation Engine

In the next procedure, you continue to use the Vertex Deformation Engine. The default Falloff values for skin wrap might not produce perfect results so you select control points and edit the envelopes.

1. Continue from the previous exercise or open *knightSkin06.max*.
2. Make sure you are out of sub-object mode.
3. Choose the high-poly mesh.
4. On the menu bar, choose Views > Shade Selected.
5. Right-click the Perspective viewport label and then choose Wireframe and Edged Faces.

   All objects, except the high-poly knight, is in wireframe.
6. Use the time slider to go to frame **30**.

7. In the Perspective viewport, press **L** to go to the Left viewport.

   The hip area needs some work since it is deforming in a very soft curve compared to the control mesh.

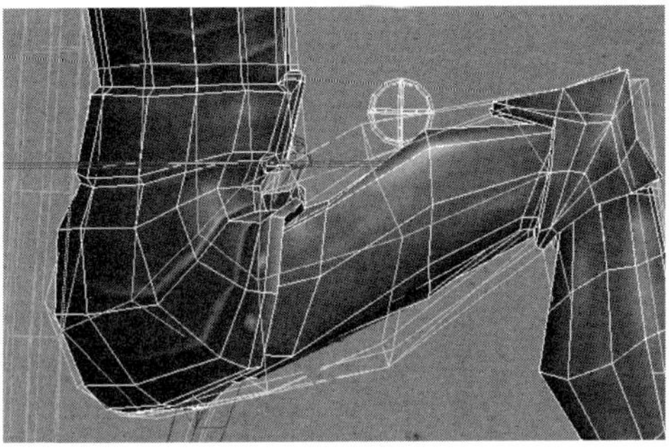

8. In the Parameters rollout, set the Falloff to **3.0** and Distance Infl. to **0.8**.

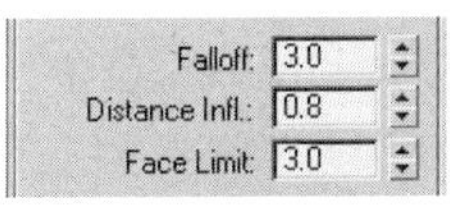

   These are global controls. Falloff determines the extent to which the control vertices affect nearby points in the base object. Distance Infl(uence) determines the distance of influence, in system units, for control vertices in the control object.

   Distance Influence is a multiplier. It looks at the length of each edge that touches each control vertex. For each vertex, it averages all lengths and then multiplies the average by the Distance Influence value. It lets vertices that touch only small faces to affect a small area, and vice versa. The higher the influence value, the smoother the deformation, but each vertex has less individual control For best results, keep this value between **1.0** and **2.0**.

9. By making these global changes, you see the hip area following the control mesh better.

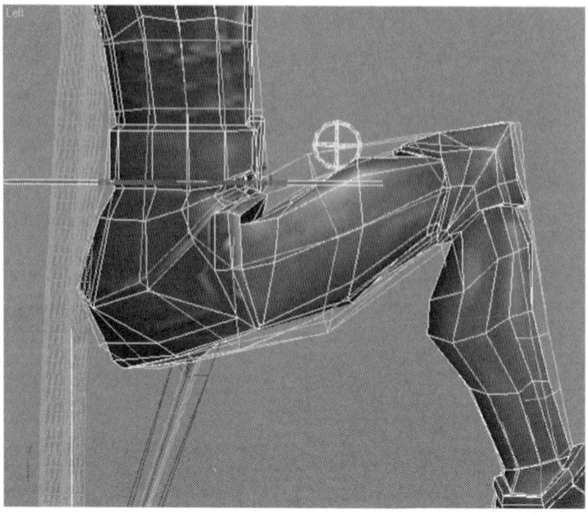

Global settings only get you so far. Manual adjustment is likely in most rigs, especially in areas such as the hips.

10. In the Modify Stack display > Skin Wrap, choose sub-object Control Vertices.

11. Make sure you are still at frame **30**.

12. In the Left viewport, select the control vertices in the front hip area.

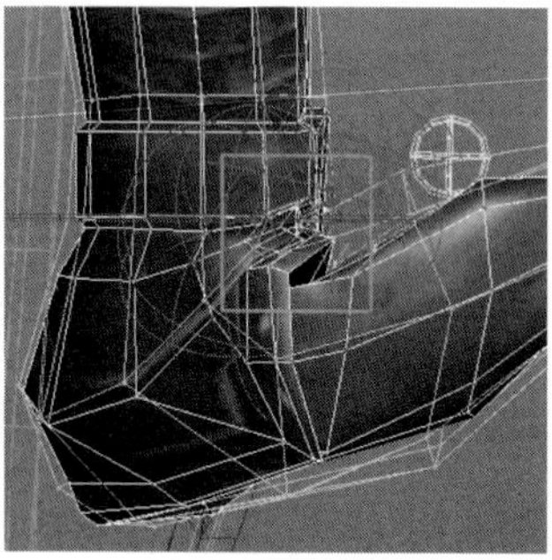

Large red orbits surround each control point; they are the envelopes. Notice the Local Controls are now available.

13. In the Parameters rollout, set the Local Scale Mult. to **0.7**.

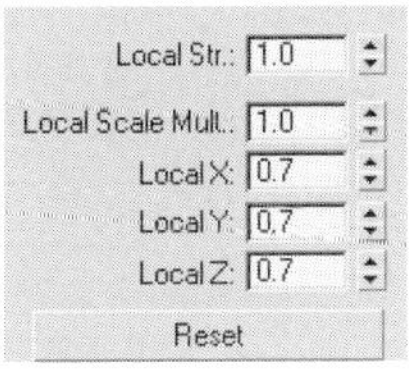

Scale each selected control-object vertex's volume of influence uniformly. Default=**1.0**.

Note: If you press Reset, only these vertices are affected and their settings return to **1.0**. If you don't Reset, and re-select the vertices, the Scale setting is remembered.

14. In the Left viewport, select the control vertices around the thigh area.
15. In the Parameters rollout, set the Local Str. (Strength) to **4.0**.

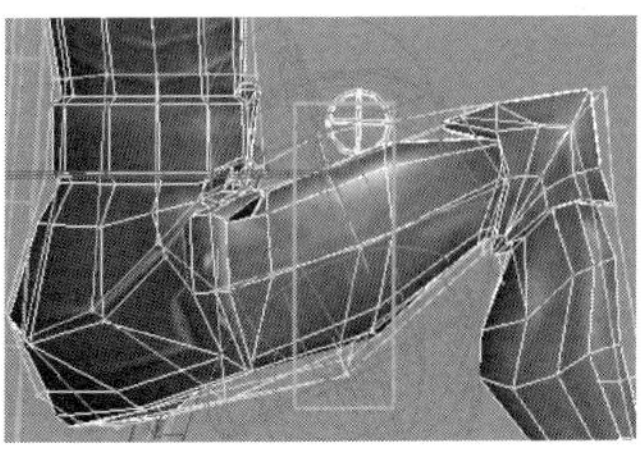

This setting determines the power and direction by which the control-object vertex affects points under its influence in the base object. A positive value pulls the points toward the vertex; a negative value pushes them away. Default=**1.0**.

16. Select the control vertices around the knee.
17. Set the Local Scale Mult. to **0.47**.

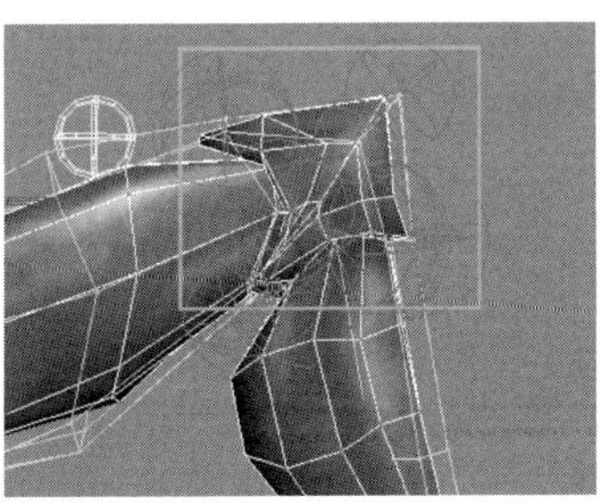

This isolates the effect the knee has on the rest of the leg.

18. Scrub the time slider.

    Use the options you learned to continue to edit various joints.

19. Save the file as **knightSkin07.max**.

Using Convert to Skin

The Skin Wrap modifier produces data unrecognizable to game engines. Notice the high-resolution knight is animated but does not have its own Skin modifier, which a game engine recognizes. Skin Wrap has a Convert to Skin option which intelligently "bakes" the animation into the geometry and applies a Skin modifier. You try this next.

1. Continue from the previous exercise, or open *knightSkin07.max*.
2. Select the Knight_GEO_BodyHighRes object.
3. Make sure you are at frame **0** and out of sub-object mode.
4. In the Parameters rollout, choose Convert to Skin.

   A Skin modifier is applied above the TurboSmooth modifier and Skin Wrap is turned off.

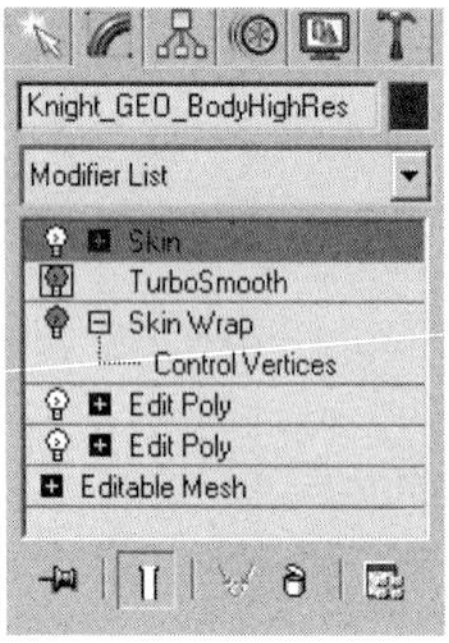

5. Scrub the time slider.

   The animation is replicated from the Skin Wrap modifier. The Skin modifier contains all bone assignments from the original Skin modifier, but with completely rebuilt weight settings based on the base-object weights created by the Skin Wrap modifier.

6. In the Skin modifier > Parameters rollout, choose Edit Envelopes.
7. Scrub the time slider to frame **50**.
8. In the Parameters rollout, turn on Vertices.

9. In the Bone List, choose Knight_Bone_Lleg00.

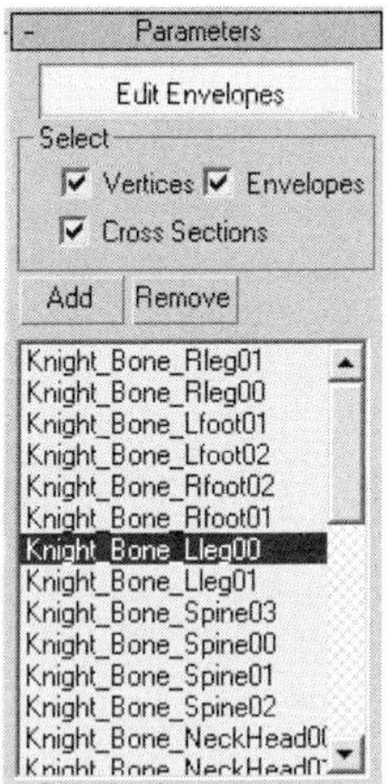

10. In the Perspective viewport, choose the following vertex.

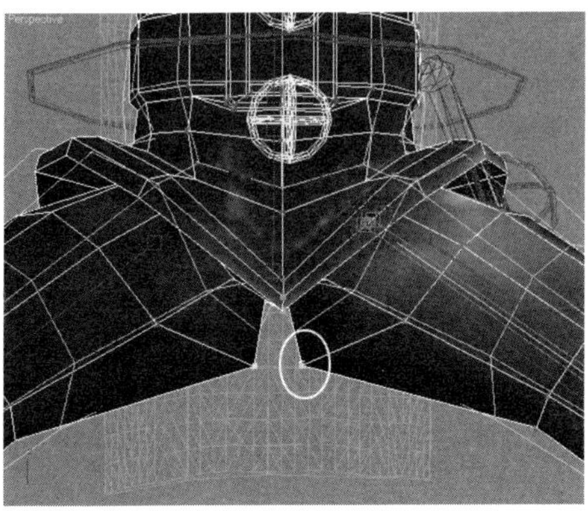

11. In the Weight Properties group, choose Weight Table.

12. In the Skin Weight Table dialog, choose Selected Vertices from the drop-down list near the bottom left of the dialog.

13. In the table, double-click under Knight_Bone_Lleg00 and then type **1.0**.

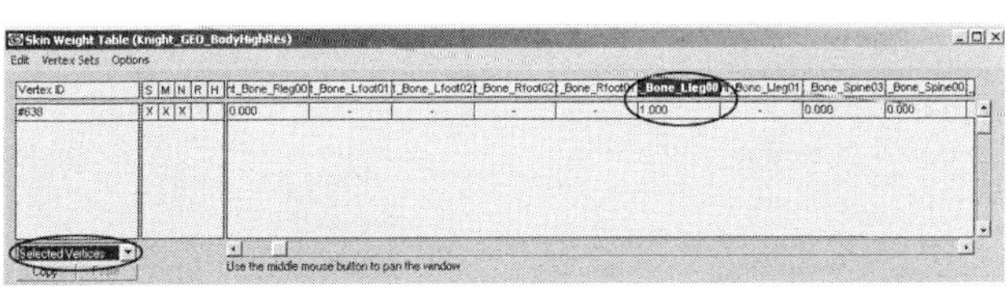

This sets Knight_Bone_Rleg00 and Knight_Bone_Spine03 to **0.0**.

14. Repeat the previous steps for the opposite bone envelope (Knight_Bone_Rleg00) and vertex.

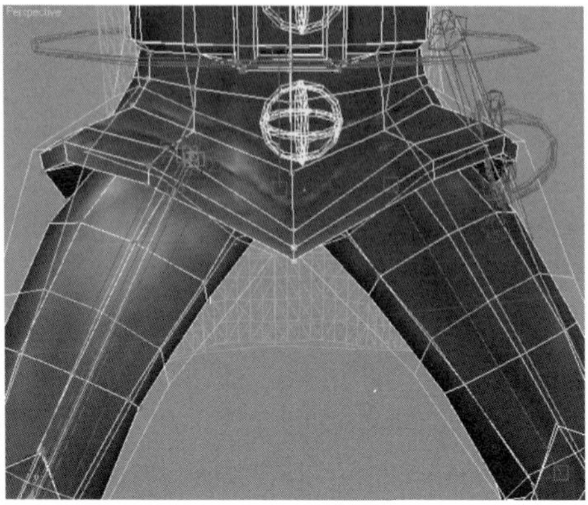

The data you currently have is now acceptable for a game engine.

15. Continue to edit any other weighted vertices you feel are necessary.

Skin Wrap and Reactor Cloth

In the next example, you use Reactor Cloth with Skin Wrap. You set up a simulation using cloth dynamics on the low-resolution cape and then use Skin Wrap for the high-resolution mesh. This saves computing power and time because the dynamics are done on the low-resolution objects.

1. Open *scene01.max*.

   The Reactor icons from the modeling chapter are in the scene. The rigid body collection is removed because you bind the cape to the deforming mesh for animation.

2. In the User viewport, choose Knight_GEO_LowResCape01.
3. On the Modify panel > Modifier List drop-down, choose reactor Cloth.

   First, you want to make sure that the cape stays with the character as it moves. Using Select and Link does not achieve this when the simulation is run.

4. On the Modify Stack display, open the reactor sub-object level, and choose Vertex.

5. In the User viewport, region-select the first two rows of vertices on the front part of the cape where it meets the pendant.

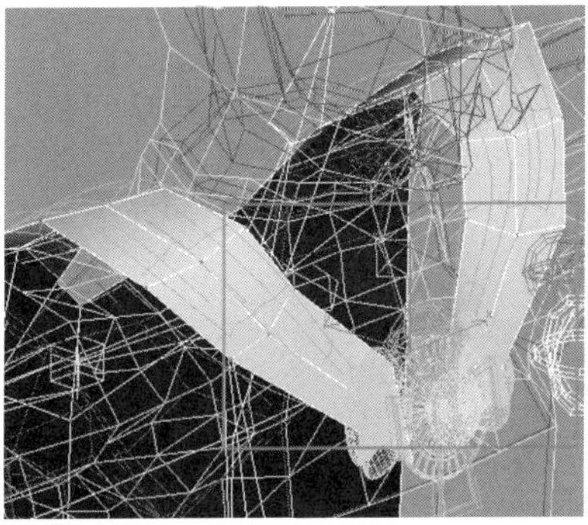

6. In the Constraints rollout, choose Attach To DefMesh.

   This adds a new constraint to the list.

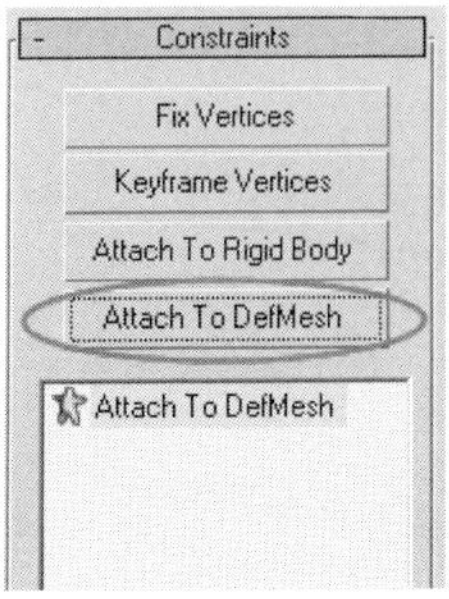

7. Choose Attach To DefMesh from the list.

   A new rollout is displayed above the Constraints rollout called Attach To DefMesh.

8. In the Attach to DefMesh rollout, choose None and then select Knight_GEO_BodyLowRes.

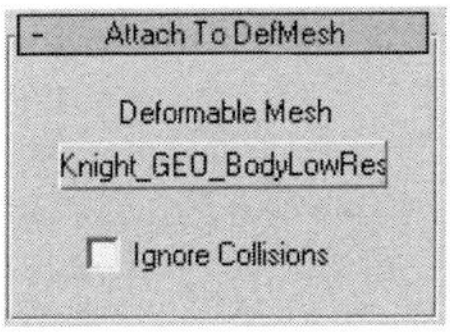

Next, you change settings in the Properties rollout to get the cloth to work correctly. This is a trial-and-error process. Once you do several simulations in a variety of circumstances, you become familiar with the changes required.

9. In the Properties rollout, make the following changes:
   Mass: **5.0**
   Friction: **1.0**
   Rel Density **10.0**
   Air Resistance: **20.0**
   Stiffness: **1.0**
   Dampening: **1.0**

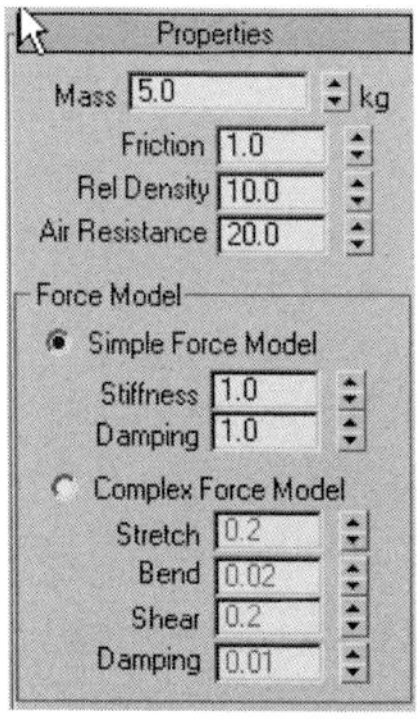

10. Near the bottom of the Properties rollout, turn on Avoid Self-Intersections.

    This stops the object from passing through itself.

11. Save your file.

Adjusting Reactor

Approximating real-world scale for your scene and objects is important while using dynamics simulation tools such as Reactor. Since this is not the case for this particular scene, you change many of the default settings of the Reactor engine to reflect the scene scale.

1. Continue from the previous procedure, or open *scene02.max*.

2. On the command panels, choose Utilities.

3. On the Utilities rollout, choose reactor.

   This opens the global tools for reactor dynamics.

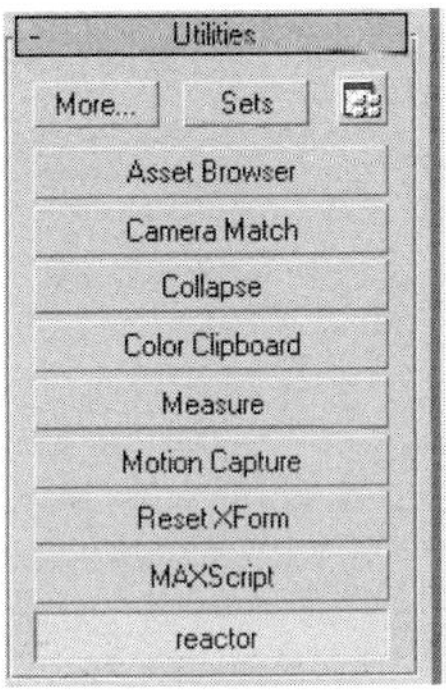

4. In the World rollout, make the following changes.
   Gravity Z: **–4850.0**
   World Scale 1m=: **251.0**
   Col Tolerance: **18**

   The gravity needs to be increased and so does the world scale to allow for the scene scale issue. The Col Tolerance controls how close the cloth mesh gets to the collision mesh before colliding with it. It took trial and error to arrive at this value.

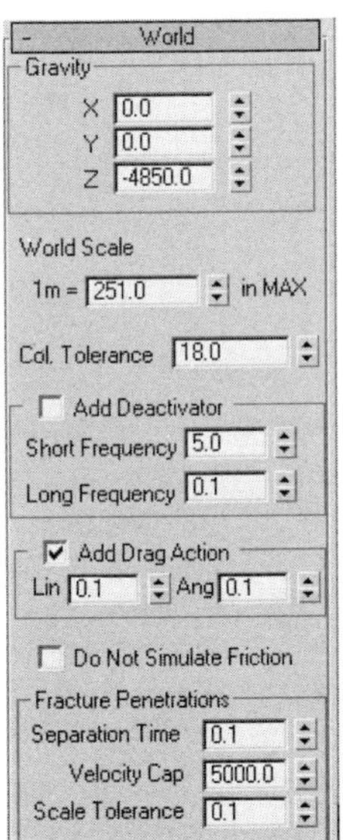

5. On the main menu bar, choose Tools > Layer Manager.

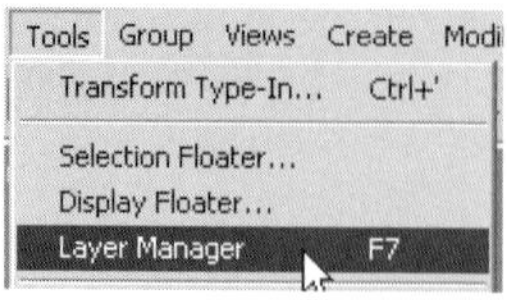

6. In the Layer Manager dialog, unhide the Horse Layer.

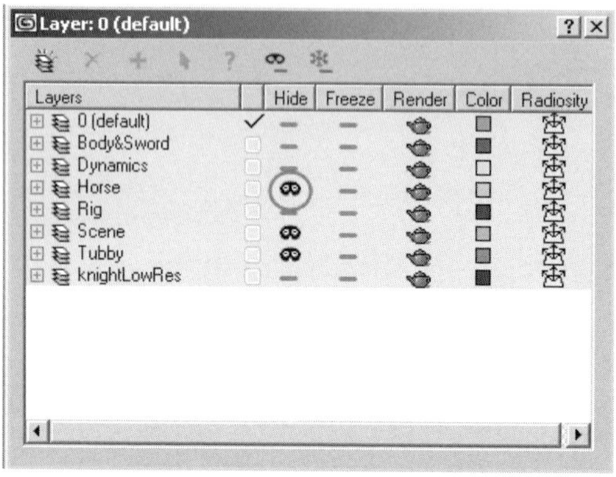

7. In the viewport navigation controls, choose Zoom Extents.
8. Close the Layer Manager dialog.
9. Scrub the time slider.
10. The knight jumps on the horse's back.
11.  On the reactor toolbar, choose Create Animation.

    This starts the dynamics simulation, which can take several minutes to calculate all the frames in the animation. The time varies depending on the speed of the computer you are using.

12. Scrub the time slider.

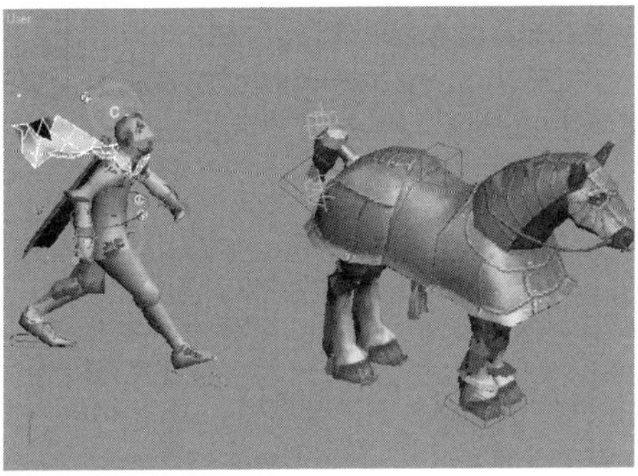

The low-resolution cape follows the low-resolution version of the knight like a cloth would. The high-resolution cape is not affected at all. You use Skin Wrap to bind the low-resolution cape.

13. Scrub the time slider to **0**.
14. In the User viewport, choose Knight_GEO_HighResCape01.
15. On the Modify panel > Modify Stack display, choose Editable Mesh.
16. On the Modifier List drop-down, choose Skin Wrap.

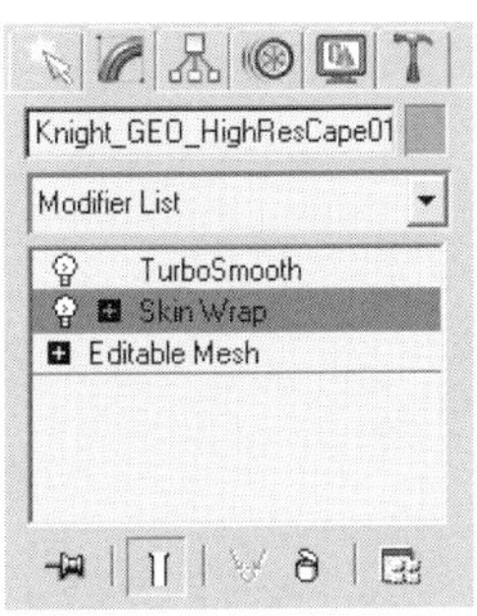

17. In the Parameters rollout, choose Add.
18. In the User viewport, choose Knight_GEO_LowResCape01.
19. Turn off Add.
20. Turn on Weight All Points.

21. Scrub the time slider.

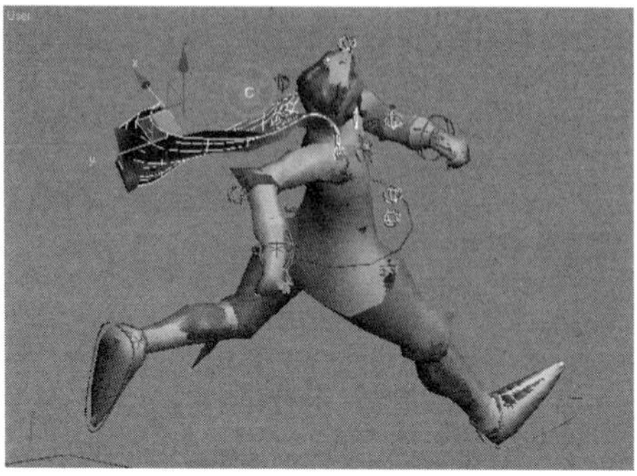

The high-resolution cape follows the low-resolution cape.

22. Save your file.

This approach is a fast and efficient way to work with dynamics since there are fewer vertices to calculate. You can update or replace the high-resolution cape at any time and not have to recalculate the cloth.

Parameter Collector

Next, you use another new feature in **3ds max 7** called Parameter Collector. This is a useful tool for both technical directors and animators.

This tool allows you to sort and present animatable parameters in an organized dialog that you design. You find Parameter Collector by choosing ALT+2 or choosing Animation > Parameter Collector from the menu bar.

Before Parameter Collector, you had to choose the bone, helper, or control object you wanted to animate and then go to the Modify panel and adjust its custom attributes over time to create keyframes. Now, you can create a floating dialog with all custom attributes in one location, which makes setting keyframes for one or multiple custom attributes fast and efficient.

Why Use Parameter Collector?

This tool was made with the technical director (TD) in mind. The TD can create custom, stand-alone dialogs so the animator can view all animatable parameters in one location.

One of Parameter Collector's most powerful features is the ability to change all parameters in a collection simultaneously, in absolute or relative mode. So if you're animating a character's hand, for example, you can use Parameter Collector to easily make all the fingers curl up together to form a fist.

Typical Parameter Collector Workflow

- Rig the character using control splines and/or helpers.
- Apply Custom Attributes to the control splines and/or helpers.
- Use Parameter Collector to organize all Custom Attributes in one dialog.
- Use Auto Key or Set Key to animate one or more of the custom attribute spinners in the Parameter Collector dialog.

Parameter Collector UI

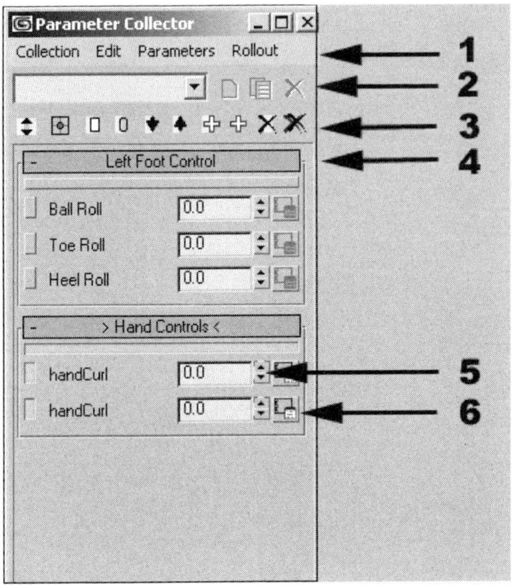

1. Menu Bar – Many of the tools found here are also available on the toolbar.

2. Collection Toolbar – You give collections a unique name by typing it into the drop-down list and then pressing ENTER. You organize your collections in this area rather than having all the custom attributes in one long rollout.

3. Parameter Collector Toolbar – You use the options found in this toolbar to organize parameters in the rollouts. You can add or delete parameters to rollouts, and decide if you edit one parameter or more at the same time.

4. Rollout – This rollout was created by choosing Rollout > New Rollout from the menu bar. Once a rollout is added, you can add parameters and rename the rollout. Below the rollout is a long horizontal bar that you can choose. Once chosen, it turns yellow and makes the controls in this rollout active.

5. Animated Spinner – You can animate parameters using Auto Key or Set Key.

6. Properties – Once a keyframe is created, you can access the Key Info dialog.

Using Parameter Collector

Next, you use the Parameter Collector to animate the hands to curl.

1. Open *KnightSkin08.max*.
2. In the Perspective viewport, choose Knight_GEO_BodyLowRes.
3. Right-click and then choose Hide Selection from the quad menu.
4. On the menu bar, choose Animation > Parameter Collector.
5. On the Parameter Collector menu bar, choose Rollout > New Rollout.

   A new rollout named Parameter 1 is created. You change the name next.
6. On the menu bar, choose Rollout > Rename Rollout.
7. In the Rename Rollout dialog, type **Hand Curls**.

8. On the Parameter Collector toolbar, choose Add to Selected Rollout.

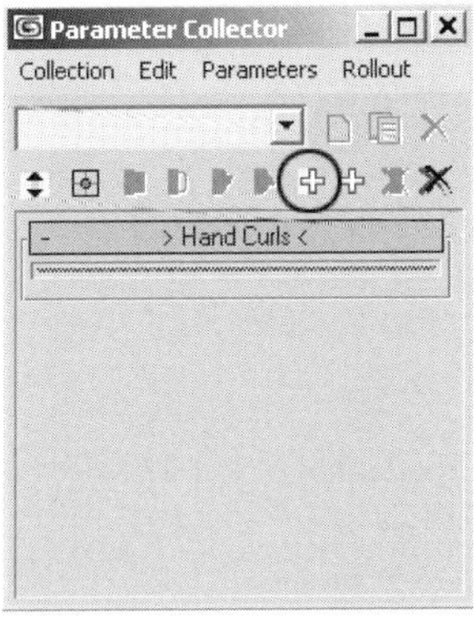

The Track View Pick dialog is displayed. It is going to be difficult to find the objects you want. Instead of hunting through the dialog, go into Isolate mode and then re-open the dialog.

9. Close the Track View Pick dialog.
10. In the Perspective viewport, choose Knight_CNT_Rhand and Knight_CNT_Lhand.

    These are the two control splines that contain the control the hand's custom attributes.

11. Press ALT+Q to enter Isolation Mode.
12. In the Parameter Collector toolbar, choose Add to Selected Rollout.

13. In the Track View Pick dialog, open Objects.

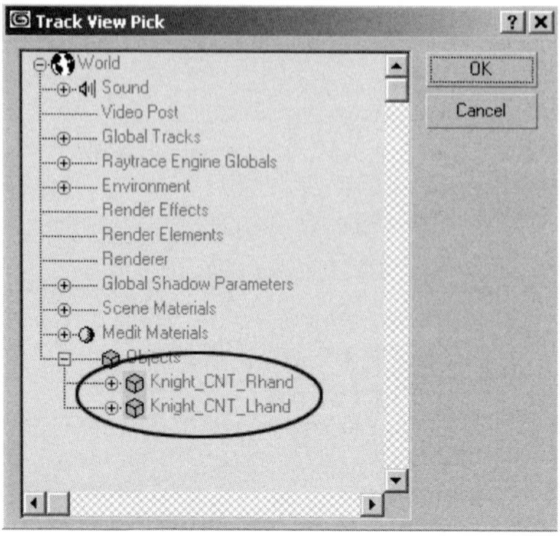

Only the Hand Controls are displayed in the Track View Pick dialog.

14. Open their settings and choose their Custom Attributes.

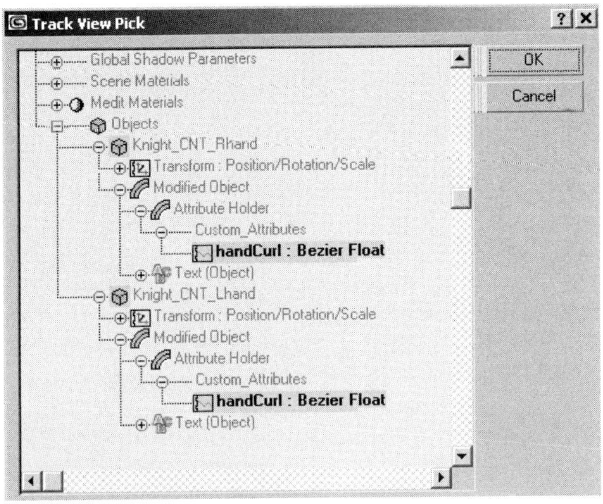

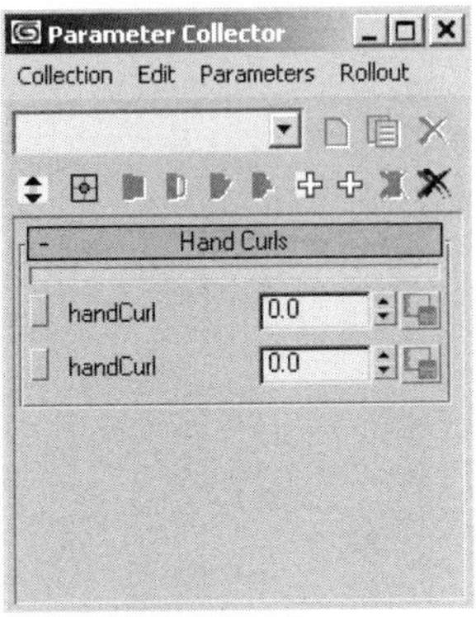

Both Hand Curls are displayed in the Hand Curls rollout.

15. Exit Isolation Mode.

Editing the Controls

Next, you learn how to edit the controls and set keyframes.

1. Continue from the previous exercise.
2. Use the time slider to go to frame **80**.

3. In the first Hand Curl setting, type **45**.

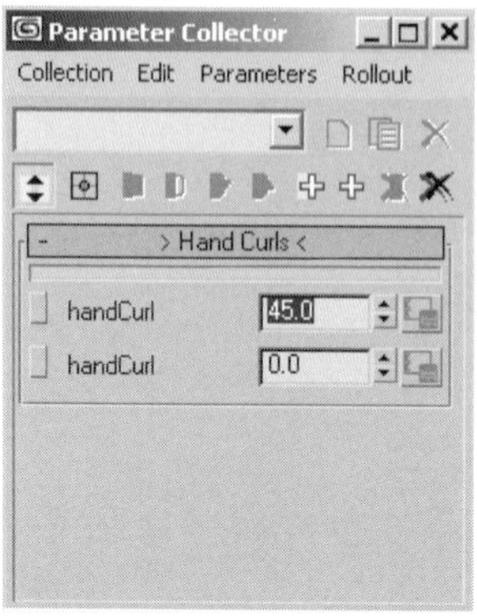

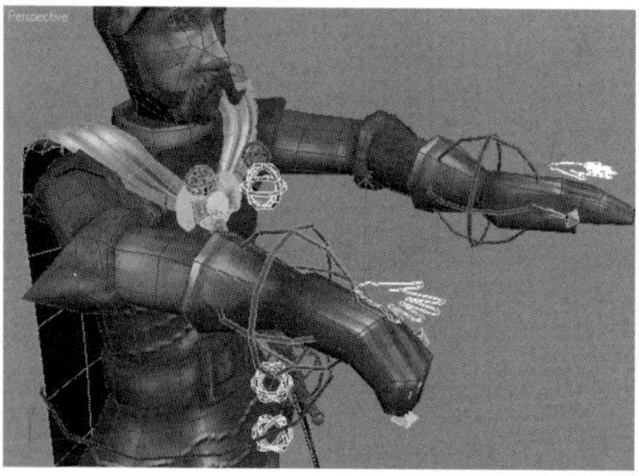

The hand curls. Next, you want to adjust one control but affect both hand controls.

4. Set the Hand Control to **0**.
5. In the Parameter Collector toolbar, choose Multiple Edits.
6. In the Parameter Collector dialog, choose the Select Parameter button to the left of the Control name.

7. Set one of the controls to **45**.

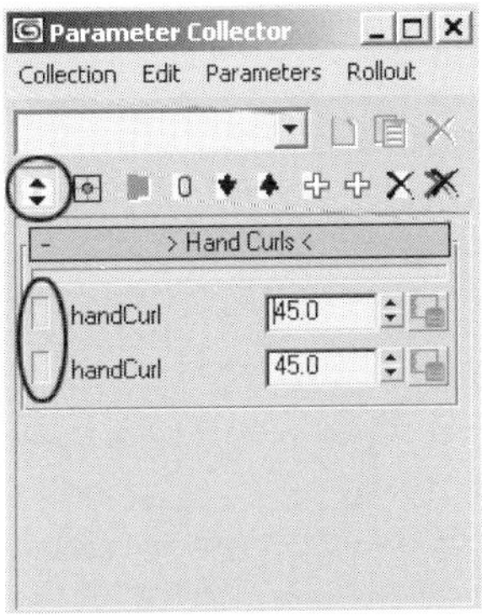

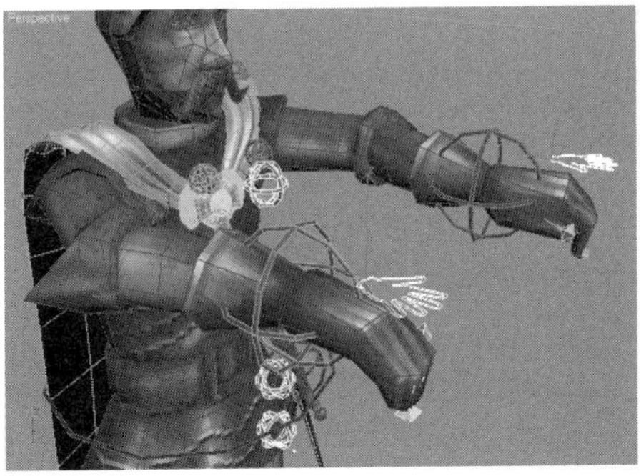

8. Both controls are affected and both hands curl in the viewport.
9. Right-click one of the spinners to set it to **0**.
10. Turn on Auto Key.

    Note: You can use Set Key as long as you set the Filters in the Animation Controls.

11. Set one of the controls to **45**.
12. A keyframe is created at frame **80** and the start keyframe is at frame **0**.
13. In the Parameter Collector dialog, the spinners are highlighted in red, just like any other animated parameter.

14. In the Parameter Collector dialog, choose the Properties button next to the top spinner.

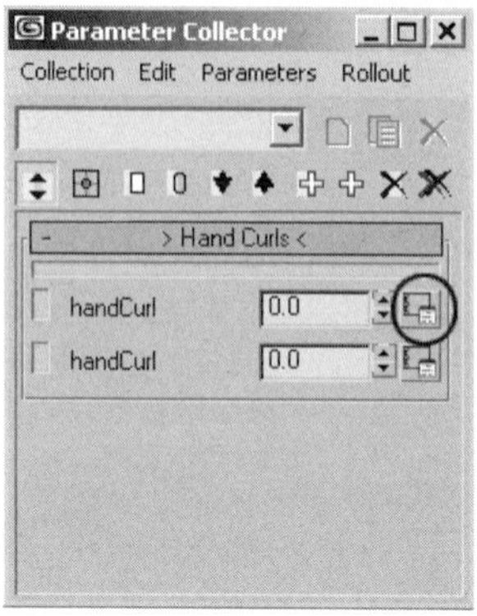

The Key Info dialog is displayed.

15. In the Key Info dialog, go to keyframe **1**.
16. Set the Time to **75**.

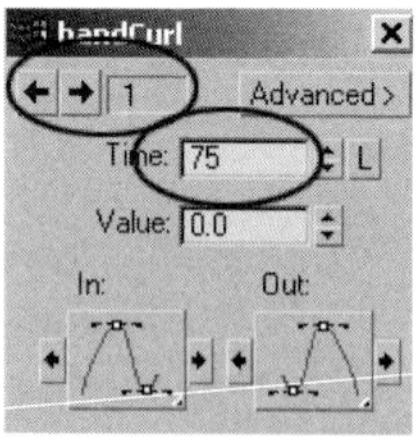

17. This does not move the key for both hands, so repeat the steps for the second hand curl.
18. Go to frame **85** and set the curl to **0**.
19. The hands begin to curl at frame **75** and returns to its starting position at frame **85**.
20. Turn off Auto Key.

Organizing the Collections

1. Continue from the previous exercise.
2. In the Parameter Collector dialog Collection toolbar, type **Arm Controls** in the drop-down list and then press ENTER.

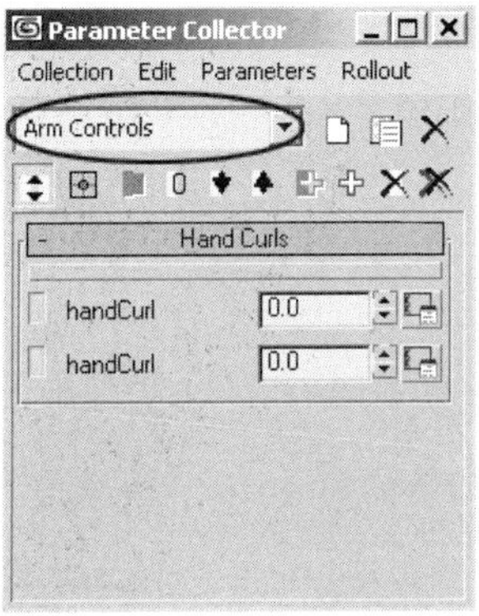

3. In the Collector toolbar, choose New Collection.
4. In the drop-down list, type **Foot Controls** and then press ENTER.
5. On the menu bar, choose Rollout > New Rollout.
6. On the menu bar, choose Rollout > Rename Rollout.
7. In the Rename Rollout, dialog, type **Leg Controls**.
8. In the Perspective viewport, choose both foot controls.
9. Press ALT+Q to enter Isolation Mode.
10. In the Parameter Collector toolbar, choose Add to Selected Rollout.

11. Add the controls to the rollout, the same way you added the hand controls.

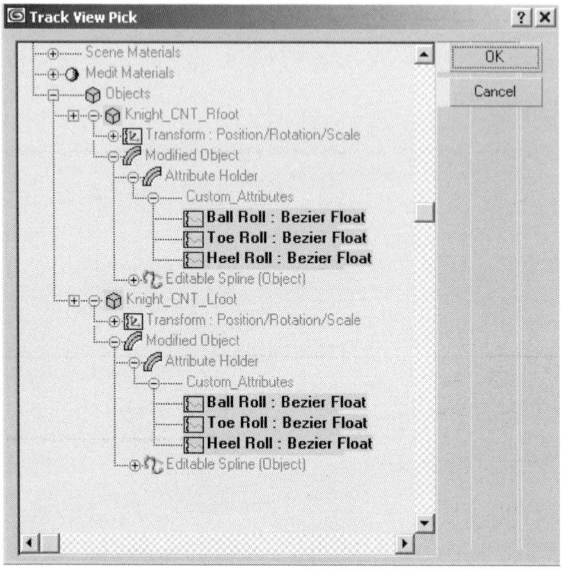

12. In the Parameter Collector dialog, all foot controls for both feet are in the dialog.

13. Exit Isolation Mode.

14. In the Parameter Collector dialog > drop-down list, you now have two collections.

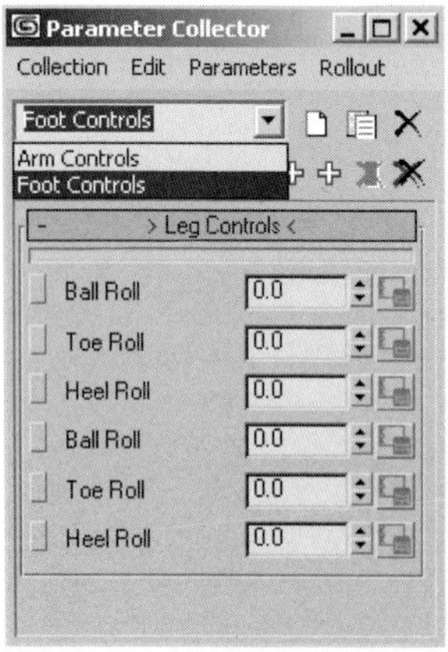

15. From the drop-down list, choose Arm Controls.

    This is how you organize your controls. You can continue to add arm controls to the Arm Controls collections and foot controls to the Foot Controls collection.

Conclusion

In this chapter, you used three new features in **3ds max 7**: Skin Morph, Skin Wrap, and Parameter Collector. These features extend the product's flexibility in character setup and animation.

5 Scene Assembly, Lighting, and Rendering

Objectives

After completing this chapter, you should be able to:

- Organize and manage a complex scene via the Layer Manager.
- Use mental ray lights and renderer.
- Use Render to Texture and mental ray to create shortcuts for render efficiency.
- Use the new Camera Map feature for detailing your scene via a matte painting.
- Create a high-resolution poster to promote your new short film.

Introduction

In this chapter, you look at the importance of scene assembly. You take everything you've been working on and assemble it to prepare for final rendering and compositing.

You start by merging various elements into the final scene and then making sure the file is organized and managed correctly. Next, you set up the lighting, and in the process, create some rendering shortcuts through the use of Render To Texture. Finally, before moving onto the actual final render and compositing in Chapter 6, you render a high-resolution still for a promotional poster.

Scene Assembly

Well before you begin, you need to collect all your 3D assets. These assets include the animated knight, horse, and the set.

Typically in a production, some elements are animated or modeled independently of the final version of other elements. The reason for this is efficiency. Rather than waiting for each successive piece of the scene to finish at the final state, working this way allows multiple people to work with the elements simultaneously. Low-res proxies, or representations, of the final objects are used as stand-ins for the animators so they know where there characters are vis-à-vis each other and the environment. Once all the elements are finished and saved as independent files, it is the responsibility of the Scene Assembler, or quite frequently the Lighting/ Rendering TD, to bring everything together.

In your case, these elements were brought together into a scene in the last chapter. However, other than the knight and the merge animation tools, the process was not described nor was the final scene organized. To understand scene assembly and organization, you are going to back things up a bit.

1. Open *Knight_Animation.max*.
2. Scrub the time slider.
3. The final animation for the knight is displayed.
4. On the main toolbar, choose Layer Manger.

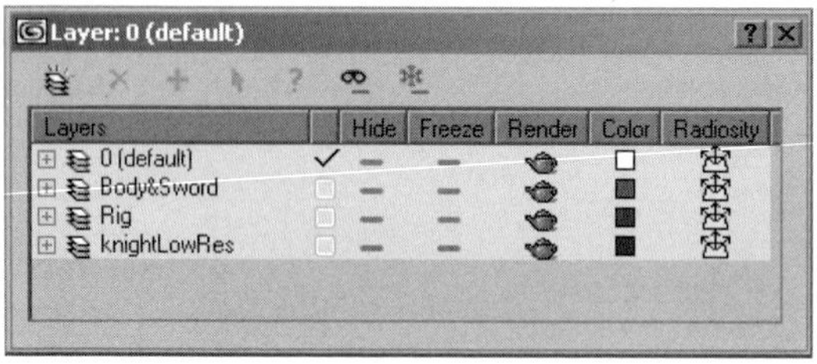

The Layers are set up properly and everything is easy to navigate. There are separate layers for the renderable geometry, the animation rig, and the low-res control mesh. This scene is almost ready for scene assembly, but first you adjust a few elements.

5. In the Layer Manager, choose the knightLowRes layer.
6. On the Layer Manager toolbar, choose Select Highlighted Objects and Layers.

   This selects everything on the selected layer.

7. In the Layer Manager dialog, choose the layer Rig.
8. On the Layer Manager toolbar, choose Add Selected Objects to Highlighted Layer.

9. In the Layer Manager dialog, choose the knightLowRes layer.
10. On the Layer toolbar, choose Delete Highlighted Empty Layer.

    You transfered the objects in the knightLowRes layer to the Rig layer. The reason for this is that while it was convenient for them to remain on separate layers when working with the knight, they do not need separate layers now. You don't want to have so many layers that management becomes tedious.

    Next, since there is more than one character in the scene, and you have more than one rig layer, you need to rename this rig so you know it belongs to the knight.
11. In the Layer Manager dialog, choose the Body&Sword layer.
12. Right-click the name and then choose Rename.
13. Rename the layer Knight_Render.

    Tip: Notice the use of underscores instead of spaces in the names to separate words. This is another good organizational habit to get into when naming anything within a file. The reason for this is the problem spaces in names cause in other areas of **3ds max**, such as scripting.
14. In the Layer Manager dialog, choose the Rig layer.
15. Right-click and then choose Rename from the right-click menu.
16. Rename the layer Knight_Rig.
17. In the Layer Manager dialog, choose the icon under the Hide column to hide this layer.

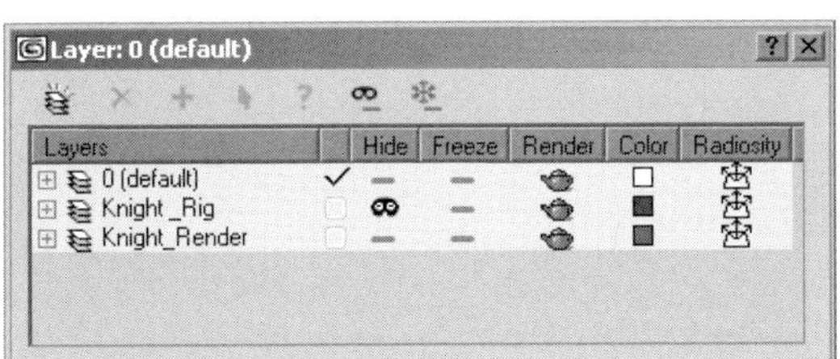

18. Close the Layer dialog.
19. Save the file as **MedievalSceneAssembly_01.max**.

Replacing the Pendant

In Chapter 2, you created a low-resolution version of the pendant that, when rendered, looked almost identical to the high-res version. You merge the low-res file into the scene next.

1. Continue from the previous exercise or open *MedievalSceneAssembly_01.max*
2. On the menu bar, choose File > Merge.
3. In the Merge File dialog, choose *pendant_Final.max*.
4. In the Merge dialog, choose All and then click OK.

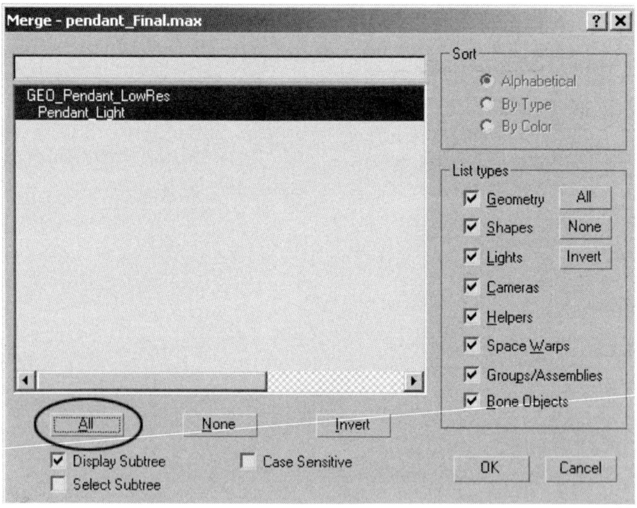

The textured low-res version of the pendant is displayed. Next, you delete the old one anddd this new one to your organized layers.

Tip: If everything in the Shaded viewports is black, press CTRL+L to display the default lighting.

5. Right-click to activate the Left viewport, and press ALT+W to maximize the viewport.
6. Zoom into the pendant.
7. Press **H** and make sure GEO_Pendant_LowRes and Pendant_Light are selected.
8. On the main toolbar, choose Select and Move, and Local from the Reference Co-ordinate drop-down list.

9. In the Left viewport, move them out slightly from the chest of the knight so that they match the position of the high-res pendant.

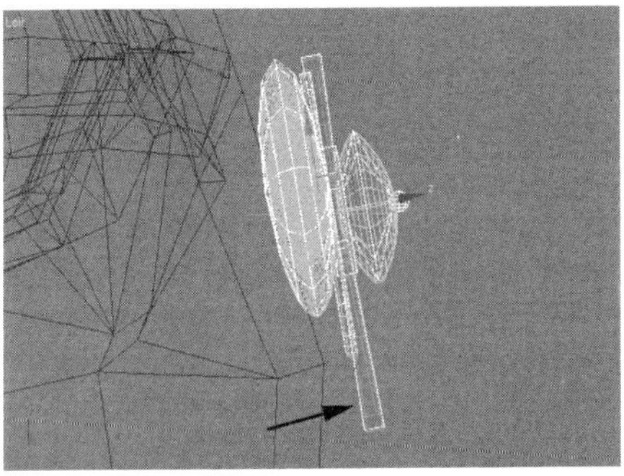

10. Press **H** and then choose Knight_GEO_pendantBack, Knight_GEO_pendantCenter, Knight_GEO_pendantKnots, Knight_GEO_pendantTop, Knight_GEO_pendantTop01, Knight_GEO_pendantTop02, and Knight_GEO_pendantTop03. Click Select.

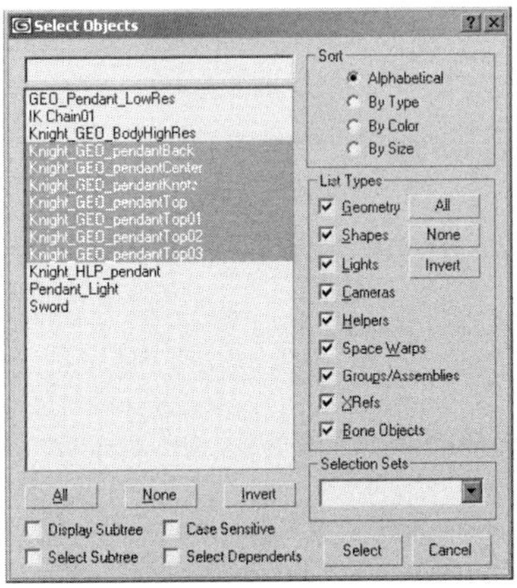

11. Press DELETE on the keyboard.

12. Press H and then choose GEO_Pendant_LowRes and Pendant_Light.

13. On the main toolbar, choose Select and Link.

14. In the Left viewport, click and drag from the selected object to Knight_HLP_pendant.

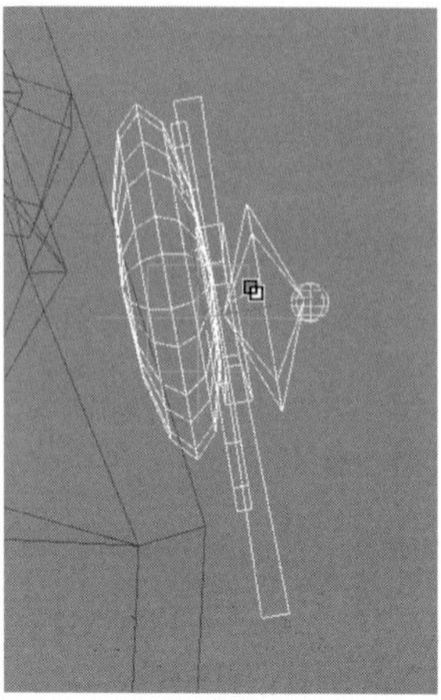

15. On the main toolbar, choose Select and Move.
16. On the main toolbar, choose Layer Manager.
17. In the Layer dialog, choose the Knight_Render layer.
18. On the Layer toolbar, choose Add Selected Objects to Highlighted Layer.
19. In the Layer dialog, choose the Pendant LowRES layer.
20. On the Layer toolbar, press DELETE.
21. Close the Layer dialog.
22. Save your scene as *MedievalSceneAssembly_02.max*.

Getting the Horse

Next, you merge the horse into the scene.

1. Continue from the previous exercise or open *MedievalSceneAssembly_02.max.*
2. On the menu bar, choose File > Merge.
3. In the Merge File dialog, choose *Horse_Animation.max*.
4. In the Merge dialog, choose All and then press OK.
5. Adjust the Perspective viewport to see both the knight and the horse.

6. Scrub the time slider.

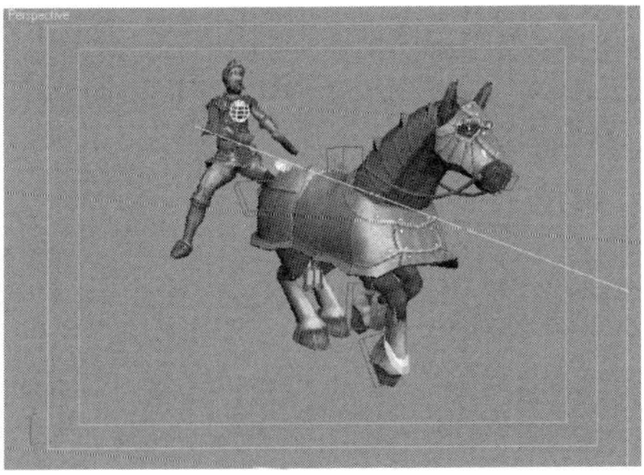

The Knight jumps up onto the horse's back, but when the horse rears and runs away the knight doesn't go with him. You fix this next.

7. Scrub the time slider to frame 0.
8. On the main toolbar, choose Layer Manager.
9. In the Layer dialog, unhide the Knight_Rig layer.

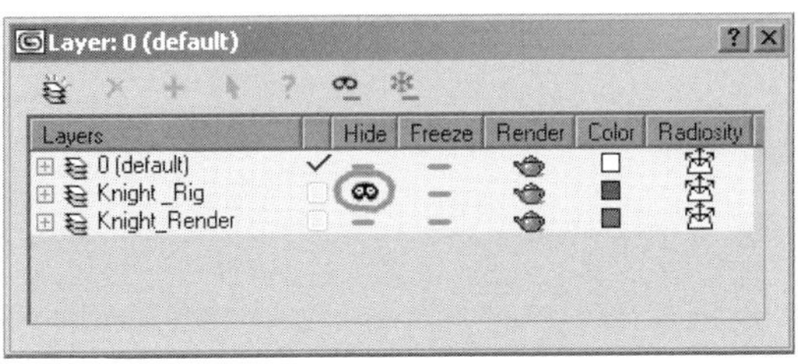

10. In the Left viewport, choose Knight_CNT_Main.

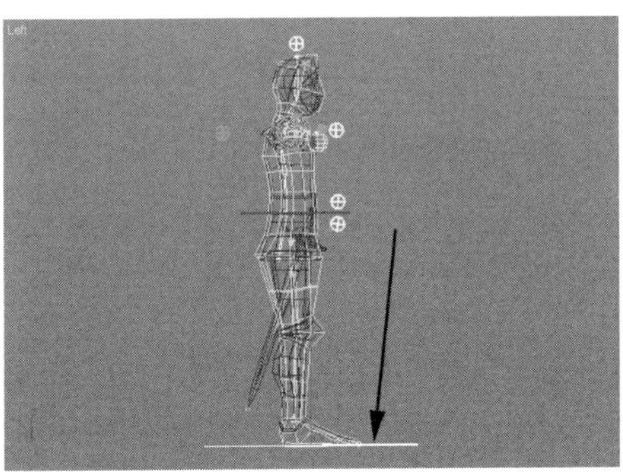

11. On the main toolbar, choose Select and Link.

12. In the Left viewport, click and drag from Knight_CNT_Main to Knight Link.

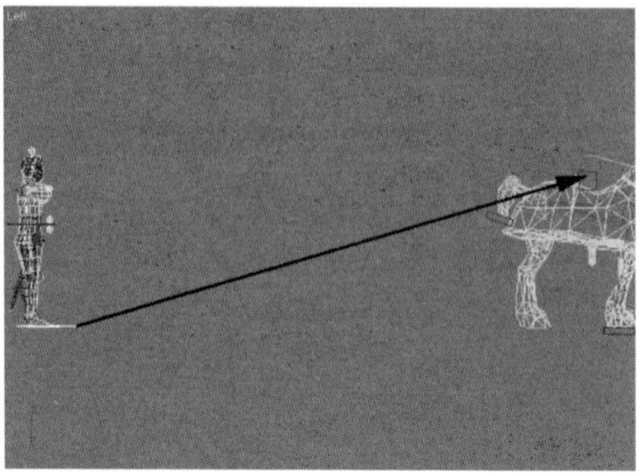

13. Scrub the time slider.

    The knight stays with the horse. Knight Link is a dummy object with a Link Constraint assigned.

    Next, you organize the horse.

Organizing the Horse

1. On the main toolbar, choose Select and Move.
2. Press **H** and type **BH** in the Select Objects dialog.

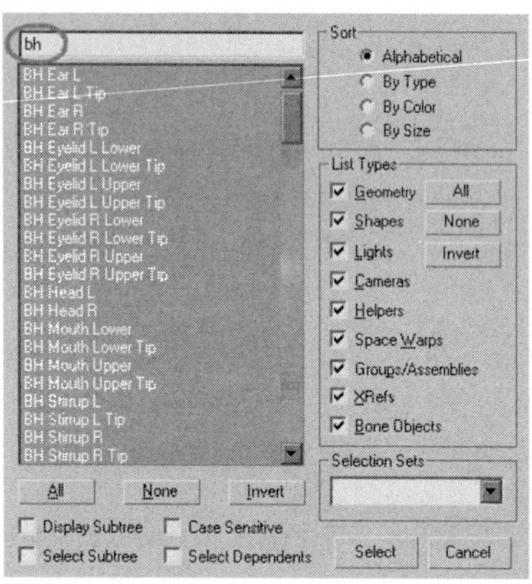

3. Click Select to close the dialog.
4. On the main toolbar, choose Layer Manager.

5. On the Layer toolbar, choose Create New Layer (Containing Selected Objects).

   A new layer named Layer01 is created. All selected objects are in this layer.

6. Rename the layer **Horse_Rig**.
7. Press H and then choose all objects beginning with HorseBip.
8. In the Layer Manager dialog, make sure the layer is selected.

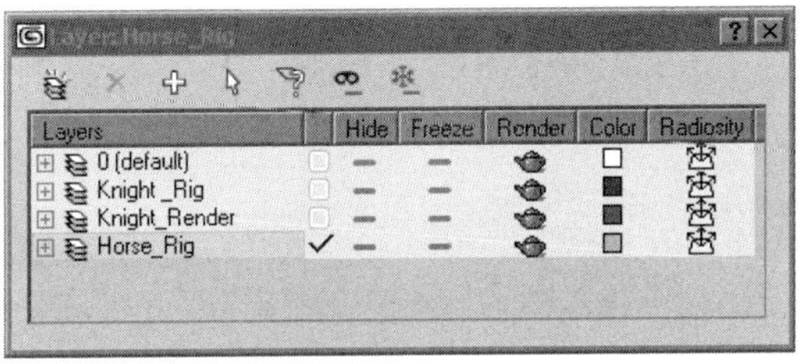

9. On the Layer Manager toolbar, choose Add Selected Objects to Highlighted Layer.
10. In the Layer dialog, hide the Horse_Rig layer.

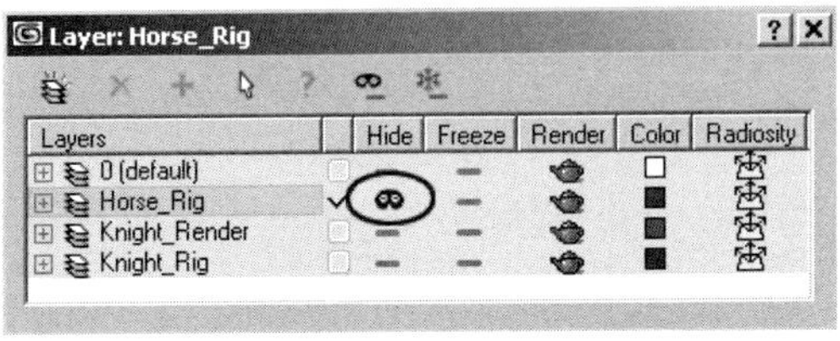

The reason you hide the layer is so you can see what is added to the rig layer (and what's missing). Now that the layer is hidden, you clearly see a few helper dummy objects have not been added.

11. In the Left viewport, choose the five dummies (not the Toe0Nub dummies).

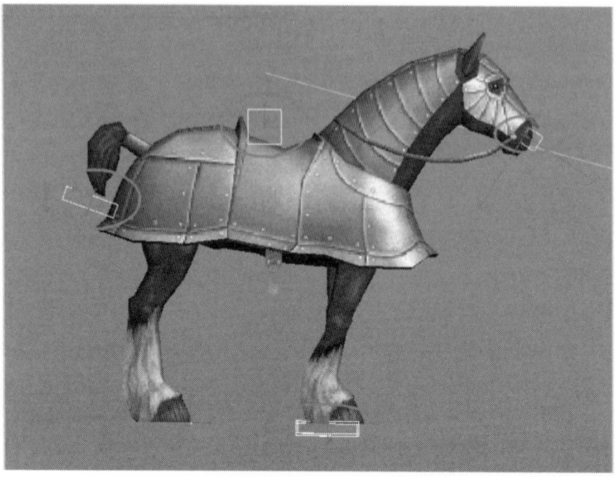

12. Make sure the Horse_Rig layer is selected.
13. In the Layer Manager toolbar, choose Add Selected Object to Highlighted Layer.

    The dummies disappear automatically because the layer is hidden.
14. In the Left viewport, choose Armored Horse.
15. Rename the object Armored_Horse_GEO.
16. In the Layer Manager dialog, choose Create New Layer (Containing Selected Objects).
17. Rename the layer **Horse_Render**.

    Note: The horse might disappear after it's placed in the layer. If it does, choose the icon under the Hide column to unhide the layer.

18. In the Layer dialog, make sure Knight_Rig and Horse_Rig are hidden.

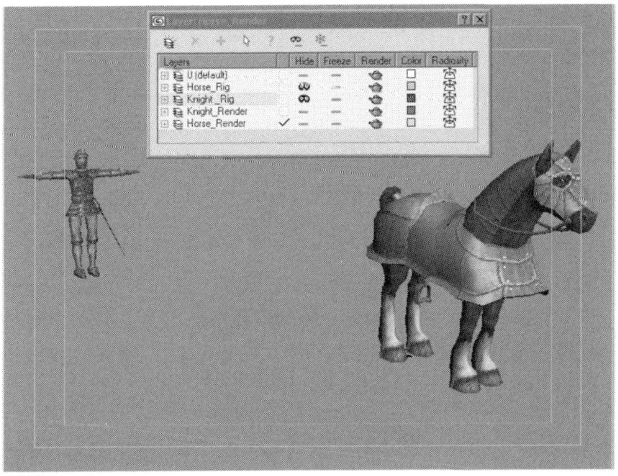

19. Close the Layer Manager.

    Next, you clean up the viewport display. A camera was included in the horse file and a light was merged with the Pendant. You hide them instead of using layers.

20. Press SHIFT+L.

    This hides all lights by category.

21. Press SHIFT+C.

    This hides all cameras by category.

22. Save the file as **MedievalSceneAssembly_03.max**.

Merging the Environment

The Knight and the Horse are the only objects in 3D space. Next, you merge an environment.

1. Continue from the previous exercise or open *MedievalSceneAssembly_03.max*.
2. On the menu bar, choose File > Merge.
3. In the Merge File dialog, choose *Medieval_Set.max*.

4. In the Merge dialog, choose All and then click OK.

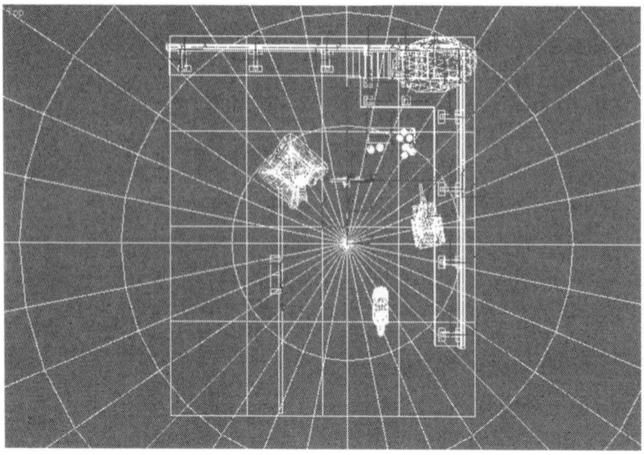

A lot of objects are merged into the scene. The advantage of using Layers and properly organizing your scene is you won't have to go hunting in the Select Object dialog.

Next, you organize the objects that are part of the environment.

Tip: It's a good idea to use layers since layer names are remembered when merging files.

5. Right-click to activate the Top viewport, and then choose ALT+W to maximize it.
6. In the viewport navigation controls, choose Zoom Extents.

   Tip: The sky dome object does not zoom out all the way, that is it omits the sky dome. The reason is that in the Sky's properties, Ignore Extents is on.

7. Select the Sky object and right-click.
8. Choose Properties from the quad menu.
9. In the Display Properties group, Ignore Extents is turned on.

   This is a great organizational method for limiting the zoom on certain objects. This way you are forced to stay closer to your main objects.

10. On the main toolbar, choose Layer Manager.

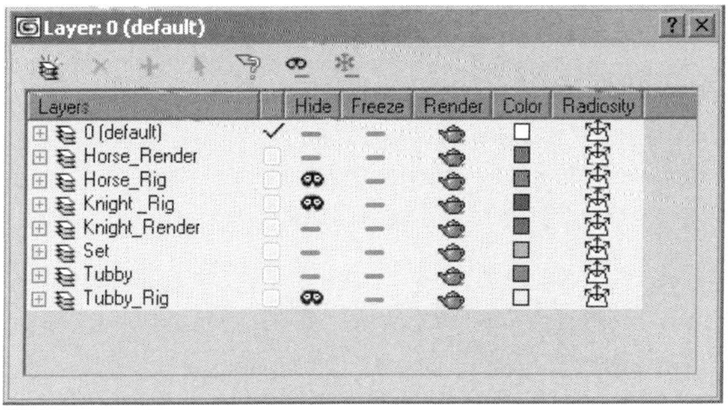

The layers from the environment are displayed. The names of the layers along with their settings are kept.

11. In the Layer Manager dialog, hide and unhide the various layers to get familiar with all objects in the scene.

    Next, you adjust the start for the animation.

12. In the Time Controls, choose Time Configuration.

13. In the Time Configuration dialog > Animation group, set the Start Time to **1**.

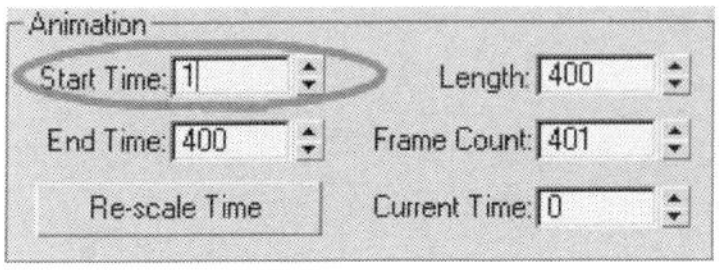

Frame zero is the reference pose and not needed for the animation.

Tip: Place the cursor on the time bar and use the following keyboard shortcut combinations to adjust the configuration.

CTRL+ALT+LMB – Change the start time.
CTRL+ALT+MMB – Set a Range of frames.
CTRL+ALT+RMB – Change the End time.

14. Save your file as *Medieval_Lighting_01.max*.

Setting Up Lights and Using Mental Ray

For this scene, you use both renderers that come with **3ds max**: mental ray and scanline. You use both renderers because there are advantages to both. Mental ray has a large feature set and can produce high-quality renderings. However, you sacrifice speed for that high-quality image. You use the scanline renderer because it's fast and can produce very good renderings.

You use mental ray in the following procedures to generate high-quality images in conjunction with features such as Camera Mapping and Render to Texture.

Setting Up for Mental Ray

Next, you change the scanline renderer to the mental ray renderer.

1. Open *Medieval_Lighting_01.max*.
2. On the menu bar, choose Tools > Light Lister.

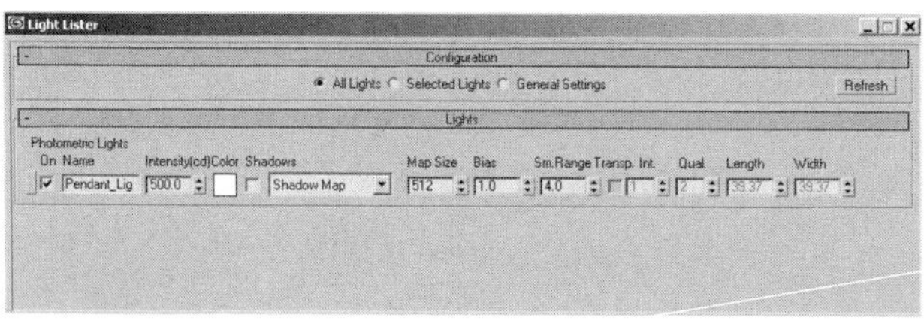

   This scene has one Photometric Point Light.

3. Close the Light Lister.
4.  On the main toolbar, choose Render Scene.
5. In the Render Scene dialog > Common Tab > Assign Renderer rollout, choose the button next to Default Scanline Renderer.

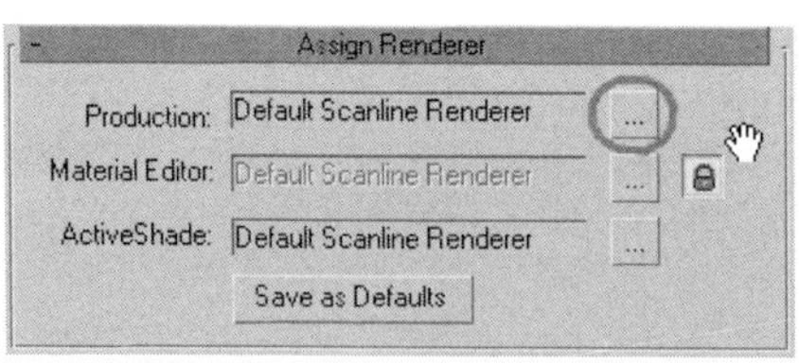

6. In the Choose Renderer dialog, choose mental ray.

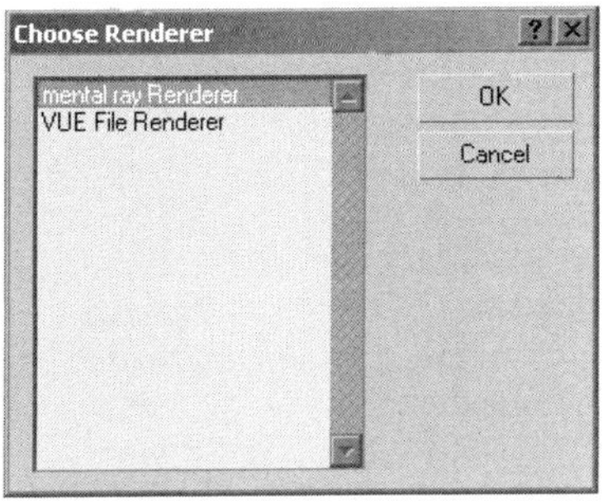

Override Material Setup

Next, you look at some features exclusive to mental ray that make your renderings efficient. You create a simple gray material and apply it to all objects in the scene. You can imagine how time-consuming and cumbersome to then re-apply the original Materials that include Maps onto the objects in the scene. However, mental ray comes equipped with a feature called Override Material. This feature sets the original textures onto the objects after you use the gray material to set up your test renders.

1. Continue from the previous exercise.
2.  Press **M** to open the Material Editor.
3. Choose an empty sample slot.

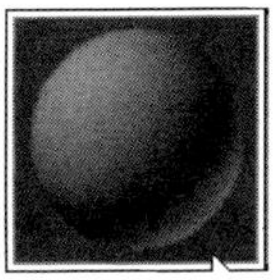

4. Change the name of the Material to Plaster.
5. In the Blinn Basic Parameters rollout, make the following changes.
   Ambient: **127**
   Diffuse: **127**
   Specular: **229**

Specular Level: **10**
Glossiness: **10**

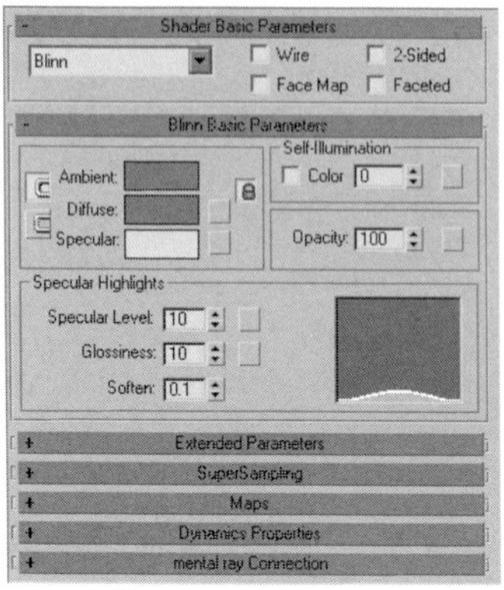

This Material is 50 percent gray and helps clearly show lighting effects better than your Materials with textures. Using this type of Material for test renders works better with light temperature and color, and also renders a lot faster.

6. Press **M** to close the Material Editor.

7.  In the Render Scene dialog > Processing tab > Translator Options rollout > Material Override group, turn on Enable.

8. Choose the None button next to Material.

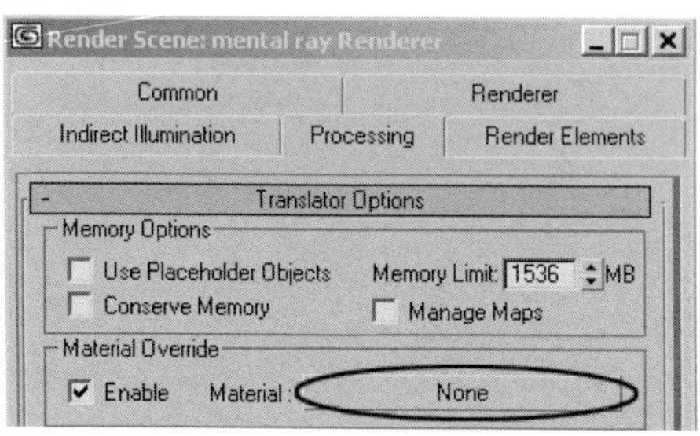

9. In the Material/Map Browser dialog > Browse From group, choose Material Editor.

10. Choose Plaster from the list and then click OK.

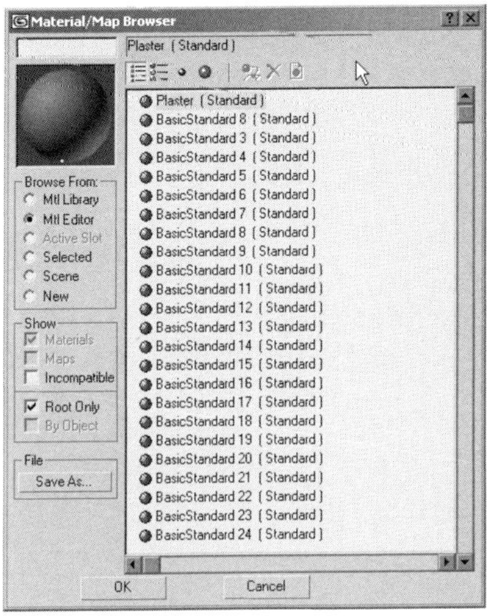

11. In the Instance or Copy? dialog, choose Instance.

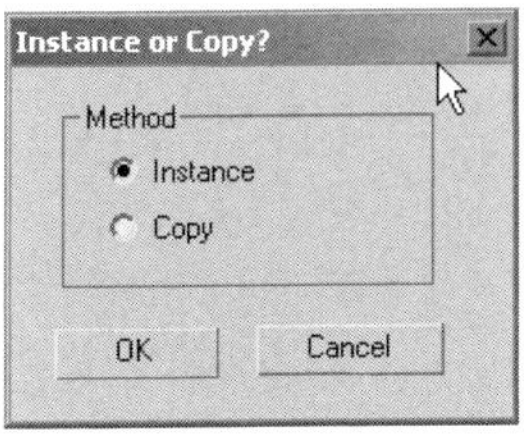

You have created a simple 50 percent gray Material to use for test renders. When you want to return to the original Materials, you simply turn off Enable. Since there is only one light in the scene, it's not worth rendering right now. You set up the rendering for optimization and then you merge the lights before you start rendering.

Efficiency in Render Tests

Next, you make optimizations to the renderer. To do this, you need to identify the features you want to use so you know the type of adjustments to make. Basically, you use all the bells and whistles with Final Gather, Global Illumination, and Displacement. However, later in this chapter, you learn how to bake these elements so you don't have to recalculate them.

1. Continue from the previous exercise.
2.  On the main toolbar, choose Render Scene.
3. In the Render Scene dialog > Indirect Illumination tab > Caustics and GI rollout > Global Illumination group, turn on Enable.

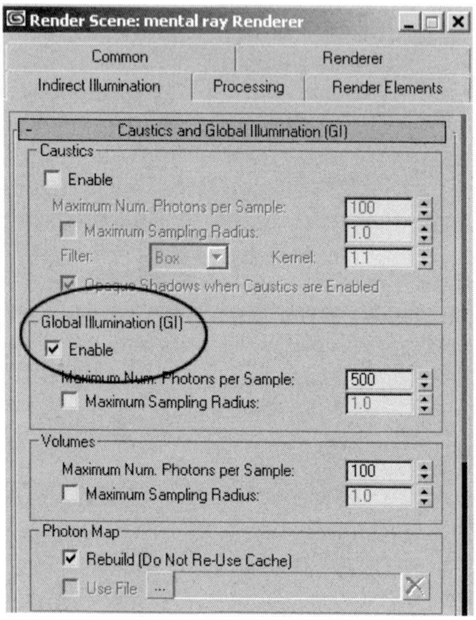

4. In the Final Gather rollout, turn on Final Gather.

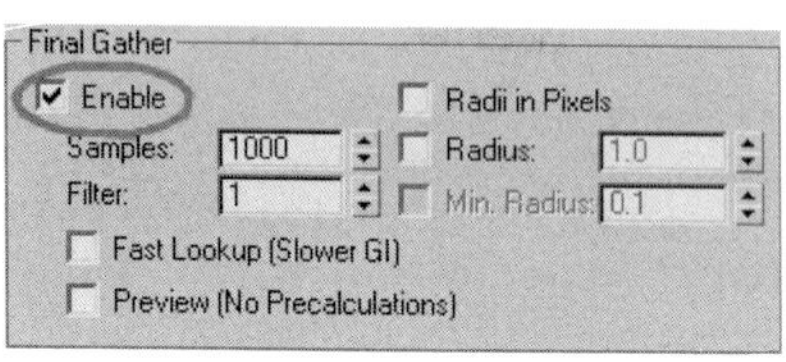

5. In the Render Scene dialog, choose the Preset drop-down list.

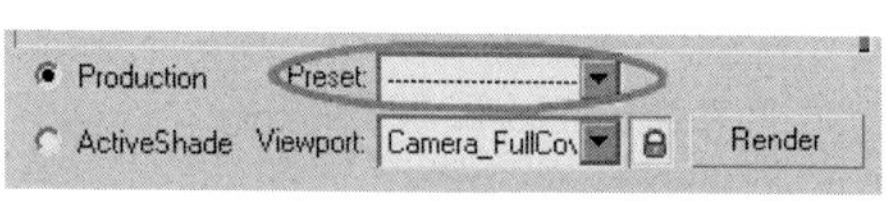

6. Choose Save Preset from the list.
7. In the Render Presets Save dialog, type **No_Optimizations** and then press Save.

8. In the Select Preset Categories dialog, make sure everything is selected and then choose Save.

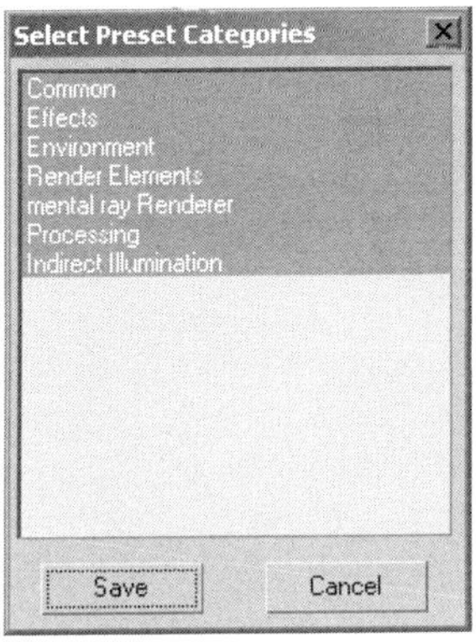

You set up a preset so that once all the optimizations are done, you can switch to the default settings. Doing so enables you to perform time comparisons between renderings.

Setting Up Optimizations

Now you set up the optimizations.

1. Continue from the previous example.
2. In the Render Scene dialog > Indirect Illumination tab > Caustics and GI rollout, make the following changes.
   GI Enable on: **True**
   Maximum Num. Photons per Sample: **250**
   Max. Depth: **32**
   Max. Reflections: **16**
   Max. Refractions: **16**
   All Objects Generate & Receive: **True**

Global Energy Multiplier: **2**
Decay: **1.8**

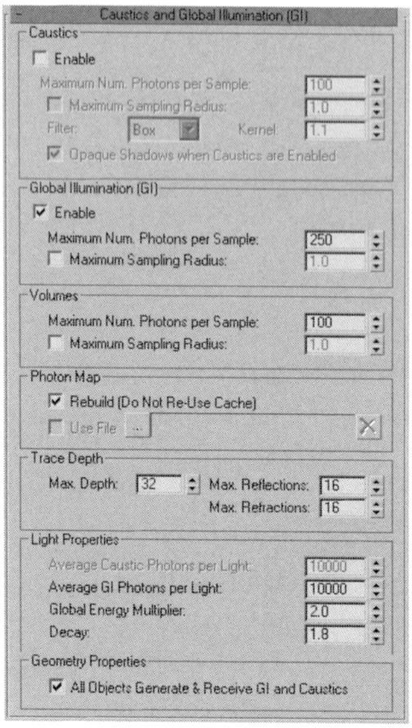

Increasing the Max. Depth, Reflection, and Refractions, "pushes" the light farther into the shadowed areas. The Global Energy Multiplier and Decay also help to push light into shadows.

3. In the Final Gather rollout, make the following changes.
   Final Gather Enable on: **True**
   Samples: **250**
   Radius on: **True**
   Radius: **1000**
   Min. Radius on: **True**
   Min. Radius: **500**
   Filter: **1**
   Max. Depth: **2**

Max. Reflections: **1**
Max. Refractions: **1**

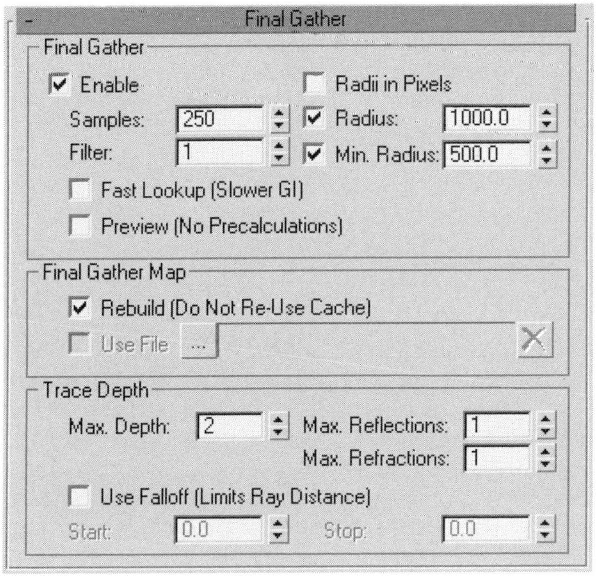

Global Illumination can appear patchy without final gathering, but it increases rendering time.

Increasing the Radius and Min, Radius values drastically reduces render times.

4. In the Render Scene dialog, choose the Renderer tab.
5. In the Sampling Quality rollout, make sure the following options are set.

Minimum: **¼**
Maximum: **4**

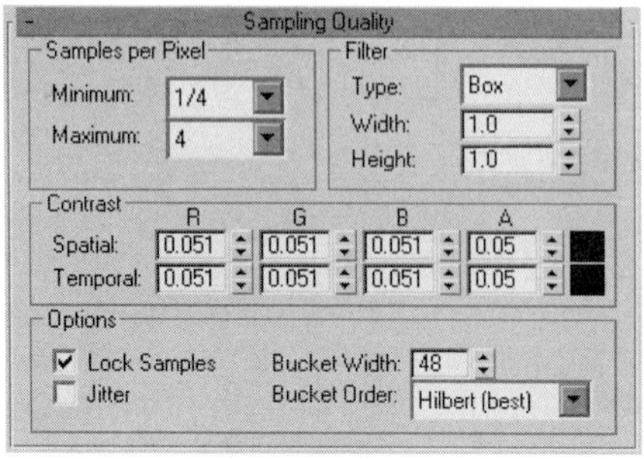

If you see a lot of aliasing in your renders, increase the Maximum setting to **16**. However, this adds significant time to your render. When you do lighting tests, it's better to keep the value lower and increase it for the final render.

6. In the Renderer tab > Rendering Algorithms rollout, make the following changes.
   Raytrace Acceleration Size: **5**
   Raytrace Acceleration Depth: **30**
   Max. Depth: **1**
   Max. Reflections: **0**
   Max. Refractions: **0**

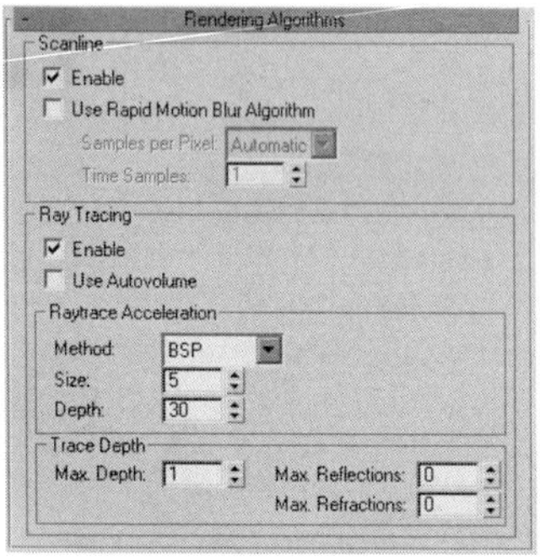

The controls in this rollout enable you to choose whether to render using Ray Tracing, Scanline rendering, or both. You can also choose the method used to accelerate Ray Tracing.

The controls in the Ray Trace Depth group limit the number of times each ray is reflected, refracted, or both.

By default, both Ray Trace and Scanline are enabled, which lets the mental ray renderer use a combination of ray tracing and scanline rendering to render the scene. Scanline rendering is used for direct illumination (primary rays) only; ray tracing is used for indirect illumination (caustics and global illumination) as well as reflections, refractions, and lens effects.

Note: All options in the Camera Effects rollout (Depth of Field, Motion Blur, and Contours) should be turned off, except for Camera Shaders.

7. In the Shadows and Displace rollout, make the following changes:
Shadows Enable on: **True**
Displacement View on: **False**
Edge Length: **2**
Max. Displace: **200**
Max. Level: **6**

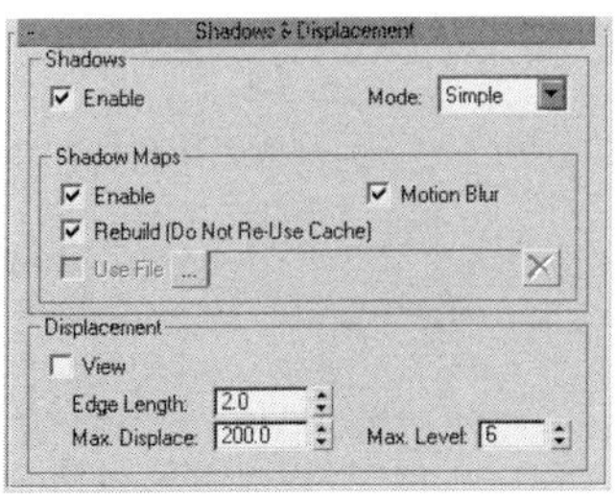

The options in this rollout affect shadows and displacement.

Tip: During lighting renders, the displacement is turned off to save render time. For final render, you turn it on.

8. In the Render Scene dialog > Common tab > Common Parameters rollout, make the following changes:
Single: **True**
Output Size drop-down list: **HDTV**
Width: **500**
Height: **281**

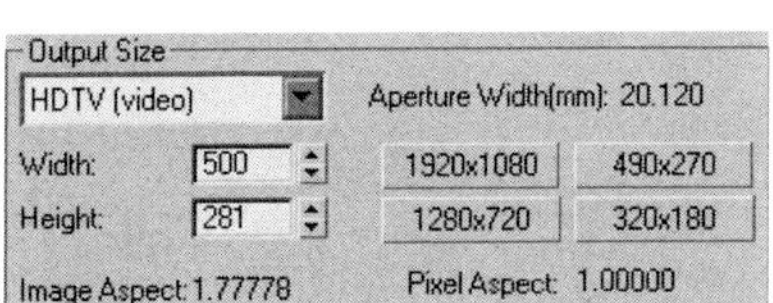

Next, you save another Preset named Optimized.

9. In the Render Scene dialog, Preset drop-down list, choose Save Preset.
10. In the Save Preset dialog, type **Optimized**.
11. In the Select Preset Categories dialog, make sure everything is selected and then press Save.

    Saving Presets is a useful production feature for the following reasons:

    - Switch between different settings to see quality and speed differences.
    - Share render setups with your entire team so that renders are consistent.
    - Set up a variety of different render passes that require different settings. Simply set them up by loading a preset.

Setting Up the Lights

Next, you merge the lights into the scene.

1. Continue from the previous exercise.
2. On the menu bar, choose File > Merge.
3. In the Merge File dialog, choose *Medieval_Lights.max*.
4. In the Merge dialog, choose All and then click OK.

5. Press SHIFT+ L to unhide the lights.

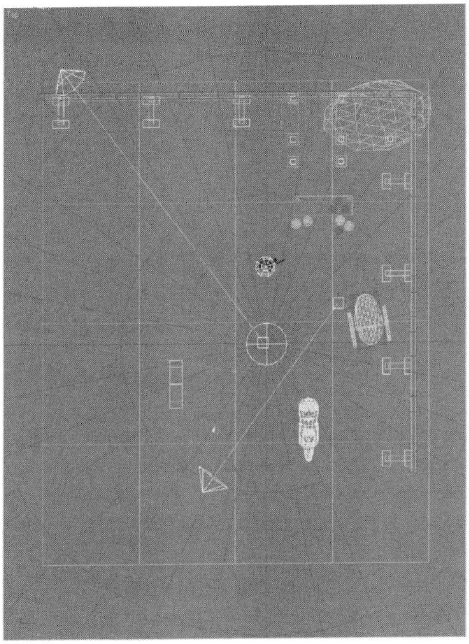

6. On the main toolbar, choose the Filters drop-down list, and then choose Lights.

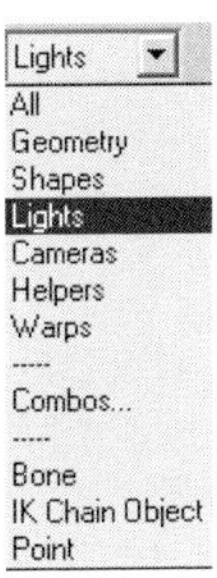

This ensures you only choose lights when you click in a cluttered area.

7. In the Top viewport, choose the skylight named Sky01.

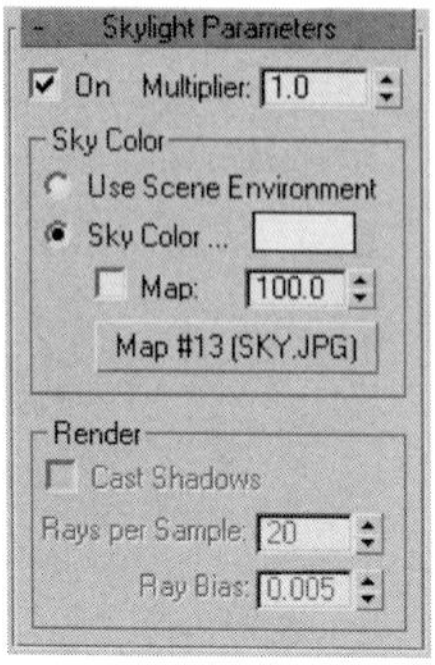

The Multiplier's value remains at **1**. Sky Color is chosen instead of Use Scene Environment because it's faster. Since mental ray is the renderer, and you have a Skylight in the scene, Final Gather must be turned on, which you did in the previous procedure.

8. In the Top viewport, choose mr Area Spot01.
9. Rename the light **mrArea_SUN**.

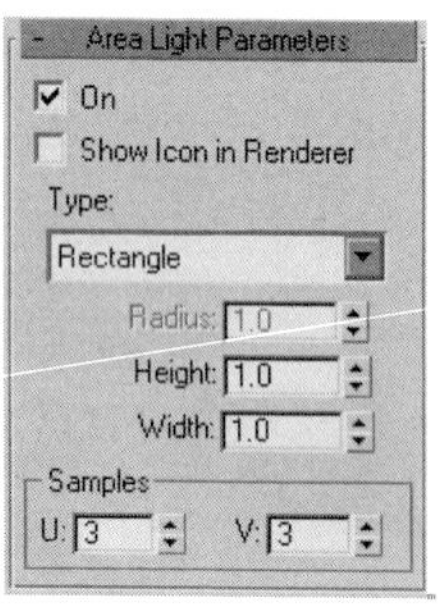

Most of the defaults are kept for this light. One setting that does change is in the Area Light Parameters rollout. The Samples are set to 3 for optimization.

10. In the Intensity/Color/Attenuation rollout, the light color is set to R=255, G=239, and B=213, which is a yellow tint.
11. In the General Parameters rollout > Light Type group, turn off the Light.

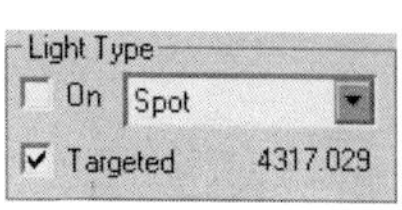

12. In the Top viewport, choose mr Area Spot02.

13. Rename the light **mrArea_FILL**.

    The settings are the same as the previous light except the color is set to R=213, G=228, and B=255, which is a blue tint.

14. In the General Parameters rollout > Light Type group, turn off the Light.

    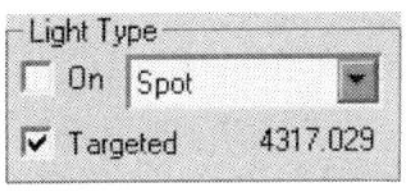

    You turn off the lights so you can see how each light affects the rendering. It's better to start with one light in the scene and then slowly add others where you notice light is needed.

Lighting Tests

Next, you start rendering.

1. Continue from the previous example or open *Medieval_Lighting_02.max*.
2. Right-click in the Top viewport and then choose Unfreeze All from the quad menu.

   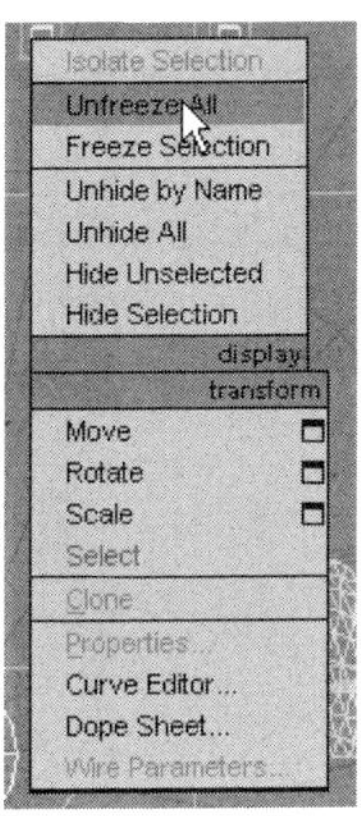

3. On the main toolbar, set the Filters to All.
4. In the Top viewport, choose the Sky object.
5. In the Top viewport, right-click and then choose Hide Selection.

6. Right-click the Camera viewport to make it active and then press ALT+W.

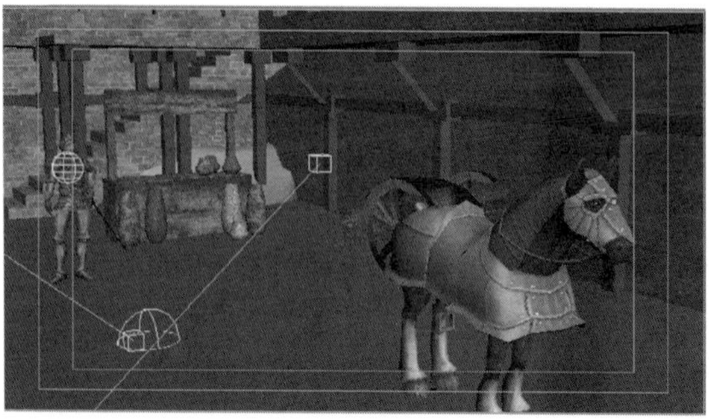

7. On the main toolbar, choose Quick Render.

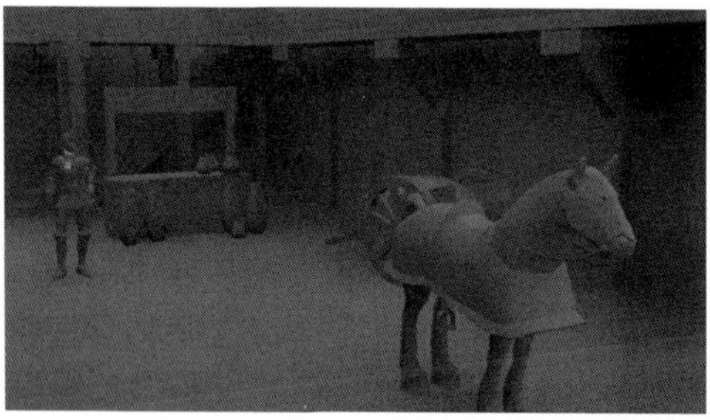

You get an image similar to the previous one. The image renders rather quickly with some aliasing. This is expected since this is a render test. You can always increase the sampling in the final render to fix the aliasing problem.

What you want to look for in this rendering is the intensity of the general ambient light. It looks good, so next you turn on the Key light, which is the Sun.

8. In the Top viewport, choose mrArea_SUN and turn it on.
9. Press F9 to render the last viewport, which is the Camera viewport.

Note: Earlier in the chapter, you locked the Camera viewport so every time you press Render, the Camera viewport renders.

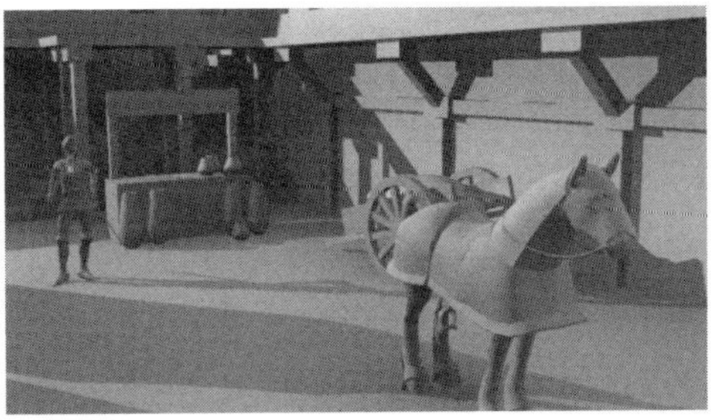

Notice a slight yellow tint in the scene and the direction of the shadows, which is what you want from the Key Light. Next, you turn on the Fill light, which is closer to the camera and the horse.

10. In the Top viewport, choose mrArea_FILL light and turn it on.
11. Press F9 to Render.

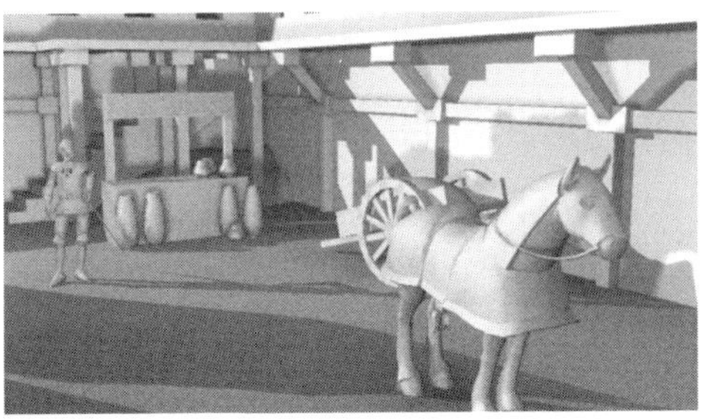

Notice the shadows around the stairs and overhang are washed out. You adjust this next.

12. Make sure the fill light is selected.
13. On the Modify panel > Intensity/Color/Attenuation rollout, change the Multiplier to **0.8**.

14. In the Decay group > Type drop-down list, choose Inverse.

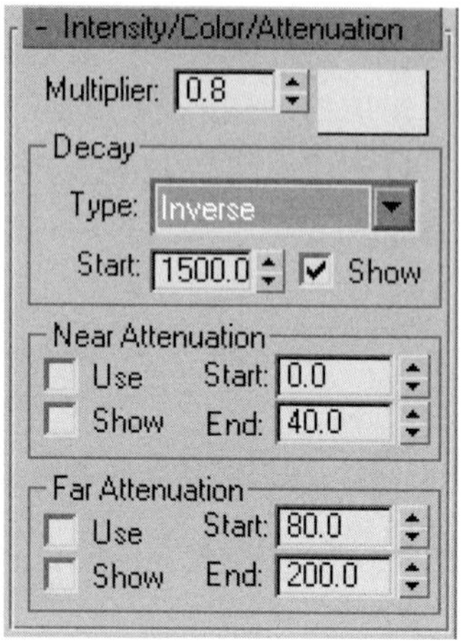

You want the light to fill the area around the horse only.

15. In the Top viewport, you see the green start gizmo display for the decay.

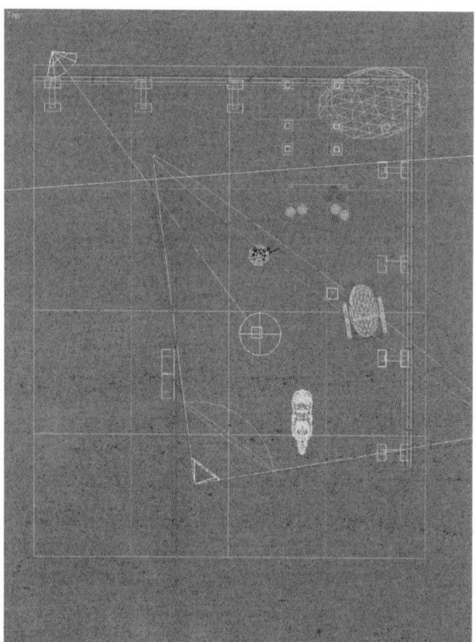

16. Press F9 to Render.

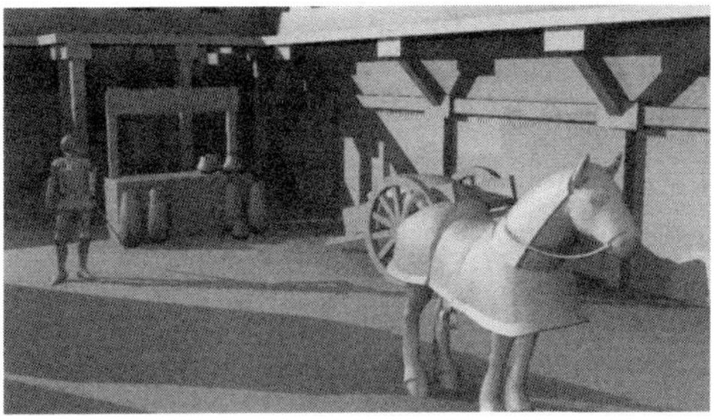

The scene is not washed out. Next, you turn off Material Override and render with the textures.

17. Continue from the previous exercise.
18. On the main toolbar, choose Render Scene.
19. In the Render Scene dialog > Processing tab > Translator Options roll-out, turn off Material Override.

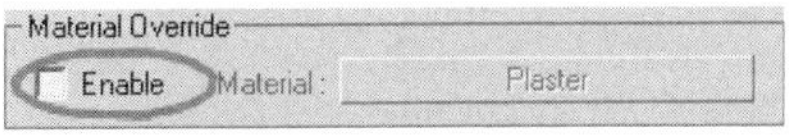

20. In the Render Scene dialog, choose Render.

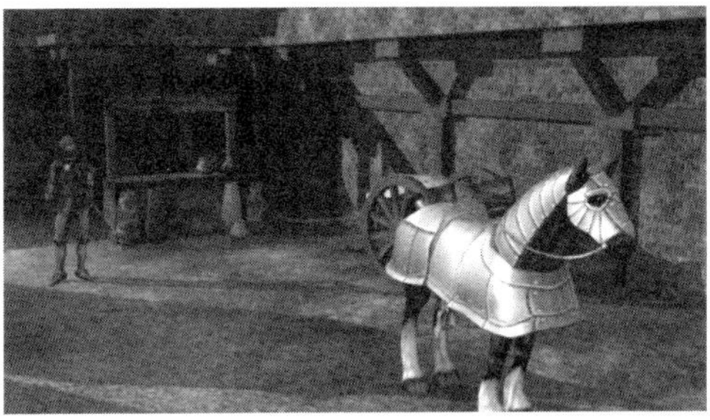

The rendering looks quite good, except the ground looks too flat. You fix this next.

Getting Your Displacement Set Up

You add a mental ray displacement shader to the Ground material. It's a subtle effect but definitely gives the grass a more realistic look.

1. Continue from the previous exercise.
2. Press **H** and then choose Ground.

3. On the Modify panel, change the Length and Width Segments to 40.
4. In the Render Multipliers group, change the Density to **3**.

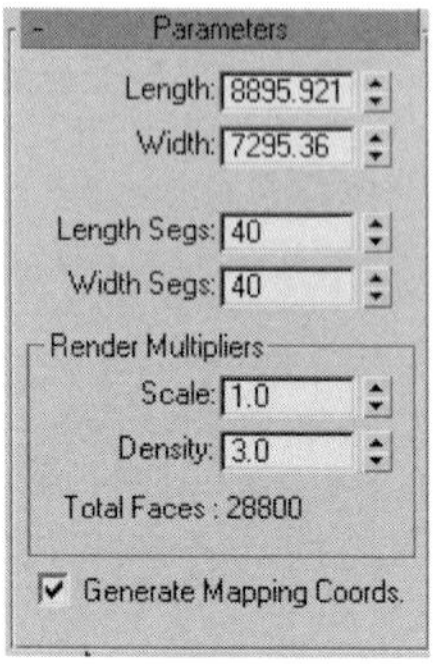

5. 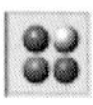 Press **M** to open the Material Editor.
6. In the Material Editor, choose an empty sample slot.
7.  In the Material Editor > bottom toolbar, choose Get Material.
8. In the Material/Map Browser dialog > Browse From group, choose Selected.
9. In the Material/Map Browser dialog, double-click Ground.
10. Close the Material/Map Browser dialog.
11. In the Maps rollout, turn off Bump maps.

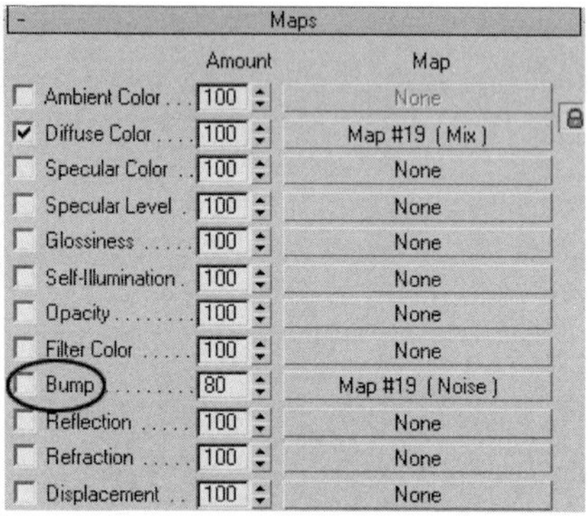

12. Open the mental ray Connection rollout.

13. In the mental ray Connection rollout > Extended Shaders group, turn off Lock next to Displacement.

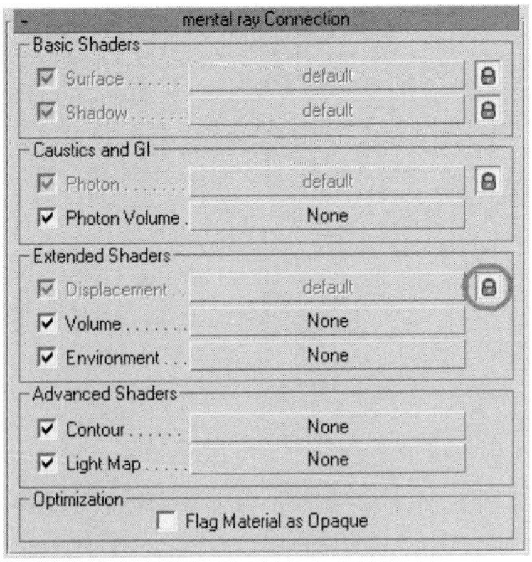

14. Choose the None button next to Displacement.

15. In the Material/Map Browser > Browser From group, choose New and then double-click the 3D Displacement shader.

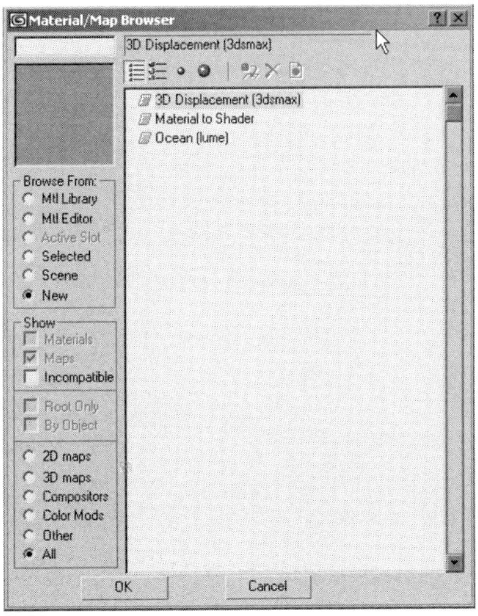

16. In the Material Editor > side toolbar, choose Material/Map Navigator.

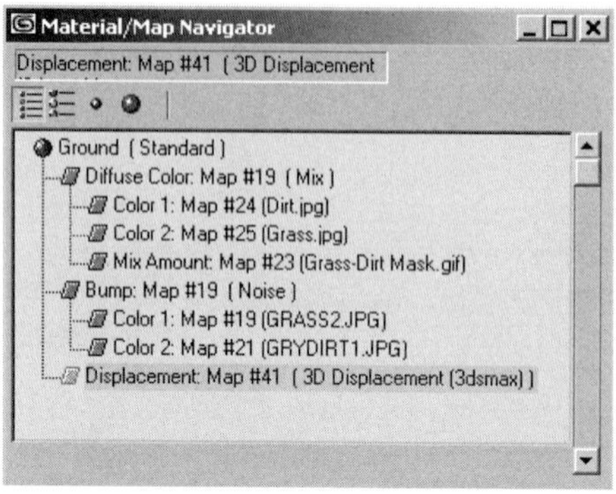

Note: Mental ray shaders are usually assigned to **3ds max** Material Types such as Standard, Raytrace, etc. You add the shaders through the mental ray Connection rollout, which determines the Map Channel it affects. The shader displays with a yellow parallelogram to indicate mental ray shaders, not **3ds max** Map Types.

17. In the 3D Displacement Parameters rollout, choose the None button next to Extrusion Map.

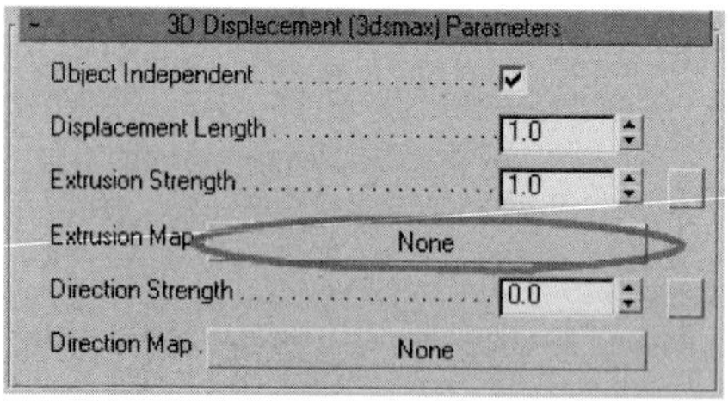

18. In the Material/Map Browser dialog > Browse From group, choose Selected.

19. Double-click *GRASS2.jpg*.

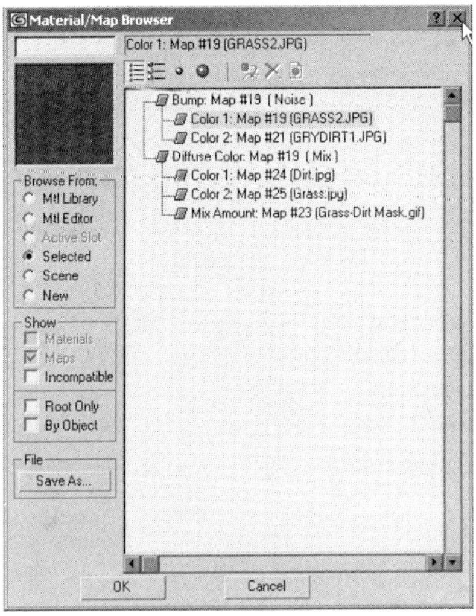

20. In the Instance or Copy? dialog, choose Copy.
21. In the Material/Map Navigator, choose Displacement.
22. In the Shader rollout, choose the None button next to Extrusion Strength.

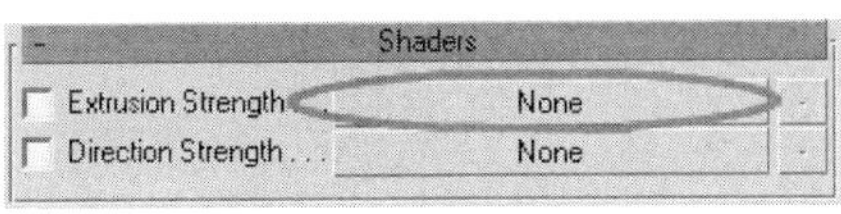

23. In the Material/Map Browser, double-click *Grass-Dirt Mask.gif*.

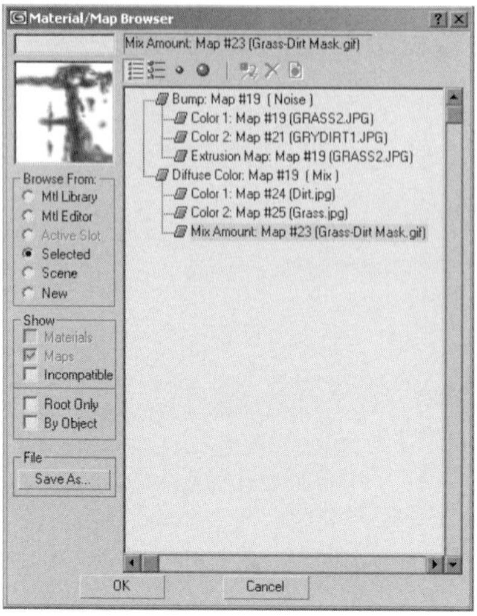

24. In the dialog, choose Copy.

25. In the Material/Map Navigator, choose Displacement.

26. In the 3D Displacement Parameters rollout, set the Length to **50** and Extrusion strength to **80**.

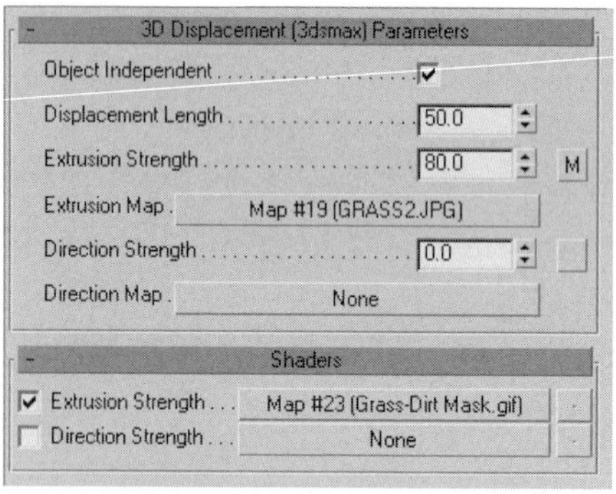

27. Press F10 to open the Render Scene dialog.

28. In the Renderer tab > Shadows & Displacement rollout Displacement group, turn on View.

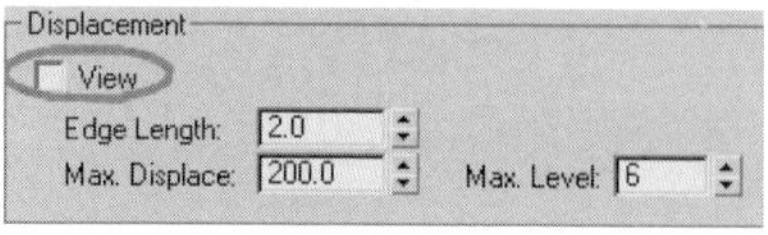

29. On the main toolbar, choose the Layer Manager.
30. In the Layer dialog, hide the Knight_Render and Horse_Render layers.

    This way you can see the grass clearly.

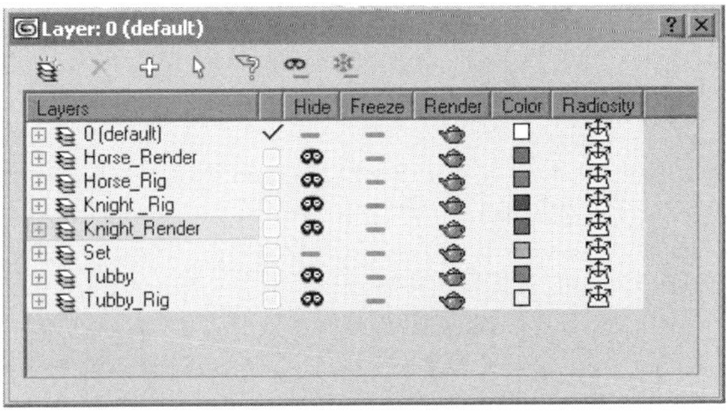

31. Make sure the Camera viewport is set to Camera_FullCoverage.

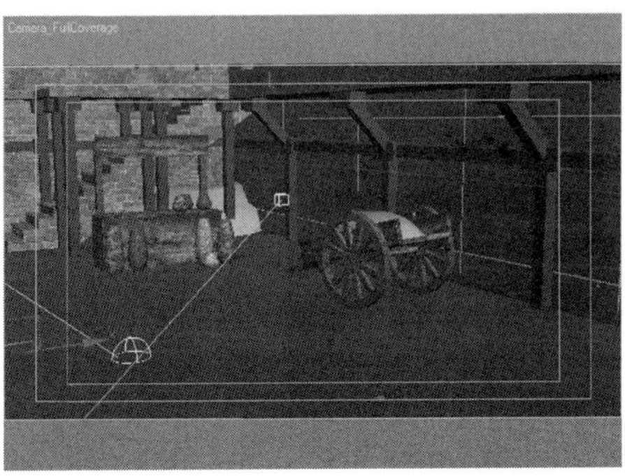

32. On the main toolbar, choose Quick Render.

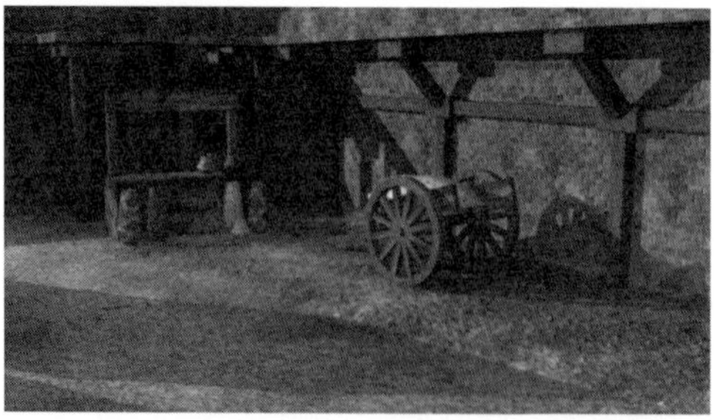

With Displacement

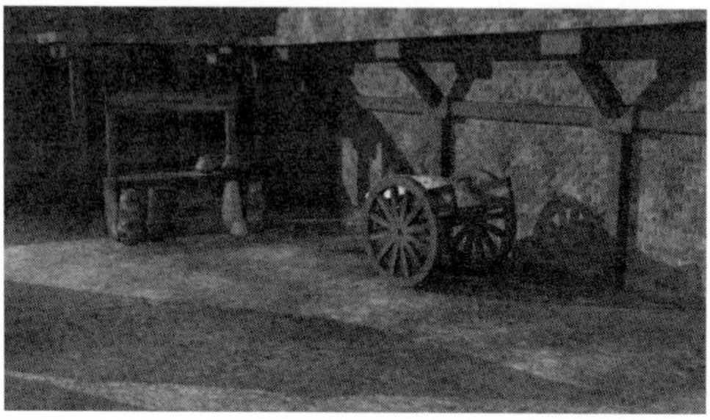

Without Displacement

Clearly you can see the difference between the images with and without displacement.

Note: This effect is even more visible at low camera angles.

Next, you set up the scene for print.

Rendering for Print

Projects often require promotional prints. Since printing does not work the same as pixels per screen, deciding the size to render your image can be difficult. However, using the Print Size Wizard inside **3ds max** makes printing easy.

Calculating Print Settings

1. Open *Medieval_Lighting_03.max.*
2. Scrub the time slider to frame 174.

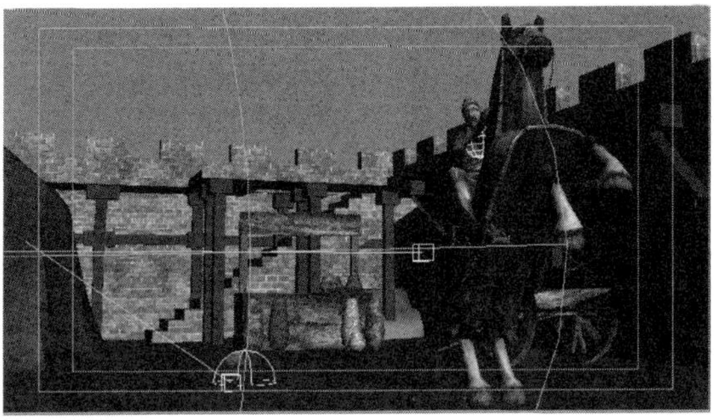

3. On the menu bar, choose Rendering > Print Size Wizard.
4. In the Paper Size group > DPI value, choose **300**.
5. Set the Paper Width to **5** and Height to **3**.

   The Image Width and Height changes to 1500 × 900.
6. In the Rendering group, turn on Save File.
7. Choose the Files button and give your file a unique name on your local directory.

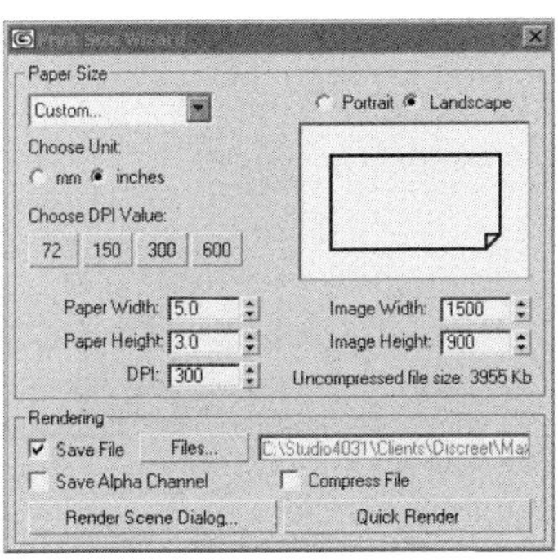

8. In the Print Size Wizard dialog, choose Quick Render.

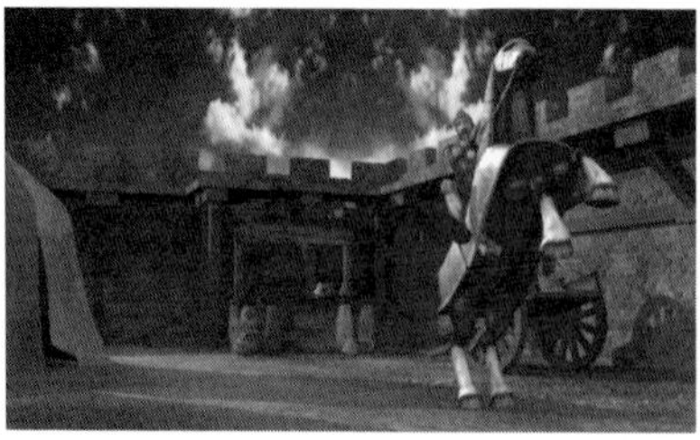

Next, you optimize the scene for rendering.

Creating Render Shortcuts

Up to this point, you have used mental ray with acceptable results and rendering times. Next, you switch to scanline rendering and get the same results in a fraction of the time using some new features in **3ds max 7**.

Mental Ray and Render to Texture

Next, you use Render to Texture with the mental ray renderer to back the textures into the geometry. Render to Texture is not new but using it with mental ray is.

1. Open *Medieval_Lighting_04.max*.
2. In the viewport navigation controls, choose Zoom Extents All.
3. Region-select everything in the Top viewport.

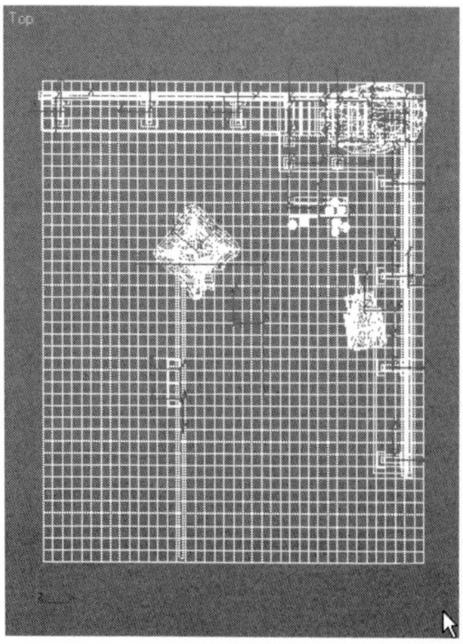

Note: In this file, the characters are all hidden and only the set is visible.

4. Press 0 to open Render to Texture.
5. In the General Settings rollout > Output group, choose an output path.

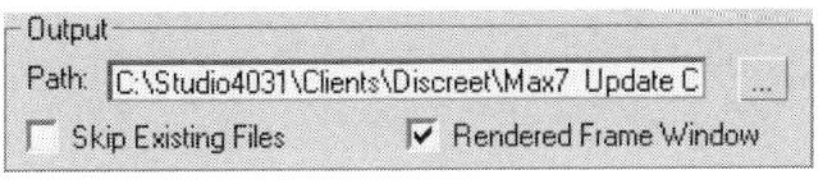

6. In the Objects to Bake rollout > Selected Object Settings group, turn on Enabled.

   Note: Click this check box a few times to ensure the checkmark is black, not unavailable.

7. Enable Projection Mapping.
8. In the Projection Mapping group, turn off Sub-Object Levels.
9. In the Mapping Coordinates group, leave Use Automatic Unwrap on and the Channel set to **3**.

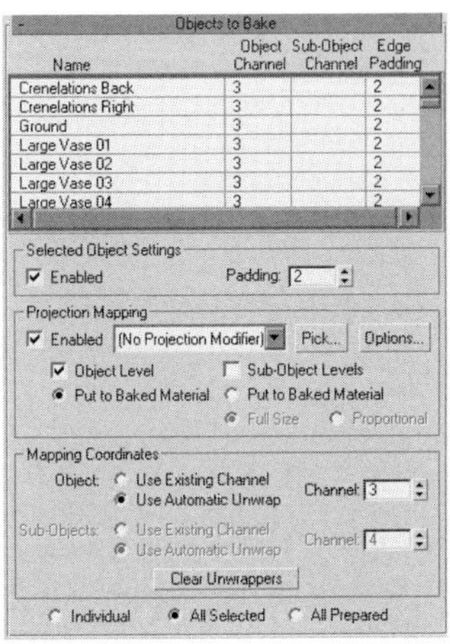

10. 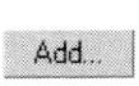

In the Output rollout, choose Delete to delete all entries.
11. 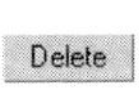

In the Output group, turn on Add.

12. In the Add Texture Elements dialog, choose CompleteMap and then choose Add Elements.

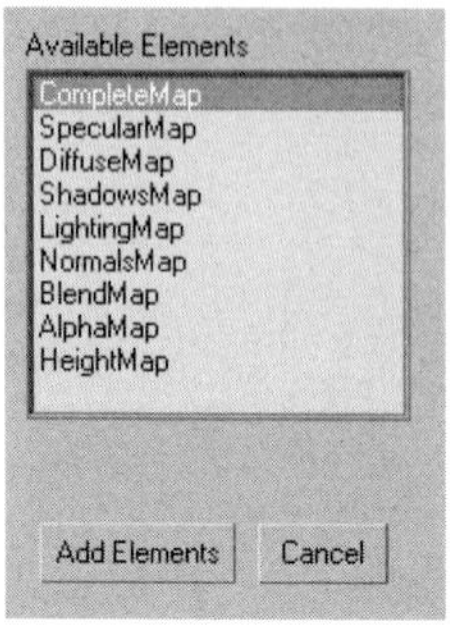

13. In the Select Element Common Setting group > Target Map Slot drop-down list, choose Diffuse Color.
14. Set the Output Size to **512**.
15. In the Selected Element Unique Settings group, maker sure Shadows are on.

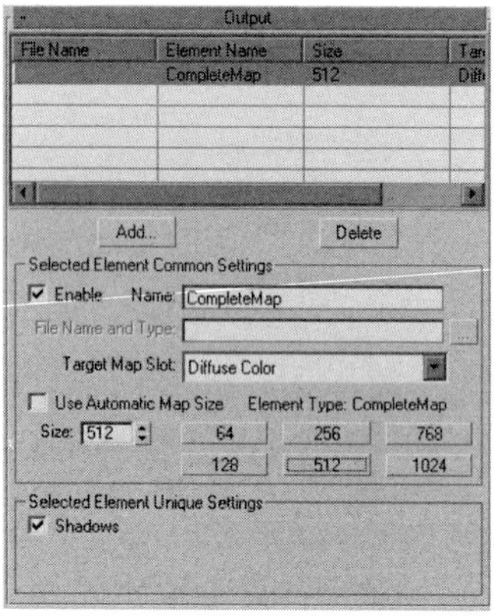

16. In the Baked Material rollout, make sure Save Source (Create Shell) and Duplicate Source to Baked are selected.

17. Make sure Keep Source Materials is chosen.

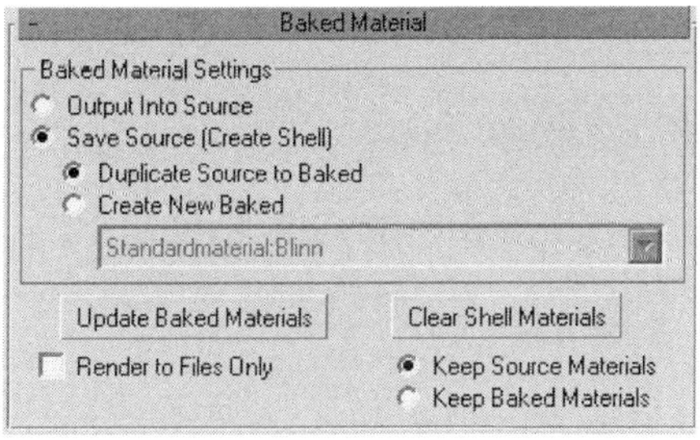

18. At the bottom of the dialog, choose Baked for both Views and Render.

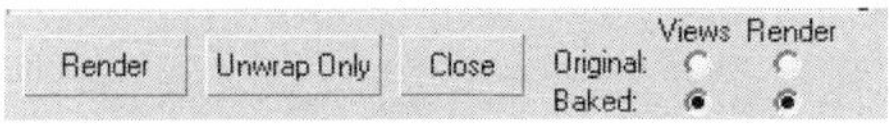

19. In the dialog, choose Render.

The result is that mental ray is rendering with its lights and shadows and that information gets baked into the geometry. This allows you to render with no lights and use the scanline renderer, which renders even faster since it doesn't calculate any shadow information.

Note: The shaded viewport displays the shadows.

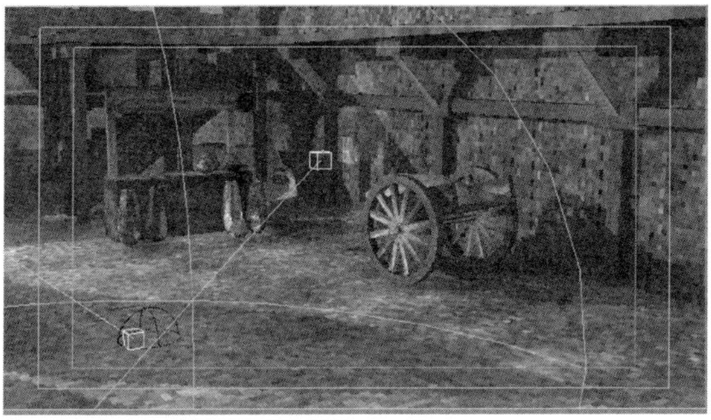

The reason you use this technique for the objects is that you render objects in layers. In the next chapter, you take a different approach for the characters.

Next, you see how fast the scene renders.

20. On the menu bar, choose Tools > Light Lister.

21. In the Light Lister dialog, turn off all lights except for the Pendant light.

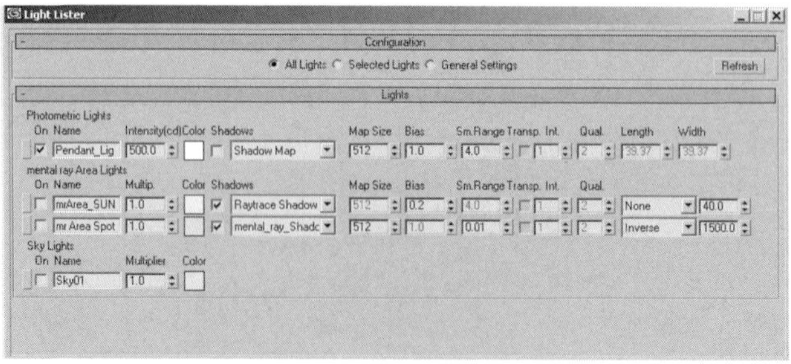

22. Close the Light Lister.
23. On the menu bar, choose Rendering > Environment.
24. In the Common Parameters > Global Tinting group, set the Ambient light color to R=**165**, G=**165**, and B=**165**.

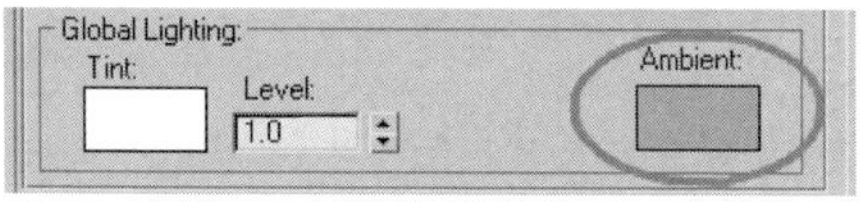

Note: You do this to see the textures when you render. You don't need lights in the scene because they are baked into the textures, but you still need light in the overall scene so it is not black.

25. Close the Environment and Effects dialog.
26. Press F10 to open the Render Scene dialog.
27. In the Assign Renderer rollout, change the Renderer to Default Scanline.

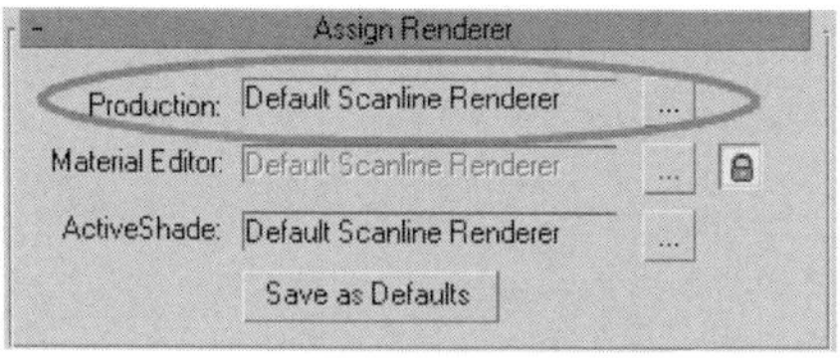

28. Right-click the Camera viewport and then press C. Choose Camera_FullCoverage.

29. In the Render Scene dialog, choose Render.

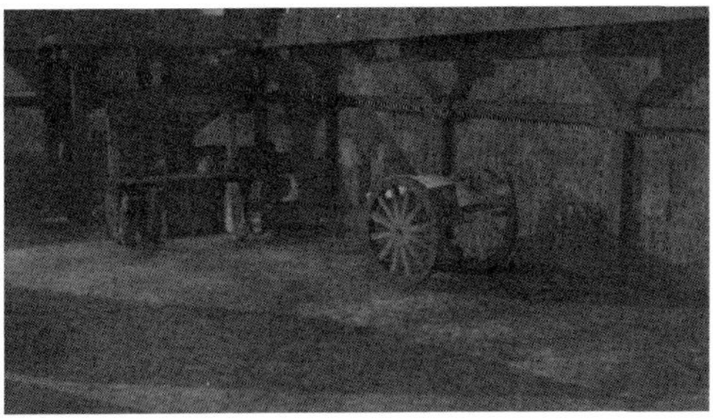

Notice the rendering time is much faster and that the shadows display in the viewport because the information is baked into the texture.

Per-Pixel Camera Mapping

Next, you use Per-Pixel Camera Map type to improve render speeds. The Camera Map Per Pixel enables you to project a map from the direction of a particular camera. However, the real power in this tool lies in matte painting. You can paint extra detail in the resulting map that would prove difficult and time-consuming to do in 3D.

1. Open *Medieval_Lighting_04.max.*

   This scene uses the mental ray renderer.

2. 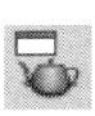 Press F10 to open the Render Scene Dialog.

3. In the Common Tab > Common Parameters rollout > Output Size group, choose 1920×1080.

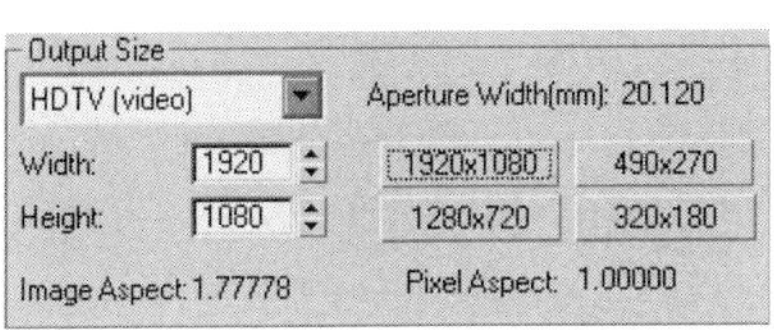

4. Make sure Camera_Promotional is active.

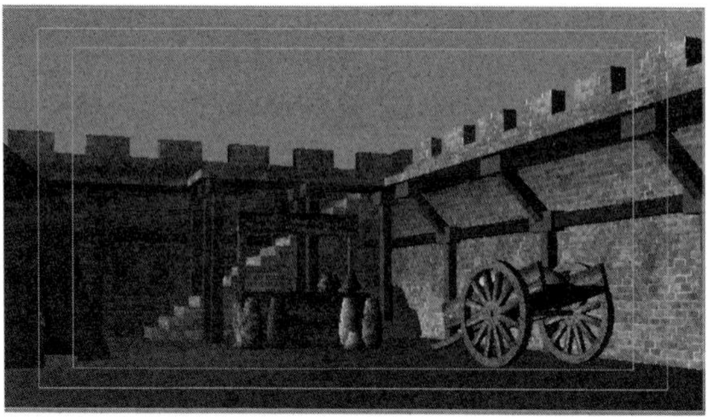

5. In the Render Scene dialog, choose Render.
6. In the Rendered Frame Window, choose Save and save the files as *Medieval_CameraMap,tga.*

   Now you have an image you can use to paint more detail and create a matte painting. Assume this step is done and use Camera Per Pixel to map it back onto the geometry.
7.  Press **M** to open the Material Editor.
8. Choose an empty sample slot.
9. Right-click in the active viewport, and choose Unhide by Name from the quad menu.
10. In the Unhide Objects dialog, choose Sky.

    You unhide the sky object because to project a texture there needs to be an object to project onto, if there is no object then artifacts occur.
11. In the Top viewport, select all objects in the scene.
12. In the Material Editor > bottom toolbar, choose Assign Material to Selection.
13. In the Blinn Basic Parameters rollout, choose the Map button next to Diffuse.

14. In the Material/Map Browser dialog, double-click Camera Map Per Pixel.

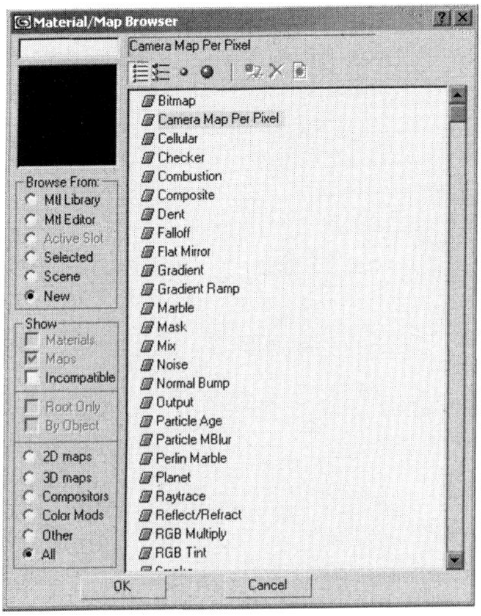

15. Choose SHIFT+C to unhide the cameras.

16. In the Camera Map Parameters rollout, choose the None button next to Camera.

17. Press **H** and then choose Camera_Promotional.

    This is the camera you used to render the image.

18. In the Camera Map Parameters rollout, choose the None button next to Texture.

19. In the Material/Map browser, double-click Bitmap and choose the rendered image.

20. In the Material Editor > bottom toolbar, choose Go to Parent.

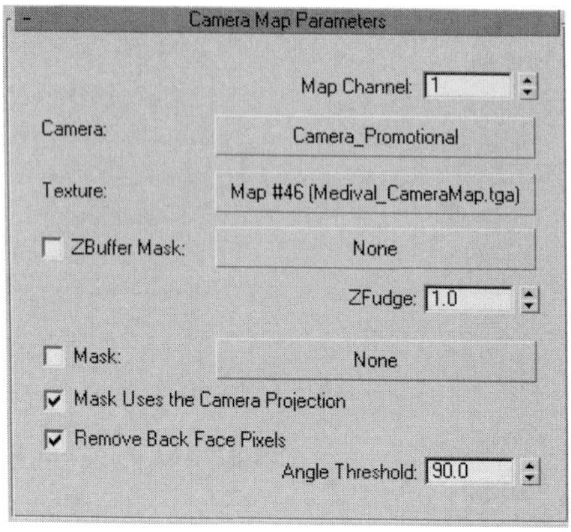

21. Choose Go to Parent again.

22. In the Blinn Basic Parameters rollout, set the Self-Illumination value to **100**.

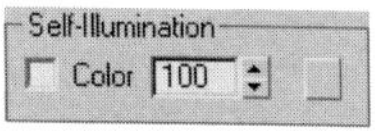

23.  Press F10 to open the Render Scene dialog.

24. In the Assign Renderer rollout, make sure the renderer is set to mental ray Renderer.

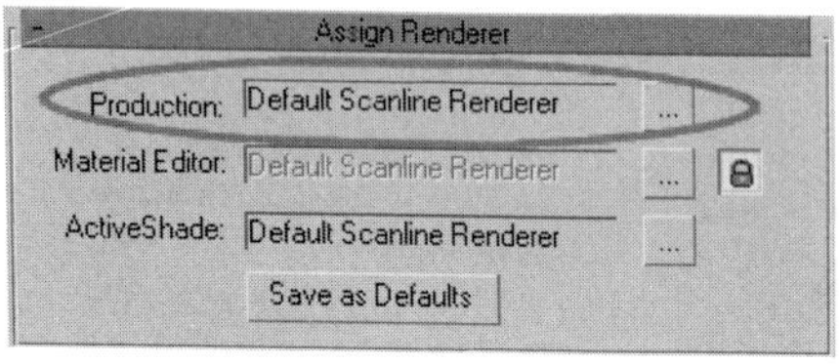

Note: Make sure the renderer you used to produce the image for the camera map is the same renderer you use at this stage. If you use another renderer, in the image below, Scanline, you might get artifacts due to the subtle differences in how each renderer calculates.

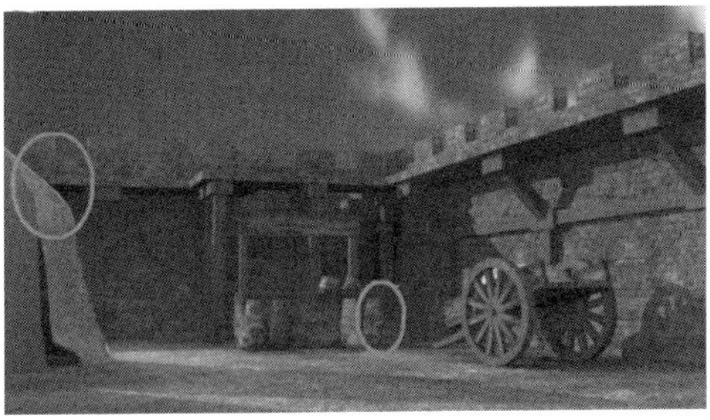

25. Turn off all lights in the scene.

    The Pendant Light doesn't affect the scene since it's the set you render.

26. Make sure the camera you rendered from and picked in the map type is active.

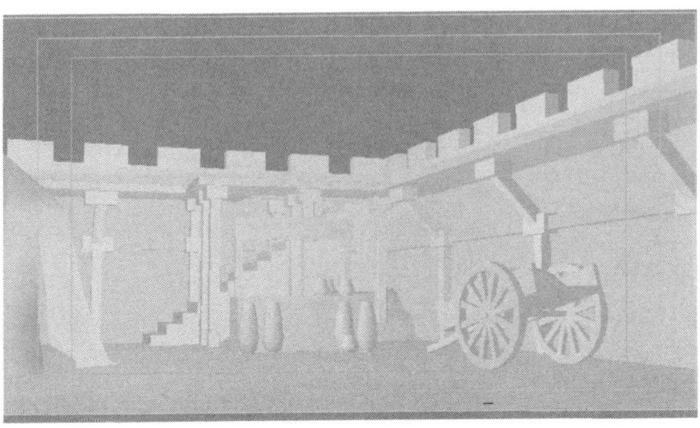

27. In the Render Scene dialog, choose Render.

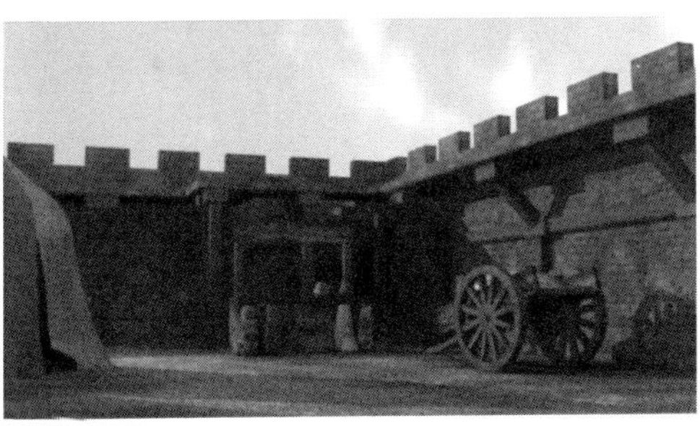

Conclusion

This chapter concentrates on the importance of organization and management for scene assembly. You worked with the mental ray renderer and shaders, and learned how to optimize the rendering process. You used Render to Texture with mental ray, and the Camera Map Per Pixel map type to further improve render times.

6 Rendering and Compositing

Objectives

After completing this chapter, you should be able to:

- Use the new Walk-Through mode to create and set up cameras interactively.
- Set up renders with multiple layers and multiple passes and elements.
- Have **3ds max** communicate with **combustion** and rebuild rendered elements into **combustion** workspaces.
- Use newly found powers to adjust/control your composite because of the many layers and elements.

Introduction

In this chapter, you continue preparing your scene for final render. You use a new feature in **3ds max 7** to navigate around your environment and experiment with camera angles until you are satisfied. To optimize render speeds, you use render elements and other render settings for full control.

You leave the familiar 3D environment and enter the world of 2D for compositing. You realize the importance of planning to split render passes that take advantage of the communication capability between **3ds max** and combustion. It provides complete control and incredible speed, thus completing the production tour.

Camera Setup

Before any rendering occurs, you need to create cameras. To create cameras, you need to break down the action in the scenes and decide on timing along with the total number of shots.

1. Open *MedivalNoCameras.max*.

   This scene is similar to the one from the previous chapter. There are slight changes discussed later in the chapter, but notice the two leftover cameras. The scene is ready to accept more cameras.

   A shot list that breaks the scene down in action blocks follows.

Shot 1 (fr. 001-043)	Character Establishing	Knight standing proud
Shot 2 (fr. 007-036)	Close-Up	Knight hears something
Shot 3 (fr. 030-101)	Environment Reveal	Reaction, runs & mounts horse
Shot 4 (fr. 100-165)	Action Cut-Away	Knight landing on horse, takes a backward glance
Shot 5 (fr. 130-400)	"Punch-line"	Knight gallops off to reveal a mere boy

   Note: You don't have to follow the shot list exactly, however it enables clear instruction later in the chapter.

   Now that the shot list is established, you create the camera angles using the camera interactive walk-through mode.

Knowing the Controls

Walk-through mode is an option available as part of the Pan flyout in the viewport navigation controls. It resembles a game cam and commonly is referred to as the Quake Cam, with one main difference; it does not support collision detection. Walk through is similar to ghost mode in Quake. This option gives you an interactive and immersed sense of your environment.

1. Before creating your camera angles, explore the location of options in the user interface to access all settings.
2. On the menu bar, choose Customize > Customize User Interface.
3. In the Customize User Interface dialog, make sure Keyboard is chosen.

4. In the Group drop-down list, choose Walk Through.

   You see the controls set for Walk Through. You can customize all default settings.

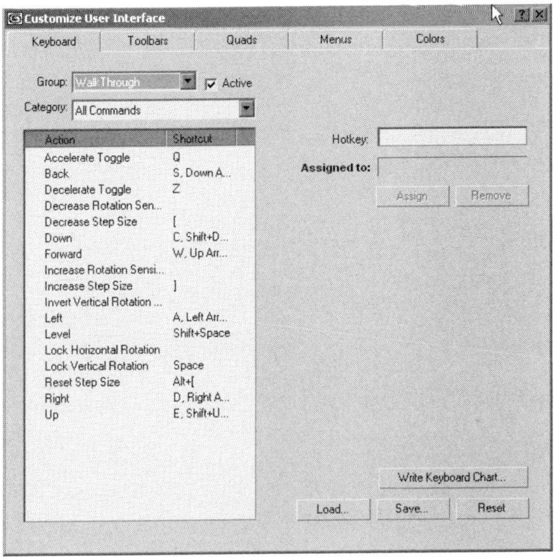

5. Close the Customize User Interface dialog.

   The following table organizes the default keyboard shortcut options.

Walk-Through mode – Position keyboard shortcut controls	
Forward	W, UP ARROW
Back	S, DOWN ARROW
Left	A, LEFT ARROW
Right	D, RIGHT ARROW
Up	E, SHIFT+UP ARROW
Down	C, SHIFT+DOWN ARROW
Increase Step Size	)
Decrease Step Size	(
Reset Step Size	ALT+(
Accelerate Toggle	Q
Decelerate Toggle	Z

Walk-Through mode – Aim keyboard shortcut controls	
Aim	RMB drag
Level	SHIFT+SPACEBAR
Lock Horizontal Rotation	
Lock Vertical Rotation Space	SPACEBAR
Invert Vertical Rotation Toggle	
Increase Rotation Sensitivity	
Decelerate Rotation Sensitivity	

Next, you use the default controls to create camera angles.

6. Right-click to activate the Camera_Promotional viewport.
7. Choose ALT+W to maximize the viewport.
8. Press **P** to set the viewport to Perspective.

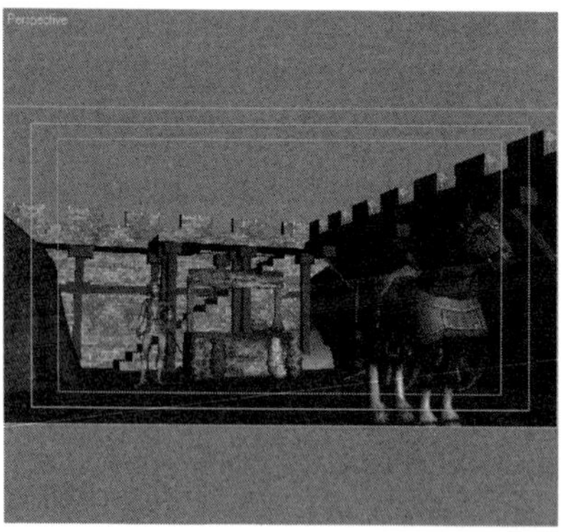

Note: In this case, you want to use Perspective to set a new camera angle. You can use Walk-Through mode in a Camera viewport if you want to change its position.

9.  In the viewport navigation controls, hold down Pan and then choose Walk Through.

You are now in Walk-Through mode. Next, you test the sensitivity and make any necessary adjustments.

10. In the Perspective viewport, click and drag to take a look around.

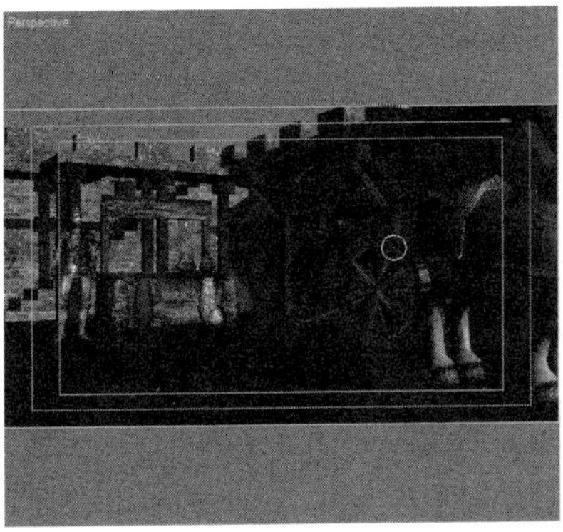

11. Press **W** while you click and drag to move forward.

    Tip: If you are moving slowly, press **Q** to accelerate. If it is still too slow, press] continuously to increase the step size.

12. Press **E** and **C** to move up and down respectively.

    Tip: Press SHIFT+SPACEBAR to reset your aim and be level with your position.

    Before you continue, make sure you are familiar with the controls.

Setting Up Cameras Using WTM

Next, you create cameras.

1. Continue from the previous exercise.
2. Press **C** and then choose Camera_Promotional.
3. Press **P** to change to the Perspective view.
4. Turn on Walk Through.

5. Move around your scene until you have a camera angle similar to the following image for Shot 1.

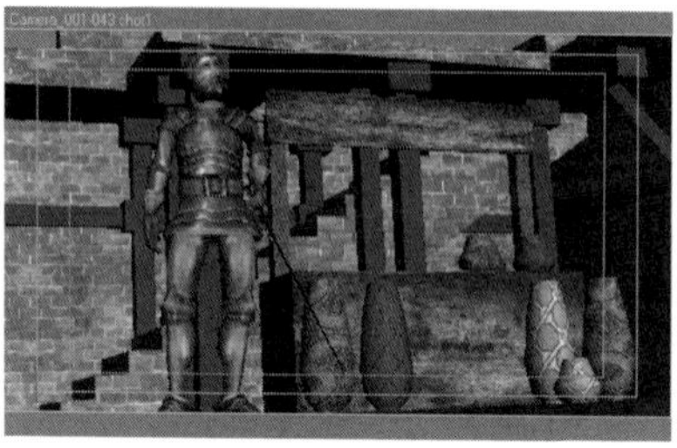

Tip: Shot 1 is an establishing shot of the knight. You want the knight to be the proud, brave hero.

6. Press CTRL+C to create and activate the new camera.
7. In the Name and Color rollout, type **Camera_Shot1_001-043**.

Tip: Giving your camera a name that contains the frame numbers improves workflow and eliminates potential for confusion.

8. Use the camera navigation controls to adjust FOV, Dolly, and Camera Roll.
9. Follow the following images and text to create the remaining cameras based on the shot list.

Reminder: Change the active Camera viewport into a Perspective viewport before using Walk Through. This prevents you from affecting the current Camera angle.

Various camera angles and times are displayed in the following images. Shots 2 and 5 have animated cameras. Use Walk Through to create the intial position and then animate the camera using transforms.

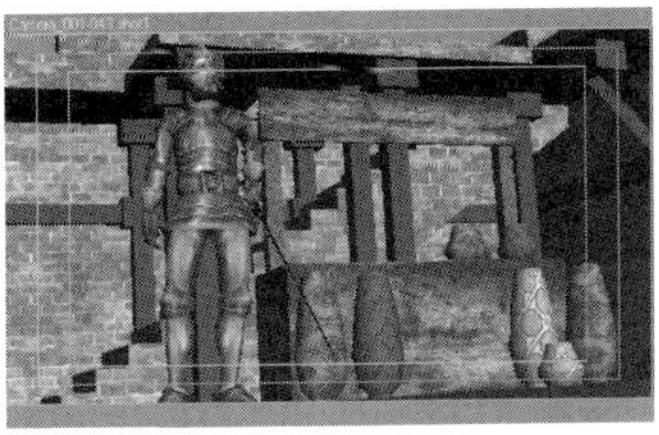

Shot 1 frames 001-043

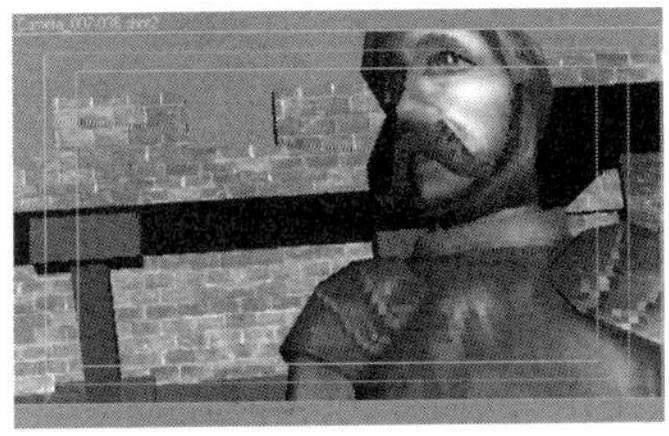

Shot 2 frames 007-036

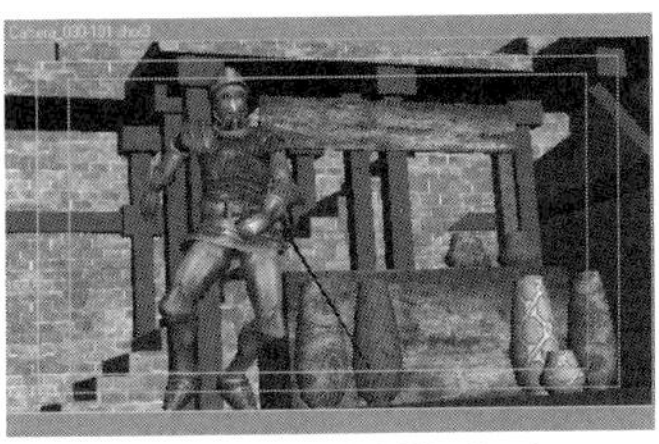

Shot 3 frames 030-101 start

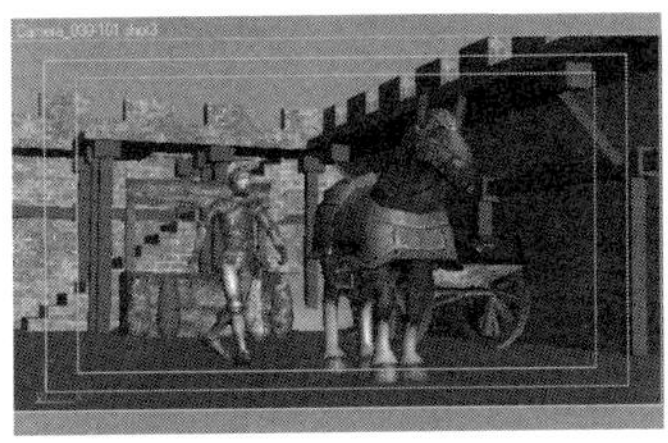

Shot 3 frames 030-101 end

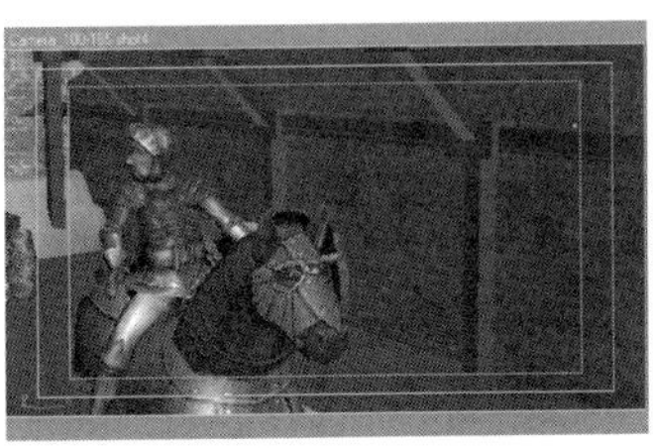

Shot 4 frames 100-165

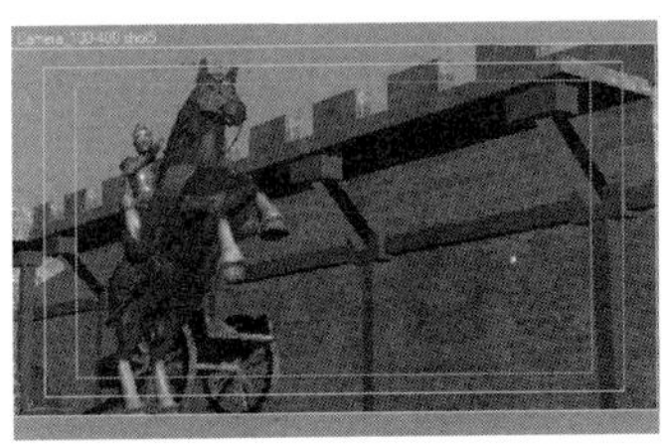

Shot 5 frames 130-400 start

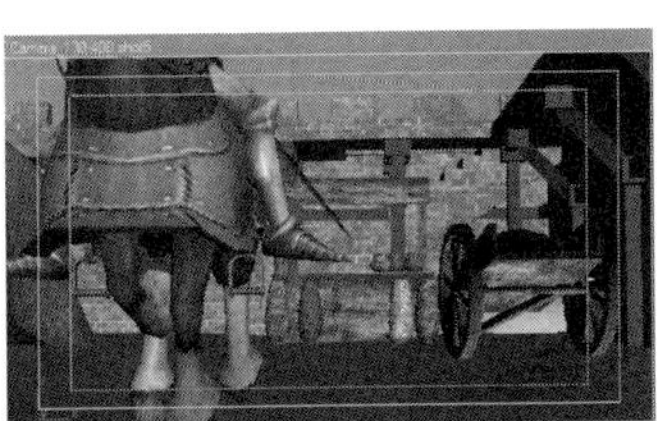

Shot 5 frames 130-400 middle

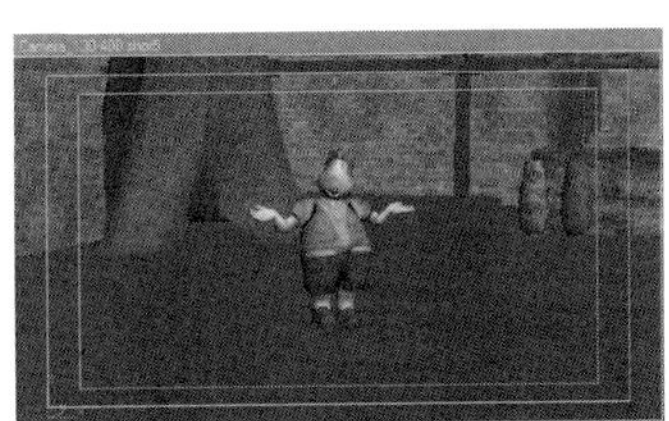

Shot 5 frames 130-400 end

Tip: Boris Petrov, aka Bobo, created a script named *RecordNavigationPath_05.ms*. It generates an animated camera based on the movement you make using Walk-Through mode. So you can actually use it to record your movements and create an animated camera to match them. It can be a great way to create an architectural walkthrough or a simulated steady-cam shot.

10. Open *MedivalFinalCameras.max* to view the final camera setup.

Rendering the Sequence

Now that the cameras are complete, you render the sequence. You decide to render the background and characters separately. Continue with the following procedures to organize each sequence.

Splitting Up the Scene

The scene is split in two: background (or the set) and characters. You render each of these components with multiple render passes.

1. Continue from the previous exercise or open *MedivalFinalCameras.max*.
2.  On the main toolbar, choose Layer Manager.
3. In the Layer Manager dialog, hide all layers except for the layer named Set and layer 0.

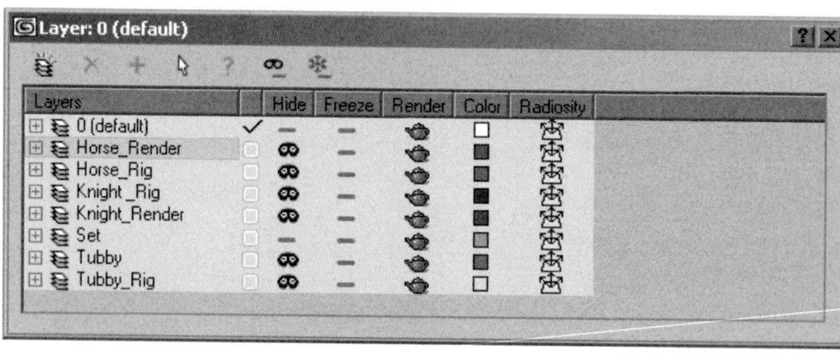

4. On the menu bar, choose File > Save As.
5. In the Save As dialog, type **Medival_Environment.max**.

   This file is the base for the various render passes for the environment. Next, you create a base file for the character layer. To do so, you first create a Matte Shadow material for the environment.

6. Close the Layer Manager dialog.
7. 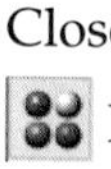 Press M to open the Material Editor.
8. In the Material Editor, choose an empty sample slot.
9. Rename the Material MATTE.
10. Choose the Standard Material Type button.

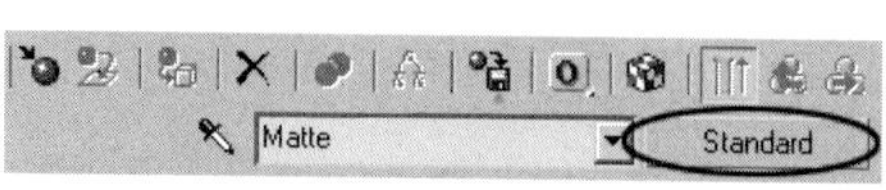

11. In the Material/Map Browser dialog, double-click Matte Shadow.
12. Leave the default settings as is.

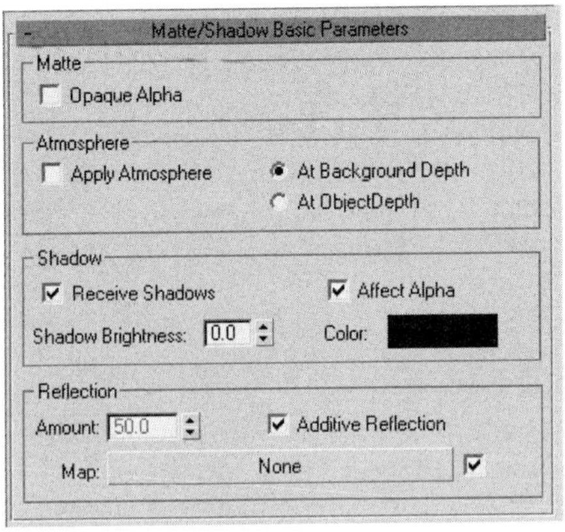

13. Drag and drop this Material into an empty sample slot.
14. Rename this new copy **MATTE_noShadows**.
15. In the Matte/Shadow Basic Parameters rollout > Shadow group, turn off Receive Shadows.

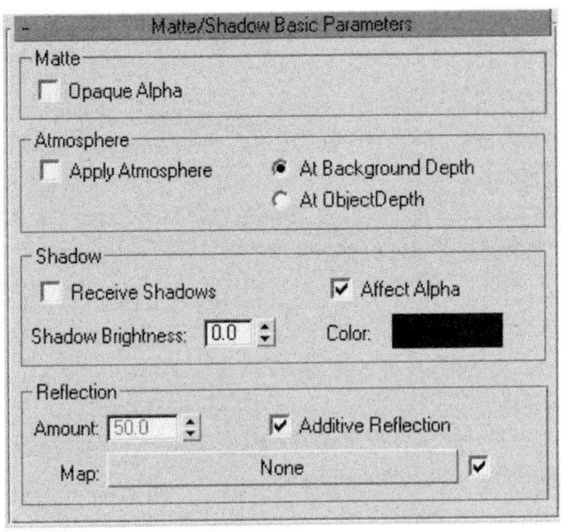

The Matte materials for the environment are created. The materials allow the environment to both block light and receive shadows, but not render shadows. Next, you assign the materials to the set.

16. Activate the Top viewport.
17. In the Top viewport, region select all objects in the scene.
18. Hold down ALT and then select the Ground to deselect it.

19. In the Material Editor, make sure MATTE_noShadows is active.
20. In the Material Editor > bottom toolbar, choose Assign Material to Selection.
21. Right-click and then choose Properties from the quad menu.
22. In the Object Properties dialog > Rendering Control group, turn off Receive Shadows.

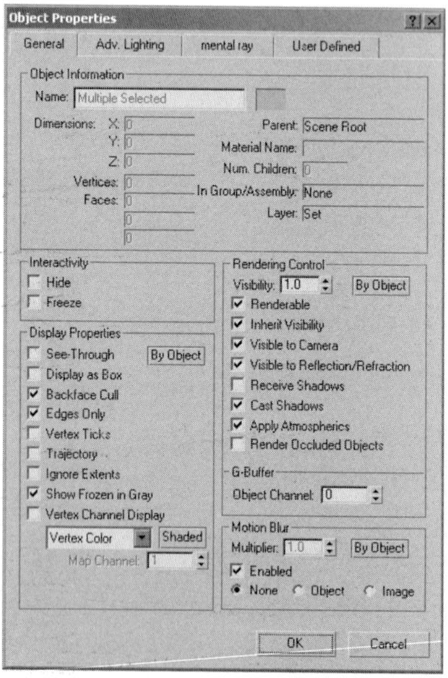

23. In the Top viewport, choose Ground.
24. In the Material Editor, choose Matte.
25. On the bottom toolbar, choose Assign Material to Selection.

    The set now has the matte materials assigned. The final adjustment you make is to the light source. You adjust the light because it is too bright for the character pass. This is an adjustment you would acknowledge during test renders, however adjusting it now saves time.

26. On the command panels, choose Display.
27. On the Display panel > Hide by Category rollout, turn off Lights.
28. Press **H** and then choose mr Area Spot02.

29. On the Modify panel > Intensity/color/attenuation rollout, change the Multiplier to **0.35** and set the Decay Start to **1000**.

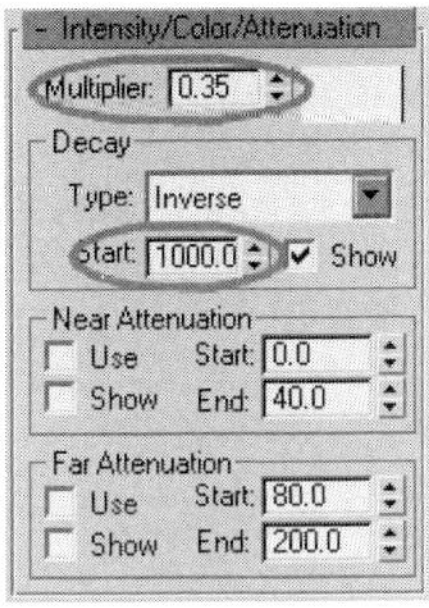

30.  On the menu bar, choose Layer Manager.

31. In the Layer Manager dialog, unhide the Knight_Render and Horse_Render layers.

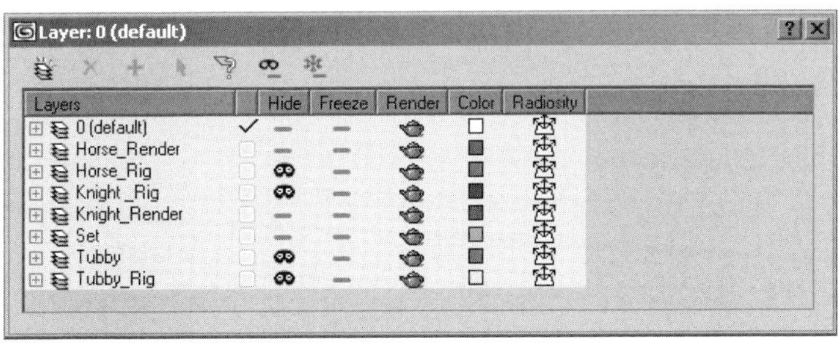

32. On the menu bar, choose File > Save As and save the file as **Medival_Characters.max**.

    Your two source files are created and now it's time to set up the render specifics for each render pass.

Rendering the Background

You begin by rendering the environment because it's less complicated to set up and faster to render. You render two passes: Diffuse and Lighting/Shadows. These two passes are composited to form a complete image of the background. You have control over both individual layers in **combustion**.

Note: All images are supplied on the courseware CD so you don't have to render each frame.

Assigning a Diffuse Layer

1. Continue from the previous file or open *Medival_Environment.max*
2. Resave this file into a directory separate from the courseware files as **Medival_Environment_diff.max**.

   This file represents the Diffuse pass.

   Note: Resave the file immediately to prevent an accidental file overwrite.
3.  On the main toolbar, choose Render Scene.
4. In the Common tab, open the Assign Renderer rollout.
5. In the Assign Renderer rollout, set the Renderer to Scanline.

   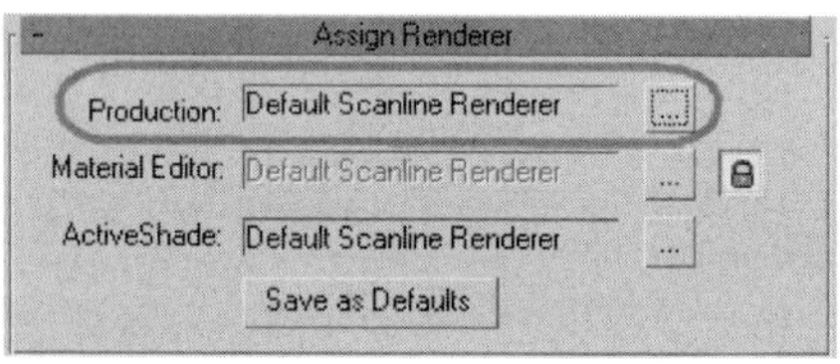

   Note: You use Scanline for two reasons: to show you can mix renderers and so you can use mental ray for the lighting pass because it's fast.
6. In the Render Scene dialog, choose Render Elements.
7. In the Render Elements rollout, make sure Elements Active is turned on.

   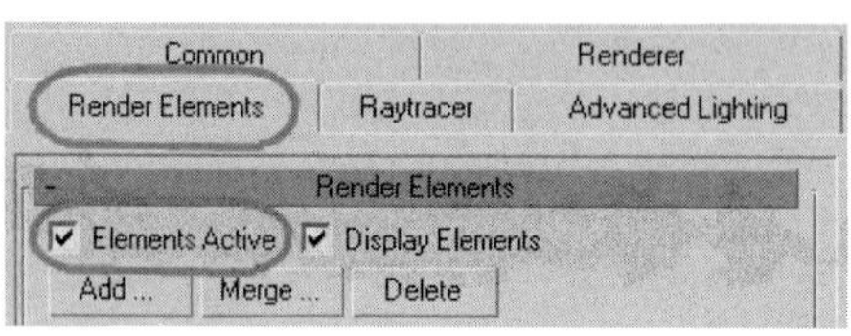

8. 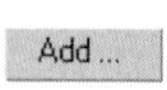

   Choose Add.

9. In the Render Elements dialog, choose Diffuse and then click OK.

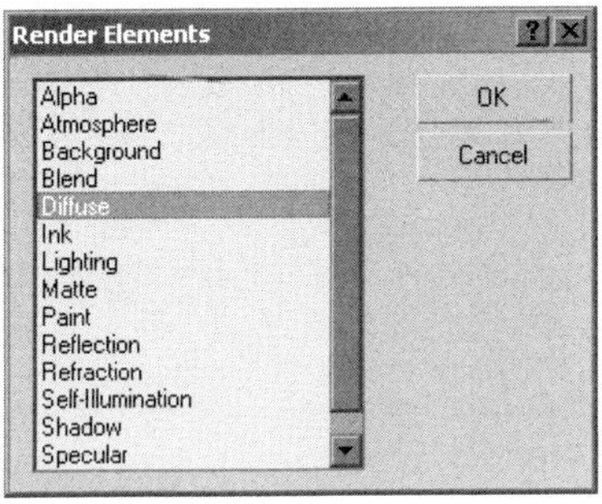

10. In the Selected Element Parameters group, make sure both Enable and Enable Filtering are on.

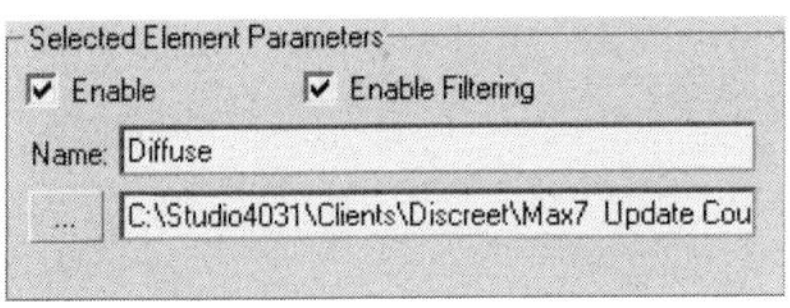

11. In the Render Element Output File dialog, choose a sensible output and file name.

    Note: For the file name, use a format like this: Shot number, followed by the current layer, followed by the pass. Use an underscore to separate each segment. If you were rendering shot 1, the file name would look like this:

    Shot_1_BG_diff_.png, where

    Shot_1 = Shot number
    BG = The rendered layer (background)
    Diff = The rendered pass (diffuse)
    _ = The last underscore, used to separate the frame numbers, is added when rendering
    .png = The file format

12. In the Diffuse Texture Element rollout, make sure the Lighting check box is on.

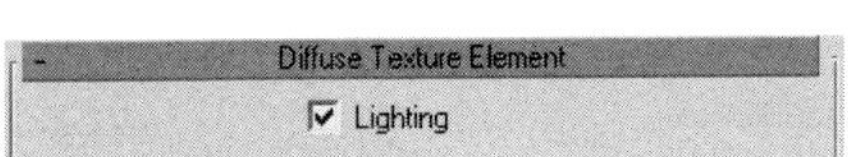

13. Save your MAX file.

Setting the Time

The scene's environmental/background diffuse pass is ready to render. Next, you set up common parameters appropriate for the five individual cameras.

1. Continue from the previous exercise.
2. In the Render Scene dialog > Common tab > Common Parameters rollout > Time Output group, choose Range.
3. Set the range to match the currently active camera range (the camera you wish to render).

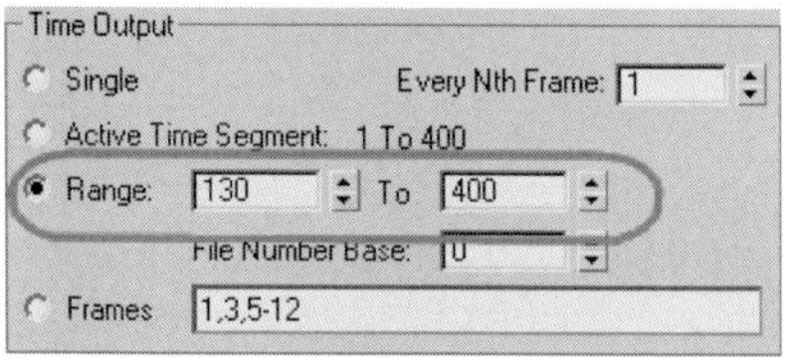

Tip: When you render background layers, if the camera is stationary, then render one frame only and add more frames in the composite. Slight motion can be added in the composite.

4. In the Output Size group, choose HDTV (video) from the drop-down list.
5. Set the Width to **500** and the Height to **281**.

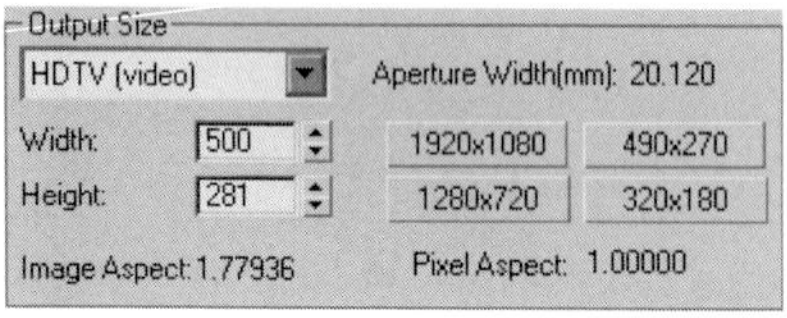

6. In the Render Scene dialog, choose Render.

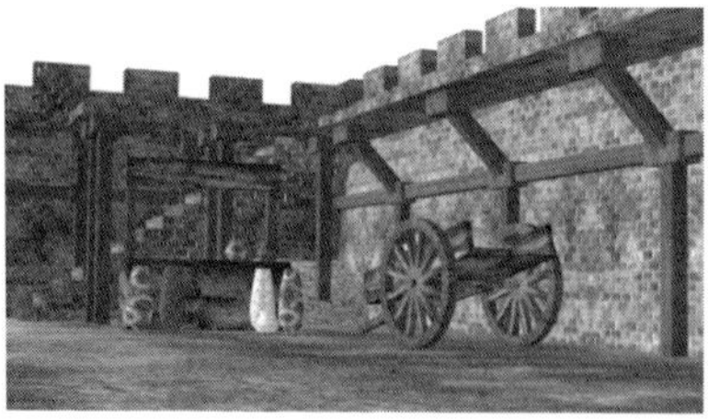

Rendering the GI/Shadow Pass

1. Open *Medival_Environment.max*.
2. On the menu bar, choose File > Save As and resave the file to **Medival_Environment_GI.max**.

   The _GI represents the Global Illumination pass.
3.  On the main toolbar, choose Render Scene.
4. In the Assign Renderer rollout, notice the mental ray renderer is chosen.

   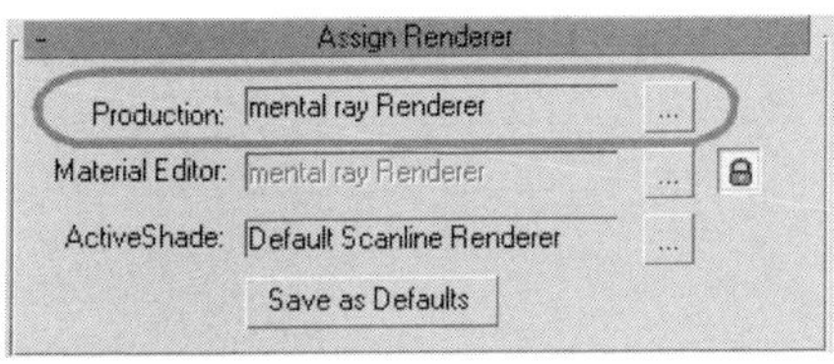

   Note: You use mental ray for its Displacement and Global Illumination options.
5. In the Render Scene dialog, choose the Renderer tab.
6. In the Sampling Quality rollout > Sample per Pixel group, change the Maximum number to **16**.

   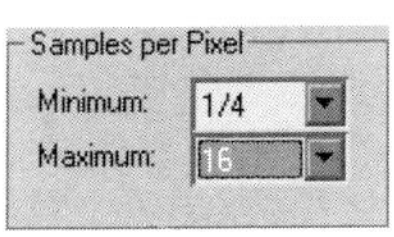

   If neighboring samples find a difference in contrast that exceeds the contrast limit, the area containing the contrast is subdivided to the depth specified by Maximum.
7. In the Shadows & Displacement rollout > Displacement group, turn on View.

   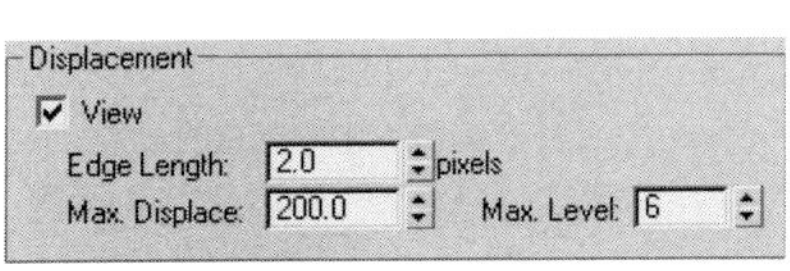

   Note: Depending on the camera you use and where it is placed, you might want displacement enabled. If the camera is either sitting on the ground or underground, then turn off this option because the rendering takes too long to calculate due to the camera's proximity.

8. In the Render Scene dialog, choose Indirect Illumination.
9. Use the following image to make sure all the settings are the same.

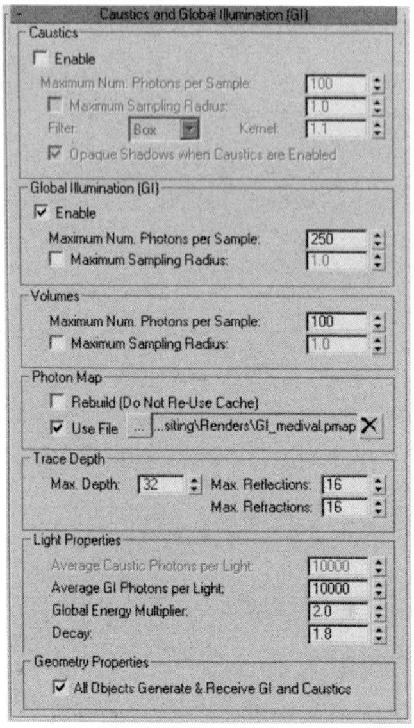

10. In the Photon Map group, turn on Use File and then choose an Output Path and Filename.

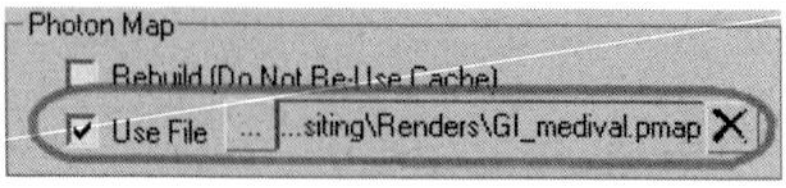

Tip: You turn on this option because although the camera is moving, the geometry is not relative to the lights. In other words, the light calculations are the same from frame to frame. Instead of recalculating the same thing over and over, you calculate it once and reuse the information.

11. In the Indirect Illumination tab > Final Gather rollout, make sure the settings match the following image.

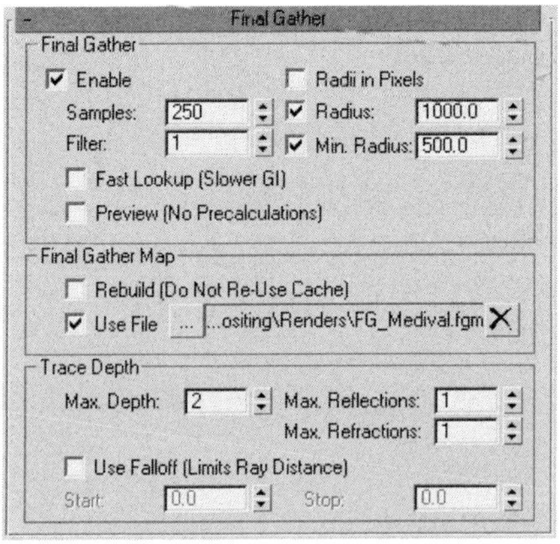

12. In the Final Gather Map group, turn on Use File and then choose an Output Path and Filename.

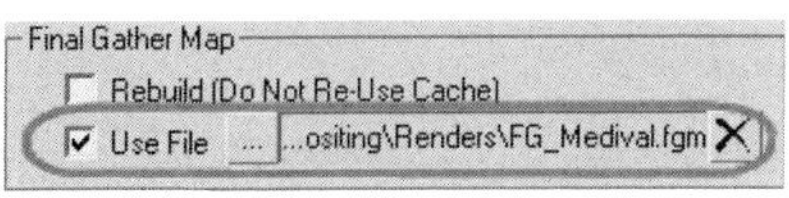

13. In the Render Scene dialog > Processing tab > Material Override group, turn off Enable.

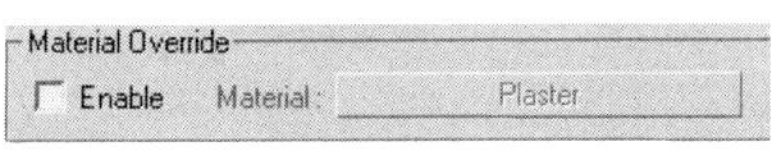

14. In the Memory Options group, turn on Conserve Memory.

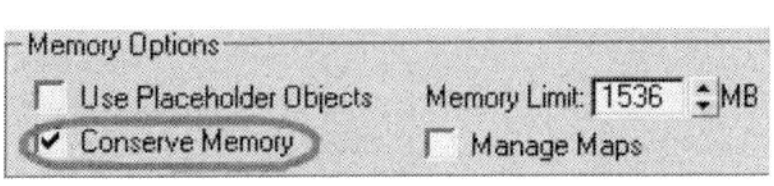

The rest of the Render Scene dialog settings are again limited to the Common tab and are adjusted based on the camera, just like in the previous diffuse pass setups.

Note: At this point, choose Render Elements and add Lighting and Shadows just as you added Diffuse.

There is one last setup for the GI pass. If you render, the Diffuse maps and textures are active. You want the environment to render at a 50 percent gray material with lighting, shadow, and displacement information, not textues. In previous chapters, you created a Plaster material. You load it and confirm it has a Photon Base shader assigned.

15.  Press **M** to open the Material Editor.
16. Choose an empty sample slot.
17. In the Material Editor > bottom toolbar, choose Get Material.
18. In the Material/Map browser dialog > Browse From group, choose Scene and then double-click Plaster.

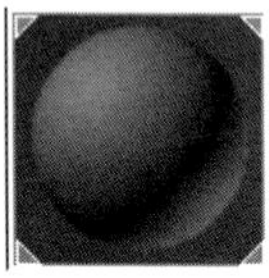

19. In the Material Editor dialog, open the mental ray Connection rollout.
20. In the Caustics and GI group, notice the Photon Basic shader is assigned.
21. In the Top viewport, choose Ground.
22. In the Material Editor, choose an empty sample slot.
23. In the Material Editor > bottom toolbar, choose Get Material.
24. In the Material/Map Browser dialog > Browse From group, choose Scene and then double-click Ground.

Note: You need this to create the Ground's GI texture pass.

25. In the Material Editor, drag and drop the Plaster material onto an empty sample slot.
26. Rename the material PlasterGround.
27. In the mental ray Connection rollout > Extended Shaders group, unlock the Displacement map.

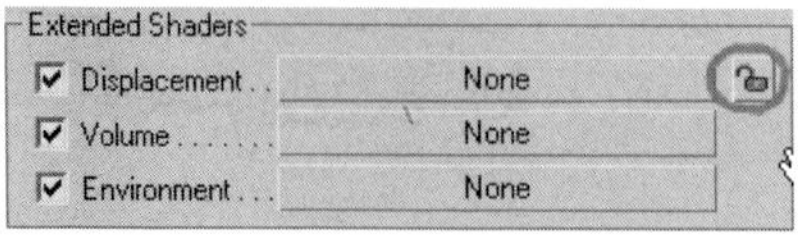

28. Choose None next to Displacement.
29. In the Material/Map Browser dialog > Browse From group, choose Selected.
30. Double-click Displacement Map for the Ground object and then choose Instance.

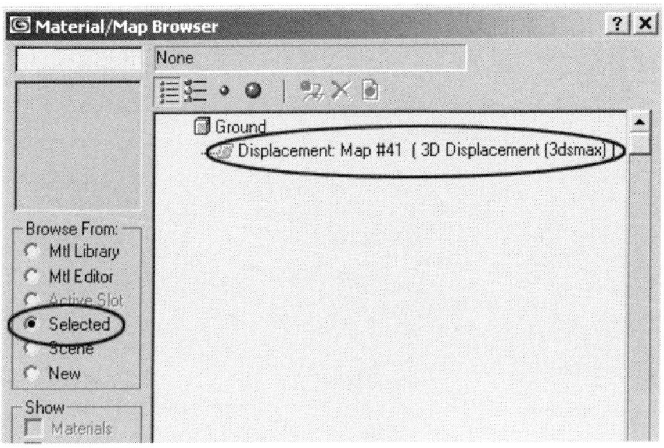

Assigning the Materials

1. Continue from the previous exercise.
2. In the Material Editor, choose PlasterGround.
3. In the Material Editor > bottom toolbar, choose Assign Material to Selection.
4. On the menu bar, choose Edit > Select Invert so everything except the Ground is selected.
5. In the Material Editor, choose Plaster.
6. In the Material Editor > bottom toolbar, choose Assign Material to Selection.
7. In the Top viewport, choose Ground.
8. Save your file.

   Again, many of the notes regarding camera specific settings and the single frame trick are the same as previously described for the background's diffuse pass.

9. Right-click in the Camera view. Type C and then choose Camera_Promotional.

10. In the Render Scene dialog, choose Render.

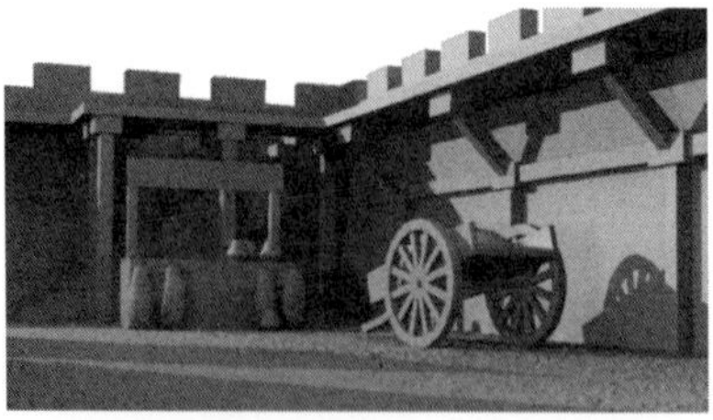

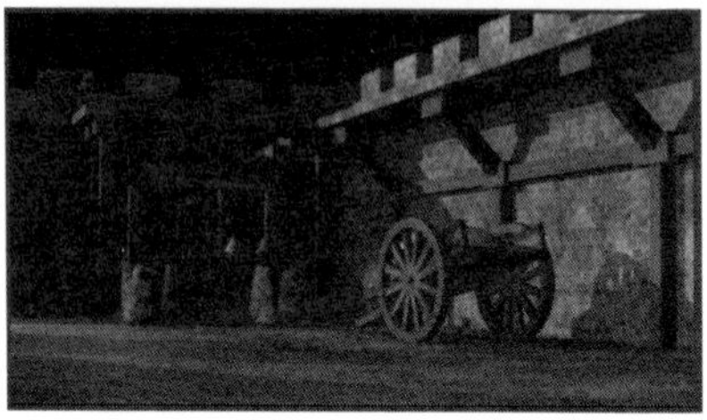

Here is what the two composited passes look like. The GI pass is used with an overlay filter.

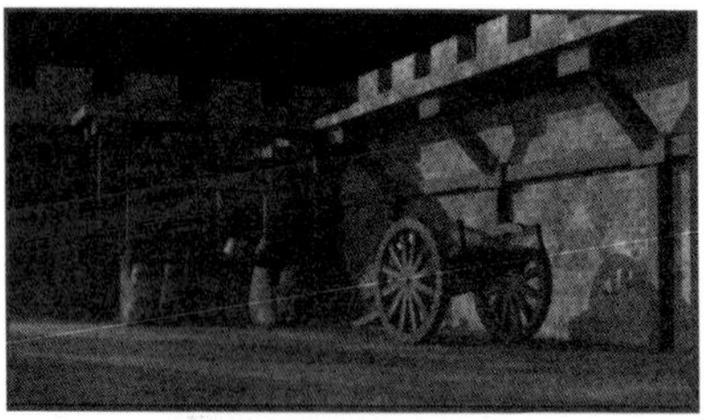

Rendering the Character in Elements

Next, you organize the characters. You create more layers, however they are easier and faster to set up.

1. Open *Medival_Characters.max*.

   Most of the preparation is done from the last exercise. This file uses the mental ray renderer.

2.  Press F10 to open the Render Scene dialog.

3. In the Render Scene dialog > Common tab > Common Parameters rollout, set the Range as **1 – 43**.

4. In the Output Size group, choose HDTV (video) from the drop-down list. Set the Width to **500** and the Height to **281**.

Note: Remember these settings are dependent on your camera.

5. In the Render Output group, save the file as **Shot_1_Knight.png**.

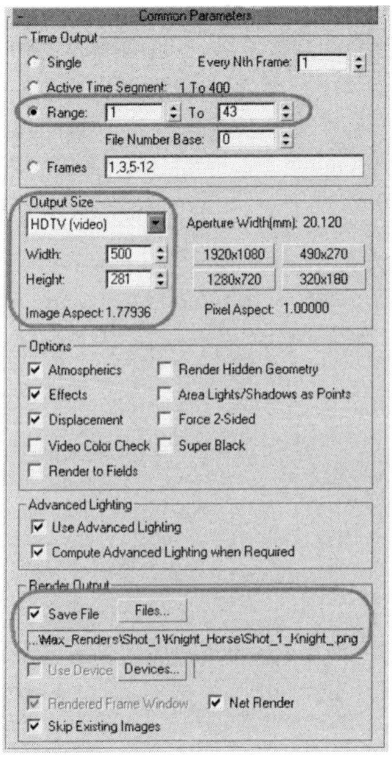

Note: When you use Render Elements later in the chapter, the files automatically use the path and saved file name as a base.

6. In the Render Scene dialog > Renderer tab > Sample Quality rollout Samples per Pixel group, set Maximum to **16**.

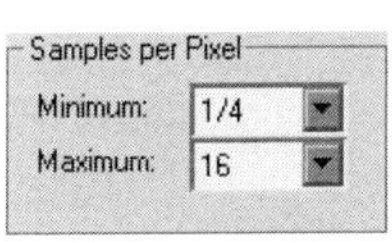

7. In the Shadows & Displacement rollout > Displacement group, turn off View.

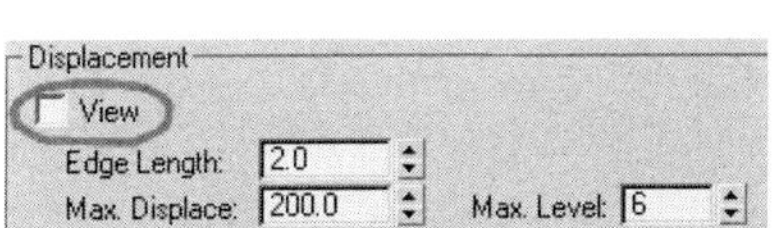

8. In the Render Scene dialog > Indirect Illumination tab, compare your settings with the following image.

9. Make sure Photon Map is turned on and then choose a Filename and Output Path.

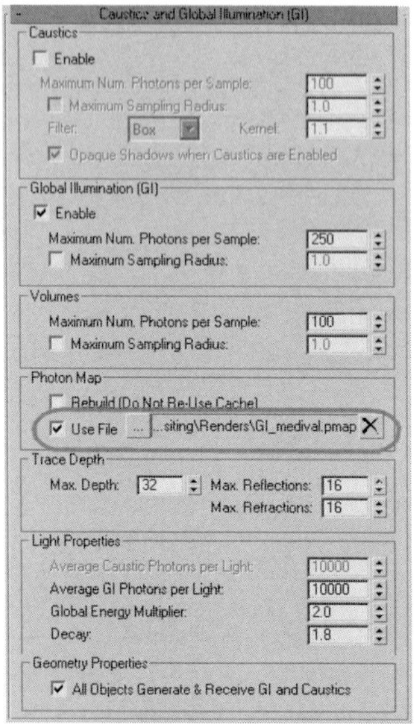

Note: You use the same technique for storing the photon maps as you did in the environment pass to save time. However, you recalculate the Final Gather map because the characters are moving through the scene.

10. In the Final Gather rollout, Final Gather Map group, make sure Rebuild Final Gather Map is on.

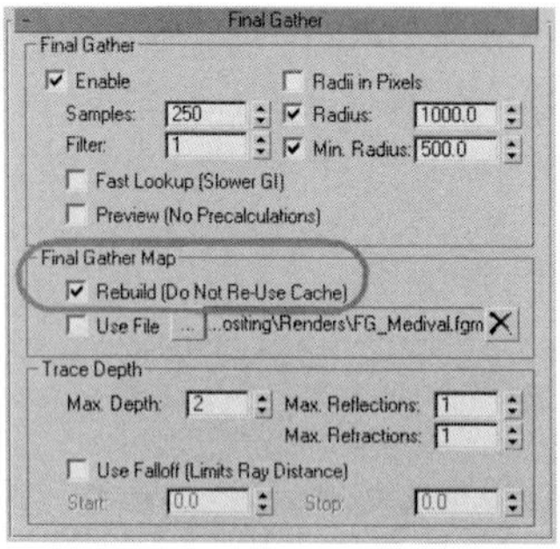

11. In the Processing tab > Material Override group, turn off Material Override.

12. In the Render Scene dialog, choose Render Elements.

    This is the most important location for rendering the characters.

13. In the Render Elements rollout, make sure Elements Active is on.

    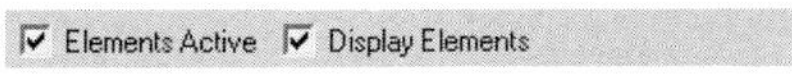

    The following elements are already chosen: Diffuse, Specular, Shadow, Alpha and Z Depth. If not, continue with the following steps.

14. 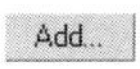

    Choose Add.

15. In the Render Elements dialog, choose:
    Diffuse
    Specular
    Shadow
    Alpha
    Z Depth

    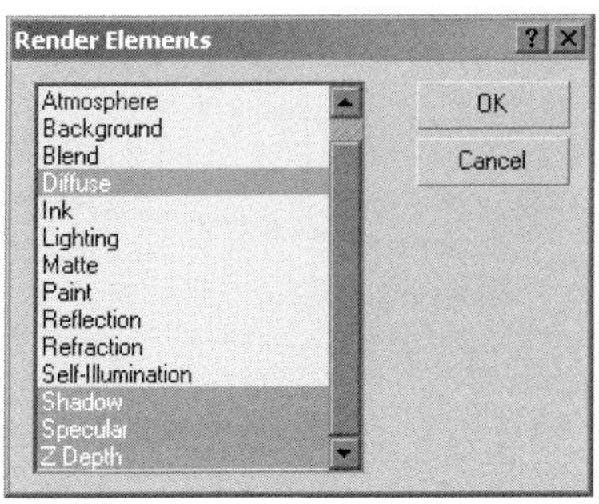

    Note: Most of the Layers, except for Z Depth, might be subtle. You choose Z Depth to create depth effects such as Depth of Field and Fog. Ultimately, you want to give the compositor as much control as possible.

16. Make sure all elements have both Enable and Enable Filtering check boxes turned on.

    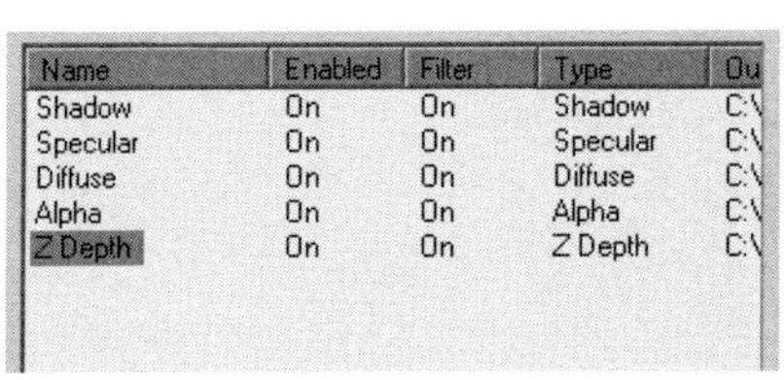

17. In the Output to **combustion** group, turn on Enable and then choose a Filename and Output Path.

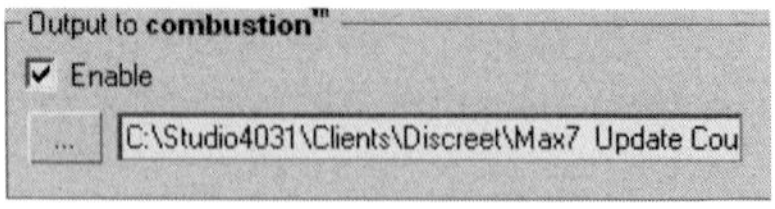

Tip: This option creates a **combustion** CWS file.

18. Select the Diffuse element.

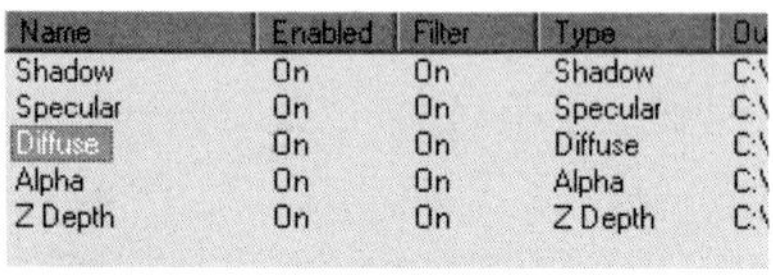

19. In the Diffuse Texture Element rollout, make sure Lighting is on.

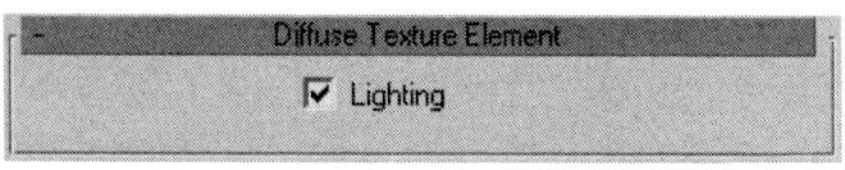

20. Select the Z Depth element.

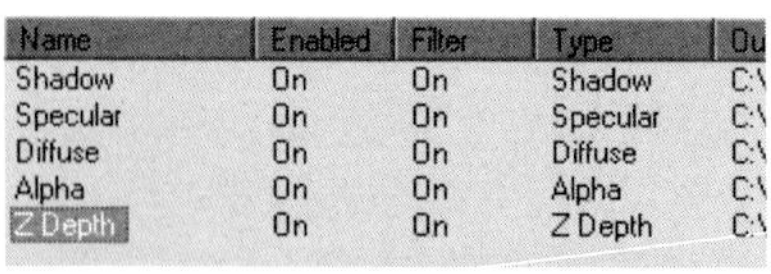

Note: In the Z Element Parameters, there are Z Min and Z Max settings. These values need to change based on the camera you render from. You derive these values by using Expose Transform node.

21. In the Top viewport, make sure the Cameras are visible.

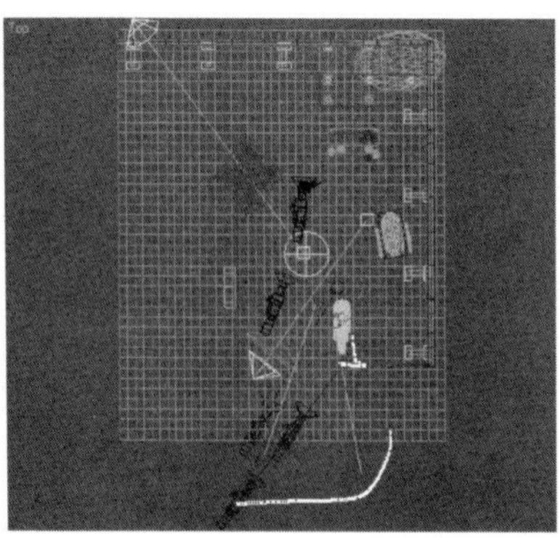

22. Press ALT+W to maximize the Top viewport.
23. 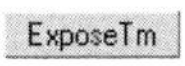

On the command panels, choose Create > Helpers.
24. In the Object Type rollout, choose ExposeTM.
25. Click anywhere in the Top viewport.
26. On the command panels, choose Modify.
27. In the Parameters rollout > Objects group, choose None under Expose Node.
28. Press **H** and then choose Camera_001-043.

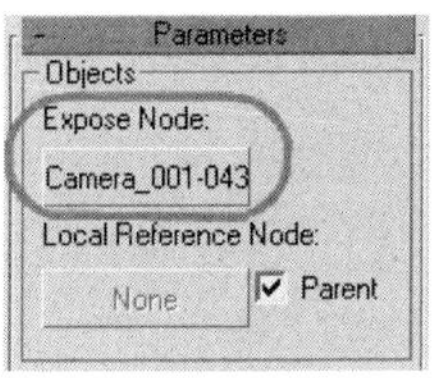

29. Turn off Parent.
30. Choose None under Local Reference Node.
31. Press **H** and then choose Knight_GEO_BodyHighRes.

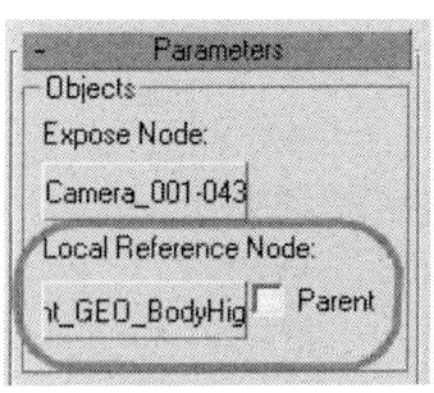

32. In the Exposed Values group > Distance To Reference group, the value logs the distance between the camera and the character. Write this value down.

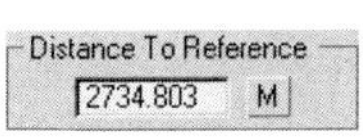

33. In the Parameters rollout, choose the button below Local Reference Node.

34. Press **H** and then choose the Stairs.

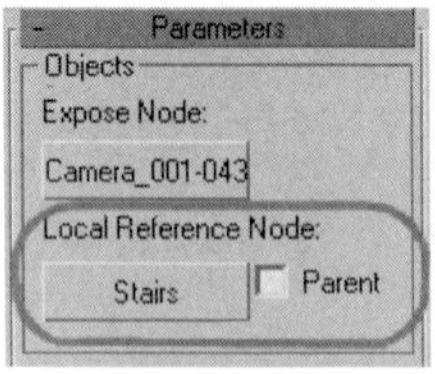

35. In the Exposed Values rollout > Distance To Reference group, make a note of the number.

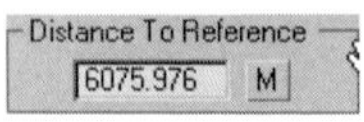

These values are the basis for setting the Z Depth Min. and Max.

36. In the Render Scene dialog > Render Elements tab, choose Z Depth.

37. In the Z Element Parameters rollout, enter the values you wrote down for the Z Min. and Z Max.

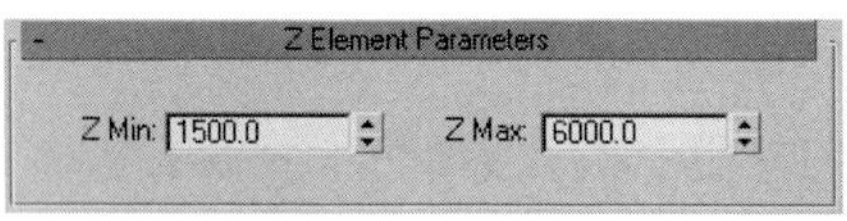

The Min. value should be slightly less than the distance between the camera and the knight. The Max. value should be slightly more than the distance between the camera and the stairs.

Tip: You can modify these numbers since they are guidelines only. For instance, if you want finer detail in the Z Depth pass, particularly on the character, bring the values closer together. The best advice is to remember to do a couple render tests on still frames.

38. Save your MAX file.

You might want to save a file for each camera setup.

Here's how the rendered element looks.

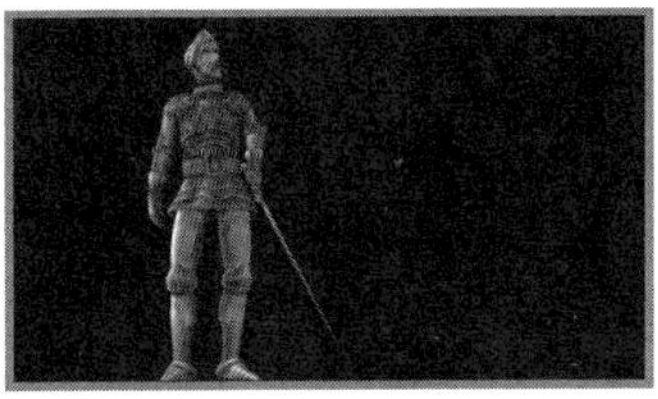

Shot 1 Diffuse Pass

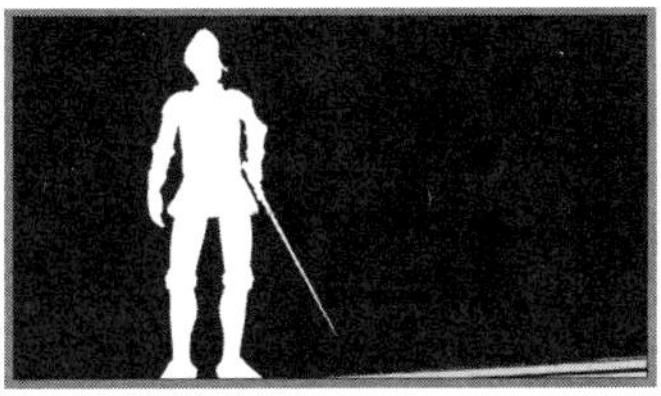

Shot 1 Alpha Pass

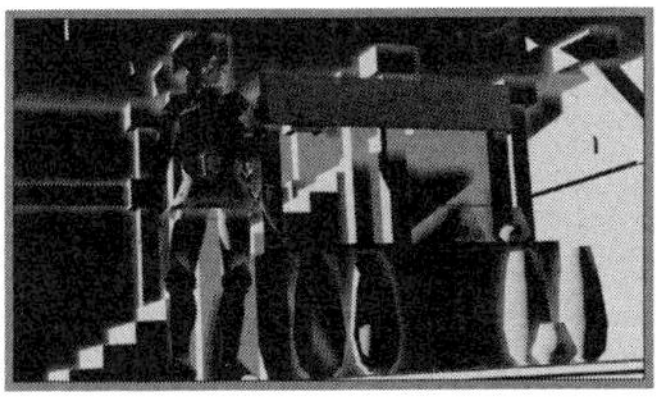

Shot 1 Shadow Pass (alpha)

Shot 1 Specular

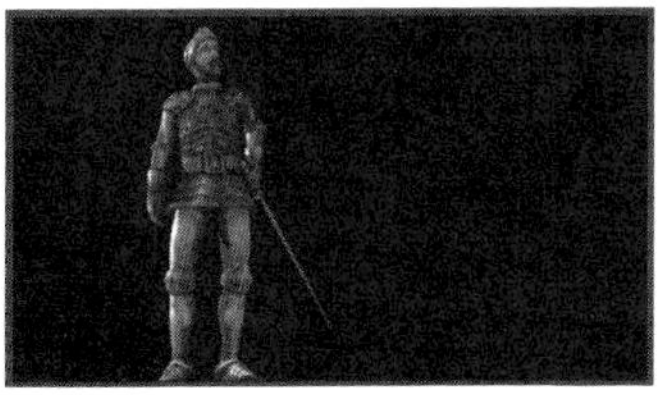

Shot 1 Comp Assembled

The render sequences are supplied so you don't need to wait for renderings.

Compositing and the Power of Layers

Next, you use Discreet compositing software called **combustion**. The methods and theory you learn in this chapter are transferable to other 2D compositing tools.

Combustion-3ds Max Connection

1. Open **combustion 3**.
2. On the menu bar, choose File > Open Workspace.
3. In the Open Workspace dialog, double-click *Shot_1_Knight.cws*.

   Make sure the PNG files for each element are mapped to a directory so **combustion** can read the files when it opens the CWS file. You might have to redirect **combustion** to that specific directory location when this file opens.

4. Choose Viewport Layer List, and then choose Dual.

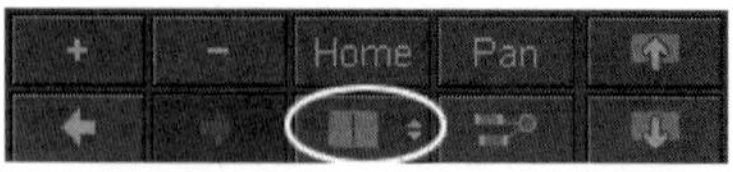

5. Click the Left viewport and then choose F12.

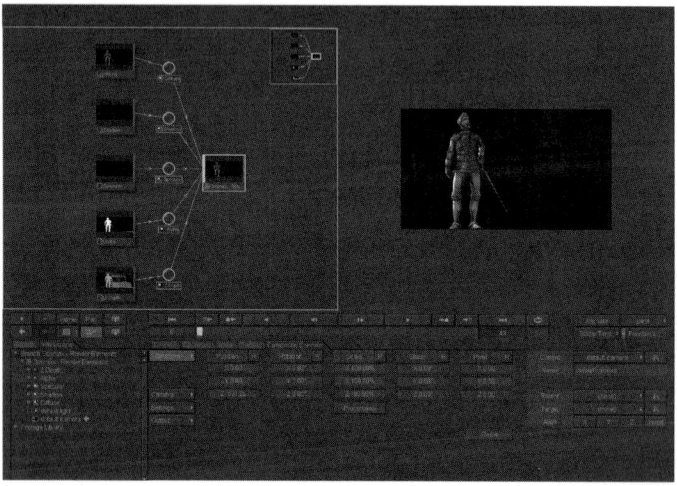

Schemative view is active. This is a graphical representation of the composite flow.

The composite is set because you rendered with Render Elements and saved a CWS file in **3ds max**. This means the **combustion** workspace is assembled with all render elements properly arranged. You look at that next.

6. In the Workspace tab, choose Specular.

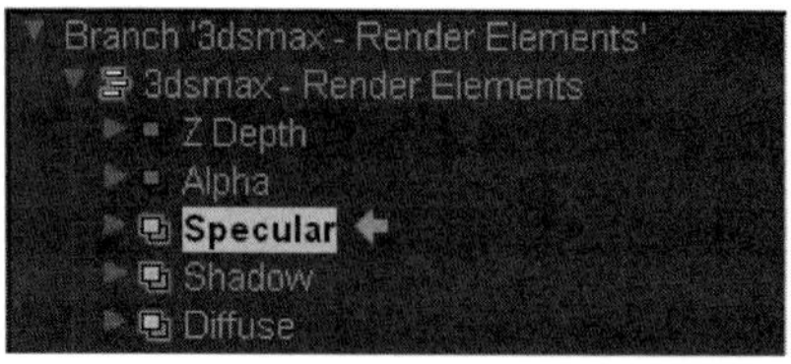

7. In the Composite Controls tab, choose Surface.

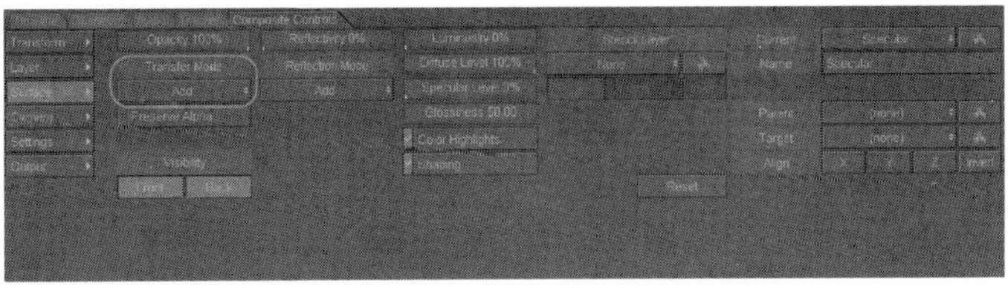

Note: The Specular layer's Transfer mode is set to Add. You can also use Screen.

8. In the Workspace panel, choose Shadow.

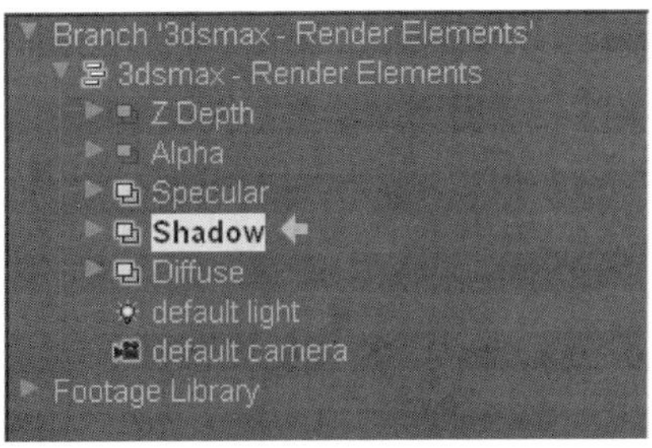

9. In the Composite Controls, choose Surface.

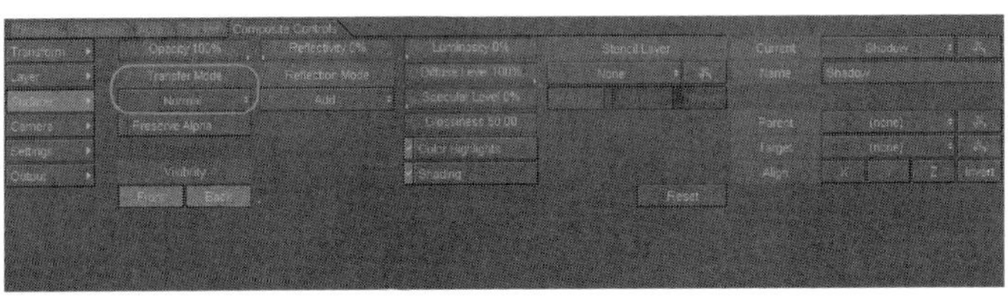

Note: The Shadow Layer's Transfer mode is set to Normal. Since it has an Alpha channel, it correctly composites over the Diffuse channel. You can also use Multiply.

10. In the Workspace tab, choose either the Z Depth or the Alpha Layer.

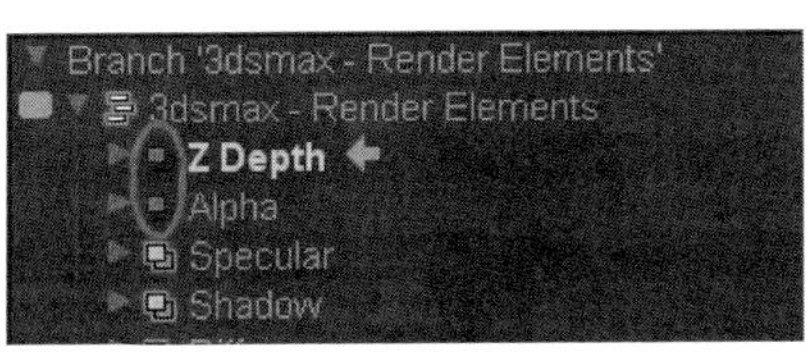

Note: Both of these layers are turned off for the display of the composite. Both **3ds max** and **combustion** know these layers are used as control layers.

Clearly, you see the communication between these programs. Next, you identify the importance of rendering separate layers rather than rendering a single pass.

Understanding the Power of Layers

While you use the composite from the previous exercise, it is not part of the final composite. You work on a fast and simple example to help you understand the power of rendering with layers in **3ds max**.

1. Continue from the previous exercise.
2. On the menu bar, choose File > Save Workspace As, and then type a unique name so you can get back to your file.
3. In the Workspace tab, choose Shadow.
4. In the Composite Controls > Surface, change Opacity to **50%**.

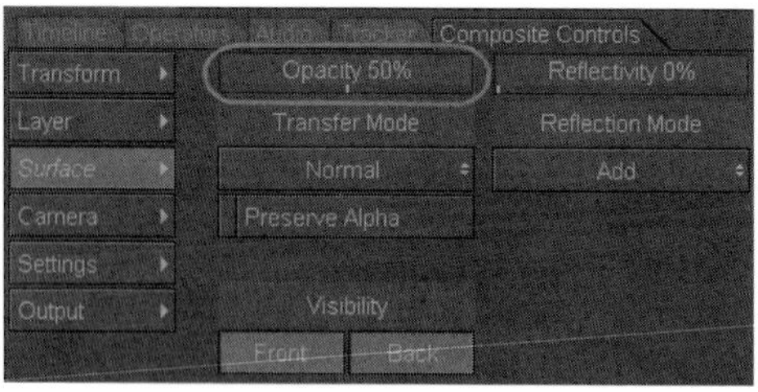

Note: The Shadows on the knight lighten interactively based on the opacity value.

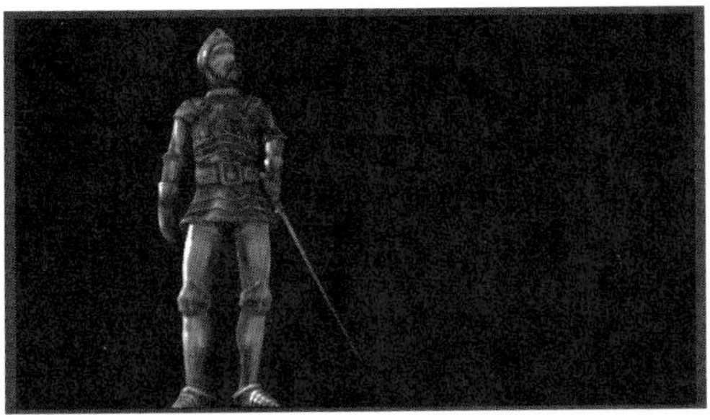

Shadow Opacity 50%

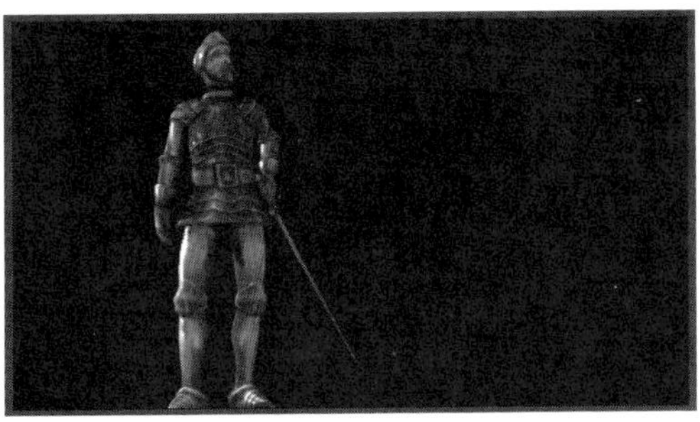

Shadow Opacity 100%

5. In the Schematic viewport, choose Shadow layers root footage.

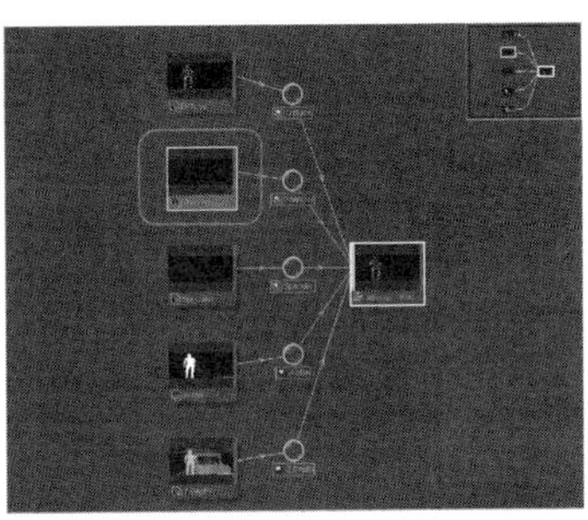

6. Right-click and then choose Add Operator > Blur/Sharpen > Box Blur.

   This adds a Box Blur operator to the Shadow layer.

7. In the Schematic viewport, double-click Box Blur.

   This makes it active.

   Note: Once active, the Box Blur tab is active.

8. Change the radius value to **1**.

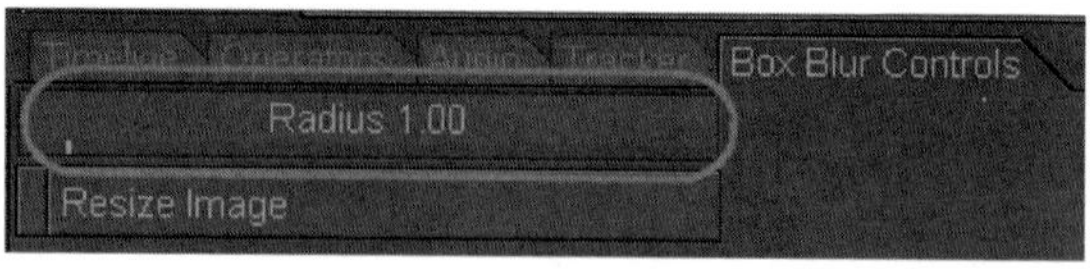

This softens the shadows.

9. In the Workspace tab, choose Specular.

10. In the Workspace tab, right-click and then choose Operator > Blur/ Sharpen > Gaussian Blur.

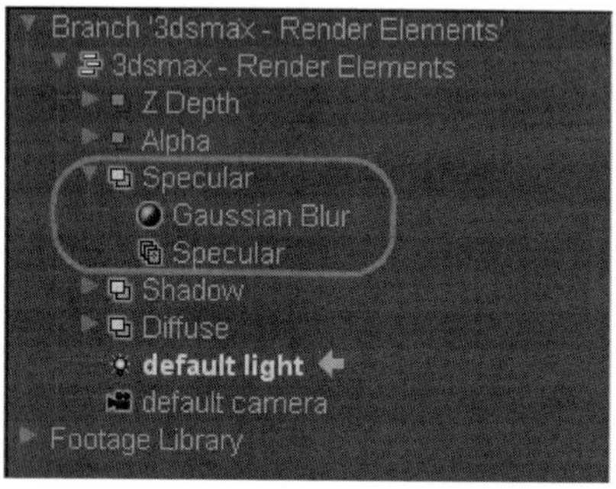

Note: This is another way to add an Operator.

11. In the Workspace tab, choose Specular.

12. Right-click and then choose Copy.

13. Right-click and then choose Paste.

A new layer called Specular(2) is created.

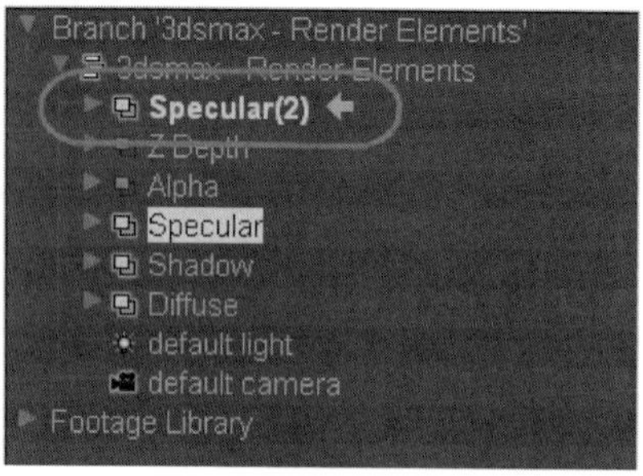

14. In the Workspace tab, choose the sphere next to Gaussian Blur to turn it off.

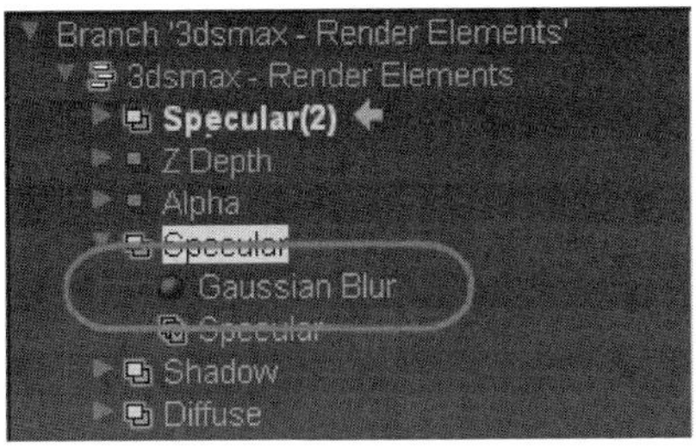

15. In the Workspace tab, open Specular (2) and then choose the Gaussian Blur Operator.
16. Change the Radius to **3**.

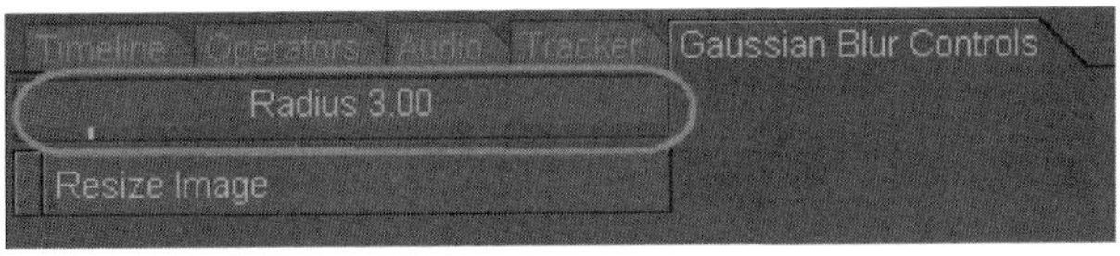

You doubled the Specular layer and slightly blurred the second layer to create what's commonly referred to as a Specular Bloom. Use this option to give you more realistic highlights. This effect is easy to achieve when you use Render Elements in **3ds max**.

17. Open *Shot_1_LayersExample.cws* to see the final sample workspace.

Tip: You might notice Schematic view looks disorganized since you added operators. To fix this, right-click and then choose Flow Direction > Flow Right.

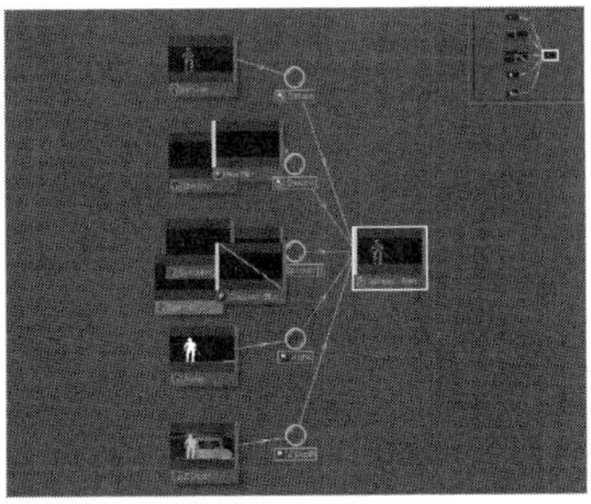
Before Update Flow Direction

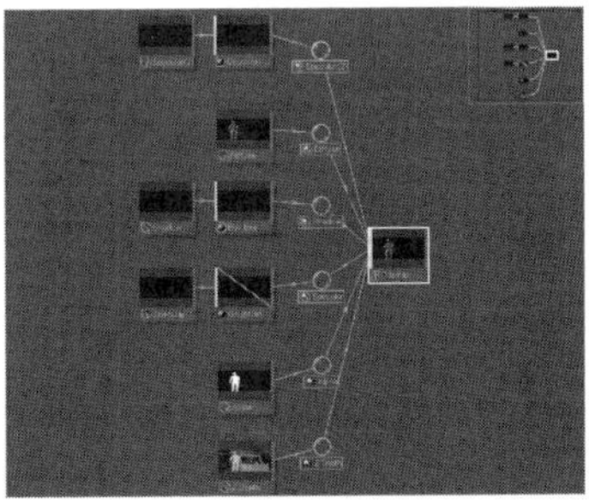
After Update Flow Direction

Note: As you continue, this option is referred to as Update Flow Direction.

Putting it All Together

Next, start with the original comp to finish the composite.

1. Open the workspace you previously saved, or open *Shot_1_Working_01.cws.*
2. On the menu bar, choose File > Import Workspace.
3. Choose *Shot1_background.cws* and make sure to choose the correct path.

   This is a simple background setup. The time ranges and appropriate blend modes are set. You make the remaining changes.

   Note: There are currently two separate composites. You bring them together to make one.

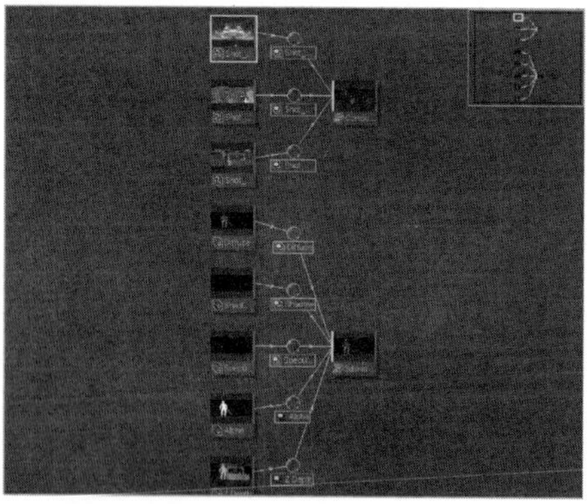

4. In the Workspace tab, choose *3dsmax – Render Elements*.

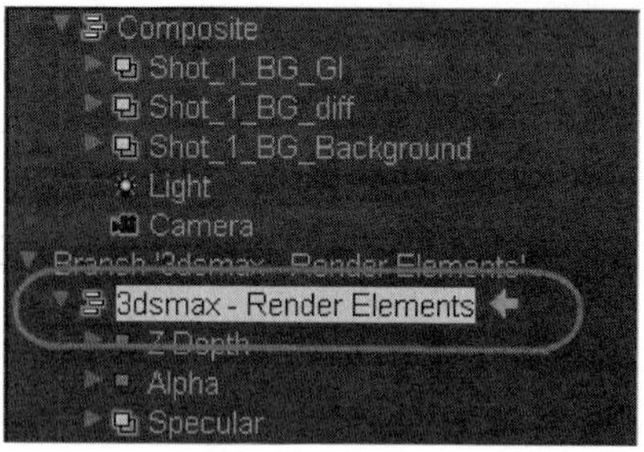

5. Right click and then choose Nesting.

6. In the Nesting Options dialog, type Knight as the Composite Name and then click OK.

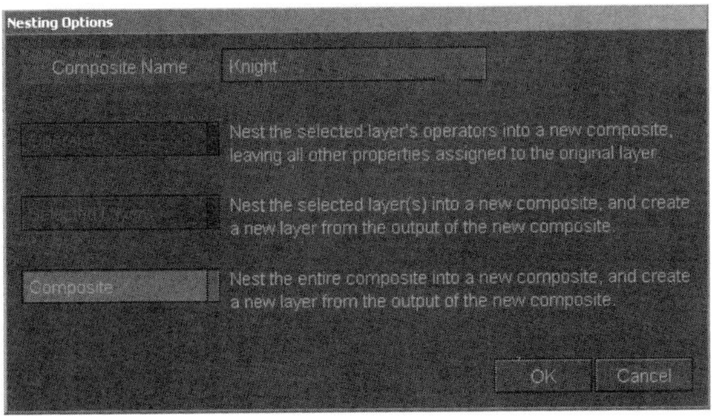

Note: You compiled all knight's layers into a single composite within the existing composite. All layers for the knight can be treated as a single unit or individually as sub-units.

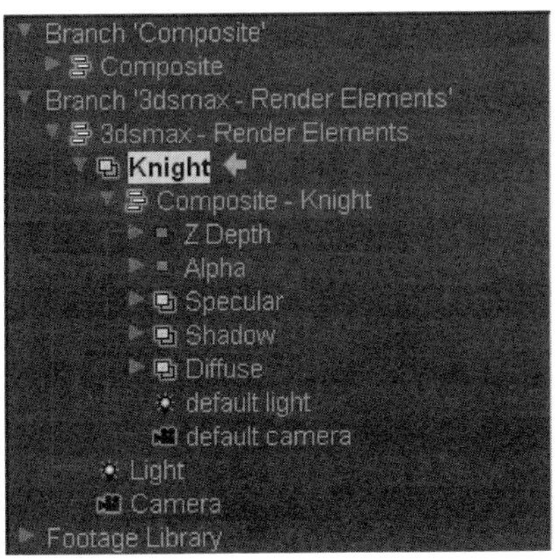

7. Update Flow Direction.
8. In the Schematic viewport, choose the Background Composite node.

9. Click drag from the right edge of the node and connect it to the 3dsmax – Render Elements Node.

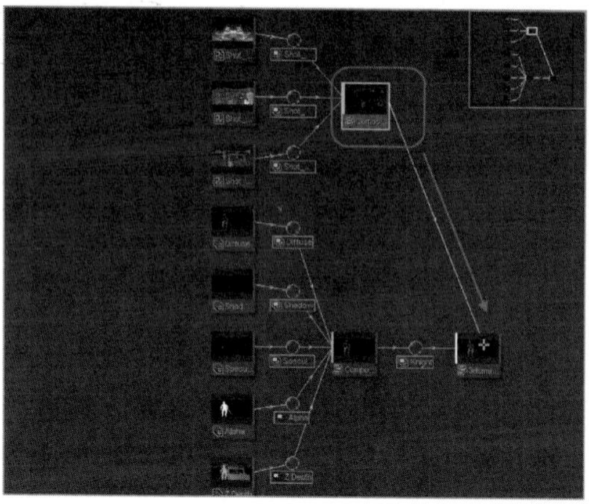

10. From the menu, choose New Layer.
11. In the Workspace tab, rename the composite Background.

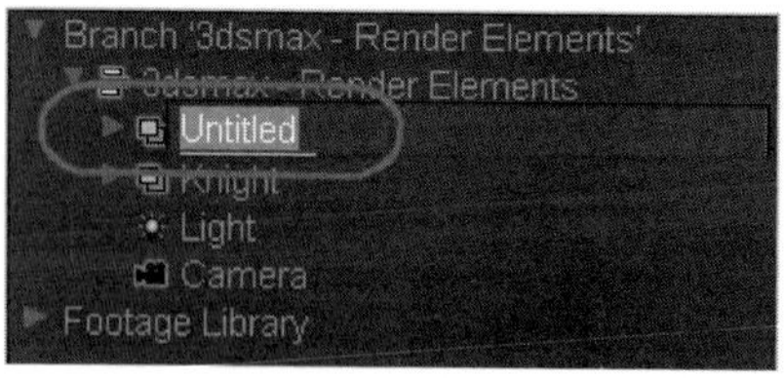

The Knight and Background are part of the same composite. However, the Background is on top rather than behind the character layer. You fix this next.

12. In the Workspace tab, choose the Background layer and drag it below the Knight Layer.

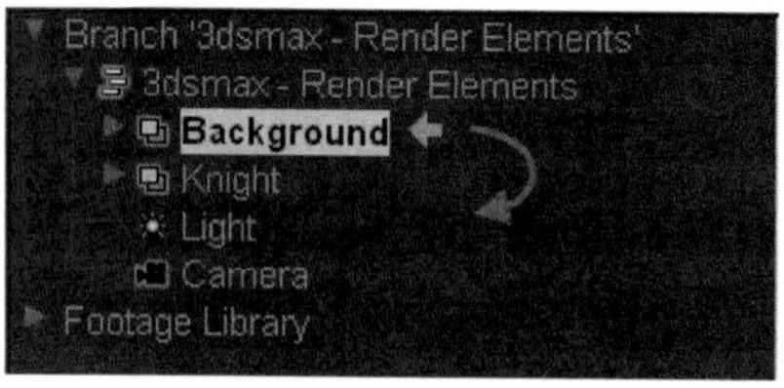

13. Update Flow Direction.

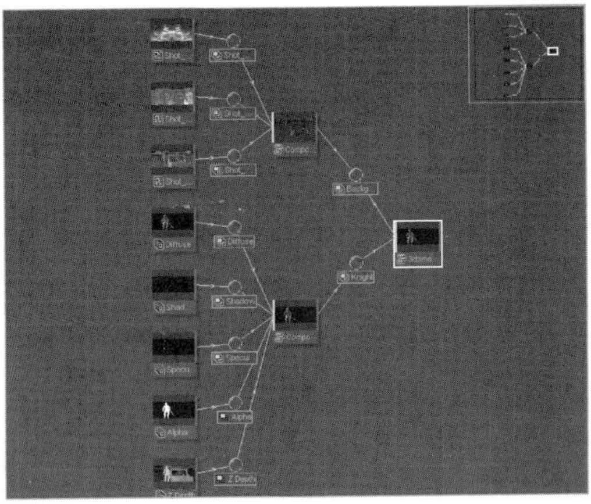

14. In the Workspace tab, open the Knight Layer and then choose the Knight layer.

15. Right-click the Knight layer and then choose Operators > Channel > Set Matte.

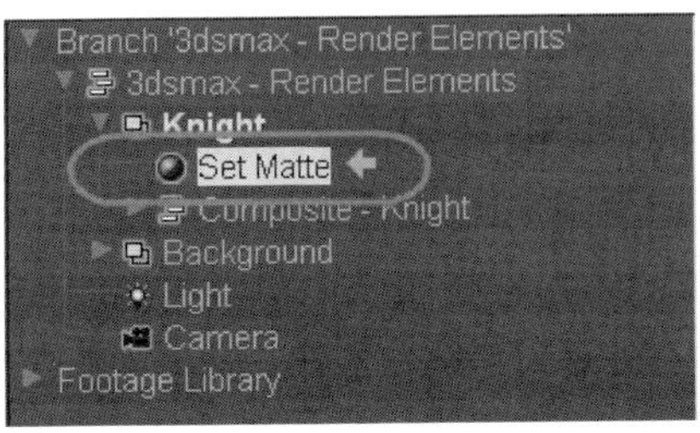

16. In the Workspace tab, choose Set Matte.

17. In the Set Matte Controls tab, choose (none) next to Layers.

18. In the Layer dialog, double-click Alpha.

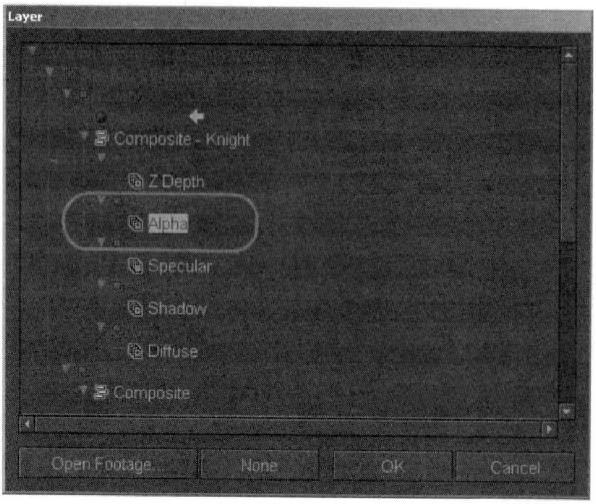

19. Set the Input to Alpha.

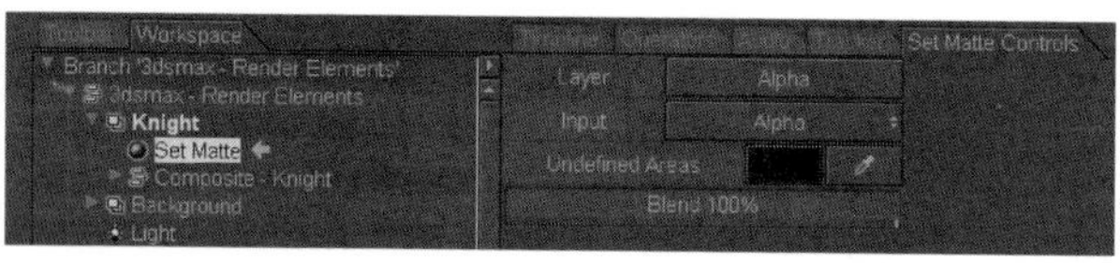

20. Update Flow Direction.

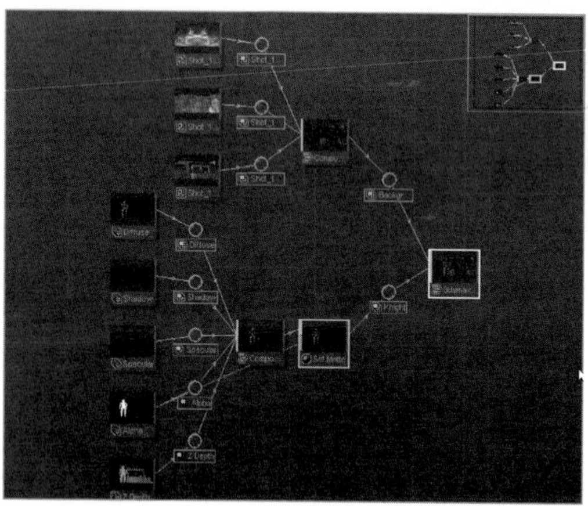

In the Camera viewport, you see the background behind the character.

Adding Specular Effects

Next, you use the same procedure as you did in the sample example to create a Specular Bloom effect.

1. Continue from the previous exercise.
2. In the Workspace tab, choose the Specular layer for the Knight composite.

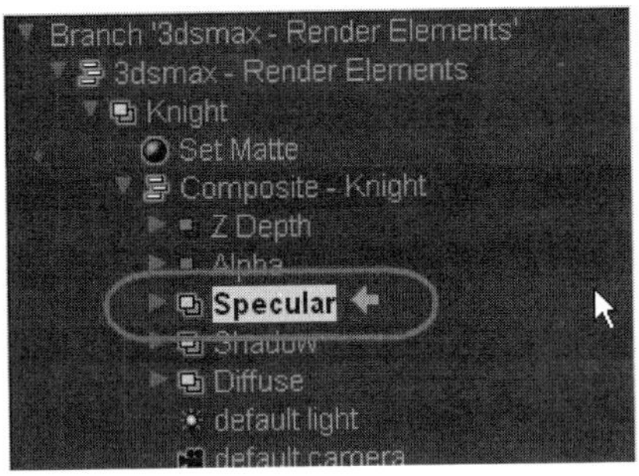

3. Right-click the layer and then choose Copy from the right-click menu.
4. In the Workspace tab, choose 3dsmax – Render Elements Node.

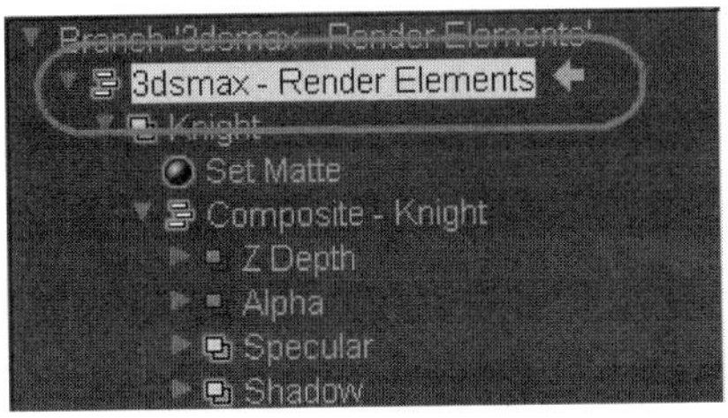

5. Right-click and then choose Paste.

   Note: In the workspace window, there is a new entry under 3dsmax – Render Elements called Specular. You apply the effect here because it is located above both the knight and the background layers, therefore affecting both.

6. In the Workspace tab, choose Specular under 3dsmax – Render Elements.
7. In the Composite Controls tab, choose Surface.

8. Change the Transfer mode to Screen.

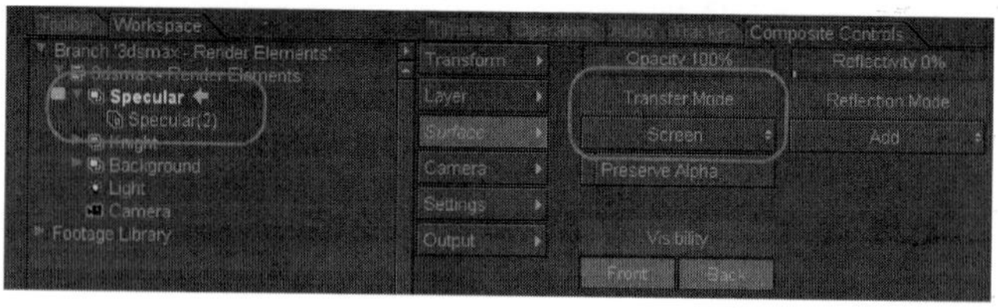

9. In the Workspace tab, rename this layer **Knight Specular Bloom**.
10. Make sure the schematic view is active.
11. In the Workspace tab, double-click Knight Specular Bloom. This changes the Schematic viewport into this layer's viewport. This way you can see the changes you make and how they affect the final image.

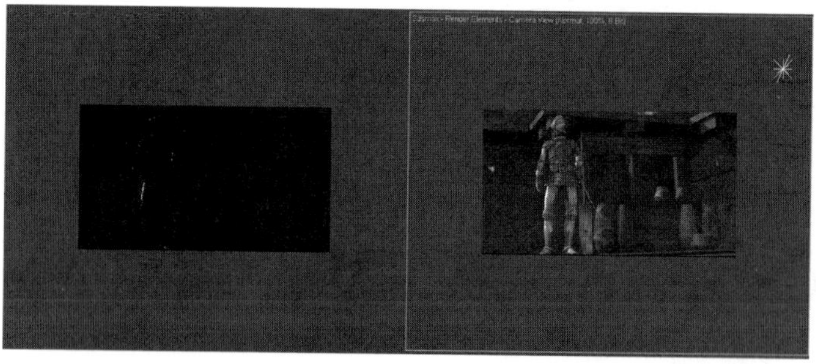

12. In the Workspace tab, choose Knight Specular Bloom.
13. Right-click the layer and then choose Operators > Color Correct > Discreet CC Basics.
14. In the CC Basic Controls tab, change the Gamma value for RGB to 2.

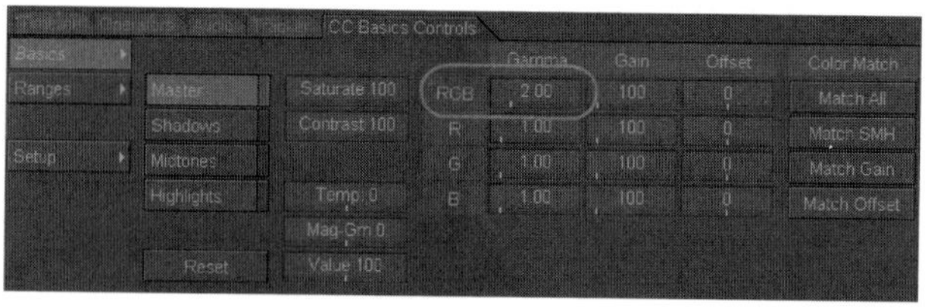

15. In the Workspace tab, right-click Knight Specular Bloom and choose Operators > Blur/Sharpen > Gaussian Blur.

16. In the Gaussian Blur Controls tab, change the Radius to **3**.

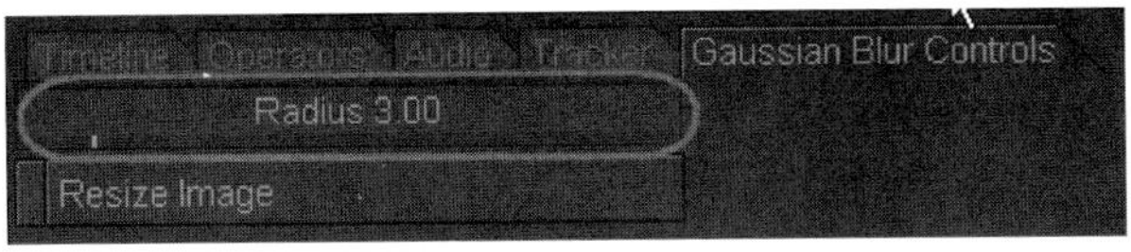

A specular bloom effect from the knight's armour is displayed.

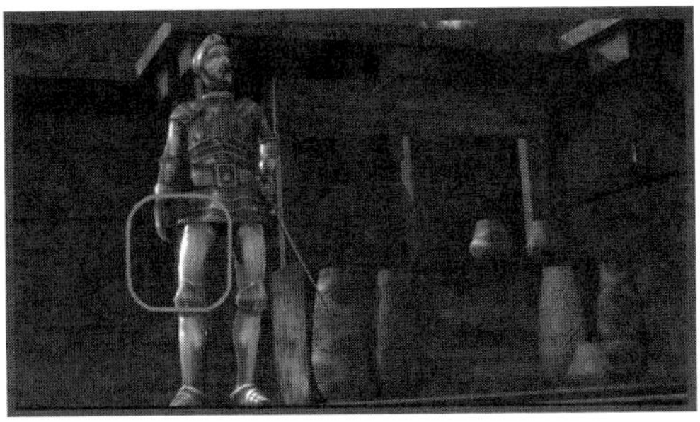

17. In the Specular layer view, choose F12.
18. Update the Flow Direction.
19. Save your workspace.

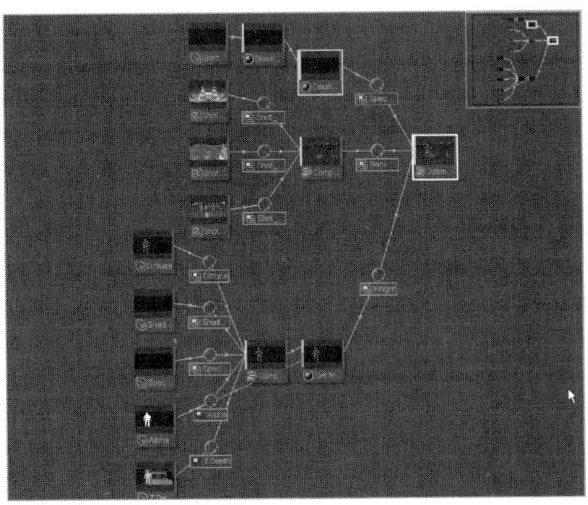

Background Layers

The knight is done, now you concentrate on the background layers.

1. Continue from the previous exercise.
2. In the Workspace tab, select and expand the Background Layer and Composite so you see all the individual layers.

3. In the Workspace tab, choose Shot_1_BG_diff.

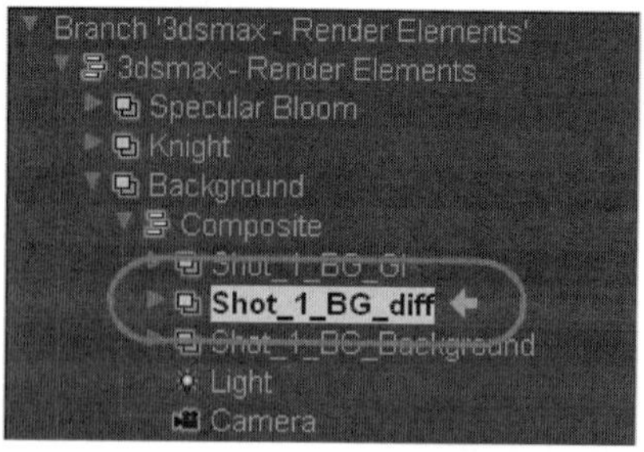

4. Right-click the layer and then choose Copy.
5. Right-click the layer and then choose Paste.
6. In the Workspace tab, choose the new layer and rename it Shot_1_BG_screen.
7. In the Composite Controls tab, choose Surface.
8. Change the Transfer mode to Screen and the Opacity to 10%.

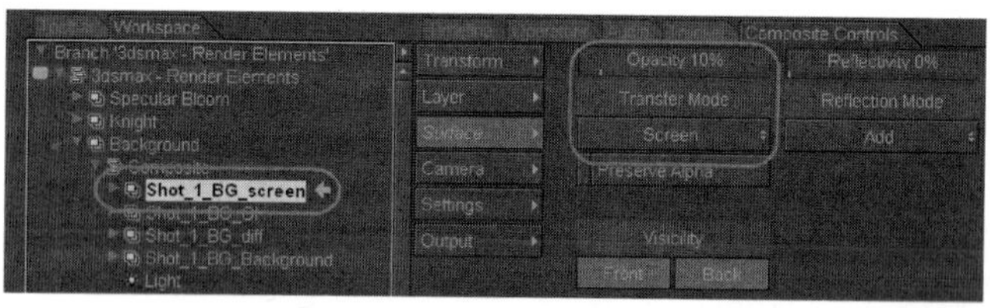

9. In the Workspace tab, right-click and then choose Operators > Blur/Sharpen > Box Blur.
10. In the Box Blur Controls tab, change the Radius to **1**.

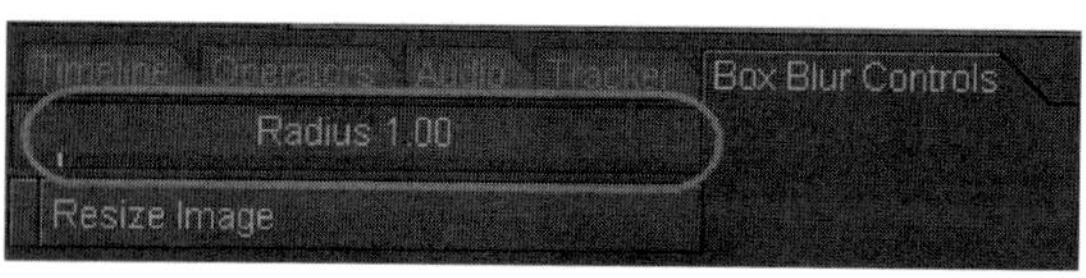

11. Update Flow Direction.

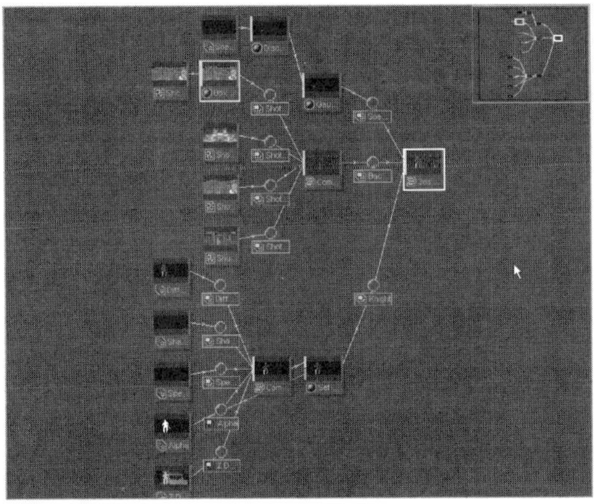

This effect is subtle, yet the background appears slightly brighter. Next, you add contrast while adding specular effects.

12. In the Workspace tab, choose Shot_1_BG_GI.

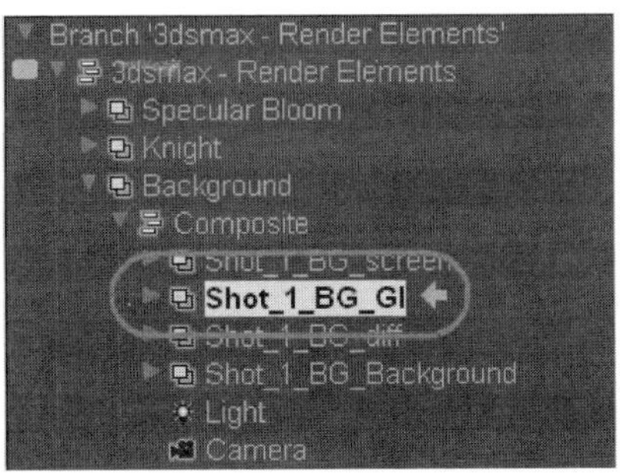

13. Copy and then Paste the layer.

14. Rename the new layer Shot_1_BG_Glow and make sure it's selected.

15. In the Composite Controls tab, choose Surface.

16. Change the Transfer mode to Overlay and the Opacity to **12%**

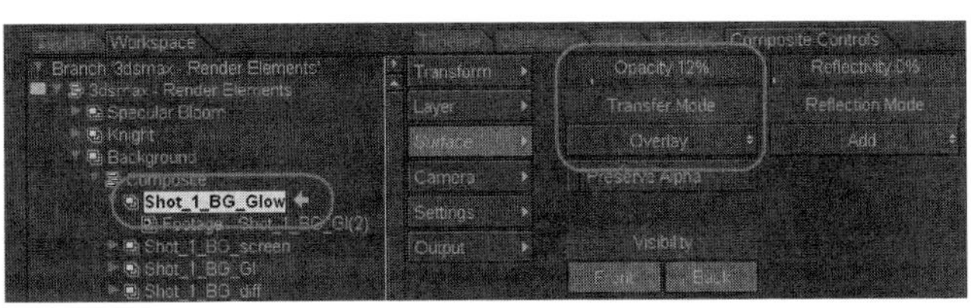

17. In the Workspace tab, right-click Shot_1_BG_Glow and then choose Operators > Color Correct > Discreet CC Histogram.
18. In the CC Histogram Controls, move the high and low value arrows towards the center of the graph. Low=**90**, High=**127**.

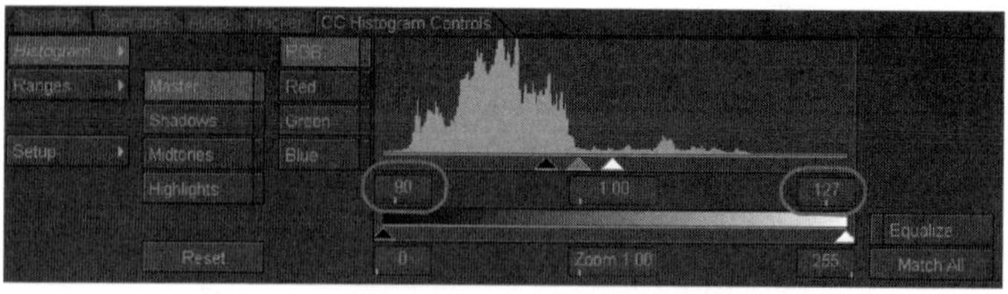

Tip: Double-click the layer to see the changes you make and then switch back to Schematic View.

19. In the Workspace tab, right-click the layer and then choose Operators > Blur/Sharpen > Box Blur.
20. In the Box Blur Controls, change the Radius to **5**.

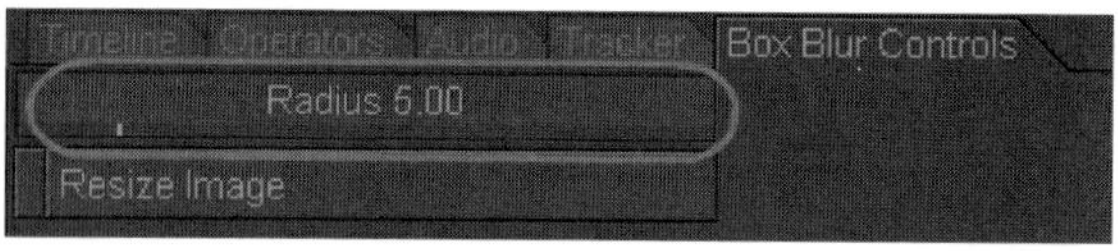

21. Update Flow Direction.

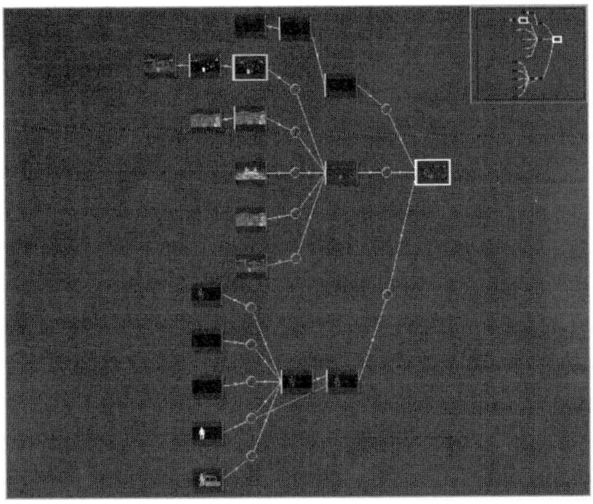

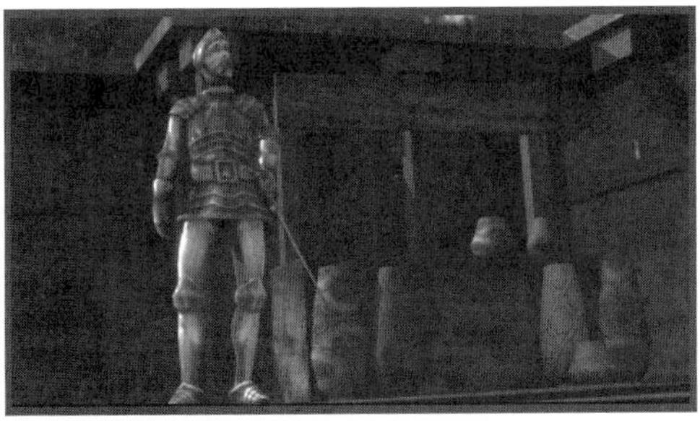

Before lighting adjustments

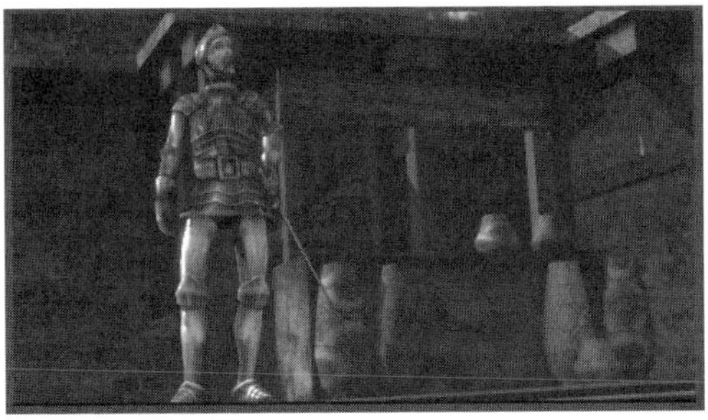

After lighting adjustments

Adding Depth of Field

Next, you use the Z Depth layer to help you create a Depth of Field effect.

1. Continue from the previous exercise.
2. In the Workspace tab, choose the Background Composite.

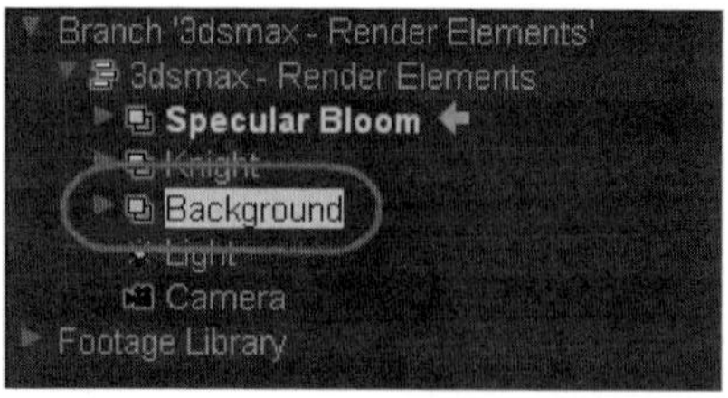

3. Right-click and then choose Duplicate from the right-click menu.

   Tip: Duplicating creates an Instance. This means anything you do to the individuals on one is applied to the others. However, anything you apply above the existing layers is applied only to it.

4. In the Workspace tab, choose Background (2) and move it so it is above the original Background.

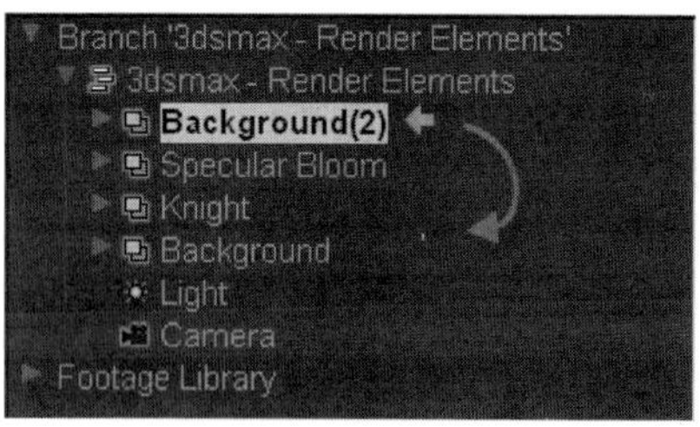

5. Rename it Background Blur.
6. In the Workspace tab, right-click Background Blur and then choose Operators > Blur/Sharpen > Gaussian Blur.
7. In the Gaussian Blur Controls tab, change the Radius to **1.5**.

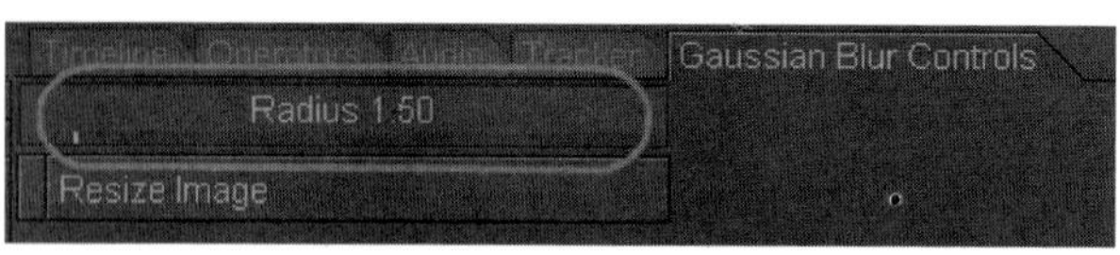

8. Right-click and choose Operators > Channel > Set Matte.

9. In the Workspace tab, choose Z Depth in the Knight layer.

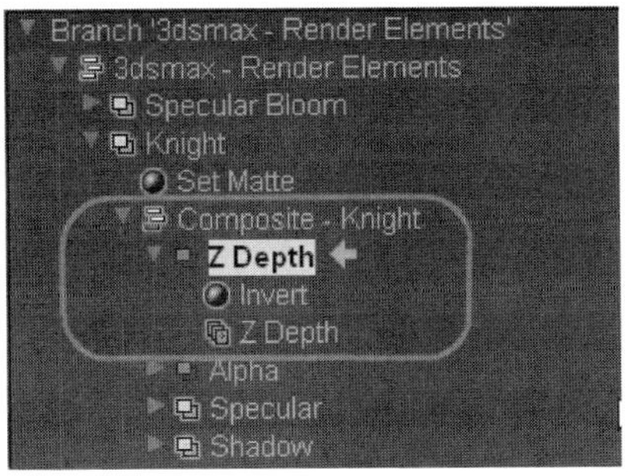

10. Right-click and choose Operators > Channel > Invert.
11. In the Workspace tab, choose Background Blur > Set Matte.
12. In the Set Matte Controls, choose None next to Layer.
13. In the Layer dialog, choose Invert.

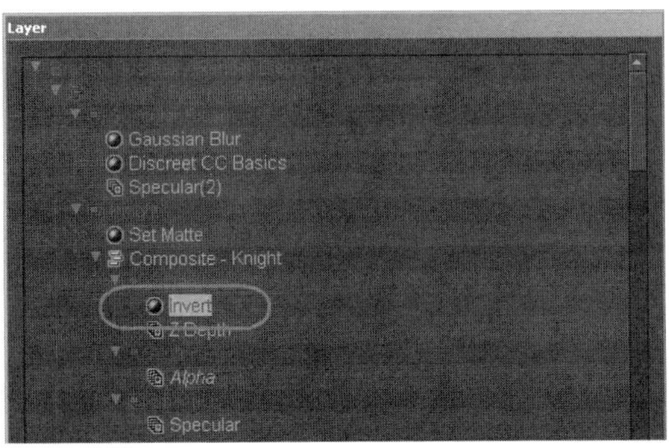

This completes the depth of field effect. The Z Depth pass acts as a control for matting out the blurred background. Effectively fading the effect in based on the distance to camera. Rather than rendering a time-intensive 3D depth of field effect, you can set this one up and have the effect be interactive and non-destructive.

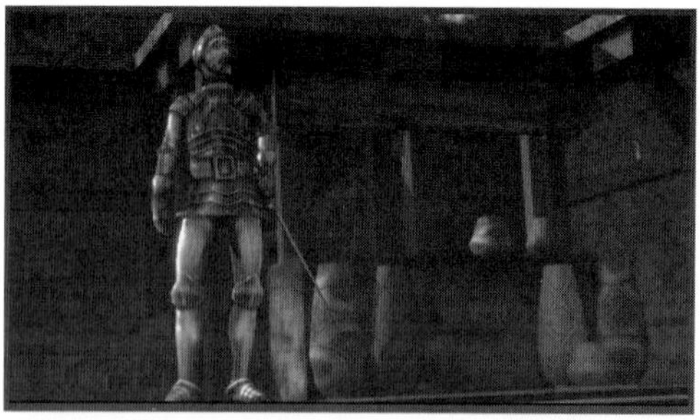

Before Depth of Field

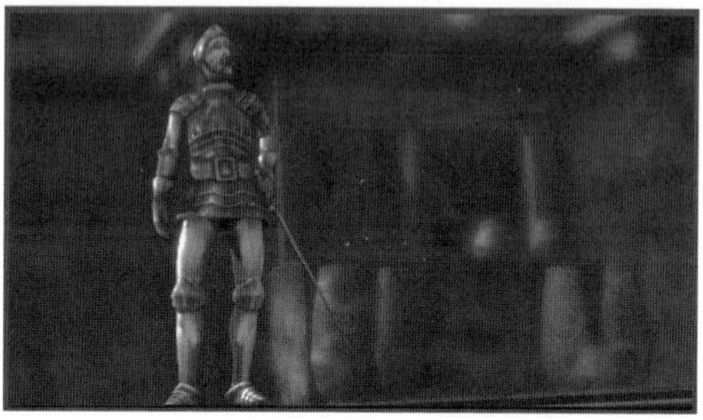

After Depth of Field (exaggerated to see the effect more clearly)

Adding Color Correct

Next, you add a global Color Correct Operator.

1. Continue from the previous exercise.
2. In the Workspace tab, choose Branch '3dsmax – Render Elements'.

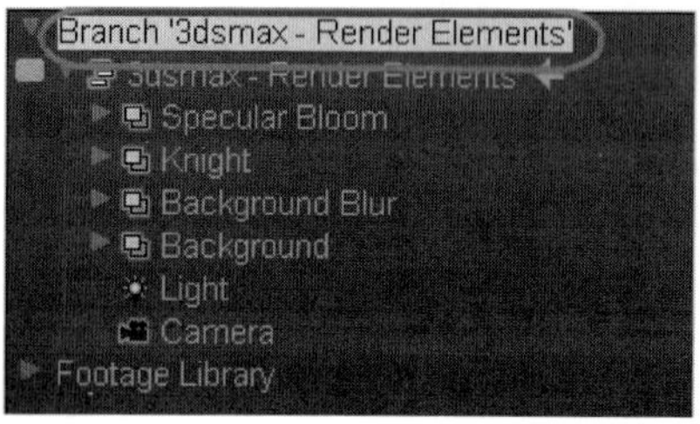

3. Right-click and then choose Add Operators > Color Correct > Discreet Color Corrector.

   Adding the Color Correct Operator here affects all layers.

4. In the Workspace tab, choose Discreet Color Corrector.
5. In the Color Correction Controls, choose Setup.

6. In the Color Correction Controls, choose Import.

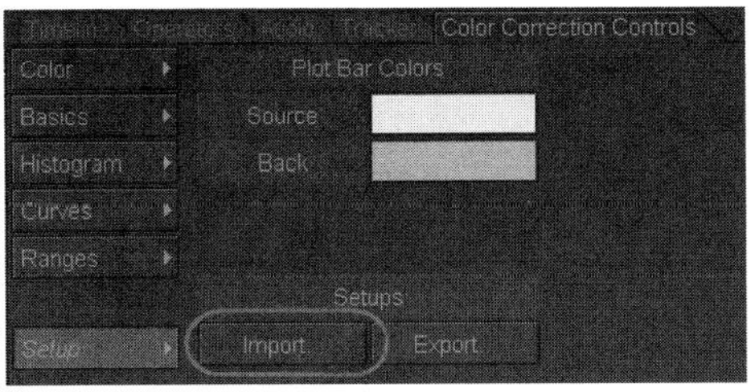

7. In the Import Color Correction Setup dialog, choose *ColorCorrectMaster.correct.*

   Tip: By exporting and importing color correction files, you maintain a common look throughout various shots.

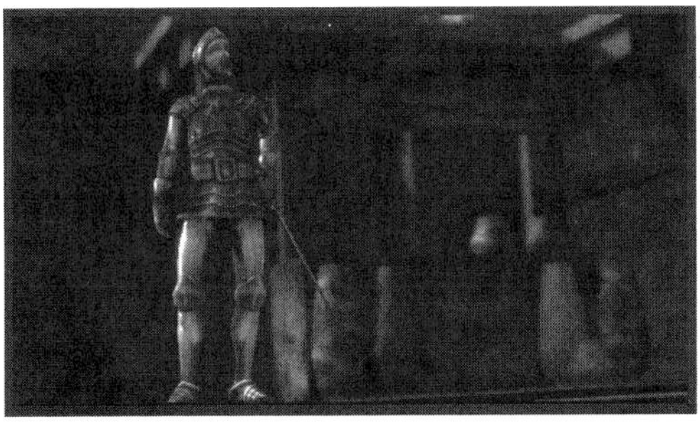

Before Color Correction

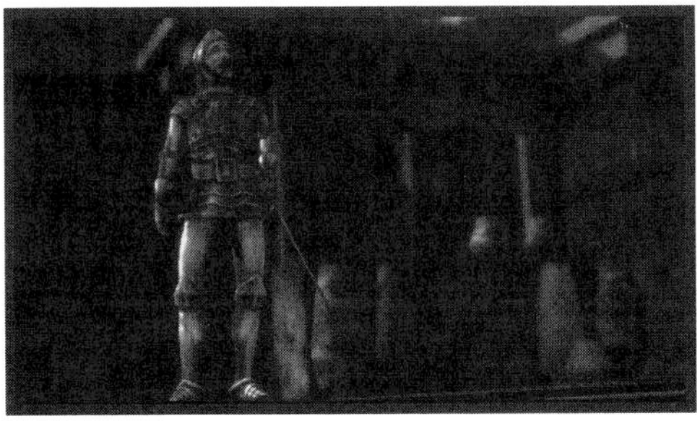

After Color Correction

8. You can continue to adjust the settings if you are trying to achieve a different look.

   This completes the composite for Shot 1.

Conclusion

This chapter concludes the Update Courseware for **3ds max 7**. You have used many new features and some favorites that have weathered the test of time. You experienced the power of **3ds max** for games and entertainment. Most importantly, you have experienced its flexibility regardless of the application. Continue to use the tools and immerse yourself in the power of **3ds max** and **combustion**.